The Communist Parties of Eastern Europe

The Communist Parties of Eastern Europe

Stephen Fischer-Galati, editor

New York Columbia University Press

Library of Congress Cataloging in Publication Data
Main entry under title:

The Communist parties of Eastern Europe.

Includes bibliographical references and index.
1. Communist parties—Europe, Eastern. 2. Communism—Europe, Eastern. I. Fischer-Galati, Stephen A.
JN96.A979C65 329'.02'0947 79-13016
ISBN 0-231-03591-8

Columbia University Press
New York Guildford, Surrey

Printed in the United States of America

10 9 8 7 6 5 4 3 2

Contents

The Communist Parties of Eastern Europe

Stephen Fischer-Galati
Introduction

Today, some thirty-five years since the "liberation" of Eastern Europe by the Soviet Union, the Communist parties have consolidated their power. Their raison d'être and legitimacy, however, remain rooted in the military power of the USSR. None, not even the League of Communists of Yugoslavia, can relax its vigilance toward internal and external enemies bent on or favoring the overthrowing of the ruling cliques. The "enemies" are easily identifiable. Theoretically, they comprise the Western imperialists headed by the United States, the practitioners of apartheid, the Zionists, all internal opponents to Communist rule and, at least in the case of Albania, also the "revisionists" in the Kremlin. In practice, the only enemies are the vast majority of the peoples of Eastern Europe and the men in the Kremlin who have the ultimate power over the very survival of the Communist leaders of these countries.

Given these "objective conditions," the Communist parties of Eastern Europe are severely limited in their exercise of power. It is true that over the years certain variations in the character of Communist rule have been recorded throughout the region. But, with the possible exception of Yugoslavia, there have been no true national roads to communism. Accommodations to specific historic and political circumstances have always been a function of relations between the leaders of the Communist parties of Eastern Europe and the Kremlin. These are the paramount factors which must be understood in any study of the Communist parties of Eastern Europe. The differences recorded in the ensuing essays are, as the authors indicate, illustrative of specific national and international considerations conditioned by the political dynamics of the intrinsically static and rigid Soviet system.

All of the Communist parties of Eastern Europe are theoretically committed to socialist modernization. The Yugoslav, East German, and Hungarian have each, in their own way, devised blueprints for economic development which appear to be at variance with those of the more rigidly centralized ones enforced in the USSR, Romania, and Albania, for instance. Similarly, the agricultural systems of Yugoslavia and Poland differ from those of the other Communist countries of Eastern Europe. Yet, in the last analysis, no matter what the blueprint, modernization remains hampered by constant ideological and political restraints directed against the resurgence or development of "bourgeois" tendencies within the socialist camp and of ideological contamination by nonsocialist modernizers from without the camp.

The Communist parties of Eastern Europe have also sought a degree of identification with historic traditions in an effort to strengthen their legitimacy as executors of the social and national revolutionary legacies of their countries. Thus, the parties seek to gain a modicum of popular support at home through implied denial of their subservience to the Soviet Union and, in most cases, to negate Western contentions regarding the monolithic character of Russian imperialism. Yet this Communist nationalism is politically fabricated and, as such, transparent even to the staunchest opponents of Soviet domination of the area—the rulers and peoples of Yugoslavia, Albania, and Romania.

In their attempts to secure their positions vis-à-vis the Kremlin and to avoid the possibility of armed intervention by the Soviet Union or its agents, the Communist leaders of Romania, Yugoslavia and, in their own way, also of Albania have pursued foreign policies often at variance with those of other Communist parties in Eastern Europe. But even these deviations have been conditioned by fears of ideological contamination and of possible reprisals from Moscow. The foreign policies of all other Communist parties in Eastern Europe are indistinguishable from those of the Soviet Union.

There are, to be sure, differentiating characteristics among the parties and party states of Eastern Europe. Nationalism and the cult of personality are more manifest in "Peronist" Romania, Stalinism and revolutionary radicalism are most acerbic in Albania, coexistence with the powerful Catholic church is manifest in Poland, liberalism toward intellectuals and relaxation of internal political controls are most evident in Yugoslavia and Hungary. There are also differences to be noted in the relative sizes of the parties, in the composition of their membership, and even in their organizational structure. Nevertheless, potentially meaningful deviations from Soviet norms such as Titoism or any other variant of "socialism with a human face" can never hope to become prototypes for change within the Soviet bloc.

The cracks in the "granite-like" structure and unity of the Soviet camp in Eastern Europe are discernible to the quantitative analyst of East European communism. The qualitative analyst, however, will have to conclude that the rock is solidly embedded in the principles and practices of Soviet communism, the ultimate protector of the Communist parties of Eastern Europe against political earthquakes or neutron bombs.

Peter R. Prifti

1. The Labor Party of Albania

According to classic Communist doctrine, of all the countries in Europe, Albania was the least qualified candidate for communism. With a backward, semifeudal social and economic order, Albania in 1944 was farther removed than any other European nation from the industrialized capitalist society that Marx believed to be a prerequisite for transition to socialism and communism. Yet for the past three decades, Albania has been ruled by the most doctrinaire and orthodox of all the ruling Communist parties in Europe.

THE DISSENTING VOICE IN EUROPEAN COMMUNISM

An examination of the current positions of the Albanian Communist party—known officially as the Albanian Party of Labor (APL)—reveals that on a surprising number of issues, the party stands apart from all the Communist parties in Eastern Europe. Indeed, in some respects it stands out from all the other parties in the socialist world.

Unlike other East European parties which, in the wake of the Twentieth Congress of the Communist Party of the Soviet Union (CPSU) in 1956, abandoned Stalinist practices—to a greater or lesser degree—in their domestic and foreign policies, the Albanian party successfully resisted all pressures to decentralize and liberalize its policies. Consequently, Albania at present has the distinction of being the last stronghold of Stalinism in Europe. The only Moslem country in the world to have adopted communism to date, Albania is currently the most isolated country in Europe—ideologically, politically, and in most areas of her cultural life. She attained this position as a result of the break between the APL and the CPSU in 1961, and the hostile foreign policy which the Albanian party subsequently pursued toward both Eastern and Western Europe. On the question of the Warsaw Pact as well, the Albanian party stands apart from other East European parties.[1] Following the invasion of Czechoslovakia in 1968 by members of the Warsaw Pact, Albania made history in Eastern Europe when she formally withdrew from the Pact in September of that year—the only East European country to sever ties with the Warsaw Pact. The leaders of the APL felt compelled to denounce the Pact, convinced that the East European collective security system had become, in the hands of the Soviet leaders, an instrument of aggression against the very member states it was designed to defend.

Unlike all other socialist countries in Eastern Europe, Albania refused to take part in the European Security Conference that was held in Helsinki in July 1975. This dramatic boycott of the conference underscored the Albanian party's rejection of détente politics in Europe and of all efforts to relax tensions between NATO and the Warsaw Pact countries.[2] Far from supporting the trend toward détente, the Albanian party in the late 1970s stood out among the East European Communist parties as the lone defender and propagator of cold war politics.

As a result, the APL held the distinction among Europe's Communist parties of being the "fiercest enemy" of the Soviet Union. A major reason for the Albanian party's hostility toward the Soviets was its position on the question of revolution versus peaceful coexistence with capitalist countries. Unlike other Communist parties in Europe, which had long ago accepted peaceful coexistence as the general line of the socialist camp in its relations with the capitalist West, the Albanian party put its trust in revolution; that is, in armed struggle and the violent seizure of political power as the only reliable strategy for ensuring the victory of socialism and communism over the capitalist world.

A striking fact about the APL which is not generally known—even among some specialists in Communist affairs—is that it was the only Communist movement in Eastern Europe to seize power without the direct aid of the Red Army. Albania achieved liberation from the Nazi-Fascist occupation armies by her own efforts, though she received considerable military material from the Anglo-American allies.

Western tourists to Albania almost invariably comment on the fact that there are no churches or mosques open for public worship in that country. This has been a feature of Albanian society since 1967. In this respect also, the Albanian party stands alone in Eastern Europe—and indeed in the entire socialist world—for it is the only Communist party in existence to have institutionalized atheism.[3] In the area of "manners and morals," too, the Albanian party occupies an extreme position compared with those of other East European parties. Visitors to Albania have reported that bearded and long-haired men, for example, were not allowed to enter the country unless they first groomed themselves in a "respectable" manner. That points to another distinct feature of Albanian communism. Although the Albanian party leaders abolished the religious establishment and proudly proclaimed Albania as "the first atheist country in the world," in their public attitude toward morality and personal habits and tastes, they project an image that is closer to that of the Grand Inquisitor than to modern libertarians and advocates of the sexual revolution. As a consequence, Albania stands out as the country with the most puritanical communism in Eastern Europe.

Visitors to Albania are fascinated by the virtual absence of automobile traffic in Tiranë and the rest of the country. It is a unique phenomenon among the countries of Eastern Europe, and a reflection of Albania's economic system. The absence of private cars in Albania is chiefly the result of the economic policy that has been practiced by the party leaders in their efforts to industrialize the country. The Albanian leadership directs a highly centralized economic system in a relatively undeveloped country where priority has been given to the development of heavy industry, rather than to the production of consumer goods, least of all "luxuries" such as civilian cars.[4]

In all of these respects, the Albanian Party of Labor has stood out as the dissenting voice in European communism—a loner party that not only seems convinced of the correctness of its lonely path, but has presented Albania as the model for the future social and political development of the nations of Europe.

THE MAINSPRINGS OF APL POLITICS

Before proceeding with a discussion of the Albanian party's position on domestic developments and of the international situation in recent years, it seems worthwhile to determine as far as possible the mainsprings or primary motives which underlie the party's activity.

Perhaps the most important factor in this regard is the nationalism of the Albanian party leaders. The evidence for nationalism as a motivating force in the policies and actions of the APL's leaders is incontestable. It is present in the homage they pay to Albania's national figures, above all the Skënderbeu—the medieval national hero—and to the leading patriots of Albania's national movement for independence: Kristoforidhi and Naim Frashëri, writer-patriots; Abdyl Frashëri, statesman; Isa Boletini and Çerçiz Topulli, freedom fighters; and Ismail Qemali, the venerable patriot who in 1912 proclaimed Albania's independence from the Turks. Nationalism is apparent in the attention given to the observance of important anniversaries in the country's history: the League of Prizren (1878), which sparked the movement for independence; the Congress of Manastir (1908), a milestone in the standardization of the Albanian alphabet; and the Battle of Vlorë (1920), which resulted in the expulsion of Italian occupation forces from Albanian territory seized during World War I. It is evident in the care taken by the regime to preserve national monuments, including castles, towns of unusual historical interest, such as Krujë, Berat and Gjirokastër (now officially "museum cities"), and even certain churches and mosques of rare architectural and artistic value. It manifests itself also in the party's stress on preserving and enhancing the nation's cultural heritage—folk costumes, folk songs and dances, and the treasury of national folklore. Truly, there is no lack of evidence to support the claim that nationalism is a dominant force in the politics of the Albanian party.

It is perhaps not too difficult to understand why Albanian party leaders value nationalism and use it to win popular support for their policies. Albanians have been fiercely proud of their country, and are renowned for their spirit of independence. They have been conquered many times, but never wholly subdued. Albania, moreover, was the last country in the Balkans to win its independence from the Ottoman Empire. Having emerged from nearly five centuries of Turkish dominion, the Albanian people are understandably jealous of their newly-won national independence and sovereignty. The fact, too, that even after 1912 their nation was seriously threatened with partition by the neighboring countries has made them still more nationalistic, wary of foreigners, and extremely sensitive to threats—whether real or imagined—to their national existence and security. Patriotic and national feelings and considerations played a major role in the efforts of Albanian party leaders to resist Yugoslav encroachment on Albania's sovereignty in the 1940s, and to weather successfully the unsettling effects of the split with the Soviet Union in the 1960s. Such, it appears, is the background and the soil in which the nationalism of the Albanian party leadership is rooted, takes its nourishment, and operates as a vital force in contemporary Albanian politics.

Another motivating force that has helped to shape the politics of the Albanian party is ideology. First Secretary of the APL Enver Hoxha has always insisted that the break with Moscow in 1961 was due to ideological and political differences between the two former allies.[5] While that is an oversimplification of the matter, it is nonetheless true that ideology has been one of the more important mainsprings in the APL's activity throughout its history. Albanian party leaders are convinced that ideology, or the mastery and practice of Marxism-Leninism, is indispensable for victory over the class enemy, and for the successful construction of a socialist society. They are persuaded that only correct political ideas can lead to correct political action. Such orientation, they believe, is provided only by the principles of Marxism-Leninism, which are universally true at all times inasmuch as they derive from the science of dialectical materialism. To be sure, these principles have to be adapted to the particular conditions of the country in which they are to be applied, but they must not under any circumstances be revised, as the "modern revisionists" have done, under the pretext that this or that principle or doctrine has been outdated by events. The Albanian party insists that the Marxist-Leninist ideology is a powerful weapon in the hands of Communists, and an infallible guide to the inevitable triumph of socialism over capitalism. Accordingly, the party has expended vast amounts of energy and resources in propagating its conception of Marxism-Leninism, both at home and abroad.[6]

The Albanian party's interpretation of Marxist-Leninist ideology is exceptionally orthodox, the emphasis being placed on the revolutionary aspects of that ideology. The revolutionary world outlook is thus another characteristic feature of the APL. Albanian leaders assert that revolution is the distinctive feature of the present epoch. They claim that Marxism-Leninism is essentially a revolutionary ideology, a blueprint for the violent seizure of political power. Consequently, the APL draws a clear demarcation line between the forces of revolution and progress on the one hand, and the forces of reaction and revisionism on the other. In the true spirit of the cold war era, the APL scenario divides the world rather neatly into two distinct, irreconcilable camps, destined by historical forces to struggle against each other until the old order gives way to the new. The scenario rejects such "anti-Leninist" doctrines as "peaceful coexistence" in the ideological sphere, détente, negotiations, and collaboration between East and West, and instead hails the politics of revolution: confrontation, open polemics, and relentless class struggle against the enemies of socialism. From the Albanian party's viewpoint, the two opposing camps are engaged in a life-and-death struggle that embraces all fronts—political, economic, cultural, and military.

In looking further for an explanation of the APL's passionate advocacy of revolutionary politics, one finds helpful clues in Albania's history and in the APL's own past. First, the Albanian people are noted for their martial traditions, especially in northern Albania, where until very recently the rifle was considered a man's best friend. Second, Albania won her independence and defended her territorial integrity against foreign aggression in large part through the force of arms. This historical fact is reflected in Albania today in Hoxha's oft-quoted observation that "the Albanian people have hacked their way through history sword in hand." Third, the APL's great trust in arms also springs from the fact that the party came to power by means of an armed struggle. Albanian leaders point to their successful guerrilla war as proof that only through revolutionary warfare can the working class, the peasantry, and all oppressed peoples of the earth seize political power from the hands of their oppressors.[7]

The fourth mainspring of the APL's politics is the commitment to the modernization of Albania. The drive to modernize stems mostly from historical and political factors. The leaders of the Albanian Party of Labor are anxious to overcome Albania's age-old poverty and backwardness—a bitter legacy of her semi-feudal past and centuries of Ottoman misrule. They are painfully conscious of the public image of Albania abroad as "the most backward country in Europe" and of the phrase "darkest Albania" that still circulates abroad.[8] They are eager, therefore, to bring Albania into the twentieth century as rapidly as possible. APL ideologists often remark that there are two kinds of liberation: one political, the other socioeconomic. When Albania won her independence in 1912, they say, she achieved only political liberation, and as a result the country's internal conditions hardly changed in the following three decades. It was only in

1944, when the partisans seized power, that Albania not only regained her political liberation, but for the first time in her history embarked on the road of complete social and economic liberation for the Albanian masses.

The APL's desire to modernize Albania is also rooted in Communist dogma. Being highly doctrinaire Communists, Albania's leaders are striving to carry out faithfully Lenin's thesis that "communism is Soviet [or people's] power, plus electrification."[9] Their objective, it appears, is to make Marxist-Leninist Albania a show-case of all-around progress in Europe, and a concrete and inspiring example of the power of a genuine socialist state.

The method chosen by the Albanian party for modernizing Albanian society is tight centralism. This is a system of central control that in terms of its severity and the extent of its reach into all aspects of Albanian life probably has no equal in Eastern Europe. "Extremist centralism" thus emerges as another distinguishing trait of the Albanian party. Almost from the beginning of APL rule, Hoxha, Mehmet Shehu (now premier of Albania), and other party leaders made centralism a guiding principle of their regime. They were convinced that strong centralized rule was indispensable for political stability and the modernization of the country. Centralism in the Albanian context means both centralized planning and direction of the economy, and central control of the political, social and cultural life of the country. It is a form of oligarchy that is intended to ensure the party's leading role in all phases of Albanian life. From the APL's point of view, centralism is not only a valuable administrative technique, but also serves a vital political end. It helps to guarantee the "dictatorship of the proletariat" in socialist Albania, a term which party spokesmen define as "the rule of the working masses."

There are reasons, of course, why this extremist form of centralism became a dominant feature of the ideology and practice of the Albanian party. As in so many other instances, these reasons are rooted for the most part in Albania's past. Tightly centralized political authority came rather naturally to a country which in the past had known almost nothing but conditions of near-anarchy and autocratic rule.[10] Two other social conditions that prepared the ground for strongly centralized Communist rule were the factionalism of the clans and tribes of prewar Albania, and the intense localism and provincialism of the population which served to divide and weaken the country. In addition, the primitive and largely disorganized economic life of presocialist Albania generated strong popular sentiment in favor of a regulated, centralized economic system. In the old society, the average working man and peasant lacked the habits of discipline and industry. Hence a tight, centralized economy, capable of mobilizing the nation's manpower into a unified labor force, seemed to be the logical solution to the problem of worker lethargy and lack of discipline.

The sixth mainspring of the APL's activity is its radicalism. The Albanian Party of Labor has gone further, it appears, than any East European Communist party in resorting to radical solutions in the building of socialism. In this regard, the APL has lived by the book, for it has consistently sought to be faithful to the letter—if not always to the spirit—of the teachings of Marx and Lenin. In line with orthodox Marxist doctrine, the Albanian party has nationalized all industry and commerce, and collectivized all agriculture. In other words, it has socialized the entire wealth of the country, thus completing the transition from private to public ownership of the means of production. The absence of ranks or gradations in the Albanian armed forces is further testimony to the party's radical bent. The most dramatic and notorious example of the party's radicalism is its abolition of the religious establishment in the country.[11] Albania's Ideological and Cultural Revolution—carried out over a four-year period (1966–69)—also testifies to the party's radical posture in grappling with social, economic, and other problems.

Classic Communist ideology has been an important formative influence on the APL's radical character. But an even more important influence, perhaps, is to be found in Albania's history. The extreme radicalism of the APL is a measure, as well as a product, of the extreme conditions which prevailed in prewar

Albania: crushing poverty, overwhelming illiteracy, rampant superstition, blood feuds, and ravaging epidemics—above all malaria and syphilis.[12] To deal effectively with those conditions, Albanian party leaders apparently found it both reasonable and necessary to take strong measures, and to develop a style of rule encompassing features which, taken together, make up what we today call Albanian Stalinism.[13]

In the preceding discussion, an attempt has been made to identify the mainsprings of the politics of the Albanian Party of Labor, both on the domestic and foreign levels. We have tried in this manner to describe the main features of the party's character: nationalism, ideology, revolutionary militancy, modernization, centralism, and radicalism. There are other features in the APL's political make-up, such as utopianism, conspiracy, nepotism, ruthlessness, and even elements of messianism. But these are probably not as important as the features discussed above, and need not be treated at length here. Let us now examine in some detail the practical experience of the APL, especially in relation to recent developments in Albania and abroad.

THE POLITICS OF THE APL

The Domestic Experience of the Party

The road traveled by the Albanian Party of Labor since its founding may usefully be divided into three periods or stages. The first stage covers the war years, and extends from the founding of the party on November 8, 1941, to the seizure of power by the party-controlled National Liberation Front on November 29, 1944. The essential character of this stage is political, since the main aim of the party at this time was to liberate the country from the Nazi-Fascist occupiers and their Albanian collaborators, regain national independence, and install Communist rule.

The second stage covers roughly the first two decades of Communist rule in the country (1945–65). It is this time-frame that is commonly referred to by APL historians as the stage of the construction of the economic base of socialism in Albania. During this period the party leadership was preoccupied chiefly with socioeconomic questions, above all with programs designed to effect public ownership of the nation's wealth through the nationalization of industry and commerce, and the collectivization of agriculture.

The third stage began in 1966 with the launching of the Ideological and Cultural Revolution and is currently in progress. This stage has been designated by party ideologists as that of "the complete construction of socialism" in Albania. During this period the APL has been, and will continue to be, concerned mostly with the solution of problems of an ideological and cultural character. The overall goal in this connection is to stamp out "bourgeois and revisionist ideas" from the consciousness of the Albanian masses, and to imbue them instead with the Communist world outlook and morality. The idea is to create the "new Communist man," in preparation for entrance into the Communist society that lies somewhere in the distant future.

These stages interlink and overlap with one another, since the questions and problems dealt with in one stage have existed in some measure in the other two stages. Nevertheless, there has been a shift of emphasis from political, to socioeconomic, to ideological and cultural goals in the activity of the party over the entire period.

As a monolithic political organization of a militant character, the APL exercises a monopoly of power in the Albanian regime. Modeled on the 1936 constitution of the Soviet Union, the party has a three-tier structure, with the base organization at the local level, the district organization at the regional level, and the all-party organization at the national level. At its Seventh and most recent Congress (1976), the party numbered 101,500 members in a country with 2.5 million people, a far cry from the 2,800 members it had in November 1944.[14] The party currently has a

Central Committee of 115 members—in contrast to the 21 members it had at its First Congress in 1948—and a 17-member Politburo.

Since the Politburo is the real seat of power in the party hierarchy and in the nation, the decisions taken by that body, and approved by the Central Committee, constitute the line of the party and may not be questioned by party members, or by the rest of the citizenry.[15] Party policies may be discussed by party members, provided such discussions do not lead to decisions or actions that conflict with the line of the party. The Albanian party insists on ideological unity in its leadership, and "steellike" political unity between the masses and the party. It views such unity as a prerequisite for the effective implementation of its general line. It does not tolerate opposition to its policies, whether organized or merely vocal. It interprets such opposition as "factionalist activity" designed to break up the unity of the party.[16] Whenever it has detected or suspected tendencies toward factionalism, it has reacted with great severity against the alleged offenders. Hence its long record of purges against dissenters, as for example in 1946, when Sejfulla Malëshova, the leading party ideologist, fell from power; in 1955, when Politburo members Tuk Jakova and Bedri Spahiu were dismissed; and the more recent shake-ups in 1973–75, which will be discussed later.[17]

The Albanian Party of Labor represents itself as the "organized vanguard" of the working class, and as a "detachment of the international Communist movement." According to Albanian leaders, the APL has been a revolutionary party from the outset, and is comprised of revolutionaries bent on advancing the process of the "uninterrupted revolution" in the country.[18] Statutes regulating party life say that the primary political, economic, and social tasks of the APL on the domestic front are: to "strengthen the dictatorship of the proletariat" in order to assure the political unity of the party and the working masses, a unity which is indispensable for safeguarding the revolution and for building socialism; to transform Albania from an agrarian-industrial society into an industrialized country with a modern agricultural system; and to advance toward an egalitarian society by gradually narrowing the differences between the working class and the peasantry, between towns and villages, between theory and practice, and between mental and physical labor.[19] On the foreign front, the APL—true to its dogmatic interpretation of Marx and Lenin—is pledged to an irreconcilable struggle against imperialism ("headed by the United States") and modern revisionism ("headed by the Soviet Union"); to the support of all revolutionary Marxist-Leninist parties and groups and of national liberation movements of oppressed peoples throughout the world, and to solidarity with the workers in capitalist countries who are struggling to overthrow monopoly capitalism. The Albanian party, in brief, is resolved to do its part, however minute, to advance the cause of world revolution in the interest of socialism.[20]

The leader of the Albanian Party of Labor, Enver Hoxha, has served as its First Secretary since the formation of the APL in 1941. Mehmet Shehu, the second-ranking member in the party hierarchy, has held the post of prime minister of the Albanian government since 1954. In view of the fact that these two men are primarily responsible for charting the APL's course and giving it its particular temper and character, it will be instructive to consider briefly their background.

Hoxha, a skillful organizer and versatile politician with a flair for public speaking, has one of the best records for political longevity among leaders in the Communist world. He was born in the town of Gjirokastër in southern Albania on October 16, 1908. In 1930 he graduated from the French Lyceum in Korçë, reportedly with a brilliant record, and with a good foundation in the humanities. In 1931 he enrolled at the University of Montpellier in France, on the strength of a scholarship granted him by the Albanian government. While in France, he wrote articles for the French Communist party organ, *L'Humanité*, denouncing King Zog's government, an action that led to the termination of his scholarship. He then moved to Brussels, where he took a job as a private secretary at the Albanian Consulate. At the same time, he studied law and continued his anti-Zog activities, until he was detected and dismissed from his post.

In 1936 he returned to Albania, where he taught first at the Tiranë Gymnasium and later at the Korçë Lyceum. He lost his job again—shortly after the Italian invasion of Albania in 1939—on charges by the Fascist authorities that he had engaged in subversive pro-Communist activity among his students. Hoxha then moved to Tiranë where, behind the facade of a tobacco shop, he worked underground as a leader of the Tiranë Communist group. When the Albanian Communist party was formed in Tiranë in November 1941. Hoxha was chosen as head of a seven-member Provisional Central Committee.[21]

Hoxha is a nationalist, a doctrinaire Communist, and an intellectual who admires both Stalin and the genius of men like Balzac, Montaigne, Shakespeare, and Molière. He combines in his person ruthlessness toward "enemies of Albania, socialism, and the party," a certain fondness for conspiracy, messianic zeal for the propagation of the "Communist faith" in the world, and great trust in the efficacy of radical measures for the modernization of Albania. With a background in Western education and experience as a liberal arts college professor, Hoxha seems to be well informed about literature, the theater, and philosophy, particularly the philosophy of education. He is fluent in French, and has knowledge of Russian, English, Italian, and Serbo-Croatian. He might well be pictured as holding the sword of the dictatorship of the proletariat in one hand and the Western lamp of learning in the other.

Five years younger than Hoxha, Mehmet Shehu has a reputation as a brilliant army commander, and as the most ruthless leader of the Albanian regime. He was born on January 10, 1913, in Çorrush, a village in the Mallakastër region in southern Albania. After graduating from the American Vocational School in Tiranë in 1932, he went to Italy where he enrolled at the Military Academy in Naples, but was expelled four months later because of his pro-Communist sympathies and activities. When the Spanish Civil War broke out, he joined the "Garibaldi" International Brigade and fought as commander of its Fourth Battalion. He spent three years (1939–42) in a concentration camp in France, then returned to Albania, where he joined the newly-founded Albanian Communist party and the anti-Fascist resistance struggle.

Shehu was the Man of the Hour for the partisan cause. Owing to his professional military training, his battleground experience in Spain, his natural gifts as a commander, his fanatic zeal for communism, and his ruthless disposition, he soon became the most renowned commander in the partisan army and the scourge of the *Balli Kombëtar* (The National Front), the partisans' leading contender for power during the war. It has been said by some *Balli Kombëtar* leaders that without Shehu the Communists could not have won the war and come to power in Albania. Following the war, Shehu held a number of high military, party, and government positions, such as army chief of staff, APL-CC secretary, and minister of the interior. At present, he holds the posts of Prime Minister and Minister of Defense.[22]

Opinions vary concerning the relationship between Hoxha and Shehu, some saying that external fear—formerly of Yugoslavia, and now of the Soviet Union—has been the basis of their cooperation, while others believe that they have managed to share power principally for internal reasons, above all the need to maintain the balance of power within the country. More likely, the main reason the two have ruled together successfully is that they are the strongest symbols of the national liberation struggle, Hoxha in the political field, and Shehu in the military arena. They appear, moreover, to complement each other, in the sense of compensating for each other's weak points. Shehu's image as an uncompromising, authoritarian figure is probably as useful to Hoxha in maintaining control in the country as Hoxha's image as a man of broader sympathies and a skillful, versatile statesman is useful to Shehu.

Internal Life of the Party

In order to preserve its "ideological purity" and revolutionary orientation, as well as to strengthen its working-class base, the

Albanian party—as is customary with militant, monolithic organizations—has been constantly preoccupied with the question of the quality of its members. The party leadership has voiced frequent complaints over the petit bourgeois background of many of its members, their low level of education and culture, and over recurring violations of party regulations in the selection of candidates for membership. Apparently, candidates in many cases are selected not according to party criteria—character, morals, spirit of sacrifice, and political and ideological maturity—but rather on the basis of "nepotism, family relations and friendship."[23] In order to deal with this situation, the party has, from time to time, carried out "purification of ranks" campaigns which have resulted in the expulsion of thousands of members and candidate members.[24]

Above all, the leadership has sought to increase the percentage of workers in the party, at the expense of intellectuals, students, and bureaucrats—those regarded as less reliable politically than members of the working class. As a result of strenuous efforts by the party, and the swelling of the ranks of industrial workers with the gradual development of the nation's industry, the membership of workers in the party increased from 15 percent in 1945 to 37 percent in 1976. The working-class representation in the party became the dominant group in 1971. Commenting on this long-awaited event at the Sixth APL Congress, Enver Hoxha said: "It is a great joy and victory for the party and all the people that now, for the first time in the history of our party, the worker Communists occupy the first place in party membership."[25] He added that "the evil" which befell many Communist parties in revisionist Eastern Europe stemmed from the fact that their ranks were "deproletarianized," for they were filled with technocrats, bureaucrats, and intellectuals. The implication was that the Albanian party was now much less prone to such a disaster, but, as later developments showed, it had not yet overcome the danger of "degeneration."

It will be recalled that the third stage of Albania's "uninterrupted revolution" has as its main goal the cleansing of the superstructure of Albanian society by uprooting "alien ideologies" from the consciousness of its citizens. It is a goal that involves every citizen in a continuous struggle against bourgeois and revisionist ideas, against liberalism and conservatism. The object of the Ideological and Cultural Revolution in 1966–69 was essentially to make "a great leap forward" in this direction. At that time, the struggle focused on wiping out the harmful effects of bureaucracy which threatened to alienate the party from the masses and to remove its social roots, i.e., backward customs, patriarchy, superstition, and vestiges of feudalism and oriental influence that were stifling Albanian society.

These anachronistic concepts and practices, as well as "harmful alien influences" from Western and Eastern Europe, had become widespread among cadres in party and state apparatuses, creating numerous problems of administration for the regime and causing great alarm among the party leaders. One of the more persistent problems was that many party cadres confused the roles of the party and the government, and instead of simply directing and supervising the work of government workers—as they were supposed to do—often took over the functions of the latter, and ended by botching both their own jobs and those of the government workers. A more serious problem that developed in the mid-1960s was the gap between party cadres of limited education and culture and the more advanced body of citizens they were expected to lead in the building of a modern, progressive society. Reacting to this situation, Enver Hoxha asked, in April 1966: "How can one seriously believe that party members in the villages, some of whom are illiterate, or with only a grade school education . . . can advise or direct the army of teachers, agronomers, doctors, veterinarians that dot the countryside?"[26] Ironically, this problem was created by the very modernizing process that the Communist regime had set in motion twenty years earlier.

Perhaps the best summation of the major problems in the APL's internal life was made by the party's First Secretary in a speech to the Politburo in February 1966, at the beginning of the Cultural Revolution. While reaffirming the long-held position that "the line of the party in all matters has been basically correct." Hoxha nonetheless was unusually frank in discussing the bureaucratic problems that have plagued the party since the late 1940s. He spoke of his frustration in trying to communicate with local and regional party leaders about the problems they faced. All too frequently, it turned out, their reticence was but a device to cover up their incompetence, their ignorance, and violations of "party norms" and "socialist legality." Some of the bureaucratic vices to which they had become addicted were thievery, favoritism, "bossism" toward subordinates, and indolence. Hoxha said that the cadres "had become captives of conservatism."[27]

He complained that too many Communists preferred "desk jobs" to working on the production line because they had the mistaken antiegalitarian notion that office work is more "honorable" and more "worthy" than manual work. He labeled these people "petty tyrants," whose "sick psychology" leads them in the end to embrace antirevolutionary and even antiparty positions. Another common failing of cadres was their reluctance or refusal to leave the city and work in the countryside, on the pretext that they were frail, or that it would interrupt their children's education, or that their expertise was such that they were irreplaceable, or similar "petit bourgeois" excuses.

A disturbing consequence of these bureaucratic practices was that the bureaus of the state and mass organizations, both in the cities and in the countryside, had become overstaffed with party cadres, thus hampering their efficient operation and threatening to negate the all-important political goal of the revolutionary transformation of Albanian society. Hoxha has on many occasions touched on this problem, speaking with indignation about the disproportion between Communists and non-Communists in various bureaus, including the ministries in Tiranë. In a major speech on April 26, 1972, he remarked that of the total number of cadres in the central organs of the ministries, the Communists accounted for 45.5 percent, and that in some ministries the figures were even higher.[28] He asked: "Why on earth are so many Communists needed [in these ministries]?

Wouldn't it be better for many of the Communists . . . to go without delay to the grass roots, where the practical struggle is being waged to supply the people properly and to serve them better?"[29]

The First Secretary also denounced repeatedly the enormous growth of the "paper bureaucracy," which paralleled the staffing of state organs, as well as organs of mass organizations, with superfluous personnel. As a result, the administrative machinery of the regime groaned under the weight of myriad laws, decrees, rules and regulations. An ever more refined government code for doing even the simplest job generated an endless stream of mostly meaningless figures and statistics. The condition provoked Hoxha to cry out. "We are obsessed with figures and statistics."[30] He condemned the judicial authorities for trying to codify everything under rules and regulations, and for creating, along with other bureaucrats, a potentially dangerous gulf between the party and the people.

The rampant growth of the bureaucracy in the Albanian regime confronted the APL with still another problem—the propensity of cadres to act in an arbitrary manner. Certain Communists operated under the assumption that "the party is infallible," or that "the party has unlimited rights" and therefore can do anything it pleases, or that "the party must not be criticized" because criticism impaired its authority.[31] In some cases, such arbitrary acts were due to wrong interpretations of party regulations, while in other cases they were subterfuges by individuals to hide their own mistakes and to evade criticism of their conduct by using the party's authority as a protective shield. Addressing this issue, Hoxha informed party cadres that "the party has some rights, but it does not have unlimited rights over everything; it cannot act at will."[32]

As mentioned earlier, the official party line is that the dangerous disease of "bureaucratism" is the offspring of alien ideologies, principally conservatism and bourgeois and revisionist influences. However, in his February 3–4, 1966 speech (delivered apparently over a period of two days), Hoxha took the extraordinary step of going beyond the official position, and attributing most of the blame for "the evils of bureaucratism" to the party leadership itself. He said:

> It is important to understand that . . . we, the leaders, are the biggest culprits for this condition.
>
> We, the leadership, demanded to be . . . consulted over almost everything; we insisted on giving guidance in everything. . . . No one could operate outside that framework.[33]

Albania's top leader noted that the policy of unrestricted "control by the leadership over everyone and everything" had proved to be wrong. He added that as long as the administrative apparatus is not under the complete control of the people, bureaucratism "with all its evils will surface again and again" in Albania.[34] Hoxha, in effect, admitted that tight centralism as a guiding principle for governing Albania was at least open to question, if not totally discredited by the mid-1960s, however useful or necessary it may have been in the early years of the regime.

Drawing the logical conclusions from his own analysis of the problem of bureaucracy and its corrosive effects on the party and the country, Hoxha proposed a daring solution. He suggested that the party open itself up to questioning and criticism by rank-and-file members. He said that no one should hesitate to criticize the distortions and the errors that may be made by the Central Committee, the Politburo, or any of their members.[35] Hoxha repeated this proposal six years later, in his February 26, 1972 speech, when he said—in language reminiscent of Mao's "Let one hundred flowers bloom" campaign—"Let everything seethe within the organization. Even if someone comes up in opposition to the line of the party, let him oppose it."[36] The fact, however, that he repeated the proposal means that nothing was done about his original proposal in 1966, which in itself is an indication of the difficulty of the problem or, as is more likely, that the party leadership had no intention of making such a basic reform in its style of rule.

Other steps actually taken or proposed since 1966 as a means of overcoming the paralyzing effects of bureaucracy, and "perfecting" the internal life of the party included the reduction of personnel in state organs, requiring administration workers and intellectuals to do physical labor for one or more months a year, and increasing "workers' control" by giving the working masses greater power in the management of the economy and a wider role in the work of the state apparatus.[37] All of these measures aimed ostensibly at bringing the regime closer to the people by making the government more responsive to their needs and aspirations, and by strengthening the bonds between them and the party. Another step along this line was the suggestion that more attention be given to electing "the best people" to office, people who are honest, courageous, hard workers, "revolutionaries . . . who know the problems of the people, live and work with the people."[38] The suggestion implied that "right government" is a function—at least in part—of "right people," and not merely the result of an ideology, or a particular economic system or social order.

Despite, however, the actual and potential value of these measures, the party leadership viewed them as stop-gap, rather than long-term, solutions to the problem of bureaucratism. The long-term solution, in the APL's view, was above all a question of education: of raising the ideological consciousness of the cadres, the workers and the collectivized peasantry; strengthening their revolutionary spirit so that they may shun the comfortable and easy life and choose instead the life of hardships and self-denial; and putting politics ahead of everything, which meant judging all things from a political viewpoint. More specifically, "putting politics ahead" in this context meant asking whether a particular action, policy, or proposal was in the interest of the people, the country, and socialism, or simply in one's personal interest.[39] It meant giving politics priority over economic, technical, and pragmatic considerations in the performance of one's job and the solution of the nation's problems. These ideas motived to a large extent the reform of the education system in 1969 and the series of propaganda campaigns that were carried out in recent years. The party leaders hoped through these efforts to "revolutionize the life of the country" and deal a crushing blow to the endemic problem of bureaucratism. They warned constantly that it was precisely "the worm of bureaucratism" that gnawed at the vitals of the CPSU and brought on the tragedy of revisionism in the Soviet Union. They were determined not to allow a recurrence of that tragedy in Albania.

In spite of the problems facing the APL in the "third stage" of its path and development (the ideological and cultural stage), Enver Hoxha was able to report to the Sixth Party Congress in November 1971 that during the period from the Fifth to the Sixth Congress (1966–71), "not the least sign of hostile work, or of inconstancy in the [party] line" had appeared "either in the party as a whole, or within the ranks of the Central Committee."[40] It seems likely that the stability experienced by the Albanian party during the late 1960s encouraged the Politburo to toy with the idea of relaxing the APL's stand and moderating its rule to a degree. This notion is reflected in a number of speeches Hoxha made at party meetings in 1972, in which he invited criticism of the party line "from below," and the abolition of "excessive secrecy" in the work of the party.[41] On the question of secrecy he said the times had changed since the National Liberation war: the "antagonistic classes" had been smashed; therefore, there was no longer any reason for excessive secrecy. It was a potentially significant moment in the history of the party's domestic policy, but it produced no fruit.

The APL's hesitant steps toward relaxation and limited dialogue with the Albanian masses came to an end within a year. Alarmed by the liberal and reformist trends in the country, which by the end of 1972 had gathered much strength, the party reverted to its customary Stalinist position. It fell back on the trusted mechanism of the purge as it set out to curb the deviationists and dissenters and reestablish the familiar pattern of extremist centralism.

External Life of the Party

The term "external life" of the party is used to mean the APL's relations with organizations and groups in Albanian society outside the party organization. In the discussion that follows, we shall deal principally with the APL's relations with three representative sectors of Albanian society that were much in the news in Albania during 1973–75. These are the youth and intelligentsia, the army, and the economy, all of which experienced upheavals and reshuffles in their leaderships.

According to APL theoreticians, the remnants of bourgeois ideology are most prevalent among intellectuals, then among peasants, and least among workers.[42] It was no accident therefore that the first wave of repression, begun by the party in 1973, was directed against the intellectuals of the country. The repression was carried out under the banner of the struggle against "liberalism"—a term used by Albanian propagandists to describe attitudes, conduct, positions or trends of individuals or organizations that did not conform to "strict proletarian discipline" and to the party's position on art, literature, and cultural life in general.[43] To be sure, there was some justification for concern on the part of Albania's rulers over so-called manifestations of liberalism, both in the area of the arts and among youth. In 1972, for example, there was a sharp increase in youthful hooliganism and crime; in the rate of failures, repeats, and expulsions among students at the University of Tiranë; and in the spread of the more vulgar Western life-styles among young people. Antisocial attitudes of this sort had spread even among children of party members, provoking Hoxha to ask: "How can Communists, whose children turn into hooligans, vagabonds, and purveyors of extravagant bourgeois fashions and tastes, be in the vanguard and set an example for others?"[44] Party leaders, however, moved to condemn not only such negative manifestations, but the more legitimate and reasonable aspirations of youth and intellectuals for autonomy, experimentation, self-expression and dialogue with the outside world, particularly the West.

The growing divergencies between the party and the young generation became evident in a most revealing confrontation at a meeting of the APL Secretariat on February 23, 1973. The meeting was presided over by Hoxha, and was called to discuss a report by the leadership of the Labor Youth Union of Albania

(LYUA).[45] The youth report complained that the party leadership did not seem to understand "the concerns, requirements, interests and problems" of young people. The report was critical of the fact that partisan war themes dominated the lives of youth, from history books in school to literature for the young, in films, the theater and so on. In an apparent effort to help redress the balance, the report called for more books by foreign authors in Albanian libraries and bookstores. More important still, the LYUA report seemed to question the validity of one of the party's most cherished slogans: "Albania is building socialism under conditions of a fierce encirclement by imperialist and revisionist enemies." It is a slogan the party has used with obsessive intensity to justify its hard-line centralist rule and militant ideology, fuel its vitriolic polemics against the Soviet bloc and the West, whip up revolutionary fervor among the masses, and accelerate the pace of modernization in the country. The report of the youth leaders left no doubt that the young people in Albania did not share the revolutionary fervor of Hoxha's generation, and were restive over the APL's isolationist politics. They were looking toward links with the continent as an alternative to isolation.

The pressures to broaden contacts with Europe came also from the ranks of the artistic intelligentsia—from writers, painters, critics, entertainers, and others who had come to question the guiding principles of "socialist realism" in the arts, under which they labored. There were calls from this sector and from the youth that the party relinquish its close supervision of the LYUA and of the LAWA (League of Albanian Writers and Artists). The argument against party tutelage and in favor of autonomy, made by the intelligentsia and the youth, had won support even from some party members—a fact that caused much distress in the leadership of the party.

In spearheading the APL's drive to silence dissent among the intelligentsia and the youth, Hoxha said that the party was "opposed to tutelage and to dictatorial methods," but at the same time it was "opposed to any weakening, however slight, of [its] leadership in the mass organizations."[46] He took issue with almost every point raised in the February 1973 report of LYUA leaders. Contrary to the negative impression the report gave concerning young people, Hoxha said: "I am of the opinion that our youth are the happiest and most cheerful in the world," and then went on to give a vivid description of the benefits enjoyed by youth in contemporary Albania.[47] He insisted that partisan war themes were "the most suitable" of all themes for socialist Albania's youth since they must learn of the heroic sacrifices made by the makers of Albania's revolution. He said that the imperialist-revisionist encirclement of Albania called for constant vigilance, particularly ideological vigilance, since the encirclement was more ideological than geographical in nature. The encirclement was the sum total of myriad pressures exerted through literature, radio, TV, tourists, trade, fashions, etc., and was aimed at confusing the gullible, creating disorder in the country's economy, and causing political and ideological degeneration among the masses, above all among youth and intellectuals.[48]

In brief, the enemy's goal was to destroy socialist rule in Albania "by encouraging liberalism . . . and opening the way to the introduction into [the] country of alien influences."[49] Hoxha denounced those who advocated that Albania "should follow . . . the course of European development," saying: "No, comrades, we cannot and should not follow 'the European road'; on the contrary, it is Europe which should follow our road, because from the political standpoint, it is far behind us . . . far from that for which Marx, Engels, Lenin and Stalin fought."[50]

The APL's First Secretary mounted his attack on the intelligentsia at the Fourth Plenum of the party's Central Committee on June 26, 1973. He tried to show that the most serious international questions, such as détente and European security, cannot be divorced from seeming trifles such as miniskirts, pickpocketing, and rock-and-roll music. In the APL's vocabulary, détente means liberalism, and liberalism means degeneration and ruin for Albania's political system and social order. The Albanian party was opposed to European bourgeois culture not only for ideological and political reasons, but because of a certain puritanical element in its character. It was jealous of its socialist culture, and feared that exposure of European cultural influences would impair its "purity" and destroy its usefulness in building a morally sound and vigorous society. After denouncing every aspect of the bourgeois way of life, Hoxha concluded: "We have nothing to learn from this culture; we have no reason to impart it to our masses and youth, but should discard it contemptuously and fight it with determination."[51]

A special term used by Albania's officialdom to describe collectively the peculiar weaknesses and failings of the intelligentsia was "intellectualism." The term was applied to those who emphasized the role of reason and intellect in society, downgraded the value of physical work, and relied chiefly on argument and abstractions for solving complicated social problems, rather than on the proper combination of theory and practice, and the "teachings of life itself."

The Fourth Party Plenum in June 1973 expelled from the party two prominent Central Committee members: Fadil Paçrami, secretary of the Tiranë Party Committee and an influential playwright; and Todi Lubonja, director of Albanian radio and television. Paçrami was accused of being a "right-wing deviationist" with "liberal-anarchist" views, while Lubonja was said to harbor "liberal-opportunist" views and to have developed a strong taste for "modernist esthetics."[52] Rudi Monari, first secretary of the youth organization, also lost his post, and Dhimitër Shuteriqi was dismissed as president of the League of Writers and Artists of Albania after serving in that post since 1957.

The purge of the leaders of the youth organization and the intelligentsia revealed a gap in the understanding of Albanian reality by the Hoxha-Shehu team on the one hand, and the youth and intellectuals on the other. The divergence in views between the two sides brought into question many of the basic premises or mainsprings of the party's general line: its militant ideology, its revolutionary orientation, its extremist centralism, even its conception of Albanian nationalism. The doubts expressed by youth and members of the intelligentsia about the reality of "enemy encirclement" of Albania were part of the attack on the APL's ideology concerning such issues as isolationism, polemics, détente, and peaceful coexistence. Criticism of partisan war themes implied rejection of the party's class- and revolution-oriented art and culture, the militancy of the "uninterrupted revolution," and the "war psychosis" that pervaded Albanian society. In short, it implied a rebellion against the perpetuation of the cold war atmosphere in the nation.

Moreover, the objections voiced by the intelligentsia against the strictures of "socialist realism" and against the APL's paternal attitude toward artists and intellectuals amounted to an attack on the party's rigid centralism, that is, on its insistence to determine, direct, and control every facet of the country's cultural life. Finally, the desire of young people, artists, writers, students, and others to reach out toward other nations in Europe and establish meaningful communications with them bespoke conception of Albanian nationalism different from that of party leaders. Compared with this new idea of political identity, Albania's rulers were guilty of "narrow nationalism," for they stood for a form of patriotism that seemed to be both politically unenlightened and a hindrance to the modernization of the country. In light of the above, the purge of the intelligentsia in the name of antiliberalism and antimodernism was not likely to suppress dissent from this sector for very long.

In July 1974, Albania's ruling hierarchy met in plenary session to discuss matters of national defense. The plenum apparently decided to dismiss Albania's minister of defense, Politburo member Gen. Beqir Balluku, a long-time associate of Hoxha. In October, Balluku's downfall was indirectly confirmed when it was announced in Tiranë that Premier Shehu had been appointed minister of defense. The charges against the purged defense minister were not made public until November 1976, when the Seventh Congress of the Albanian Party of Labor convened in Tiranë. Speaking at the Congress, the party's First Secretary made a fierce attack on Balluku and his two chief subordinates, General Petrit Dume, the army's chief of staff and a candidate member of the Politburo, and Hito Çako, head of the army's Political Directorate and a member of the party's Central Committee. Hoxha accused the trio of being "a traitorous and putschist group," which operated as "a faction at the head of the army" and which intended "to overthrow by force" the party and the Stalinist social order in Albania.[53] He said that in this plot they relied also "on armed intervention from abroad," but failed to reveal the identity of the alleged alien conspirators. In a letter to the Chinese leadership, dated July 29, 1978, Albania further charged that Balluku had come under the influence of the Chinese, and had advocated a defense policy for Albania that was suggested by China, but was contrary to the position of the Albanian party. The charge cast Balluku in the role of a Chinese agent who "worked in secret" to carry out China's "hostile strategic plan" against Albania.

The fall of these three also brought down General Rahman Perllaku and Halim Ramohito, both of them APL-CC members and immediate subordinates of Dume and Çako. It was the greatest upheaval in the military establishment of postwar Albania. It was also the most significant, because it marked the most serious cleavage between the party and the military establishment in the history of socialist Albania.

The party's confrontation with the army apparently involved both foreign and domestic issues. An esoteric reading of Albanian sources indicates that the clash was the result of a variety of factors: nationalistic, ideological, institutional, and personal. It seems that Hoxha and Balluku held conflicting positions on the question of Albanian foreign policy and national defense policy.[54] Published Albanian reports implied that the general was not enthusiastic about the official defense policy, which is based on the doctrines of the people's war and the citizen-army, and favored instead the development of a modern professional army, and giving greater emphasis to advanced military technology.

On an institutional level, the army sometimes resisted party scrutiny or control of its affairs. The party in turn became concerned over the erosion of its authority in the army establishment. There was also a personal element in the controversy: the party's First Secretary apparently suspected Balluku of plotting to seize power and establish military rule in the country. In spite of Balluku's unblemished public record of loyalty and support of the First Secretary, Hoxha looked upon the defense minister as a personal rival who threatened his power and position as Albania's leader.[55] Army discipline, as well, became an important issue in the developments that led to Balluku's expulsion. Press reports told of a breakdown of discipline among soldiers and officers that threatened army morale and the efficiency of military operations. After examining this situation, party officials explained it by the standard formula. They attributed the army's problems mainly to manifestations of "liberal and bureaucratic attitudes" within the military establishment, but this could hardly be called a realistic analysis of the situation.

The dominant motive behind the shake-up in the army was probably the party's resolve to reaffirm its "leading role" in the military establishment and to keep intact the hard-line centralism of the regime. The party's confrontation with the army's leadership illustrated some of the basic features of its character and style of operation. The priority given to "guerrilla warfare" in the nation's defense policy revealed the party's continuing faith in the revolutionary strength and potential of the masses. And Hoxha's rather paranoic fear of an army coup led by Balluku showed that suspicion and intrigue—long institutionalized under the APL's Stalinist reign—continued to exert their influence on Albania's domestic politics.

Turning to the economic sector, when we consider the extremely backward economy of prewar Albania and the vast destruction caused by the war, the gains achieved by the Communist regime in developing the country's economy are indeed remarkable. The positive results of modernization are evident in all areas of the economy: industry, agriculture, communications, housing, transportation, and so on.[56] Some students of Albanian affairs are convinced that such progress could not have been made except by means of a centrally directed economy. They believe that the strong discipline of an authoritarian regime was necessary in order to overcome the country's legacy of backwardness and set it on the path of modernization.

Lately, however, the question has arisen whether the policies and methods that made rapid economic progress possible during the early postwar period have not become a stumbling block to further progress. The evidence suggests that the economy is facing serious problems in planning, production, organization, and management. Some of the problems are: lack of discipline on the job, high labor absenteeism, theft of "the public's wealth," damage to and destruction of "socialist property," exaggerated reports of overfulfillment of production norms, wasteful use of raw materials, and the sacrifice of quality for quantity in the production of goods in order to exceed production quotas. This last point is of special significance because of its effect on the country's foreign trade. Albanian officials have noted that some big countries buy Albanian goods for political reasons, even when such goods are of inferior quality. Referring to the Chinese, Hoxha has said: "Very often, they shut one eye with regard to the quality of our goods."[57]

Socialist Albania's economic problems are not new. They have bedevilled party and government officials since the early postwar years.[58] As usual, party leaders have assessed the problems of the economy from a political and ideological standpoint, rather than raising more pragmatic or technical questions that might have a bearing on such problems. In a speech in June 1973, Hoxha said that the "faults of the economy do not stem either from our system of management, or from the economic policy of our party. . . . [They] stem from the influence and pressure which the capitalist-revisionist encirclement exerts on our people, from the old petit-bourgeois mentality, and a narrow interpretation of the party's directives."[59]

In line with this analysis, APL leaders have laid the blame for the failures of the economy to "bureaucratism, intellectualism, and technocratism." The last term, technocratism, is used to attack those elements who seek to limit the participation of the working class in "the technological and scientific revolution"—which allegedly is now in progress in Albania—and who, in addition, look upon engineers, technicians, and specialists as the prime movers of industry and the economy.[60]

As in the case of the intelligentsia and the army, the Hoxha-Shehu team has been concerned over the party's "leading role"—that is, its prestige, authority, and monopoly of power—in the economic sector and in the Trade Unions of Albania (TUA), which is the mass organization of the working class. This concern stems especially from the fact that influential elements in the economy and the state administration have lately come to conceive of mass organizations such as the TUA, the LYUA, and the UAW (Union of Albanian Women) as "independent" units, even as "parties" rather than as "transmission belts" or instruments of the Albanian Party of Labor. Such a trend, of course, worried party leaders, who were quick to condemn it as "a dangerous deviation," and to attack "reformist enemies" of the party for trying to transform the APL from a revolutionary party into an organization that would perform only an educational or economic role in society. Speaking for the party on this subject in March 1975, Ramiz Alia, a Politburo member and a leading Albanian ideologist, denounced those who identified the working class with the trade union organization, rather than with the APL, and warned bureaucrats and technocrats to desist from attempting to subvert the party's leading role in the nation by placing "the caste of functionaries and technicians" above the party, and at the head of the country.[61]

To counter these threats and to invigorate the economy, the party leadership made great efforts for more than two decades to establish "workers' control" in the economy. "Workers' control" in the Albanian context means acknowledging the working class as the decisive force in production, and "as the sharpest weapon in the struggle against bureaucratism."[62] The Albanian regime sees workers' control primarily as a political weapon in its struggle against the domestic class enemy rather than as a pragmatic tool for achieving specified economic goals. These efforts have never proved very successful in spurring production, particularly food production, in which Albania traditionally has had a shortage. Since the early 1960s, the regime has depended mainly on China to meet the country's food needs, and to achieve the overall goals of the five-year economic plans. But as Hoxha once admitted, China had to make sacrifices in order to assure Albania of the foodstuffs it needed.[63] In 1975, problems of economic planning, allocation of resources, labor, use of funds, and production worsened. The situation was aggravated by restrictions on basic research in educational and research institutions, the inability of Albanian agriculture to produce enough food to meet the country's needs, and above all by China's reduction of aid and credits. The cutback in aid was reflected in Tiranë's cool reaction to the signing in Peking in July 1975 of a five-year economic agreement in connection with Albania's Sixth Five-Year Plan (1976–80).[64]

The aggravation of the economic situation produced a crisis within the party Politburo and led to a far-reaching shake-up in the economic sector. The reshuffle of personnel brought down two Politburo members: Abdyl Këllezi, a deputy prime minister, chairman of the State Planning Commission, and president of the Albania-China Friendship Society; and Koço Theodhosi, minister of industry and mining. Another cabinet member, Kiço Ngjela, minister of trade and a member of the party's Central Committee, also lost his post. There were unconfirmed reports that scores of other officials, accounting for as much as one-fourth of the personnel in the Albanian administration, were dismissed from their jobs. The three cabinet members who were expelled were replaced by relatively unknown party officials: Petro Dode, Pali Miska, and Nedin Hoxha, respectively.[65]

The evidence indicates that the purged leaders had advocated a significant reform of the country's economic system, aimed at decentralizing the planning and administration of the economy, as well as at broadening economic relations with other countries. They had argued, in effect, that the economic policy of Hoxha and Shehu amounted to "narrow nationalism" and a closed economic system. Their downfall presumably was also linked to the change in Albania's economic relations with China. The drop in Chinese aid apparently provoked serious controversy in the party Politburo over the economy, with the Këllezi group arguing for reform, and the Hoxha-Shehu leadership standing firm.

The nature of the controversy and the basic causes of the purge of the Këllezi group were publicized for the first time by the Albanian leadership at the party's Seventh Congress in November 1976. Both Hoxha and Premier Shehu made strong attacks on the dismissed leaders of the technocratic intelligentsia. They alleged that Këllezi, Theodhosi, Ngjela, and their followers had "renounced the principles of centralized direction" of the economy, and had attempted to introduce a form of "self-management"—apparently similar to that of Yugoslavia—into Albania's economic system. In the eyes of the APL leaderhip, however, "self-management" has always symbolized revisionism and the restoration of the capitalist system. Këllezi and his associates were accused of seeking to "depoliticize" the economy and of abandoning the principle of "class struggle" in planning and production.[66] In sum, the initiative of the Këllezi group to introduce rationalism and pragmatism into the economic system proved to be premature, and ended in failure and personal tragedy. In its refusal to revise its economic policies, the APL reaffirmed its dogmatic faith in Stalinist economics.

When in the summer of 1975 Greece proposed intra-Balkan economic cooperation, Albania rejected the plan. To be sure, in view of the great gulf between Albania's economic system and those of her immediate neighbors, Greece and Yugoslavia, as well as the serious ideological differences between Albania and the other Balkan countries, it was almost inevitable that Tiranë would spurn the Greek proposal. Yet once again, the party confirmed Albania's lonely course of isolationism.[67]

The International Experience of the Party

Over the past eighteen years, the key element in the APL's foreign policy has been unabated hostility toward United States "imperialism" and Soviet "modern revisionism" or "social-imperialism." The Albanian party has been a consistent advocate of the "twin-adversary" theory; namely, that the United States and the Soviet Union are two equally aggressive and equally dangerous superpowers, bent on world hegemony. According to this theory, the two characteristic features of the relationship between the United States and the USSR are collaboration and rivalry. To maintain their preeminent position in world affairs, and to continue to oppress, exploit, and manipulate other countries and peoples, they are prepared to unleash a third world war, fought with atomic weapons. The two superpowers, in the APL's view, are the source of all the evils and problems—whether economic, social, moral, racial, or ethnic—that beset the contemporary world. They are behind the Middle East conflict and the tensions in Africa, Korea, the Mediterranean, and elsewhere.[68] They are thus the greatest threat to world peace and to the security and well-being of peoples.

Starting from this general theoretical framework, the other elements in the APL's foreign policy follow more or less logically. The Hoxha leadership considers it its proletarian internationalist duty to call on all workers, revolutionaries, and all progressive peoples of the world to wage a relentless struggle against the two superpowers until those enemies are completely destroyed. In fact, the Albanian party has sought to encourage the creation of a united front of "the peoples of the world" against Soviet-American power. Accordingly, the APL opposed the 1975 Helsinki Conference on ESC, as well as all summit conferences between Soviet and American leaders, arguing that such talks do not advance the cause of peace, but merely cloak American and Soviet plots for aggression. On the military front, the Albanian party attacked NATO and the Warsaw Pact on the ground that the two blocs were under the control of the superpowers. On the economic front, the party opposed both the Common Market and the Comecon, since they allegedly did not serve the economic and national interests of the member states. Similarly, Albanian representatives at the UN utilized every opportunity to "unmask" the "savage features" of American and Soviet imperialism, and warned the rest of the world not to be misled by the détente politics of Moscow and Washington.

In spite of Hoxha's hostility toward Moscow, the Soviet leaders continued their decade-old efforts to draw Albania back into the Soviet orbit.[69] Hoxha and Shehu, however, rejected with scorn all Soviet bids to normalize relations, and instead continued to hope for—indeed to urge—a "second October Revolution" in the USSR, one which would sweep away the center of modern revisionism in the world.[70]

The most significant event of the 1970s, in terms of the international experience of the APL, concerned relations with Communist China, Albania's closest ally since the break with the Soviet Union in 1961. For a decade (1961–71), relations between the smallest Communist party in Eastern Europe, and the largest Communist party in the world were nearly ideal, based as they were on an almost perfect identity of views on foreign and domestic issues. During this period, Albania and China served as an outstanding example of harmonious relations between a big and a small country, and of socialist solidarity in the Communist world.

However, cracks began to appear in the alliance in 1971, with the start of an improvement in relations between China and the United States. Albanian leaders did not like this development, and began to make oblique attacks on their Chinese allies, warning that "you cannot rely on one imperialism [United States] to oppose another [USSR],"[71] and that any wavering or relaxation of the struggle against the United States was fraught with dangerous consequences. They were also unhappy over China's support of NATO and the European Common Market, both of which Albania denounced.

By 1975, the political and diplomatic divergences between China and Albania had affected their economic relations as well. The five-year economic pact (1976–80) provided evidence of this fact, and suggested that a turning point had been reached in the economic relationship between the two allies. Conclusive evidence of the changed relationship in this area came to light in the proceedings of the Seventh Party Congress (November 1976), when Premier Shehu barely mentioned China in his economic report.[72]

Accumulated tensions reached the crisis point in 1976 with the death of Mao Tse-tung and Chou En-lai (the architects of the Sino-Albanian entente), the fall of "The Gang of Four," and the rise of Hua Kuo-feng to the highest position of power in China. Albania's Stalinist leaders were sympathetic to the fallen hard-line, militant Politburo members of the Chinese Communist party, and therefore did not endorse their dismissal. The growing tensions between Albanian and Chinese leaders surfaced in July 1977, when Albania launched a strong attack on China's foreign policy, calling it "opportunistic" and a "flagrant departure from the teachings of Marxism-Leninism."[73] The Albanian statement took issue with China's revision of her policy toward the two superpowers, and with the view that the Soviet Union is a more aggressive and more dangerous power than the United States. The focus of the Albanian attack, however, was on the Chinese theory of "The Three Worlds" which, according to Hoxha and Shehu, aligned China with the most reactionary regimes of the developing countries, and against the proletariat and revolutionaries of the world. Albanian leaders denounced the theory as thoroughly pernicious and antirevolutionary. A third major point of friction between Hoxha and the Chinese was China's reconciliation with the "renegade" Yugoslav leadership, and her endorsement of Tito's nonalignment foreign policy. Albanian leaders have consistently assailed that policy as counterrevolutionary, its aim being to smother national liberation movements and to preserve Western imperialist influence and power in the world. Tito's historic visit to China in the summer of 1977 served to reinforce Albania's conclusion that China had abandoned the cause of the proletariat and the revolution, and had become a revisionist country, no different in principle from Yugoslavia and the Soviet Union. Indeed, by early 1978 Albania had gone so far as to label China's foreign policy "social-chauvinism."

Albania's ideological polemics against her former ally were neatly summarized by Premier Shehu on November 29, 1977, on the occasion of the thirty-third anniversary of Albania's liberation from Fascism. He declared that "to make common cause with, and reconcile yourself ideologically with the Yugoslav leadership means that you are not a Marxist, but a revisionist."[74] Continuing, he said: "The theory of 'the three worlds' is a great threat to the international Communist and workers' movement. It is the theory of unconditional capitulation to the bourgeoisie and all-round alliance with American imperialism. It is the theory of the stifling of the peoples' liberation struggle."[75]

In the meantime, the Albanian leadership mounted a vigorous campaign to win the support and allegiance of the so-called Marxist-Leninist Communist parties and groups. The campaign amounted to an attempt to wrest from Peking the leadership of the militant revolutionary forces.

The Chinese did not reply to the Albanian attack of July, 1977 until four months later, and even then only in an indirect fashion. The reply was in the form of a lengthy theoretical article entitled, "Chairman Mao's Theory of the Differentiation of the Three Worlds Is a Major Contribution to Marxism-Leninism"[76] The Chinese reply did not impress the Albanians. Tiranë continued its thinly veiled polemics against Peking's foreign policy in the months that followed. Convinced that their differences with Albania were irreparable, the Chinese took the decisive step on July 7, 1978—exactly one year after Tiranë's denunciation of Peking's theory of the Three Worlds—to cut off all economic and military aid to Albania, and to recall all their specialists working in that country.[77] The Chinese telegraphic agency reported that China's aid to Albania had totaled about $5 billion since 1954, second only to its aid to Vietnam.

Albania reacted with characteristic vehemence to the Chinese initiative. In a long and harsh letter to the Chinese Communist Party, dated July 29, 1978, the Albanian Party leadership condemned China's decision, calling it a "perfidious and hostile act" that sought to "sabotage the cause of revolution and socialism in Albania".[78] The letter complained of Chinese "big state chauvinism" toward Albania, and accused China of seeking to become an imperialist superpower. Hua Kuo-feng's August 1978 visit to Yugoslavia provided Albanian leaders with additional fuel for their anti-China polemics. They charged that Chairman

Hua's visit aimed at "creating enmities among the Balkan peoples" and inciting "a third world war".[79]

In effect, Albania's public attacks on China in 1977 and 1978 put an end to the sixteen-year-old Albanian-Chinese alliance. The rift caused a historic split in the Marxist-Leninist wing of the international Communist movement. It cost China her strongest political base in Europe, and it splintered anew the once monolithic Communist world.

At the same time, the rift with her Chinese comrades accentuated Albania's ideological and political isolation and posed problems for her economy. It also reaffirmed the APL's extraordinary commitment to cold war politics and ideology, its continuing loyalty to the Stalinist legacy, and its undiminished faith in the cause of world revolution. Furthermore, it confirmed the party's essential independence. Albania was not—as some Western observers claimed—a mere mouthpiece of Peking, but was following her own road to socialism.

A CONCLUDING NOTE

On December 28, 1976, the People's Assembly of Albania adopted a new state constitution to replace the old constitution of 1946, deemed inadequate to meet the current and future needs of the country.[80] The new document proclaimed Albania as a "Socialist People's Republic" in order to distinguish her from "so-called socialist countries," for a chief motive for drafting the new constitution was the desire to draw a clear demarcation line between the "genuine" socialism of Albania and the false socialism of the revisionist camp, headed by the Soviet Union.

The document reaffirms all of the distinguishing features that characterize the Albanian Party of Labor and the Albanian regime. The intense spirit of nationalism and concern for national security is evident in the opening paragraphs of the preamble and in the section on national defense, which prohibits the stationing of foreign troops and the establishment of foreign bases on Albanian territory. This section also contains an article which prohibits anyone from surrendering the country or allowing it to be occupied by foreign powers. Furthermore, the document provides for the creation of a defense council, to be headed by Enver Hoxha or his successor.

The new constitution sanctifies the party's dedication to ideology by asserting that "the ruling ideology" in Albania is Marxism-Leninism, and that in its policy Albania is guided "by the great ideals of socialism and Communism and struggles for their triumph throughout the world." The party's fervor for revolutionary politics is made plain in Article 4 which says that Albania "develops the revolution" through the class struggle for the purpose of "assuring the final triumph of the socialist road over the capitalist road." Preoccupation with modernization is evident in the statement that "Albania has entered the stage of the complete construction of socialism," and that "new conditions have been created" for continuous progress toward that goal.

Extremist centralism is writ large in the new constitution. Albania is "the state of the dictatorship of the proletariat"; the APL is "the only leading political force" in the nation; foreign and domestic trade are under the control of the state; and political and economic life in Albania develops "in struggle against bureaucratism and liberalism." The radical posture of the party on religion is confirmed: religion is banned from the state.

Commenting on the new constitution, Politburo member Hysni Kapo said that through it "the dictatorship of the proletariat in Albania will be kept forever pure and indomitable."[81] Indeed, the primary motive for drafting a new constitution was apparently to ensure the continuation of the general line of the Albanian Party of Labor after the deaths of Hoxha and Shehu, and thus to perpetuate Stalinism on the shores of the Adriatic. That, at any rate, is the hope of Albania's doctrinaire leaders, but the dialectical unfolding of history may have in store a different political future for Albania.

NOTES

1. Yugoslavia is an exception in the sense that she was never a member of the Warsaw Pact.

2. For the fullest account of Albania's position on détente and European security, see "The Conference of Insecurity of Europe," *Albania today* (September–October 1975), no. 5, pp. 36–39.

3. A perceptive report on Albanian atheism appeared recently under the title, "Where God Is Dead," in *The Economist*, December 27, 1975, pp. 27–28.

4. The question of heavy industry vs. light industry, that is, production of consumer goods, apparently became a central issue in high-level party discussions of economic policy in 1975. See *The New York Times*, November 23, 1975.

5. *Zëri i Popullit* (Voice of the People), daily organ of the APL, November 8, 1961; Document 14 in William E. Griffith, *Albania and the Sino-Soviet Rift* (Cambridge, Mass.: MIT Press, 1963), p. 263.

6. A good collection of the principal APL statements on revisionism is to be found in Patrick Kessel, *Les communistes albanais contre le révisionisme* (Paris: Union générale d'éditions, 1974) and in Gilbert Mury, ed., *Face au révisionisme*, containing selections from Enver Hoxha's writings (Paris: F. Maspero, 1972).

7. More recently, APL spokesmen pointed to the victorious struggle of the Indochinese peoples as further proof of the correctness of the party's thesis on armed struggle, and to the overthrow of Allende in Chile as proof by negative example of the same thesis. See "The Tragic Events in Chile—A Lesson for All Revolutionaries in the World," *Zëri i Popullit*, October 2, 1973; "Revolutionary and Fraternal Greetings to the Heroic Cambodian People," *Albania today*, (May–June, 1975), no. 3, pp. 57–58.

8. Even today, Albanian officials become indignant when tourists take photographs of peasants riding donkeys, or of quaint, dilapidated houses, instead of photographing the new railroads, factories and apartments that have been built under the socialist regime.

9. Albania completed the electrification of all towns and villages on October 25, 1970, and with a view to commemorating this accomplishment, decreed that October 25 be observed annually as "The People's Festival of Light."

10. For centuries the Albanians lived under the paradoxical "despotic-anarchic" rule of the sultans of Istanbul, while King Zog's regime (1924–39) was but a mild form of dictatorship.

11. Albania completed the collectivization of agriculture in 1967. In the same year, the regime abolished all ranks in the military forces, and closed all public places of worship. 1967 thus stands out as the year of the greatest radicalization of Albanian life under Communist rule.

12. In 1938, at least 80 percent of the population was illiterate, and large areas of the lowlands were dangerous, malaria-infested marches.

13. For a perceptive study of the nature of the Albanian state from a historical perspective, see the essay by Arshi Pipa, "Zhvillimi Politik i Shtetit Shqiptar 1912–1962" (The Political Development of the Albanian State 1912–1962). *Shqiptari i Lirë* (New York), November–December 1962.

14. At that time, Albania had a population of about 1 million. When the party was founded in 1941, it had a total of only 200 members.

15. *Statuti i Partisë së Punës të Shqipërisë* (The Statutes of the Albanian Party of Labor) (Tiranë: n.p., 1972), p. 66. Hereafter cited as *Statuti.*

16. *Ibid.*, pp. 4, 75–76.

17. Stavro Skendi, ed., *Albania* (New York: Praeger, 1956), pp. 85–86; "History of the Albanian Communist Party II," *News from Behind the Iron Curtain* (January 1956), 5(1):27–29.

18. Enver Hoxha, *Socialism Is Built By the Masses* (Tiranë: The Political Book, 1972), pp. 97, 149.

19. *Statuti*, pp. 13–15.

20. *Ibid.*, pp. 18–19.

21. See *History of the Party of Labor of Albania*, prepared by the Institute of Marxist-Leninist Studies (Tiranë: N. Frashëri, 1971), pp. 71–73; and Ramadan Marmullaku, *Albania and the Albanians* (London: c. hurst, 1975), pp. 67–71. Hoxha married Nexhmie Xhangolli in 1945, an APL-CC member since 1948 and currently Director of the Institute of Marxism-Leninist Studies. They have two sons and one daughter.

22. Skendi, *Albania*, pp. 341–43. Shehu is married to Fiqret Sanxhaktari, an APL-CC member since 1952 and presently Director of the "V.I. Lenin" Party School in Tiranë.

23. Enver Hoxha, *Speeches, 1971–1973* (Tiranë: 8 Nëntori, 1974), pp. 394–95.

24. A total of 2,865 members, roughly 10 percent of the party's membership, were expelled between 1945 and 1948; another 12,000 (more than a fourth of the party's members) were dropped between November 1948 and the end of 1951. See *Kongresi i Irë i Partisë Komuniste të Shqipërisë* (First Congress of the Albanian Communist Party) (Tiranë: M. Duri Press, 1950), p. 391; Skendi, *Albania*, p. 86.

25. Enver Hoxha, *Report Submitted to the 6th Congress of the Party of Labor of Albania* (Tiranë: N. Frashëri, 1971), p. 180.

26. Enver Hoxha, *Raporte e fjalime 1965–1966* (Reports and Speeches 1965–1966) (Tiranë: N. Frashëri, 1971), p. 335.

27. *Ibid.*, p. 230.

28. In the Ministries of Health, Commerce, and the State Planning Commission, the figures were 56.9, 52.2, and 50.5 percent, respectively. See Hoxha, *Socialism*, pp. 22–23. Communists also made up

the majority of the cadres in the youth, labor, and women's organizations, the figures for these being 52.2, 67.2, and 65.8 percent, respectively. *Ibid.*, p. 26.

29. *Ibid.*, p. 23.

30. Enver Hoxha, speech to the APL-CC Politburo on the struggle against bureaucratism, February 3–4, 1966, *Raporte e fjalime*, p. 217; PPSH, *Mbi diktaturën e proletariatit dhe mbi demokracinë socialiste* (APL, On the Dictatorship of the Proletariat and Socialist Democracy) (Tiranë: M. Duri Press, presumed date of publication, 1968), pp. 86–103. Hereafter cited as *Mbi diktaturën.*

31. Hoxha, *Speeches, 1971–1973*, pp. 136, 143–44.

32. *Ibid.*, p. 134.

33. Hoxha, *Raporte e fjalime*, pp. 228, 230.

34. *Ibid.*, p. 233.

35. *Ibid.*, p. 237.

36. Hoxha, *Speeches, 1971–1973*, pp. 132–33.

37. In the first year of the Cultural Revolution, the number of government functionaries was reduced by one-half, and some 15,000 cadres were put on "production work," especially in the countryside.

38. APL-CC "Open Letter," March 4, 1966, in *Mbi diktaturën*, p. 72.

39. *Ibid.*, p. 79.

40. Hoxha, *Speeches, 1971–1973*, pp. 75–76.

41. *Ibid.*, pp. 132–33, 152–53. It is possible, too, that there was a connection between these deliberations concerning some flexibility and moderation in the party line, and China's first significant steps toward better relations with the West.

42. Hoxha, *Speeches, 1971–1973*, p. 293.

43. The term "liberalism" was also used as a weapon to attack manifestations of laxity and complacent attitudes in the economic sector, the army, and other areas of Albanian life.

44. Enver Hoxha, Report to the Fourth APL-CC Plenum, June 26, 1973, entitled, "Intensify the Ideological Struggle Against Alien Manifestations and Liberal Attitudes Toward Them," *Speeches, 1971–1973*, p. 392. Hereafter cited as Report to the Fourth Party Plenum.

45. Enver Hoxha, "Everything In Our Country Is Done and Built for the Youth," *Speeches, 1971–1973*, pp. 238–69. Hereafter cited as Speech, February 23, 1973.

46. Hoxha, Report to the Fourth Party Plenum, p. 396.

47. Hoxha, Speech, February 23, 1973, p. 240.

48. *Ibid.*, p. 259.

49. *Ibid.*, p. 260.

50. *Ibid.*, p. 261.

51. Hoxha, Report to the Fourth Party Plenum, p. 334.

52. *Ibid.*, pp. 341, 357.

53. Enver Hoxha, *Raport në Kongresin VII të PPSH* (Report to the Seventh APL Congress) (Tiranë: 8 Nëntori, 1976), p. 144.

54. Enver Hoxha, *Our Policy Is An Open Policy* (Tiranë: 8 Nëntori 1974), p. 72.

55. Ndreçi Plasari, "The Strength and Invincibility of Our Army Lie in Its Popular and Revolutionary Character," *Rruga e Partisë* (The Party Road), monthly journal of the APL (February 1975), 22(2):40.

56. For example, between 1938 and 1973, total industrial production had grown 86 times, the area of arable land had doubled, and the area of land under irrigation had increased from 10.5 percent to 56 percent. See *30 Vjet Shqipëri socialiste* (30 Years of Socialist Albania), prepared by the General Directorate of Statistics (Tiranë: M. Duri, 1974), pp. 56, 105.

57. Hoxha, *Raporte e fjalime*, p. 43.

58. *Mbi diktaturën*, pp. 34, 36, 38.

59. Hoxha, Report to the Fourth Party Plenum, p. 368.

60. Rita Marko, Report to the Seventh Congress of the Trade Unions of Albania, *Zëri i Popullit*, May 9, 1972.

61. Ramiz Alia, "Let Us Strengthen the Leading Role of the Party In the Work of the Trade Unions," *Rruga e Partisë* (April 1975), 22(4):5–15.

62. *Zëri i Popullit*, May 9, 1972.

63. Hoxha, *Raporte e fjalime*, p. 77.

64. *Zëri i Popullit*, July 4–5, 1975.

65. *The Washington Post*, October 28, 1975; *The New York Times*, November 2, 1975. For the most informative account of the 1973–75 purges in Albania, see Louis Zanga, "Changes in Albanian Leadership Signify Struggle for Succession to Power," *Radio Free Europe Research* (Albania), November 24, 1975.

66. See Hoxha's report to the congress, *Zëri i Popullit*, November 2, 1976; and Ndreçi Plasari, "APL Has a Single Marxist-Leninist Line," *Ibid.*, February 20, 1977.

67. *The Economist*, September 27, 1975, pp. 55–56.

68. Speech at the UN General Assembly by Nesti Nase, Albanian Minister of Foreign Affairs, October 6, 1977, *Zëri i Popullit*, October 7, 1977.

69. *Izvestia*, November 29, 1975; January 13, 1976.

70. *Zëri i Popullit*, November 7 and 16, 1975. The publication in November 1975 of the nineteenth volume of Hoxha's collected *Works*, containing documents on his angry talks with Khrushchev in Moscow in November 1960, received wide publicity in the West.

71. See Hoxha's report to the Sixth APL Congress, *Zëri i Popullit*, November 2, 1971.

72. Mehmet Shehu, *Report on the 6th 5-Year Plan (1976–1980)* (Tiranë: N. Frashëri, 1976), p. 78.

73. "Teoria dhe praktika e revolucionit" (The Theory and Practice of Revolution), *Zëri i Popullit*, July 7, 1977.

74. *Ibid.*, November 30, 1977.

75. *Ibid.*, November 30, 1977.

76. *Peking Review*, No. 45 (November 4, 1977), pp. 10–41.

77. *The New York Times*, July 12, 1978; *Peking Review*, No. 29 (July 21, 1978), pp. 20–23.

78. "Letter of the CC of the Party of Labour and the Government of Albania to the CC of the Communist Party and the Government of China," 8 Nëntori, Tiranë, 1978, p. 1; *The New York Times*, July 31, 1978.

79. *Zëri i Popullit*, September 3, 1978.

80. *Ibid.*, December 29, 1976.

81. *Zëri i Popullit*, November 18, 1975. See also *The Economist*, January 31, 1976, pp. 52–53.

L. A. D. Dellin

2. The Communist Party of Bulgaria

It sounds paradoxical that the successes of the Bulgarian Communist party have been inversely related to its numerical strength, that its final victory was due entirely to the Soviet invasion, and its permanence dependent on the threat of Soviet intervention and domestic repression. Yet, the party—at least until its total "bolshevization" in the mid-thirties—had its own history and characteristics, including the largest relative following of all Balkan Communist parties.

THE PAST

From Origins to Power

The Bulgarian party prides itself on being among the oldest of Communist parties, having been formally organized as the Bulgarian Social Democratic party in 1891.[1] Its most prominent organizer was Dimitur Blagoev who had formed the first Marxist study group in Russia in 1883. While the Russian tradition was to become increasingly influential over time, the founding fathers included prominent disciples of the Western (mainly German) fountainhead, most notably Yanko Sakuzov. It soon became obvious that the two traditions were incompatible, not only for tactical and strategic but also for ideological reasons and, after repeated splits and reconciliations, the final separation occurred in 1903: then, the "revisionist" socialists under Sakuzov were expelled (aping Lenin's precedent) and the two parties added to their names the designations "broad" and "narrow" respectively, signifying their different interpretations of Marxism (evolutionary and pragmatic vs. revolutionary and dogmatic). Yet even Blagoev, the leader of the "narrow socialists," remained for years a theoretical purist, miles apart from Lenin's power-subordinated theorizing, in that he was prepared, indeed bound, to wait for the stage of developed capitalism and a dominant industrial proletariat before leading the inevitable revolution.

In Bulgaria, Marxists were faced with an underdeveloped society with a largely peasant population, yet one without striking inequalities in income, a country recently liberated from many centuries of Turkish overlordship and engulfed in nationalist-revisionist fervor. Under normal circumstances, the Marxist parties were destined for a long wait, especially as their appeal remained limited primarily to intellectuals.

The fortunes of the party became, therefore, tied mostly to outside events. The Balkan Wars (1912–13) and Bulgaria's participation in World War I (1915–19) caused, in rapid succession, disproportionate human and material losses. Disturbances within the defeated nation were conducive to Communist successes as was the postwar polarization brought about by the rule of the Agrarians under Alexandur Stamboliyski (1919–23).

In fact, the membership of the newly reconstituted Bulgarian Communist party increased to 21,000 in 1919 and to 38,000 in 1920 (the largest membership before the Communist seizure of power). At this time, the party polled about one-fourth of the votes cast (about 185,000) and became the second strongest political party, after the Agrarians, while the intimidated "bourgeois" parties lost ground. In this election, 96 percent of the party members came from the peasantry and the middle class.[2]

Infatuated with its success and unable to recognize the atypical conditions for it, the party assumed an uncompromising attitude. It antagonized Stamboliyski as well as its traditional opponents. As a result of its frontal attempt to seize power in the abortive September 1923 revolt, the party was outlawed and decimated.

Its second round of success came as a consequence of the world depression of the early thirties when, under the name of the Workers' party, it claimed a membership of 30,000, won 31 out of 274 seats in the parliamentary election in 1931, and posted a majority in the capital's municipal elections in 1932.[3] However, the dissolution of all political parties by the authoritarian Zveno Government of Kimon Georgiev, which performed a military coup in 1934, forced the party underground. It did not emerge until its own coup of September 1944, when the Soviet armies were crossing the Danube into Bulgaria.

In considering the leadership, programs, and policies of the party during its opposition period, it should be recalled that, initially, the party leadership, under Blagoev and his close collaborator Georgi Kirkov, did not expect to come to power in their lifetime. Furthermore, in their uncompromising intellectualism, they did not seek alliances with "nonproletarian" forces. Present-day Communist historians accuse the "dogmatic" party of those days with having failed to comprehend Leninism and, particularly, the need for cooperation with the peasantry and its effect on the chances for the proletarian revolution.[4]

Even after 1919, when the party—under Vasil Kolarov and Georgi Dimitrov—joined the Third International and adopted revolutionary goals, it was not yet "bolshevized." The "peasant opening" was made difficult by the emergence of the Agrarian movement—with its antiproletarian and class philosophy—which, in 1919 under Stamboliyski, gained power it did not wish to share. In fact, both parties looked with suspicion upon each other; when Stamboliyski's regime assumed dictatorial proportions and was overthrown by a broad coalition of the traditional parties under A. Tsankov in June 1923, the Communists stood idly by and even rejoiced in the elimination of a rival. However, this "passivity" was castigated by the Comintern as a cardinal error and the party was ordered to unseat the Tsankov "fascist regime" by means of a belated alliance with the Agrarians and other dissatisfied groups. The party leadership at first defended itself and its policy of neutrality but eventually submitted, with a few exceptions, and staged the unfortunate

September 1923 uprising whose easy suppression decimated the party for years to come. But Moscow's will was apparently more important than objective reality and sound judgment, thus setting a precedent for the future. After the uprising, the party leadership fled to the USSR, where Kolarov, Dimitrov, Chervenkov, and others served as Comintern functionaries until their return to Bulgaria after World War II.

The survivors at home, however, did not wish to take the defeat as conclusive, and engaged in an unauthorized "ultraleft sectarian" course which included sporadic terrorist acts, the most notorious being the bomb explosion in the Sofia Cathedral in 1925. They even wrested the party leadership from the "Muscovites" in 1929 and held it well into the mid-thirties under Iskrov and Boykov. Their uncompromising attitude toward potential allies and their belief in the self-destructiveness of the capitalist social structure came in conflict with the united-front policy of the Comintern and Dimitrov, who had been lionized at the Leipzig trial and who saw to it that the domestic leadership was purged by none other than the future "Titoist" Traycho Kostov.

By the late thirties the Bulgarian Old Guard in Moscow had restored its control and the party finally became bolshevized in Stalin's image. The period between the Popular Front of 1935 and the Fatherland Front of World War II found the party's influence as strong in Moscow as it was weak in Sofia. The loyalty of the Bulgarians (coupled with Dimitrov's saga, and—of course—ethnic, linguistic, and historic affinity with the Russians) made their contingent in Moscow increasingly important in the Communist movement, with Dimitrov now secretary-general of the Comintern. The major benefit, in national terms, was probably the support of Moscow and the Comintern for Bulgaria's national aspirations from as early as the end of World War I when the Balkan Communist Federation was formed and propounded a revisionist, pro-Bulgarian, stance on Macedonia and Thrace. This stance was gradually eroded by the need to oppose Nazi Germany and, after the outbreak of the Second World War and the emergence of Tito's growing contributions to the resistance struggle, by Moscow's endorsement of Tito's goal of a Macedonia within Yugoslavia. The Bulgarian party leadership complied, as usual, although it had taken over Macedonia's Communist party after Yugoslavia's disintegration in 1941 on the principle of "one territory—one party."

Domestically, the party was unable to attract allies in the united front (it attracted only the small radical group of Pladne Agrarians in 1936) because of its previous uncompromising stance and its reputation for terrorism. The successes of the country at that time also limited the party's growth. The peasantry reaped benefits from the higher food prices of exports to Germany. Nationalistic passions, although much more restrained than in periods past, did not provide fertile ground for Communist inroads. The vacillations in Moscow's foreign policy did not help the party either, as the party—in the span of only two years—went from opposing to supporting to again opposing Nazi Germany on the one hand, and Bulgarian revisionism on the other.

The party's efforts to attract support became mandatory after the Nazi attack on the Soviet Union, but the call for armed resistance could not rouse much enthusiasm in a country which was reaping territorial benefits as an Axis ally without engaging in military operations. The party opted for subversion instead of outright partisan warfare. Therefore, Dimitrov's appeal, made over the Soviet radio in 1942, for a Fatherland Front coalition could be implemented only in 1943, after signs of a reversal on the Eastern front became obvious. Yet, even then the coalition included only leaders of marginal groups (the Pladne Agrarians, left-wing socialists, other unattached personalities, and the Military League–Zveno group, which, however, had its supporters in the army and had staged the two previous coups in 1923 and 1934). The two major political parties, the Agrarians under Gichev and the Democrats under Mushanov, as well as the smaller yet influential Social-Democrats under Pastukhov and the Populists under Burov, refused to join the Fatherland Front and formed instead their own coalition.

The Communist resistance limited itself to political assassinations and unsuccessful attempts at sabotage by terrorists parachuted or landed from the Soviet Union, acts which provoked persecutions of both the leadership and the rank and file with the result that the party membership declined to about 8,500, and most of the leaders were sent to jail or executed. As to the partisan movement, a People's Liberation Army (Nova) formed in 1943, numbering about 500; at its height, before the seizure of power, it reached about 2,000, to which another 8,000 partisans would be added—all in all a minimal effort, despite the appreciable casualties (estimated at about 5,000) of an increasingly ruthless government campaign. Though the Bulgarian resistance was numerically small (partly because there were few Germans in Bulgaria to fight), it was still the largest resistance group in any of Germany's satellites and gave the Communists further experience in self-sacrifice as well as a lust for revenge, albeit primarily on behalf of the interests of Moscow.[5]

The Seizure and Consolidation of Power

It is now freely admitted by Communist sources that the party would not have been able to seize, let alone consolidate, its power without the entry of the Red Army and its prolonged stay in the country, unchallenged by the United States.[6]

In some respects the Bulgarian case was atypical. Thus, the country was an Axis satellite without an exile government and, therefore, not among the Western allies to be liberated; but—and this was its unique status among the Axis members—it had not declared war on the Soviet Union and had maintained diplomatic representatives, although relations were all but friendly. This not only made the work of the party more difficult but—in the eyes of the Bulgarian government—insured that, in case of a German collapse, Moscow would keep hands off Bulgaria or, at most, serve as an intermediary between Bulgaria and the Western Allies, with whom Bulgaria was at war. Because of her neutrality toward the USSR, preventing Bulgaria's active involvement in the war required some delicate justification to Hitler and the other Axis allies, an accomplishment ascribed to the personal merits of King Boris. His mysterious death was, in fact, believed to have been caused by Hitler's agents as an act of retribution, although convincing substantiation for this theory is lacking.

As the Red Army approached the Romanian border, a newly formed government (headed by the former Agrarian Ivan Bagryanov) was planning an about-face, an attempt to extricate the country from the Axis camp yet without sacrificing the territories "liberated" from Yugoslavia and Greece. Gradually, the initiative passed to the democratic opposition which, in a strong letter also signed by the members of the Communist-led Fatherland Front, urged an end to the state of war against Britain and the United States and the restoration of political freedoms. This act was a recognization of the subordinate role of the Communists, who seemed to have had no hopes of success as an independent group at that time.

When, however, the Romanians capitulated and the Red Army was approaching the Danube, the Communist attitude suddenly changed. The government was now trying feverishly to conclude an armistice with the Western Allies; but the Soviet Union, apparently seeing a chance to interfere in Bulgaria as well, intervened in the armistice process, although it had no right to do so, and the Communists called for the government's overthrow. A new government, headed by the Agrarian K. Muraviev, a nephew of Stamboliyski, united the democratic opposition parties. Muraviev's government offered the Communists and the Fatherland Front coparticipation, but the latter suddenly refused. Moscow and the Bulgarian Communists apparently were readying themselves for a takeover.

The stage was set by the unexpected Soviet declaration of war on September 5, a declaration made without consultation even with the Western Allies, at a time when Bulgaria had broken with the Axis and had decided on war against Nazi Germany. Thus, the country managed to be at war simultaneously with all warring groups. The surprise and confusion was complete when the Red Army crossed the Danube on September 8; the Government sued for an armistice, foregoing resistance by the almost intact Bulgarian army, and hoped for a Soviet halt. Instead, in the morning hours of September 9, the Fatherland Front, acting through its Military League–Zveno component (of which the minister of war, Ivan Marinov, was a secret adherent) penetrated the Ministry of War, where the government was deliberating, arrested the Cabinet, and bloodlessly installed the Communist-led coalition. The Red Army could move in, hailed as a "liberator."

These circumstances—the unexpected Soviet invasion and the resulting accession to power by the Soviet-loyal Communists—eventually determined the future of the country in a most absurd way: it tied it to the great power whose past role had once been decisive for Bulgarian liberation, but whose policies and regime were now widely feared; and it brought to power a movement which was a decisive minority, with an ideology, methods, and goals quite alien to many of Bulgaria's traditional values.

The phases of party ascendancy followed familiar patterns, yet with greater speed and ferocity than elsewhere. Although nominally a minority in the Fatherland Front government, the Communists occupied the key ministries of the Interior (police) and Justice (courts), and held control of the all-powerful local extraconstitutional Fatherland Front committees. This allowed the party to eliminate the pre-Communist leadership at the national and local levels through "people's courts" proceedings and outright police ("people's militia") and other personal-revenge measures to an extent apparently unparalleled elsewhere in the satellite states (estimates go as high as 100,000 killed, including the execution of the regents, and most ministers and deputies of all governments since 1941). Even Bagryanov was hanged and the anti-Nazi Muraviev's cabinet members received harsh prison terms. The intact Bulgarian army, a potential rival, was sent out of the country as far as the Alps to fight the German forces under Soviet command, leaving the militia as the major source of power. After the end of military operations, the leadership of the returning armies which had suffered heavy casualties (over

30,000 dead) was purged and the influence of the conspiratorial Military League ally eradicated.

The next phase of power consolidation included the gradual elimination of the non-Communist allies in the Fatherland Front itself. A United Opposition, headed by the Agrarian Nikola Petkov, who left the coalition in utter disappointment and joined the leaders of the traditional parties, staged a monumental struggle, winning about one-third of the seats to the Grand National Assembly in 1946, despite intimidation and terror. However, when it transpired that the Western powers did not intend to force compliance with the provisions of the Potsdam Declaration and other agreements, the Soviet-backed Communists, who had brought back Georgi Dimitrov from Moscow as the new Bulgarian prime minister, decimated their opponents and hanged Petkov in September 1947.[7] Ironically, the United States recognized the Communist-led government a week after the hanging, adding—as Bulgarians claim with justification—insult to injury. The Communist party, which had increased its membership to 250,000, more than ten times that of September 1944, had no one to fear from the outside any longer. A "people's republic" with a new "Dimitrov Constitution" replaced the monarchy and the parliamentary form of government, and the Moscow contingent of Bulgarian Communists, led by Dimitrov and Kolarov, secured the country as a Soviet stronghold.

The third phase centered on an intraparty conflict with a purge of real or imaginary deviationists, most notably Traycho Kostov, party secretary and logical successor to Dimitrov. Kostov was accused of Titoist crimes and duly executed in 1949.[8] Dimitrov himself, who had been in favor of a Balkan federation with Tito's Yugoslavia and even of a larger East European federation, was quick to purge the "Kostovites." His brother-in-law, Vulko Chervenkov, assumed the leadership in 1950, after the deaths of both Dimitrov and Kolarov. Chervenkov ruled the country in Stalinist fashion, isolating it from the West, purging Party membership by about one-fourth, and turning Bulgaria into a copy of the Soviet system.

The drastic results of the *Gleichschaltung*, including the physical elimination of friend and foe alike, explain best the absence ever since of serious opposition from outside or within the party. Thus the "Thaw" after Stalin's death, and especially after Khrushchev's denunciation of his patron, was limited to some minor rebellions of collective farmers and tobacco workers in 1953 and, later on, in 1956, to some writers' and journalists' criticism of the Stalinist features of the regime. But the accumulated resentment did not explode, not only because the leadership remained united in the face of the common danger but also because, after initial caution, drastic preventive measures were taken through mass deportations and intimidations. Once the Hungarian revolution was crushed, the regime breathed more easily and congratulated itself for its successful measures as a loyal Soviet supporter.

Still, Chervenkov had to go, yet he fell from power very gradually—over a span of eight years and after a period of "collective leadership" with rival Anton Yugov and compromise choice Todor Zhivkov. Elected First Secretary in 1954, Zhivkov apparently benefited from Khrushchev's animosity toward Chervenkov, and by April 1956 he was selected to promote the official struggle against the "personality cult" and for rehabilitation and reconciliation with the Kostovites. By 1961, Zhivkov had maneuvered himself into the dual position of party secretary and premier, after purging his rivals and gaining Khrushchev's full confidence. In 1971, he exchanged the premiership for the head-of-state position. His reign has now lasted more than fifteen years and he has grown, with minor challenges and purges, into an undisputed leader, albeit symbol of subservience to the Soviets and of domestic suppression in a largely bureaucratic and apathetic society.[9]

THE PRESENT

Party Organization and Membership

As a faithful follower of the Soviet prototype, the Bulgarian party mirrors the Soviet organizational structure.[10] Its underlying principles are "democratic centralism" and the "territorial-production principle"; its leading role in society as well as its recognition of the Soviet primacy under the slogans of "dictatorship of the proletariat" and "proletarian internationalism" are officially stated and practiced in their Soviet form.

The latest party statute was adopted in 1962 (Eighth Congress); the latest party program, along with the new Bulgarian constitution, was voted in 1971 (Tenth Congress). The most recent (Eleventh) Party Congress took place in 1976.[11]

The Statute describes the hierarchical structure, starting with the lowest unit, the primary organization, which exists in all institutions where at least three party members are present, and ending with the Party Congress, its elective Central Committee, Politburo and Secretariat, and the First Secretary, with the familiar juxtaposition of titular and actual power. Territorially, the three-level units proceed from the municipality (*obshtina*) and city (*grad*) to the district (*okrug*) and, ultimately, the national level. Centralization is extreme, as Bulgaria is not a federal or multinational state, but a quite homogeneous one.

In 1976, party membership had reached 789,797, an increase of about 90,000 (nearly 13 percent) over 1971. This represents about 9 percent of the total population, or 13 percent of those age 18 and over. (The latest, 1978 total, was 812,000 members.) The drastic increase in membership after the seizure of power from a negligible size to a peak in 1948 points to obvious opportunism. It dropped to a low in 1954, reflecting the expulsion of the Kostovites, including about 25,000 peasants. Thereafter, membership increased relatively slowly until 1962 and then steadied at about 80,000–90,000 between congresses (a growth of 15,000–20,000 new members annually). While membership is not as difficult to obtain as it has been in the past, it remains a restricted and privileged position. The Theses of 1976 called for restricted admissions to counteract the lowered ideological and educational qualifications. Zhivkov furthermore announced the reissuing of party cards between 1978 and 1980 to weed out undesirable party members, so that a slowdown may be expected.[12]

The social and occupational distribution of party membership indicated a slowly growing share of blue-collar workers (reaching 41.4 percent in 1976) followed by a rapidly increasing white-collar group (35.6 percent) and a declining peasant share (23.1 percent). The trend is explained by the rapid industrialization, mechanization, and bureaucratization of a state-owned system and the respective decline of the peasant population. In fact, the slow increase in the share of blue-collar workers, despite the efforts of the regime, has been exceeded by that of the white-collar bureaucracy, especially in recent years (between 1971 and 1976 their share increased by 1.8 percent as against 1.3 percent for the workers), and presents an officially admitted problem. Moreover, only 70 percent of the Communists worked in material production, which further underscores the bureaucratization of the party. About 70 percent of the members were under 50, with the average age on the increase, and the typical member being a male with a high school diploma.

The data confirmed that, compared to the occupational distribution of the population, white-collar workers were strongly overrepresented in the party, while peasants in general were underrepresented. Despite recent improvements, the shares of party women and youth (people under 30) are also smaller than their shares in the population: 27.5 of all women are members, while women make up a majority of the population, and the share of youth, which showed a dramatic drop in the late fifties and early sixties to about 15 percent of total membership, has still to regain its relative importance. All this indicates an aversion to party membership among peasants, women, and youth, due to the unpopular land collectivization and the attempts to socialize the family and to indoctrinate and discipline the young.

At the last Party Congress, in 1976, as has happened so often in the past, the leadership, and Zhivkov in particular, while expressing satisfaction with the increased membership (especially among young people), had harsh words to say about the spread of a materialistic and egotistical mentality and of personal favoritism. He criticized the membership at large and the Komsomol members in particular, many of whom subscribe to "consumerism, petty bourgeois pursuit of material well-being, and a disdain for work" instead of applying Communist virtues. Ideological deficiencies were confirmed by the demotion of the ideologue Georgi Bokov from the Secretariat and the editorship of the party daily, *Rabotnichesko delo*, as well as by the replacement of the first secretary of the Komsomol. Apathy, loose morals, and adultation of foreign things are attacked continuously. There are constant complaints about the still low educational level of the cadres. Attempts to raise it have been called a necessity if the party is to guide and control the "scientific-technical revolution" and the development of the "mature socialist society."

Leadership

The party leadership has been occupied for nearly a quarter of a century by Todor Zhivkov, which makes him the dean of the Warsaw Pact leaders. Born in 1911, he joined the party at 19 years of age while a printer in the capital; he made his career there, ultimately as a partisan leader, taking part in the 1944 takeover and immediately organizing the militia as an instrument of terror. He made the greatest advances during the 1950–54 period, becoming secretary and Politburo candidate in 1950 and full member in 1951, and was considered one of Chervenkov's protégés. After his election to First Secretary in 1954, he maneuvered carefully among the heavyweights and managed by 1962 to eliminate all of them, presumably with the support of Khrushchev. By 1971, he had become the established leader, combining the top party and state positions. Since then he has enhanced his stature to the point of becoming an object of adulation, as Brezhnev is in the USSR. At the same time, Zhivkov pays lip service to collective, "Leninist" principles, which he associates with the "historic" April 1956 Plenum, at which the Stalin-type personality cult was officially condemned.

There has been no known serious challenge to his leadership since the April 1965 conspiracy of the partisan-military group, headed by Ivan Todorov-Gorunya who, incidentally, was reported to have committed suicide after the discovery of the plot. What is significant and sets apart the Bulgarian case is that the conspiracy was apparently based on considerable support in the armed forces (a Communist version of the Military League), and that a subsequent purge of first party secretaries of many districts suggested a general malaise and possible widespread opposition to Zhivkov's leadership and policies. The most plausible speculation about the motives for the planned coup is that Zhivkov's subservient attitude toward Moscow and the examples of Yugoslavia, Albania, and even Romania must have rekindled desires for greater independence in men who had, in the past, risked their lives as partisans. Even the official accusation of Maoist ties and goals did not belie the desire for national assertion, although it implied a stricter domestic dictatorship, which may or may not have been the case.[13]

In recent years, the challenges have been more of a personal and isolated nature. But Zhivkov has not been lax in purging or demoting any actual or potential rival, especially among the younger men who, as the leader advances in age, must be jockeying for position in the inevitable succession struggle. The most prominent targets have been Mitko Grigorov, Luchezar Avramov, Venelin Kotsev, Ivan Abadzhiev and, in 1976 and 1977, the older Zhivko Zhivkov and the number two man, Boris Velchev, a close friend and Politburo member in charge of cadres and foreign relations, who was flatly dismissed in May 1977. It should be noted, however, that most of these persons have retained their party memberships, and even places in the Central Committee, and some have been restored to previous positions.[14]

The Politburo's full membership was reduced to eight after Velchev's dismissal, but was restored to its eleven-person size at the end of 1977, with the inclusion of Defense Minister Dobri Dzhurov, Foreign Minister Petur Mladenov, and the new star, Ognyan Doynov, age 41, who epitomizes the typical *apparatchik*, possessing technical skills and some foreign experience. It still included two near-octogenarians, the "legendary" Tsola Dragoycheva, its only woman, and Ivan Mikhaylov, a general with active Soviet service. Although two older members have been dropped, the average age is still 60; the only other member under 50 is Aleksandur Lilov, the ideologist, who together with Grisha Filipov, an economist reared in the Soviet Union, and Premier Stanko Todorov, seem to be Zhivkov's closest collaborators. Pancho Kubadinski and Tano Tsolov complete the list. The number of Central Committee secretaries was expanded to eight. promoting mainly heads of departments of the Central Committee itself.

There is little doubt that the new leadership members serve also at Zhivkov's pleasure and that before his death no serious challenge is likely. In fact, the current power of Zhivkov is such that he has moved his daughter Lyudmilla to the Central Committee and into the eleven-person Bureau of the Cabinet as well as to the chairmanship of the Committee on Culture, to which the propaganda and educational apparatus is subordinated.

The Central Committee's full membership increased from 147 in 1971 to 154 in 1976 and again to 173 in 1978, while its candidate membership zigzagged from 110 up to 121 and down to 106. The recent turnover denotes Zhivkov's hand in replacing potential Velchev supporters and guaranteeing the security of his own position.

A closer look at the full membership elected by the Eleventh Congress (no similar details are yet available on the 19 members added in 1978) revealed a drastic increase in the average age; whereby the majority consisted of persons in their late fifties and early sixties, i.e., the generation of partisans and pioneers in the consolidation of the new regime. While most of the total membership were below 60, the age shift was clearly evident from the fact that the 51–70 age group had about doubled in size since the Fourth Congress; those above 70 years of age now numbered 45, whereas there were only 12 members under 40, a substantial drop, and the 41–50 age group had also declined, from 120 to 80. Although this trend follows the aging of the Bulgarian population at large, it dramatically emphasizes the great reliance on the "tested generation" and explains the latent conflict between old and young.

It should also be pointed out that women numbered only 27 out of the 275-strong Central Committee, a gross underrepresentation in a regime that claims equality between the sexes.

As to the occupational distribution of the membership, government officials not only held but continued to increase their relative majority; they were followed at a distance by party (CC) functionaries, scientific and cultural workers, and employees of various mass organizations, i.e., a composite of state and party bureaucrats and intellectuals, while blue-collar workers were at the bottom of the scale (thirteen, of whom only six were full members). It is interesting to note that the number of district and local party functionaries who are full members had been cut almost in half. This is explained partly by promotions to government service but also denotes a trend toward centralization and lesser attention to the provinces. It appears that no representative of the agricultural sector sits on the Central Committee and that only one economic manager has been elected to it, emphasizing further the role of political positions.

The educational level of the Central Committee members had improved somewhat for obvious reasons, as the old generation with less formal education leaves the stage and the party-state bureaucracy takes the lead. Of the total membership, over 80 percent were reported to have had higher education (against 75 percent in 1971), and 2 percent to have had only elementary education (against 9 percent).

It also appears that the only sizable ethnic minority, the Turks, is severely underrepresented, with only one full member and four candidates, while the Turkish population amounts to nearly 1 million out of a total population of 8.7 million. By contrast, there are three members out of a 5,000-strong Jewish community.

As is known, while the Central Committee is formally the policy-making body, it meets quite infrequently, although more often than in the past, and primarily to ratify decisions taken by the Politburo. Whatever conflicts may exist, it is likely that they are suppressed, as here again Zhivkov's personal power dominates the scene, screening out even mild opposition.

The Party's Transmission Belts

The pervasive role of the party in a Communist state is well established in theory and, in the Bulgarian case, also quite pronounced in practice. As mentioned before, Zhivkov holds both the top state and party leadership posts, while Politburo members hold the premiership and all other key positions.

The current status of the Communist party is not only that of "the guiding force of society and the state" (Article 1 (2) of the 1971 Constitution), but its role is to increase further during the "current stage of building a mature socialist society" (1971 Program). The party has been called upon to provide a comprehensive "unified social management" in all fields of activity. In Khrushchevian terms, the party is moving gradually into a position as "vanguard of the entire people," not only of the proletariat. At the same time, the role of the mass public organizations and movements is to be enhanced by entrusting them with functions of social government, thus applying the "state-public" principle in practice.

Characteristic of Bulgaria is the existence of a second political party, the Bulgarian Agrarian People's Union—the same name as that of the once leading party headed by Stamboliyski and later by Dimitur Gichev (the dominant moderate wing) and Nikola Petkov (the collaborationist radical wing). After the elimination of all nonconformist leaders, including Petkov, the Communists chose to formally maintain the Agrarian party, ostensibly to use its prestige with segments of the peasantry and, more importantly, with the non-Communist world, giving the semblance of the existence of a multiparty democratic system in Bulgaria. In reality, however, the Agrarian party not only has a membership level frozen at 120,000, but is deprived by its statute from competing for power with the Communists. In word as well as deed, it supports completely the program and the policies of the Communists, serving primarily as its arm in the villages. The most recent relevant official documents even treat the Agrarians under the heading "The role of the Communist party," and it is known that the Agrarian leading cadres have been trained in the academy and schools of the Communist party.[15]

Despite the clear subordination of the Agrarian party, however, it formally maintains basic party units (*druzhbi*) and coparticipation in governmental bodies, including the Parliament (100 out of 400 deputies are Agrarians) and the Cabinet (until recently the head of state used to be an Agrarian; he now functions as deputy to Zhivkov). This serves as an outlet for those who do not wish to join outright with the Communist party or who hope that at some future time the Agrarians could play a more independent role. The Communists themselves have stressed at times, as after the death of Stalin, the increased role of the Agrarians, which has been viewed by Western observers as a sign of a certain relaxation. The avowed long-term goal of the Communists remains the elimination of all other organizations. But as long as the "cooperative-farmers" class coexists with the "working class," Communist theory does not see any inconsistency in tolerating the Agrarian "allies."

The party leads and controls the other so-called mass public organizations as well. The Fatherland Front, labeled as a "sociopolitical mass organization," numbers about 4 million members, i.e., most of the adult population, and includes as its major collective members, besides the Agrarians, the trade unions and the Bulgarian Komsomol (Dimitrov Communist Youth Union), with 2.5 and 1.4 million members, respectively. All these groups are entrusted with the implementation of party ideology and policy in their respective spheres of activity; the Front engages the population at large, primarily at the local level, and technically nominates unopposed candidates for elective office; the unions drive the workers to greater performance, besides imparting indoctrination; and the Komsomol aims at preparing the future leaders according to the prerequisites of the "new Communist man."

These mass organizations, plus the various organizations of professionals, artists and cultural workers, sportsmen, etc., have been found repeatedly wanting and short of their goals. The Theses spoke of apathy, loafing on the job, incompetence, and prejudice against manual work. Although repeated statements have been made for enlarging the role of these organizations as a sign of greater "socialist democratization," the results have been more perfunctory than real; this seems, in fact, to suit well the party elite, which prefers peace and quiet to change harboring possible surprises.

It might be added that exhortations for "proper Communist attitudes" and criticisms of behavioral shortcomings in all aspects of life have been growing in recent years. A special target has been young people for their so-called unresponsiveness to ideology and physical work, but Zhivkov went even so far as to blame the Bulgarian cultural heritage and character in general as defective in this regard. A further and as yet an officially unackowledged challenge to the regime was Zhivkov's own reference to "dissidence" in Bulgaria. Although he tried to refute it as a political phenomenon, he admitted that "a few people think differently," promising that dissidence "is condemned to inevitable failure in advance." This contradictory elaboration was supplemented by reports about the clandestine publication of a pamphlet called "Declaration 1978," listing demands for compliance with the Helsinki Declaration and even demonstration banners and leaflets marked "Down with Communism." While the success of such reactions is almost ephemeral under existing circumstances, the very fact that they were mentioned may indicate some worry in the minds of the otherwise secure leadership.[16]

The Party and the Economy

One of the major goals of general Communist policy has been the rapid industrialization of the country according to the Soviet model of development.[17] As in the Soviet Union—although on a smaller scale, of course—the Communist takeover succeeded in an industrially underdeveloped, peasant society, so that the Marxian prerequisites had to be created ex post facto.

Due to the subordinate position of the Bulgarian leadership

from the very beginning, the party copied at the first opportunity almost all institutional and policy features of the Stalinist system. Thus, not only was government ownership extended through nationalization of industry and other key economic sectors, but collectivization of the land—in the form of so-called cooperative labor farms (TKZSs)—was begun and implemented faster (by 1951–52) and more drastically than in any of the other East European satellites. Also, rigid economic planning, based on five-year plans, was adopted and continued without much relaxation.

The Soviet priorities—heavy industry with favored key branches, such as energy, machine building, etc., based on domestic resources—were also aped, although it should have been clear from the beginning that Bulgaria had nowhere near the enormous raw material base (or industrial strength) of the Soviet Union.

For a while, the period of "extensive" development, i.e., the use of easily available human and material resources (surplus rural labor, accessible raw materials, etc.), brought quick and quantitatively impressive results in the priority fields, although at a serious sacrifice of living standards. Heavy industry, receiving the prime resources and starting from a low base, grew at record rates, as did the industrial labor force within a rapidly urbanizing society; but light, consumer goods, industry, and agriculture barely moved ahead and, in view of the increasing population and urbanization, living standards dropped. At the same time, the gap between the meager resource base and the enlarged industrial capacity widened with the effect of making the country increasingly dependent on imported supplies of both equipment and raw materials. After a hectic "great leap forward" plan (1956–60)—linked to Zhivkov's ascendancy—failed to meet stepped-up targets by employing mass labor in the Chinese manner, changes became necessary. Yet, these were at first halfhearted, following again the Soviet lead. Concentration and specialization expressed themselves in merging collective farms into huge "agro-industrial complexes" (combining up to 50 villages with up to 50,000 inhabitants and an average area of about 60,000 acres) and industrial enterprises into large "trusts" (combining up to 100 enterprises). But the planning mechanism, despite the pretense of introducing economic reforms, remained substantially centralized, and quantitative targets persisted as leading indexes of success.

The seventies intensified the need for qualitative considerations, as problems of shortages and inefficiencies began piling up. The avowed goal became "intensive," cost-conscious, development. A somewhat neglected speech by Zhivkov himself in March 1974 called for increased productivity as a key factor for "building the developed socialist society" and admitted growing shortages in energy and other materials as well as a heretofore unusual shortage of labor; he also complained of the rapid obsolescence of new plants and equipment, of great material waste as well as of deficient managerial methods, all of which pointed to a greater dependence on foreign trade and aid, primarily on the Soviet Union and its bloc but also on the industrial West. Incidentally, Zhivkov reported the share of foreign trade to be two-thirds of the national income and the foreign trade growth to be exceeding that of the national income.[18]

As the 1976 Party Congress approached and a new five-year plan was to enter into effect, a more comprehensive stock-taking as well as some forecasting took place, expressed in a series of lengthy documents (Theses), including those on economic development, scientific and technological progress, and the standard of living, and culminating in the decisions of the Congress and the Seventh Five-Year Plan (1976–1980).[19]

Alongside the traditional praise and lofty promises, the balance sheet revealed a still rapidly growing economy with the familiar mix of high and low priority branches; but it also revealed growing problems, epitomized in the motto of the Congress and the Plan, "Greater Quality and Effectiveness" (borrowed, incidentally, from the Soviet Congress of the month before). Production targets were similar to those of the previous period, except that real income growth has been reduced (from 32 to 20 percent), and most targets for per capita consumer goods are set below the goals announced as early as 1972. Prerequisites for achieving these still ambitious goals are the reliance on intensive factors, such as full-capacity utilization, considerable modernization of capital stock, and the strictest economizing of domestically scarce materials, power, and labor resources. Specifically, the new plan requires a six- and even seven-day routine use of machinery, increased employment of students and even employees in production work, and stepped-up exploration of domestic resources.

Despite such rather drastic measures, which in themselves may be difficult to fulfill, the task ahead presupposes almost ideal conditions as far as productivity growth is concerned, namely, sufficient modern equipment and organization, and a qualified and devoted labor force, all of which is highly doubtful. Indeed, the first two years of the seventh five-year plan, 1976 and 1977, showed unmistakable declines across the board. Agricultural output in particular fell even below the 1975 level, making the fulfillment of the five-year targets highly problematic and forcing the regime to devote a National Party Conference in April 1978 to "improving the socialist organization of labor and the planned management of the economy," with Zhivkov the main speaker. In view of this, the best prognosis one might venture at this point is that the country's economic development will depend increasingly on foreign support—under the circumstances, mainly on the Soviet Union and its allies. It is known that the USSR, in particular, already supplies most of the petroleum, natural gas, hard coal and coke, iron ore and other metals, machines, and equipment, including turn-key installations, and also offers markets for new as well as traditional Bulgarian products. Having experienced great difficulties in competing in the industrial West, Bulgaria is now increasing even more its share of trade with the bloc (to about 80 percent, of which 56 percent is with the USSR alone). Moreover, due to the rise in the prices of oil and other raw materials, most of which come from the USSR, Bulgaria has registered for the first time in 1975 deficits in trade with its allies (deficits with the West are the rule), deficits which require further exports to the bloc and further dependence. This vicious circle is hard to break, especially since the party leadership is committed to following the Soviet connection and total integration, come what may.[20]

Foreign Policy

While party policies in the domestic field show some distinguishing characteristics, in the field of foreign relations, the party (and consequently, the country) has, due to the peculiarities of local conditions, rightly earned the reputation of being perhaps more slavishly loyal to the Soviet party and Union than any other ally. One must indeed use a large magnifiying glass to detect nuances of divergence from Soviet goals and policies. Long gone are such cases as Georgi Dimitrov's 1948 pronouncement about the desirability of forming an East European federation—including even non-Communist states such as Greece and Turkey—which, although more of an open-ended suggestion than a short-term plan, was immediately and rudely rebuffed by Moscow. So are the more tangible and immediate attempts to form a Bulgarian-Yugoslav or South Slav federation with Tito, aborted because of a coincidence of objections by England and the Soviets. Even this latter case, in which Bulgaria was to lose its part of Macedonia to Yugoslavia as well as the concession of the existence of a separate and distinct "Macedonian nation," proved more of a foreign scheme than a Bulgarian initiative.[21] Some observers have identified a few other cases of Bulgarian emphases in some actions, such as Zhivkov's proposal for an atom-free Balkan zone or attempts for inter-Balkan cooperation, but even they see the guiding hand of Moscow, as all these actions are well within the parameters of Soviet policy. There were some speculations about Chervenkov trying to side with Peking at the start of the Sino-Soviet dispute but, if true, they could best be ascribed to his fear of a personal eclipse (as a Bulgarian Stalin) wrought by Khrushchev rather than to national considerations; this episode as well as Zhivkov's "great leap forward" slogan were in any case short-lived, and at no time were there sufficient indications that a move away from Moscow was in the works.[22]

As time passed, the party leadership, epitomized by the person of Zhivkov, kept steadfastly to Moscow and its line and, in fact, became "plus royaliste que le roi." This is especially noteworthy as world communism—mainly in Western Europe, but also among the satellites, let alone in China—showed cracks, and offered challenges to Moscow's leadership with possibly unforeseeable consequences.

The attitude toward Moscow is illustrated by encomia hardly used by any other Communist leaders, expressing obedience bordering on adoration. Thus, already to Dimitrov, the Soviet-Bulgarian friendship was proclaimed "as necessary as the air and the sun is to every living creature," and Zhivkov presented the two countries as a "single organism fed by one circulatory system." This "organic unity" has expressed itself in a growing integration of economic and cultural institutions. Also, because of the identity of ideological view and political actions, the outright incorporation of Bulgaria into the Soviet Union was predicted by the Western press in 1974. No such move has yet been made and perhaps none is contemplated at this time. It is obvious that a formal annexation will have more drawbacks than advantages, as Bulgaria, as an officially independent state, has a separate vote in international organizations and can serve better as a vehicle for Soviet interest if not a component part of the Soviet Union.

In the economic field, the Soviet ties have been a mixed blessing and reveal several more or less distinct phases: the outright exploitation of the Stalinist period, which witnessed the familiar features of arbitrary plunder often under the pretense of mixed companies and which might have generated Kostov's disillusionment; the Khrushchev era of growing Bulgarian reliance on Soviet supplies of plant, energy, and material resources as well as markets to keep the industrialization drive going; and the current phase of renewed Bulgarian contributions to the Soviet economy via investments and labor for the development of badly needed Soviet resources (Bulgarian credits amounted to 280 million leva in 1976 alone), as attempts to get Western trade and aid did not meet expectations and the Soviets become more and more businesslike toward their allies.

While it is obvious that without Soviet supplies the Bulgarian economy will grind to a halt and that without the Soviet market Bulgarian exports will suffer a severe blow, the Soviet ties remain controversial. Soviet aid (which in the Soviet terminology includes also normal Soviet exports) has been more generous than to other allied states, possibly to repay the loyalty of the Bulgarian party, and has generated discussions about Bulgaria becoming a Soviet liability. But this argument, plausible in itself, does not take into account the offsetting Soviet leverage which has led not only to the familiar exploitation of the Stalinist era, but also to a likely hidden exploitation in higher Soviet import and lower Bulgarian export prices, a topic of some oblique discussion in the Bulgarian press from time to time.[23] Even more importantly, it is difficult to estimate the costs of Soviet-type industrialization in a country which lacks key heavy industrial resources but has a comparative advantage in specialized agriculture; it is even more difficult to estimate the human costs of the experiment, which might be huge. It is clear, however, that this policy has turned the country into an economic, and consequently, a political, "captive" of the Soviet Union.

The allegiance to Moscow permeates the party's attitude towards its allies, the international Communist movement, and the rest of the world. As cracks and conflicts within the movement have become more pronounced, especially with the appearance of Eurocommunism, the Bulgarian leadership has closed ranks even more tightly and slavishly behind Moscow and has indeed been selected, it appears, as a principal mouthpiece for "unity" behind Moscow and against any centrifugal tendencies. Thus, Zhivkov used several recent occasions to refute "any other road" to communism but the Soviet one and to argue, at the 1976 Conference of European Communist Parties in East Berlin, the validity of "proletarian internationalism" Soviet-style against the autonomy arguments of Tito, Ceausescu, and Western Communist leaders. Zhivkov also wrote two articles in *Problems of Peace and Socialism* (*World Marxist Review*), taking issue with the dissenters. In the first article (June 1976), he inveighed against "every manifestation of bourgeois ideology, against right- and left-wing revisionism, Maoism and anti-Sovietism," while in the second article (December 1976) he identified fraternal solidarity with the Soviet Union as the touchstone of internationalism and attacked Eurocommunism as "rejecting the objective laws of the revolutionary struggle" when opting for local peculiarities. He also praised lavishly the Soviet Union and Brezhnev. This article was displayed widely and interpreted in the West, as well as in the East, as a Soviet position without the Soviet identification. It therefore generated reactions among the Western Communist parties as well: on December 3 and 4, 1976, the Italian organ, *l'Unità*, accused Zhivkov of equating every autonomous action with anti-Sovietism and of distorting the essence of Eurocommunism.

The voice of Moscow had been heard earlier, right after the East Berlin meeting when, in *Le Monde* of August 4, 1976, Zhivkov answered a question about the compromise language in the 1976 Conference communiqué by stating that "words are of no significance" and suggested that a new conference, if it took place, should be on a world, not a European, scale since at such a meeting "over 90 percent of the parties would agree."

It has become obvious that Brezhnev appreciates Zhivkov's support and vice-versa, as high-level visits result in lavish praise and decorations reminiscent of Stalin's time, and Brezhnev has repeatedly cited the Bulgarian party as an "example of socialism in action."

Within the Soviet bloc, Bulgaria backs the Soviet leadership in all known military, political and economic deliberations and decisions and, in a tangible way, is probably playing a constraining role on Romania, as the latter is enclosed by the Soviet and Bulgarian territories. With regard to the ruling Communist parties outside the bloc, the Bulgarian leadership toes the critical Soviet line vis-à-vis China, accusing the Maoists of being bedfellows of "imperialism, fascism, and revanchism" and promising to help achieve their "political and ideological defeat." Albanian communism is also criticized, although with less vehemence, and attempts at reconciliation have become noticeable, as Tirana has shown dissatisfaction with the new leaders in Peking.

Relations with Yugoslavia—a historic foe and a special case—have fluctuated between ostensible close friendship, when common federation was the avowed goal (during the Dimitrov-Tito dialogue), and outright invective when Yugoslavia was expelled from the Cominform and on several subsequent occasions, reflecting Moscow's attitudes of the moment. The Bulgarian party was in the forefront of those who castigated Tito's "revisionism" and tried to contain contagious domestic influences, both during the purge of "Titoists" and even more so during the Khrushchev years of the acceptance of different roads to socialism. A latent issue remains, of course: the Macedonian problem, which generates occasional flareups. The Yugoslavs have acted as accusers ever since the Bulgarians reneged on their recognition of a Macedonian nation within Bulgaria and whenever they touch on the historic character of Macedonia's population, question the existence of a Macedonian nation and language, or refer to the role of the Bulgarian armed forces in the liberation of Yugoslavia. However, while attitudes remain ambiguous, official relations are correct if not friendly. An outburst of mutual recriminations occurred in 1978 when, on the anniversary of Bulgarian liberation from Turkey, reference was made of necessity to the "San Stefano" frontiers, which included almost all of Macedonia within Bulgaria. This triggered Yugoslav accusations of Bulgarian suppression of the rights of the Macedonian "minority" within Bulgaria and Bulgarian counteraccusations of "concealed territorial aspirations" by Yugoslavia. The reasons for this unusual Bulgarian escalation are not entirely clear. It might well be that Moscow keeps in store a Bulgarian card vis-à-vis Yugoslavia which could be used if and when (probably after Tito's death) the Yugoslav state comes under pressure or worse. For the time being, the Macedonian question might indeed serve as an outlet for nationalist feeling, thus possibly detracting from an accumulation of anti-Soviet bias.[24]

Bulgaria has become increasingly involved as a Soviet spearhead in Balkan matters, especially after the Cyprus dispute alienated Greece and Turkey from each other as well as from the NATO alliance. It took some time before relations with those two neighbors were normalized, as the random and mass expulsion of Bulgaria's Turks was strongly resented and as Greece did not reestablish relations with Bulgaria until wartime claims were settled. Only recently did relations become friendlier, with the Bulgarian government trying to pull the two antagonists farther away from the West by playing the role of an even-handed arbiter or intermediary. Moscow's hand is detected in Bulgaria's official preference for bilateral ties with each of the nonbloc neighbors, whereas a multilateral collective approach would seem more in the interests of an autonomous Bulgarian policy, since it could assure a joint and stronger inter-Balkan position in relation to ambitious great powers, especially the Soviet Union. But, again and again, the Bulgarian leadership has shown no inclination to take advantage of propitious circumstances and to act in its own interest. In the Near and Middle East, but also among developing countries in general, Bulgaria seems to use legitimate economic ties—selling industrial goods which have no markets in the West and buying raw materials—for the political fringe benefits of promoting the image of a more advanced socialist system and the cause of Moscow, without Moscow's direct involvement.

Relations with the West reflect the Soviet line as well. In purely ideological terms, the Bulgarian party sees the "capitalist countries" through nineteenth-century eyes, in the language of the Communist Manifesto. Its 1971 Program predicted the demise of this "exploitative system," and Zhivkov's 1976 Report pointed again to the inevitable end, accelerated by the growing strength and achievements of the socialist camp. This aggressive tone is accompanied, however, by the commitment to "peaceful coexistence" and recently to the principles of the Helsinki Accord, to which Bulgaria was a party, but many of whose provisions (especially the human rights portion) are disregarded, as is to be expected of one of the strictest Communist dictatorships.

A tangible goal which the Bulgarian regime strives to achieve by its conciliatory pronouncements is the acquisition of badly needed Western goods and technology. In fact, trade increased rapidly from the low levels of the fifties and sixties, but most recently a slowdown became obvious as deficits with the West began to pile up and assumed serious proportions. Trade volume declined in relative terms in 1975, and Bulgaria's deficits with the industrial West reached over 1.4 billion leva for the 1970–75 period, half of which was incurred in 1975 alone; they jumped to nearly $3 billion in 1977, before the country was forced to cut some exports to preserve its credit standing.[25] Due to its substantial needs, Bulgaria was ready to restore relations with West Germany in the mid-sixties, but Moscow called it to order. Now West Germany is by far the most important Western partner, and Western Europe the major area of the industrial West.

Trade with the United States is rather insignificant. Bulgaria refused to take advantage of the Trade Reform Act of 1974 because of the free-immigration provisions. In 1951, the United States broke off relations with Bulgaria as the Communist government implicated the American minister in the Kostov treason trial; although relations have since been normalized, the official Party Program still insists that "in the center of militarism, the headquarters of international reaction is the imperialism of the USA. With its brutality and adventurism, with the means for mass destruction concentrated in its hands, it threatens entire nations, hundreds of millions of peoples. Imperialism, and above all the imperialism of the USA, is an enemy of all mankind."[26] No substantive change is expected as long as the country remains so loyal and tied to the Soviets, although popular sentiments would prefer otherwise.

IN LIEU OF CONCLUSION: WHY THE SUBSERVIENCE TO MOSCOW?

The special relationship of the Bulgarian to the Soviet party does not stimulate conclusions and projections—likely to be dull and predictable—as much as plausible explanations of this unusual phenomenon. Of course, a degree of speculation and prediction is unavoidable in this attempt at clarification.

A most popular reason has remained the claim that ethnic, linguistic, religious and, in general, historic ties between the two Slav nations provide a solid foundation for their current friendship and identity of views and policies, with the emphasis on the small brother following the big. This is also one part of the official thesis. But it is hardly scientific. Ethnic and linguistic ties exist within Slavdom in general (and between Russians, Bulgarians, and Serbs, in particular), but more often than not this cultural communality has led to conflicts rather than understanding, especially in the political field (as is indeed the case with many other nations with common origin). Moreover, historically, the cultural influence moved both ways: from Bulgaria, in the Middle Ages, when the dissemination of the Cyrillic alphabet and Old Bulgarian (or Church Slavonic) literature played an important role in Russia's cultural development; and from Russia, in our time, when Bulgarians—having been under Turkish political and Greek religious domination for about five centuries—went to Russia for education and moral and material support. The modern twist of the official thesis centers on the "two-times liberation" of Bulgaria by the Russians (in 1878 and 1944), with the additional emphasis on the "selfless" motives of the liberators, all of which allegedly explains the special relationship.

It is hardly debatable that the Russo-Turkish War of 1877–78 and the ensuing liberation of the country was and could not be but greeted with joy and gratitude, as behooves a small people eager but unable by itself to obtain their freedom after centuries of foreign rule. These sentiments could have lasted much longer were it not for the fact that the tsarist officials attempted to rule the newly liberated principality with such rigor that they quickly antagonized not only the prince, whom they deposed, but also the political leaders and the population at large, thus unmasking the real aspirations of the tsars for a warm-sea outlet. As a result, the Russian officials were expelled and diplomatic relations with Russia severed in 1886 for about a decade.

Even after the restoration of relations, Russia never regained the previous affection and respect, as it often sided with rival Serbia in the Balkan squabbles. Even more significantly, Bulgarian troops fought the Russian forces in the Dobrudzha during World War I without apparent mental reservation. Finally, from the point the Bolsheviks took power, any analogy between Tsarist and Communist Russia becomes tenuous if not outrightly misleading. The degree of support of the Bulgarian Communist party from 1919 on has reflected to some extent popular attitudes toward Russia, but the war years reduced this support to a negligible minimum, as territorial gains were obtained with German help and as the country remained militarily uninvolved, with a popular king at the helm getting most of the credit. While it is known that the king rationalized his reluctance to give in to Hitler's demands for Bulgarian military participation on the Soviet front with the excuse that the Bulgarians would not fight properly against the Russians, this sounded more like a pretext to keep the country at peace than a genuine truth. In fact, anti-Soviet feeling was strong because of Soviet attempts to secure Bulgaria to its sphere of influence and because of subversive activities on Bulgarian territory and Communist partisan activities against Bulgarians, not Germans.

Most importantly, the sudden Soviet declaration of war on an anti-Nazi government and the coup against it by the Communist-led Fatherland Front was surely traumatic; the wholesale purges exposed all protestations of Soviet liberation and friendship or of Communist concern for the nation. If one adds the experience of the Stalinist years and the modest political changes thereafter, it should be clear that the close attachment to Moscow can hardly be explained by any long-lasting or uninterrupted national affinity or "fraternal feelings" toward Russia, let alone toward its Bolshevik variety. Therefore, the reason for this special relationship must be sought in the motives and perceptions of the Bulgarian Communist leadership, not the masses.

The argument of a close historic association of the Bulgarian Communists with the Russian (eventually Soviet) branch of Marxism-Leninism is a much more plausible base for explaining the connection, but it requires further clarification of underlying reasons. One set of reasons could involve the benefit for Bulgaria and its people as perceived by its Communist leaders, i.e., a "national-interest" justification. Another set could rest upon the predominance of the unity, ideological and disciplinary, of the Communist movement, taken as a prerequisite for the triumph of the Communist ideal, benefiting all mankind, i.e., the partisan "international-interest" approach. A third variant could be termed the "narrowly or personally opportunistic" motive, which could, of course, be used to rationalize any action by drawing on the national and/or international-interest justification, while in reality it serves primarily the regime and the "new class."

The national-interest motivation, while occasionally perceptible in the past, as during the inter-war revisionist period of the Balkan Federation, including the Comintern attitude toward Macedonia, has usually been subordinated to Moscow's goals, although at times Bulgarian interests have coincided with Moscow's. More recently, a strong case could be made to the effect that, with Nazi Germany's collapse seen as imminent, Bulgaria had reason to look to Moscow rather than to the Western Allies for protection of its territorial unity, since its neighbors, Yugoslavia and especially Greece, were claiming revenge. This is why prominent non-Communists like Petkov joined the Fatherland Front and even the prodemocratic Muraviev coalition tried to attract the Front and not to antagonize the Soviets. Moscow, indeed, supported the Bulgarian cause at the peace conferences, and possibly saved Bulgaria's integrity. However, in the Macedonian skirmish with Tito's Yugoslavia, the Bulgarian Communists quickly recognized a Macedonian nationality within their country's border and followed Moscow's line regardless of past commitments and potential future embarrassments. The very fact of continued subservience to Moscow ever since disposes of the national-interest motivation, it seems, satisfactorily.

The international-interest approach could be more plausible were it not that the Bulgarian Communist interpretation equates it with the interests of the Soviet Union, whereas the unity of the Communist movement has been shattered and the leadership of the Soviet party continues to be challenged, thus disposing of an ideal and of a uniform ideological or disciplinary approach to it. However, for the Bulgarian party, proletarian internationalism translates into the defense of the interests of the Soviet Union, with international Communist ideals consigned to oblivion.

This leaves the third major alternative, i.e., the opportunistic view, as the most convincing justification for Bulgaria's almost total dependence on Moscow. In fact, as has been mentioned on many occasions, the Bulgarian Communists, more often than not, had been Soviet clients spending years in Moscow, with little strength of their own, especially as they came to power solely in the footsteps of the Red Army. Their power consolidation was also the result of the presence of the Soviet forces in Bulgaria and their rule ever since has counted on the close collaboration with Soviet security forces and on the potential intervention from Moscow in case of need. Even when there were chances for asserting at least a modicum of independence, the party leadership chose not to risk it, and instead closed ranks to protect their partisan rule by backing Moscow. The reliance on Moscow has become a habit, a second nature, and has brought benefits to the faithful, headed by Zhivkov. In a curious but superficial way, it also may have raised the prestige of the country and its leaders, as they have been assigned international tasks by Moscow which few other allies have been so trusted as to obtain. Yet, on the other hand, Moscow must also have become used to taking the Bulgarian party for granted and, in the future, may have to devote more attention and resources to those of its allies who need to be catered to. Thus, the opportunistic line keeps the leadership, which relies on Soviet support for its permanence, in power, but divides it from the population and in a broader sense must affect the nation's self-esteem and inflict longer-lasting damages which are hard to estimate and might be even harder to erase.

A "redemption," i.e., a reversal of this trend, cannot, barring unforeseen circumstances, come from outside the party, as pressures for compliance, passive acceptance of the "inevitable," and even some support (especially for the social welfare aspects of Communist policies), coupled with the Soviet shadow, are ample barriers for challenging Communist rule. The challenge, if there is to be any, has to come from inside the leadership. In fact, the purge of Velchev, the old comrade and the person in charge of both party cadres and foreign relations, the ongoing purge of his followers across the country, as well as the official reference to open dissent, indicate that there might be more than a simple personality struggle involved in his removal. It might well be that the growing divisiveness within the Communist movement and the pull of Eurocommunism in particular have motivated and have made plausible attempts leading to the restoration of some modicum of independence to the once respected party and nation. It should not be forgotten that nationalism, no matter how controlled and manipulated by the regime (the alliance with the Soviet Union itself has often been rationalized as necessary for the defense of Bulgaria's national interests and goals, albeit with declining success), remains—even in Bulgaria—a potent although latent force.

NOTES

1. The major Western studies covering this period are: Joseph Rothschild, *The Communist Party of Bulgaria: Origins and Development, 1883–1936* (New York: Columbia University Press, 1959) and Nissan Oren, *Bulgarian Communism: The Road to Power, 1934–1944* (New York: Columbia University Press, 1971). Bulgarian primary sources are contained in *Materiali po istoriya na Bulgarskata komunisticheska partiya* (Sofia, 1950) and *BKP v rezolyutsii i resheniya na kongresite, konferentsiite i plenumite* (Sofia, 1957). For brief references, see "Bulgarska Komunisticheska Partiya (BKP)," in *Kratka Bulgarska Entsiklopediya* (Sofia: Bulgarian Academy of Sciences, 1963), pp. 408–13, and L. A. D. Dellin, "Bulgaria," in Witold S. Sworakowski, ed., *World Communism: A Handbook, 1918–1965* (Stanford: Hoover Institution Press, 1973), pp. 42–47.

2. Data are from official sources, with minor discrepancies in most recent Communist publications (e.g., D. Kosev, K. Khristov, and D.

Angelov, *Kratka Istoriya na Bulgaria* [Sofia: Nauka i izkustvo, 1962], p. 238). A major Western study of the party's social composition is R. V. Burks, *The Dynamics of Communism in Eastern Europe* (Princeton: Princeton University Press, 1961). On the Communist role in the labor movement, see L. A. D. Dellin, *Trade Unions and Labor Legislation in Bulgaria, 1878–1953* (New York: Mid-European Studies Center, 1953).

3. Data are from official sources.

4. The present official line is summarized in *Kratka Istoriya na Bulgaria*, pp. 202–3.

5. Communist sources usually overstate their size and role in the armed resistance considerably. The above figures are derived from reliable Western estimates (cf. Oren, *Bulgarian Communism*, pp. 214–20) and occasional Communist confirmations (cf. *Istoricheski pregled*, 1965, no. 2 and 1959, no. 4).

6. For a detailed treatment of this period, see L. A. D. Dellin, ed., *Bulgaria* (New York: Praeger, 1957) and, more recently, Nissan Oren, *Revolution Administered: Agrarianism and Communism in Bulgaria* (Baltimore: Johns Hopkins University Press, 1973). On the wartime period specifically, see Marshall Lee Miller, *Bulgaria During the Second World War* (Stanford: Stanford University Press, 1975).

7. Cf. Michael Padev, *Dimitrov Wastes No Bullets: Nikola Petkov, the Test Case* (London: Eire & Spottiswoode, 1948).

8. Kostov's case is analyzed also by Adam Ulam, *Titoism and the Cominform* (Cambridge: Harvard University Press, 1952).

9. The period of the sixties is the core of the study by J. F. Brown, *Bulgaria Under Communist Rule* (New York: Praeger, 1970). Chervenkov's rule is a typical case of rewriting recent history (compare the two multi-volume editions of the *Istoriya na Bulgaria*, the official publication of the Bulgarian Academy of Sciences). On rewriting general Bulgarian history, cf. my "Bulgarian History Revised," *Survey* (December 1961), no. 39.

10. Developments during the last three years are summarized in my profiles on "Bulgaria" in *Yearbook(s) on International Communist Affairs* (Stanford: Hoover Institution Press, 1976, 1977 and 1978), pp. 10–16, 10–18, and respectively, 8–18.

11. The respective sources are: *Ustav* [Statute] *na Bulgarskata komunisticheska partiya* in *Rabotnichesko delo* (November 14, 1962); *Programa* [Program] *na Bulgarskata komunisticheska partiya*, *ibid.* (April 29, 1971); *Konstitutsiya* [Constitution] *na Narodna Republika Bulgaria*, *ibid.* (May 9, 1971); proceedings of the Eleventh Party Congress, *ibid.* (March 30–April 3, 1976). All data referring to 1976, including Zhivkov's Report to the Congress (*ibid.*, March 30), unless identified otherwise, are taken from the Congress's proceedings.

12. Cf. *Tezisi* [Theses] *na TsK na BKP za sustoyanieto i razvitieto na Bulgarskata komunisticheska partiya i na obshtestvenite organizatisli i dvizheniya*, *ibid.* (February 5, 1976), discussing the leading role of the party, including membership, as well as the relationship with the Agrarian Union and other mass organizations.

13. For a comprehensive coverage, cf. Brown, *Bulgaria*, pp. 173–89.

14. Velchev's surprise dismissal from the Politburo, Secretariat, and Central Committee was announced on May 12, 1977. An analysis of the Politburo and Central Committee is provided by *Radio Free Europe Research*, Situation Report: Bulgaria/11, April 5, 1976, and R. N. The Central Committee After the 11th Party Congress, June 16, 1976. A most useful source is Velchev's report on Central Committee personnel before the Congress (*Rabotnichesko delo*, April 3, 1976). The most recent changes were announced by the December 19, 1977 and July 9, 1978 Central Committee plenums.

15. Cf. "Theses" and related materials cited in n. 11 and Zhivkov's Report to the Eleventh Congress. See also *Radio Free Europe Research*, Background Report/51, February 23, 1976.

16. Cf. Zhivkov's address before the Third National Conference of Young Writers in *Rabotnichesko delo*, February 3, 1978, and Western reports in *Die Presse*, April 3, 1978, and *L'Aurore*, May 24, 1978. See also L. L. Kerr, *Radio Free Europe Research*, "Dissidence in Bulgaria," July 10, 1978.

17. Much of this part is based on my previous studies, *The Bulgarian Economy and Its Foreign Trade* (U.S. Department of Commerce, January, 1975); "Bulgaria," in L. A. D. Dellin and Hermann Gross, eds., *Reforms in Soviet and Eastern European Economies* (Boston: D. C. Heath, 1972); and "Bulgarian Economic Reform—Advance and Retreat," *Problems of Communism* (September-October 1970), vol. 19.

18. Zhivkov's speech in *Rabotnichesko delo* (March 21, 1974).

19. The relevant theses are published in *Rabotnichesko delo:* on economic development (January 8, 1976), on "science and technological progress" (January 22, 1976), and on "the standard of living" (February 12, 1976). The Seventh Five-Year Plan, as adopted by the Congress and by the National Assembly, *ibid.* (April 7 and October 29, respectively), is analyzed briefly in my "Summary Evaluation of the Seventh Five-Year Plan of Bulgaria (1976–1980)" (Washington, D.C.: Chamber of Commerce of the U.S., February, 1977).

20. See my study on the Bulgarian Economy, cited *supra*, n. 16. See also G. Filipov, "Vsestranno ikonomichesko sblizhenie s Suvetstkiya suyuz—proben kamuk za istinska revolyutsionnost," in *Novo Vreme* 1977, no. 10 (October), pp. 32–44, and Zhivkov's report in *Rabotnichesko delo*, April 7, 1978.

21. For a detailed treatment of the federation plans and efforts, see my unpublished thesis, "The Bulgarian Communist Party and the Macedonian Question—A Study on Federation" (New York University, 1955), and a sequel, "Das Mazedonien-Problem in kommunistischer Sicht: ein Loesungsversuch im Rahmen einer Balkanfoederation," *Suedost-Forschungen* (Munich: Suedost-Institut, vol. 28, 1969).

22. Cf. Brown, *Bulgaria*, chap. 5.

23. For example, articles in *Ikonomika na selskoto stopanstvo*, 1975, no. 1; or in *Komsomolskaya pravda* (Moscow), July 17, 1976.

24. The 1978 escalation is best illustrated by the Zhivkov speech in Blagoevgrad (*Rabotnichesko delo*, June 16, 1978) and the declaration of the Bulgarian Ministry of Foreign Affairs (*ibid.*, July 25, 1978) and, on the Yugoslav side, by articles in *Nin* (January 29, 1978) and the resolution of the Congress of the League of Yugoslav Communists (*Tanjug*, June 23, 1978). For background details, see Robert R. King, "The Macedonian Question and Bulgaria's Relations with Yugoslavia," *Radio Free Europe Research*, Background Report/98, June 6, 1975.

25. *Statisticheski spravochnik 1976* (Sofia: Ministry of Information and Communication, 1976), p. 124, and Western estimates.

26. This phase of U.S.—Bulgarian relations is treated in my "Bulgaria," in Stephen D. Kertesz, ed., *East-Central Europe and the World: Developments during the Post-Stalin Era* (Notre Dame, Ind.: Notre Dame University Press, 1962), pp. 192–94 and "Bulgaria under Soviet Leadership," *Current History* (May 1963), 44:261.

Peter A. Toma

3. The Communist Party of Czechoslovakia

In his *Parties and Party Systems,* Giovanni Sartori refers to Czechoslovakia as a "one-party state." The reason? Because only one party exists and is allowed to exist. This party, according to Sartori, "vetoes, both *de jure* and *de facto,* any kind of party pluralism."[1] One of Sartori's indicators for the existence of the single party in Czechoslovakia is the presence of "elections resulting in the allocation of *all seats* in the legislature *to one and the same party.*"[2] Yet close scrutiny reveals that there are not one but six political parties in Czechoslovakia and that the four non-Communist parties had forty-one seats in Parliament during the past three elections. Does this mean that Sartori is wrong? Factually yes, but conceptually no.

All nominees in the Czechoslovak Socialist Republic figure as candidates of the National Front, an umbrella organization embracing all political parties and licensed mass organizations in the country. The candidates may be recommended by any of these organizations, as well as by meetings of employees in factories, schools, and offices, or army and police units. All proposals must be routed through the appropriate organ of the National Front. By virtue of being the "leading force in the society and state"[3] and, consequently, also of the National Front, the Communist Party of Czechoslovakia (*Komunisticka strana Ceskoslovenska* or KSC) wields the greatest power when it comes to decision making. All candidates for elected offices are screened, selected, and approved by the KSC. For all practical purposes, the party has a monopoly over the selecting of candidates.[4]

Although there are a total of six political parties in Czechoslovakia,the KSC is, both constitutionally and ideologically, the core institution of the authoritarian system. The other parties do not assume the role of "loyal opposition"; they do not act as a legitimate institution for articulating competitive demands of their followers; their interests and ideologies do not clash with the interests and ideology of the KSC; they exist only as a symbolic expression of socialist unity and harmless vestiges of purified traditional values. Hence, these parties play supportive rather than independent roles and therefore are viewed as auxiliary organizations of the KSC. In other words, the KSC does not aggregate or mediate six party interests but commands a monopoly in political affairs and ideological interpretation.

Since its establishment in 1921, the KSC has performed many roles and functions with different characteristics. It operated first as a nonruling party, from 1921 to 1948 (with the exception of the war years), and then as a ruling party from 1948 to present. As a nonruling party in a pluralist, democratic system of government, the KSC functioned both as an elitist and as a mass party. Before the Fifth Congress in 1929, the KSC was a mass party of a non-Bolshevik nature; after the bolshevization of the KSC in 1929, the party assumed a more militant and elitist role. With the dismemberment of Czechoslovakia in 1939, the KSC went underground, reemerging in 1945 as a mass party. Until 1948, the KSC functioned as a conspiratorial instrument of power seeking the overthrow of the Beneš regime rather than as a legitimate instrument of power in a coalition government seeking the articulation of demands for the purpose of strengthening and maintaining the system.

On the other hand, since its emergence as a ruling party, with the exception of the Dubček period in 1968–1969, the KSC has been totalitarian-authoritarian and semi-elitist in function and character. In 1968, the KSC lacked a strong ideology and a comparable mobilizational capability. Its control did not extend beyond the normal instruments of power. As a matter of fact, the KSC encouraged subgroup autonomy and competition of interests. Today, the KSC is once more a strongly ideological party; it is highly coercive, stresses mobilization, and is bent upon imposed political development. Like its mentor and idol, the Communist Party of the Soviet Union (CPSU), the KSC has been regarded since 1948 as the indispensable instrument by which the Marxist-Leninist goals of a socialist society are to be attained.

HISTORICAL DEVELOPMENT

When in Philadelphia, on October 26, 1918, Thomas Garrigue Masaryk declared his country an independent state, Czechoslovakia had already an established multiparty system but not a Communist party. Communism did not exist in Czechoslovakia until after the return of the Czechoslovak prisoners of war from Russia in 1919. Although most of the Czech and Slovak prisoners of war joined the Czechoslovak Army Corps (consisting of about 70,000 well-organized and well-equipped soldiers fighting the Bolsheviks on their way to Vladivostok) in order to be evacuated to the Western front,[5] there were some who, under the leadership of Alois Muna, decided to form a Czechoslovak Section of the Russian Communist party (Bolsheviks). However, the influence of this group on the future development of communism in Czechoslovakia was, for all practical purposes, insignificant. The Czechs had gained in both national pride and material advantage, through the formation of their new state, and the Czech proletariat—as part of the Social Democratic party, founded in 1878—profited at least as much as other classes. The feeling of nationalism proved much stronger than the appeal of proletarian internationalism. This was the case not only in the Czech Lands, where the majority of the industrial workers resided, but also in Slovakia where the abortive Communist revolution in June 1919, inspired by the Hungarian Soviet Republic, lasted only twenty days and was managed mostly by Hungarian nationals or sympathizers.[6] As a matter of fact, when the Slovak Soviet Republic was declared, the only congratulatory message from Czechoslovak Communists came from Moscow, not Prague or Bratislava. In central and western parts of Slovakia, the advancing Hungarian Red Army units were resisted by local militia organized by Slovak patriots defending the newly created Czechoslovak Republic.[7]

At that time, nationalism in Czechoslovakia played such a dominant role that socialists of various nationalities found themselves in the united National Front pitted against the Czech socialists voting with the majority. While most of the socialists of minority background in Czechoslovakia were advocates of intransigent class struggle and thus supporters of the Third Communist International (Comintern), the socialists of Czech nationality had cooperated with the Czech National Committee during the war, and, after the establishment of the Czechoslovak Republic, they were a mainstay of the new state. However, after a time, the tremendous enthusiasm of the Czech workers for the republic subsided because antagonism between the labor movement and the other parties was again preponderant, and every disillusionment worked against the out-and-out socialist patriots and for the leader of the socialist left, Bohumir Smeral.[8]

With growing unrest in the country, the left wing won a majority in Prague in late 1920 and, as a result, took over the office of the Social Democratic party located in the Lidovy dum (People's House). However, before losing the majority, the right-wing socialists had put the property deeds of the premises in a form which placed the personal property right of representatives of the right wing beyond doubt. When the party controlled by left-wing Social Democrats was ejected from the building, a row with the police ensued, blood was shed, and, in mid-December 1920, Czechoslovakia was faced with a general strike to decide the ownership of the Lidovy dum. Only the left-wing socialists took part in the strike; the socialist and nonsocialist labor organizations abstained. It was relatively easy for the government, which proclaimed martial law, to nip the movement in the bud; after a good deal of bloodshed (thirteen people killed and three thousand arrested), the strike was called off. Henceforth bitterness and antagonism drove the two wings of the socialists into separate and often hostile camps. Out of the remnants of the battered left-wing socialists, the Communist Party of Czechoslovakia was born on May 15, 1921.[9] It emerged as the result of a merger of Czech, Slovak, Hungarian and Ruthenian radical groups with the left wing of the Social Democratic party. Nevertheless, The KSC did not become a unified proletarian party until November 1, 1921. On that day the German section of the KSC, the Polish Communist party and the Jewish Communist group—upon instructions from the Comintern—were integrated into the KSC, thus creating a single proletarian party in Czechoslovakia.

Bolshevization and Mass Appeal

The Czechoslovak Communist party was founded upon the Twenty-One Conditions proclaimed by the Second Congress of the Comintern.[10] Yet the relations between the Czechoslovak party and the Comintern were cool and uneventful from the time the party was formally established. Under the slogan of proletarian internationalism, the Comintern strove to dictate the organizational framework and policies of all Communist parties, and in that regard the Czechoslovak party was no exception. Like so many other Communist parties in Europe, the KSC was seldom united on Comintern (or more precisely Soviet) policy. Comintern advisers frequently applied formulas to Communist parties which had little relevance to national circumstances. The Czechoslovak leadership felt that to abide by Comintern direction would be to sacrifice both voting strength and membership.

The card-carrying membership of the KSC fluctuated greatly. There is no precise data on the social composition or length of prewar party membership. We know that the leadership was constantly alarmed at the high rate of turnover and what this did to the party organizations on the local level. In 1921 there were 350,000 party members; in 1930 the party registered an all-time low of 30,212 members.[11] In Czechoslovakia, as elsewhere, the Communist party had never really controlled the bulk either of the unemployed or of the well-paid skilled workers.

One reason for the ups and downs in party membership was the introduction of the Russian system of nuclei into Czechoslovak factories. Their idea was that the revolutionary actions of the proletariat must start from the factories and must fail unless the Communist parties obtain a direct hold on the factories. However, in Czechoslovakia the Communist nucleus stood, first, against the majority of the socialist and trade-union workers and, second against the owners. Under these circumstances, the nuclei usually had to choose between keeping silent or seeing all their members dismissed within a short time. The members themselves regarded work in the nuclei as an almost unbearable threat to their economic existence. Hence, the majority of the members of the KSC avoided entering the factory nuclei and, in

Table 3.1. KSC Membership, 1921–30

Year	Number of Members
1921 (November)	350,000
1924	138,996
1925	93,220
1926	92,818
1927	138,000
1928	150,000
1929	81,432
1930	30,212

SOURCE: *Imprecorr* (Moscow), no. 74, 1929; *ibid.*, no. 63, 1952.

due course, the nuclei diminished and their work became less and less active. In 1930, for example, no more than 14 percent of the total membership of the Communist party was organized in factory nuclei, which does not mean, however, that the same percentage of members was working in factories—it was much higher.[12]

Another reason for the great fluctuation in KSC membership in the 1920s was the continuous rivalry among the party leaders. Soon after the merger of November 1, 1921, Smeral's centrist course was challenged by the members of the ultra-Left, headed by Bohumil Jilek, Vaclav Bolen, Alois Neurath, Karl Kreibich, Erno Seidler, Julius Vercik, Antonin Zapotocky, and others. Since the ultra-Left and the Left constituted a majority in the

Executive Committee, they also controlled the policy formulation on such issues as the nuclei in the factories, strikes and demonstrations in the trade unions, relations with the Comintern, and the general party line on strategy and tactics. Although they lacked ideological unity, the ultra-Left and the Left were credited with the early attempts to bolshevize the Czechoslovak Communist party.

At the opposite extreme of the party spectrum was the ultra-Right. Among them were such Communist leaders as Alois Muna, Josef Skalak, Bretislav Hula, Josef Hais, Josef Sykora, and J. Bubnik. While the ultra-Left found the greatest support in Slovakia, Ruthenia, and the Sudeten territory, the ultra-Right was supported by the rank-and-file members in Prague, Brno and Kladno. In 1925, the division within the party was so serious that it threatened disintegration. Consequently, in late March of that year the Executive Committee of the Comintern decided to step in and to resolve the party crisis in Czechoslovakia. Under the auspices of J. V. Stalin and D. Z. Manuilsky, the Comintern accused the KSC Right of factionalism, at the same time urging the creation of a bloc between the Left and the Center which would be strong enough to defeat the Right. After the Comintern decision, those members who had not been purged from the party either rejoined the Social Democrats or else submitted to bolshevization. It is interesting to note that according to the Comintern, the crisis in 1925 was created by both nationalist illusions among the Czech workers and the 70 percent Communist membership which formerly belonged to the Social Democratic party.[13]

After the 1925 crisis, the ultra-Left of the KSC, under the leadership of Jilek and Bolen, found it relatively easy to maintain a decisive voice in the party. In the meantime, however, struggle within the Soviet Union led to the defeat of Leon Trotsky and his followers, and had a mirror effect in Czechoslovakia (as elsewhere) with the result of purging the ultra-Left as Trotskyites. The occasion for this was the aftermath of the so-called Red Day on June 6, 1928.

The government, headed by Prime Minister Antonin Svehla,

had prohibited a festival of the Communist sports organization (Federation of Proletarian Athletic Training). The KSC decided, in accordance with the new Comintern policy of "class against class," to meet the prohibition with violence. A "Red Day" was announced and the revolutionary workers of all Czechoslovakia were called to Prague for a display of the forces of the party in spite of the threat from the police. However, on June 6, 1928, when Red Day went into effect, not five thousand demonstrators appeared in Prague, and the demonstration was called off. Moscow reacted with outrage and blamed the Czechoslovak party leadership for the fiasco. The ultra-Left resented the charge of opportunism and protested that they had been asked to perform the impossible. As a result, several leaders of the ultra-Left, including Jilek, Bolen, and Neurath, were excluded from the party. Just as in the Soviet Union the attack on Nikolai Bukharin in 1928 was waged by Stalin against alleged rightist opportunism, so in Czechoslovakia the attack by Klement Gottwald on Jilek, Bolen, Neurath, and others carried the same label. The turning point came in February 1929, during the Fifth Congress of the KSC, when Gottwald, leader of the leftist opposition, gained enough support to take over the Secretariat of the KSC from Jilek. From then on, the KSC became a mouthpiece for Stalinist policies in Czechoslovakia.

After the big slump in party membership in 1929–30, the KSC began to make a comeback. In the 1930s, party membership manifested a steady upward trend under the impact of the depression and the increasing threat to the Republic from Nazi Germany. The era of the Munich Agreement constitutes one of the great turning points in the fortunes of the Communist Party of Czechoslovakia. During the Munich Crisis, the Soviet Union declared itself ready to honor its treaty commitments to Czechoslovakia. It thus became its only ally ready to honor its obligations. However, some historians have stated that the Soviet Union was no more ready than Britain or France, and that her boldness was spurred by the certainty that Britain and France would not fulfill their obligations.[14] Nonetheless, the Soviet Union won great acclaim from wide segments of the Czechoslovak population, including those who were not normally associated with left-wing politics. Given the contempt and loathing which the Czechoslovaks felt for the West at this juncture, the Soviet Union and communism were bound to gain in popularity. The subsequent German occupation of Czechoslovakia only increased the luster of the Soviet Union. Amazingly, the Stalin-Ribbentrop–Non-Aggression Pact of August 1939 did not create revulsion against the Soviet government as it did in the West, principally because the Soviet Union, like Czechoslovakia, had been spurned by the West in its hour of crisis and, therefore, the Czechoslovak Left considered it legitimate for the USSR to undertake those measures which could buy it time and security. It is interesting to note that after the Communist takeover in 1948, the Soviets were spreading the propaganda that the Western Allies deliberately held back in the struggle against Nazi Germany because they had earlier betrayed Czechoslovakia. Be that as it may, the dismemberment of the First Czechoslovak Republic, in October 1938, also brought the end of the Czechoslovak Communist party as a legitimate parliamentary party.

The KSC During World War II

Shortly after the Munich decision to cede the Sudeten territory to Hitler's Germany, the Central Committee of the KSC decided to move the headquarters of the party to Moscow. Led by Klement Gottwald, the KSC leadership (consisting of Rudolf Appelt, Bruno Koehler, Vaclav Kopecky, Josef Krosnar, Viliam Siroky, Rudolf Slansky, Bohumir Smeral, and Jan Sverma) made its way to Moscow by the end of 1938 where it was kept in obscurity until June 22, 1941, when the two-year Nazi-Soviet honeymoon ended in an all-out attack on the Soviet Union. Because of the lack of leadership from Moscow, the illegal KSC, under the initiative of Eduard Urx in the German Protectorate of Bohemia and Moravia, formed its own Central Committee, and in London several Communist leaders joined the Czechoslovak government-in-exile as early as 1939. So in Slovakia when, under the protective arm of Nazi Germany, Rev. Jozef Tiso declared independence, two months later in May 1939, Ludovit Benada, Julius Duris and Jan Osoha organized the illegal Communist Party of Slovakia (*Komunisticka strana Slovenska* or KSS). The Slovak Communist party continued its affiliation with the illegal KSC in Prague and, therefore, never had an autonomous section in the Comintern—its existence was, strictly speaking, tactical, i.e., to weaken the opposition parties in Slovakia after the war. Hence, when the Communists took power in Czechoslovakia, in February 1948, the KSS merged with the Central Committee of the KSC, where it was outnumbered by the Czech membership and, therefore, its remaining autonomy became meaningless.

The 1938 membership of the illegal KSC was estimated at 70,000. In 1945, the party claimed that 25,000 of its members had lost their lives because they were a prime target of the German occupation. Yet, it is interesting to note that Communist resistance activity in wartime Czechoslovakia did not amount to much until 1944. Whatever resistance existed prior to 1944 was usually led by non-Communists who, due to their contacts with London and some conspiratorial experience, were more adept at clandestine activities then were the Communists. Besides, most Communists in Czechoslovakia were, after the signing of the Nazi-Soviet Non-Aggression Pact in 1939, either too confused or apathetic to resist the Nazis.

Communist participation in the Slovak National Uprising, in August 1944, was considered a political game with the objective of enabling the Soviets to gain complete control over the insurgent forces fighting for the liberation and restoration of a pre-Munich Czechoslovak Republic.[15] Of the 70,000 freedom fighters, more than 80 percent belonged to the former Slovak Army organized in military combat units under the command of the Czechoslovak government in London. Only about 10,000 insurgents, most of whom claimed to be Communists, belonged to partisan detachments under the command of Col. Alexej Nikitic Asmolov, a member of the Soviet High Command. This separation in command meant frequent misunderstandings and quarrels between the partisans (meaning guerrillas) and the soldiers and, of course, led to the eventual defeat of the Czechoslovak military units by the superior Nazi elite divisions *Das Reich*, *Deutschland*, and *Prinz Eugen*. Of the 70,000 insurgents, more than 18,000 were POWs, most of whom died in internment camps. The bulk of the non-Communist political leaders who participated in the uprising met with the same fate. As it later became evident, the Soviet government and the KSC in Moscow found it undesirable for the Slovaks to free themselves from German domination by their own valiant effort. The Soviets wanted to be the ones who would liberate Czechoslovakia and, by such liberation, to impose a sphere of influence and later domination over Czechoslovakia. One step in this direction was undertaken on September 17, 1944, when the Slovak Communists, supported by left-wing Social Democrats, succeeded in dissolving the Slovak Social Democratic party through a merger. The significance of this act was seen only after the war. With the Social Democrats eliminated from the political arena, there were only two political parties functioning in postwar Slovakia: the Communists and the Democrats. Until May 26, 1946 (the first postwar national elections), the "parity" principle gave the Communists 50 percent representation in all national and local offices in Slovakia. Yet at the polls in 1946, the Democrats received 61.43 percent of the votes while the Communists received only 30.48 percent.

The foundations of the postwar social order were set by Communist and non-Communist politicians in exile in either London or Moscow and not by a free popular expression within the country. The document encompassing the agreement negotiated between the two groups in Moscow became known as the Kosice Program.[16] According to Communist historians, in this program were embedded the Leninist principles concerning the role of the proletariat in a democratic revolution. That is to say, it placed the bourgeoisie in a disadvantageous and the Communists in an advantageous position vis-à-vis the Czechoslovak masses.

The "People's Democracy"

By the terms of the Kosice Program, a government of national unity was formed composed of the KSC, the National Socialists, the People's party, the Social Democrats, and the Slovak Democratic party. The Communists obtained the leading portfolios within the coalition Cabinet. In addition to the two vice-premierships (one Czech and one Slovak), the Communists were in charge of the Ministry of Interior, the Ministry of Information, and the Ministry of Agriculture. Although General Ludvik Svoboda, an agent of the Soviet KGB since 1940, was not yet in 1945 a member of the KSC, the Ministry of Defense which he headed was also considered a Communist outpost. Thus, from the very beginning the Communists commanded strategic heights at the national level, as well as the control of all local institutions.

The Kosice Program decreed the nationalization of all major industry, properties, and enterprises owned by Germans or their collaborators. The result was that the Communists had their hands on all institutions through which they could control the country by persuasion and threats. Through their control of the Ministry of Information, for example, they controlled all communications, and through the Ministry of Agriculture all land reforms.

It is moot speculation whether the Kosice Program represented the true will of the people. While it could be argued that the Communists arrived at major changes in society through nondemocratic means, nevertheless these changes had the support of the majority of the Czechoslovak voters. The elections of 1946 bear out this contention. After all, these were not normal times. The German occupation caused such chaos in property relationships that the subsequent nationalization was not painful to the great majority of the citizenry. There was a vast pool of industrial property which had no legal national ownership because it had been appropriated or confiscated by the Germans either through dictated purchases or confiscated from Jewish ownership. The expulsion and expropriation of millions of Germans in 1945 contributed a pool of goods from which literally millions of Czechoslovaks benefited. Despite their historic commitment to internationalism, the Communists supported the expulsions, seconded by a populace which believed that they had finally come into their national patrimony.

The elections of 1946 seemed to put a seal of approval on most of these policies. The Communists polled 38 percent of the total popular vote. The second strongest party, the National Socialists, polled only 23.66 percent, leaving the Communists by far the largest party in the field. The Social Democrats, who polled 12.1 percent, subscribed at least initially to the same program as the KSC, enabling the Communists to capture the premiership and 9 out of 26 Cabinet posts.[17] As a result of the elections, the members of the KSC chaired 55 percent of the local and 78 percent of the district national committees.

The February Coup of 1948 underscored what had been a fact since 1945, i.e., that the Communists held de facto power in the Czechoslovak system. What had changed was the willingness of the Communists to tolerate opposition and obstruction from their coalition partners. After the 1946 elections, the Communist leaders were ready to dispense with the niceties of a parliamentary regime and to apply the teachings of Leninism toward winning the socialist revolution. Many observers hold that the timing of the coup to precede the national elections, scheduled for May 1948, was of utmost importance. It was widely predicted that the Communists could not duplicate their successes of 1946 and that a defeat at the polls would automatically change the course of the people's democracy.

Since it was imperative for the Communists to be always on the offensive during the socialist revolution, pressures against the opposition, similar to those mentioned above, continued in full force until February 20, 1948.[18] Twelve non-Communist party leaders in the twenty-six-member Gottwald government, exhausted and unable to cope with such pressures any longer, resigned, and thus prompted a Communist-engendered government crisis. While the disorganized opponents were still in shock, suffering from Communist "fair play," the proponents were displaying "mass support" for Premier Gottwald by organizing workers' and peasants' demonstrations and by parading armed militiamen in the town squares. Meanwhile, pressure had been mounting long before the February crisis against a feeble old man, the president of the republic, to accept the resignations of the twelve ministers and appoint new ones, hand-picked by the Presidium of the KSC.

With the formation of a new government, the opposition suddenly disintegrated, opportunities from the other side of the aisle found new allies, and the Czechoslovak Communist party seemed to be moving steadily toward the final stage of the socialist revolution. By February 25, 1948, the transfer of power from the capitalist to the Communist elite was, for all practical purposes, completed. On June 7, Eduard Beneš formally resigned his post as president of the Czechoslovak state, and on June 27, the KSC rejoiced over the incorporation of the expurgated rump of the Social Democratic party. It has been argued that without Social Democratic support, Communist pressure "from above" would have been a fiasco and the peaceful seizure of power in February 1948 unattainable.[19]

The Communist Party in Power

After the takeover, the Communist party prepared itself to exercise control and dispensed with those organizational features which were applicable to a party out of power. The ten-man cells were abandoned in favor of the basic primary party organization which is the form prevalent in the USSR. These were established in all enterprises and working organizations. Such institutions as the factory militia (*zavodni milice*) further extended the party's control into every enterprise by the presence of armed men who were amenable to party discipline. With all organizational aspects of society firmly under the discipline and control of the party, it could now reduce its membership to more manageable proportions, and in the postcoup period, the party membership was trimmed by 823,000.[20]

During the years 1950–51, the party was shaken by the most drastic purges in the entire bloc. The purges resulted in the arrest of Rudolf Slansky, former secretary-general of the Communist party, and the subsequent execution of an entire group of Jewish and Slovak intellectuals.[21] One of the many accusations heaped on Slansky was that he transformed the party into a mass organization and ignored the principles of Leninist teaching; he was further accused of crimes ranging from Titoism to Zionism. This was a period in which the Soviet foreign policy was changing from support of Israel to the Arabs. It coincided with the campaign against "homeless cosmopolitans," most of whom turned out to be Jews. This fit the Czechoslovak purge into the scheme of grander designs of Soviet policy. All East European parties were forced to exorcize the heresy of Titoism by resolute acts of judicial murder. The execution of Titoists was thought to be an inoculation against the spread of this pernicious infection. By forcing the bloc parties to participate in the blood purges, the Soviets made them burn the bridges leading to any easy return to national communism. Since the trials in Czechoslovakia were closely assisted by Soviet "experts," they had the additional benefit of bringing the Czechoslovak secret police more closely under Soviet influence.

Slansky and his group were blamed for the Czechslovak support of the state of Israel in 1946 and 1947, a support which the Soviet Union did not oppose at the time.[22] The charges that the accused were guilty of Zionism were dubious insofar as most of them had spent a political lifetime in the service of the Communist party. The charges of Titoism contradicted those of Zionism because if Titoism had any ideological meaning, it stood for greater national independence. Until 1950, Slansky was reputed to be Stalin's closest collaborator within the KSC, hardly a Czech nationalist trying to recreate a Czechoslovak Communist party independent of Soviet influence.

Yet, there was an element of truth in the charges, as well. It was true that most levels of the party resented the extent of the close supervision they suffered from Moscow. It was even truer that Gottwald and Slansky headed separate wings of the party which despised each other. Gottwald's supporters were largely of working-class origin and came to prominence through prewar trade-union activity and other party politics. The Slansky supporters were mostly intellectuals from bourgeois families who joined the Party through intellectual processes. Many were Jews, many had fought in Spain. By utilizing folk prejudice they could be tied into a variety of sins which coincided with the interests of Soviet foreign policy. The Gottwald faction availed itself of the general political situation to victimize these tempting targets before a populace which was quite prepared to believe the worst of them.

It is difficult to overestimate the importance of the Slansky trials for the subsequent history of the KSC. An entire generation of leaders lived in the long shadow of the trials. The forces for reform hoisted the flag of rehabilitation of the Slansky group in the mid-1960s when they launched their attack on all members of the leadership who had involved themselves in the trials. The main protagonists in the political struggles of the 1960s were the vested party bureaucracy, headed by Antonin Novotny, the president of the republic, and the party intellectuals who rose to new prominence in the mid-1960s because their guidance was so badly needed by the bureaucracy in order to revitalize a retrogressive economic performance. The conservative elements tried to keep the lid down on the numerous investigations, reports, and reappraisals of the Slansky case, for the violence of the Slansky trials was not in line with Czechoslovak political traditions. A population used to the rudiments of a *Rechtstaat* was profoundly offended by the events of the 1950s, and in this climate liberals could mobilize both party and nonparty opinion around the issue of reexamination. When a full revision of the Slansky trials came during the spring of 1968, it marked the downfall of the entire stratum of leaders who had participated in those events.

Held together by a common guilt over the events of 1951, the Novotny group manifested unusual cohesion in the 1950s and weathered the Twentieth Congress of the Communist Party of the Soviet Union in February of 1956 and the subsequent Polish and Hungarian uprisings without even a ripple. The critical period for the regime came during the middle 1960s when a remarkable coincidence of circumstances cracked the unity of the leadership. A new generation which had not participated in the purges of the 1950s started contending for leadership roles which had been denied them earlier. They found the issues of the trials were useful as a lever. These trends coincided with an economic downturn which pointed up many weaknesses in the Czechoslovak economy, ranging from an imbalance of payments to an agricultural crisis precipitated by lack of investment and forced collectivization. The industrial economy was still suffering from the vast dislocations caused by the population shifts in the aftermath of World War II. The party's investment policies frequently did not prove profitable. A fundamental weakness was the Czechoslovak adherence to the Soviet model of development which stressed heavy industry. This model was perhaps successful in some underdeveloped areas where the conditions were favorable for such a development, but hardly applicable to a small industrialized society lacking in several basic resources and capital investment. The plans were mocked by the Czechoslovak economist Radislav Selucky who spoke of the "cult of the plan" as a corollary to the "cult of personality" then under severe attack within the party. As a result of the purges initiated during the de-Stalinization proceedings (which, incidentally, began in Czechoslovakia as late as 1962) and because of steady economic deterioration, President Novotny was forced to relinquish some of his dictatorial powers in favor of several moderate groups of Czech and Slovak Communists.[23] They included intellectuals and professional people, writers and journalists, trade unionists and students—all supported by the liberal wing of both the Czechoslovak and Slovak Communist parties.

From that time until 1967, Novotny and the old party stalwarts no longer controlled the machinery which was necessary for the implementation of their version of genteel totalitarianism. The leaderships of the professional organizations passed one by one into the hands of the reformers, who then used them as bastions from which to assault the remaining positions of the conservatives. Several critics of the Novotny regime called for the transformation of the party from the supreme instrument of state power into the highest embodiment of class unity. Following the Yugoslav example, the liberal Slovak Communists urged the party elite to withdraw from the daily management of state affairs and relinquish some of its decision-making power to autonomous institutions. Novotny, however, considered the liberal demands a threat to the sovereignty of the party and, therefore, in 1966 pronounced the aim of the KSC to be to harmonize group interests without permitting any sectarian stratum to deform the all-state interests. In other words, the workers, on the one hand, were to be persuaded to accept deleveling of incomes in favor of the technical intelligentsia. The technical intelligentsia, on the other hand, were to be enlisted for a more constructive role in the state without being given too much influence in the decision-making process. The alienation of youth was to be prevented from becoming a serious threat to socialist interests. Nationality groups were to be integrated into the unified state on the basis of proletarian ethics, and so on. Thus, the party's aim was to appease interest groups through party discipline and, at the same time, to prevent the formalization of their power. These tactics, however, proved ineffective in December 1967, when the intellectuals supported by Slovak nationalists under the leadership of the first secretary of the Slovak Communist party, Alexander Dubček, challenged Novotny's centralist policies and thus forced a showdown between dogmatists and progressives in the KSC in January 1968. In the meantime, Novotny in desperation tried to fire Dubček and, on the advice of Gen. Jan Sejna, mobilized the workers' militia and the First Armored Brigade to help keep himself in power. However, it was too late. Novotny and his system of dictatorship could not be saved by Soviet party chief Brezhnev's intervention in early December 1967, or by the military intervention. On January 5, 1968, Novotny relinquished his post as first secretary of the Czechoslovak Communist party and on March 22, 1968, Novotny ceased to be president of the republic.

The KSC and the Slovak Communists

The period of struggle between the various forces in the Czechoslovak Communist party which in 1968 brought down the Novotny regime was also marked by the rise of the Slovak wing of the KSC. Although still functioning under a separate label, of Communist Party of Slovakia (*Komunisticka strana Slovenska* or KSS), the autonomy of the KSS had become meaningless after its 1948 merger with the Central Committee of the KSC.[24] Nevertheless, it was Slovak proletarian nationalism that spearheaded the Czechoslovak struggle in 1968 for decentralization and liberalization of the political process.

The special position of the Slovak Communists developed as a result of the purge trials, in which they had not participated in any capacity except as victims. Although the major victim of the 1951 purges was Rudolf Slansky, in 1968 he was regarded only as a Jewish apparatchik who had been responsible for many excesses of the system. Similar views prevailed about other Czechs who had been purged about the same time as Slansky. By contrast, however, the Slovak victims of the purges, including such Jews as Eugene Loebl, were revered as genuine national heroes. The most honored among them were, of course, Vlado Klementis, Laco Novomesky and Gustav Husak.

The entire record of Communist rule in Slovakia differs from that of Bohemia-Moravia. Slovakia became the recipient of substantial investment capital and Slovak living standards climbed consistently during this period. Slovakia was an area for which the traditional mobilizational techniques seemed to be tailored. There was a substantial agricultural population to mobilize for industrialization and the statistics show a spectacular rise in urbanization.[25]

The Slovak party leaders always exhibited more independence than the Czechs. They had not been tainted by the guilt of the Slansky era. There was also no acute split between the working class and intellectual members of the Slovak Communist party. As a result, the prevailing tone of the regime in

Slovakia was more liberal. The high level of investments which Slovakia received was the object of resentment by many Czechs who felt they were called upon to subsidize the equalization of living standards between Slovakia and the Czech Lands, and were rewarded by a harsher regime. The Slovaks, the principal beneficiaries of the equalizing policies, still had grievances of their own. The Czech role in Slovakia had been and remained tutelary. For every Slovak dean at the University of Bratislava there was a Czech associate dean; this policy was duplicated in most public institutions.

The Slovaks used the ferment in 1968 to reassert their claim to national coequality through federalism. Many of the leaders of the Slovak party were not liberals in the sense that the Czech intellectuals were, but all of them believed in Slovak coequality. At that time there were many proposals; one of these was the creation of separate Czech and Slovak Communist parties, equal in all respects and joined at the national level. Until then, democratic centralism as practiced in Czechoslovakia defeated most efforts at genuine decentralization because no matter how much the government was reorganized, the orders essentially flowed from a highly centralist KSC apparatus which managed to bypass the substance of federalism as understood in the West. Much of the Slovak effort was aimed at the revival of the Slovak National Council which had directed the Slovak Uprising of 1944. The Slovaks also made efforts to vindicate the party leaders who lost their lives or were purged in 1951. In this regard, both Czech and Slovak interests dovetailed. The only reform which survived the Soviet "entry" was the Constitutional Law No. 143 of October 28, 1968, which provided Slovakia with an autonomous legislature. However, in view of the recentralization of the party after April 1969, this aspect of federalism became as meaningless as the autonomy of the KSS. Ever since the pro-Soviet Slovak Communists were placed into leadership positions in the KSC, they lost much of their erstwhile interests in the federalization of party and government. Even though economic equalization between the Czech Lands and Slovakia persisted after Dubček's removal from power in April 1969, many

Slovaks were of the opinion that economic equality could not be equated with political, social, and cultural equality.

Socialism with a Human Face

When in January 1968 Alexander Dubček replaced Antonin Novotny as secretary-general of the KSC, Czechoslovakia entered a new era of great historical significance. Some Czechs and Slovaks referred to it as the beginning of socialist democracy, while others called it a combination of enlightened socialism and Western-style personal freedom. In any case, it represented an experiment in socialism. The Slovak part in this experiment was equally significant. Under the pretext of the need to respect the specific Slovak conditions, the Slovak Communists were engaged in a struggle to gain concessions in the sphere of civil liberties for all citizens of Czechoslovakia.

Once the reformers gained power, events took their course at a rush and frequently without much guidance from anybody. Freedom of the press brought with it the abolition of censorship and the domination of the mass media by the cultural workers themselves, such as writers and journalists, and was marked by the disintegration of party control. Travel abroad, freedom of expression at all levels, and the revival of numerous voluntary organizations and associations free of party or state control all marked the phenomenon known as "socialism with a human face." The events demonstrated the fundamental superficiality of the machine which had supported the Sovietized version of communism in Czechoslovakia. There were few bastions left which the Stalinists could rely on; they had strength in institutions such as the secret police or aging factory militia, and in some quarters of the press and armed forces. Apart from these, most commanding positions were in the hands of the reformers with the enthusiastic support of the masses. All ranks of the party manifested a lack of discipline which infected even the military.[26] This general situation created dread and forboding among the Soviet and East European leaderships. They, too, had would-be reform leaders to contend with and they no doubt saw the events in Czechoslovakia as a preview of what might easily happen in their respective countries. Neither Ulbricht nor Gomułka needed much persuasion to view the Czechoslovak reformers as counterrevolutionaries or to participate in the bloc intervention of August 1968. At the same time, there were divisions within both the Soviet and Warsaw Pact leaderships as to what was the best course to follow. After the talks at Cierna-nad-Tisou, it was at Bratislava that all party leaders of the WTO, with the exception of the Romanians, met to discuss the Czechoslovak case. It was here that some of these divisions were exposed to outside observers. However, there were no divisions serious enough to prevent intervention by Warsaw Pact forces on August 21, 1968.

The subsequent internment and abduction of Dubček, Smrkovsky and Cernik to Moscow was an effort to effect splits in the leadership and create a pro-Moscow faction in Prague. These maneuvers, however, did not succeed; they only bespoke Soviet indecision. Once in physical control of the country, the Soviet leaders realized that time was on their side and that fissures would develop in the Czechoslovak leadership which they could exploit at their leisure. Gustav Husak was the first of the Czechoslovak leaders who gave the appearance of breaking ranks. From the Soviet point of view he was the ideal man because, like Kadar in Hungary or Gomułka in Poland, he had been a victim of the purges and was not saddled with the liabilities of the past. The Soviet leaders also realized that any man who worked with them would be extremely unpopular within the country and would thus become more dependent on their support. The postinvasion secret Party Congress at Vysocany demonstrated the startling discipline which the party maintained in the face of the invasion.[27] It accurately mirrored the solidarity of the country.

There was no reign of terror immediately following the Soviet invasion. The party commenced a systematic cleansing of its ranks (*proverky*) in which the credentials of each individual member had to be reverified, a program not fully instituted until the autumn of 1969. In the wake of the invasion, thousands of party members resigned individually or in symbolic mass resignations by mailing in their party cards; almost 50 percent of the members failed to pay their party dues after the invasion.[28]

In addition to those who had resigned during the first postinvasion shock, there were hundreds of thousands of others who were either expelled or crossed off party rolls in 1970. In terms of their occupations, the expelled members were the most severely penalized. They were usually forced to give up their positions altogether or perform other tasks at significantly reduced salaries. Under no circumstances could they hold positions in which they supervised personnel. Those party members who were crossed off party rolls were not only deprived of party functions, but in some cases demoted or transfered to more obscure occupational roles. The numbers affected have not been published, but a reasonable estimate runs into the hundreds of thousands.[29]

The mass expulsions had profound social consequences for the entire society. Many publications and professional associations were disbanded entirely; others were reconstituted under "reliable" party leadership. Most of the expelled party members belonged to the generation which had acquired its party membership, education, and training since 1948. In many ways they constituted the most energetic and devoted segment of the KSC. They were frequently replaced by individuals of less education and competence, and the results of this are visible in the work of enterprises and organizations. It remains to be seen if the party can afford to sacrifice a generation it struggled to educate and socialize politically. There is increasing talk of finding ways to reintegrate the expelled members into the work of the society so their talents are not entirely wasted, yet the present leaders obviously fear that placing former members in their erstwhile positions might lead to a revival of the reform movement.[30]

Federalism and the KSC

When federalism was in the making in Czechoslovakia (from April to October 1968), the overriding principle for resolving the inequities between the two nations was the effective devolution of political authority in the republic. To accomplish this task, both Slovak and Czech political leaders agreed on federalizing not only the legislative and state-executive bodies but the party structure as well. Consequently, the Draft Party Statutes prescribed the reorganization of the party along lines more or less coincident with the federal government system (Section IV, Articles 38–57).[31] Indeed, after his promotion to the rank of secretary-general, Gustav Husak reaffirmed that the intended federalization of the party would proceed and that a constituent congress of the Czech Communist party would be held subsequent to the planned KSC congress.[32] Yet, at the May, 1969 Central Committee Plenum of the KSC, Husak reversed his position and called for party unification and the preservation of its monolithic character.[33] Hereafter the existence of Czech and Slovak party organizations as "national-territorial bodies" was acknowledged, but it was stressed that the "class basis of party organizations" conferred a uniformity on the party, and obligated workers of each nation to resist granting any national-autonomous privileges to local and territorial party organizations; over-all policy and guidance were the sole prerogatives of central party bodies.[34]

As consolidation gained momentum, party federalization came more and more to be linked with revisionist designs to transform the fundamental nature and direction of the state within the structure and process of the KSC. By the end of January 1970, at the Central Committee Plenum of the KSC, it became clear that measures were in preparation to eliminate all ideas of federalism with regard to the party. Husak himself called for the elimination of "certain federative elements" which had found their way into the party.[35] Consequently, the Czech Party Bureau was presented not as the precursor of a separate Czech party but rather as a temporary creation whose function had been primarily to implement the directives of the leadership in the Czech Lands. First, Lubomir Strougal, Chairman of the Bureau, was replaced by Josef Kempny, and then other Bureau officials were removed surreptitiously. The coup de grâce came at the May 1971 Party Congress with the disbanding of the Czech Party Bureau.[36] The return to an asymmetrical party model brought the issue of party federalization to a close. Through democratic centralism and socialist internationalism, the KSC had once again assumed the role of unifier in a society of Czechs, Slovaks, and other nationalities. The party—meaning the Presidium of the Central Committee—must provide united direction to all spheres and interests of the two national republics whether they like it or not. The real meaning of federalism in Czechoslovakia lies in the class context and not in the limitation of central authority or the preservation of multinational interests. To favor the latter over the class of toilers would constitute heresy, revisionism, and opportunism.[37]

ROLE AND ORGANIZATION OF THE KSC

The KSC came into power as the result of a bloodless coup which was a feat of political organization rather than of revolutionary sang froid. Its membership and composition reflect this reality. Nearly all of the members joined since 1948; prewar party members total less than 1 percent of the total membership.[38] Therefore, in order to understand its role or sense of mission, the aspirations of the party membership must be examined.

Many of the members are of working-class origin. For these

Table 3.2. KSC Membership, 1945–48

Period	Number of Members
May 1945	27,000
August 1945	712,776
December 1945	826,527
March 1946	1,081,138
November 1947	1,281,138
January 1948	1,539,672
November 1948	2,500,000

SOURCE: Peter A. Toma, "The Czechoslovak Communist Coup in the Sino-Soviet Dispute" in *Bohemia* (Munich: Robert Lerche, 1966), 7: 383.

members, the party has provided a medium of political participation and upward mobility. The prewar Czechoslovak system placed great emphasis on the attainment of formal education and on ascribed status. Most of the present holders of primary or secondary positions within the country would never have gained comparable status roles under the ancien régime. While Lenin said that the purpose of the revolution was to place those who were on the bottom of society at the top, the Czechoslovak "revolution" has not quite attained this ideal, but it has provided a substantial portion of the population with mobility it would not have enjoyed under other circumstances. This has given the KSC a stable and faithful following at all levels of national life; everywhere there are people who may be enthusiastic by varying degrees but who share a common fear of a genuine reversal or counterrevolution. Even at the height of the Prague Spring, an opposition to the fundamental socialist organization of society was not articulated in a significant way. It is therefore fair to assume that the Czechoslovak Communist party produced a socialist state with many challenges which have centered on the issue of how to produce a more viable democratic system. For example, in 1968, the major issue was whether socialism can be reconciled with some form of parliamentary democracy. The Dubček era did not produce any movement to abolish socialism; on the contrary, it initiated a search for socialism with a human face—a demand that had the support of the overwhelming majority of the Czechoslovak people.

The Communist system in Czechoslovakia emphasizes *partijnost* as a major precondition for holding any position of authority. Consequently, all major or minor supervisory functions have to be in the hands of party members. That has left legions of discontented citizens who are willing to buy the general premises of socialism but cannot easily reconcile themselves to having their work directed by people with less proficiency and marginal educational qualifications purely because they are party members.[39] The primacy placed on party loyalty established a system of official corruption in which rewards were granted to those who externally manifested loyalty, a loyalty often on the level of lip service. This came into full view during the spring of 1968 when party members and nonparty members enthusiastically backed reforms and advocated that everybody be rewarded on the basis of qualifications.

Since the entry of Warsaw Pact troops into Czechoslovakia, the principal aim of the party has been to stabilize itself and the government. This has been a formidable task since most of the mass media was in the hands of the reformers. The task was to purge the party to a level where most of its membership would be reliable and supportive of the new political realities. There were divided opinions as to how drastic the cut should be. The conservatives in the present leadership believed along with the Soviets that the party should no longer be a semimass party; they believed that the status of the KSC as a semimass party caused the debacle of 1968 in the first place. It is reported that the Soviets advocated reducing party membership to 300,000.[40] However, the more moderate leaders, which presumably includes Husak, counseled against such a drastic purge, no doubt on the grounds that there was no need to antagonize those party members who remained loyal or at least maintained a passive stand during the Spring of 1968, and that even party members who erred but later recanted should be given a chance to mend their ways.

There are obvious differences between the hardliners and the liberals in the present leadership. Husak apparently had to fight in order to keep the hardliners from placing more individuals on trial for activities stemming from 1968. The party also remains a semimass party by the standards of other ruling Communist parties, possessing a membership of 1,382,860.[41]

Membership and Structure

Like the Soviet party, the KSC is pyramidal in structure, with final authority held by a small group at the top. Until 1953, the party's basic units were organized on a geographical basis. Since then, there has been a shift to basic organizations centered around the member's place of employment, in accordance with the Soviet model. These basic organizations are kept small to ensure greater effectiveness and easier control.

Ever since the 1960s, the party leaders have steadily complained about the lack of interest of young people in party-affiliated activities. Party membership saw a substantial upsurge during the Dubček era when young people rushed to join, but in the aftermath most of these new members were expelled. In January 1968, party membership stood at 1,699,677 members, organized in 44,179 party organizations.[42] The 1968 population of Czechoslovakia was 14,388,603, so that total party strength was close to 12 percent of the population. This is far higher than the usual Leninist norm of 5 percent of the total population. By the end of 1970, 326,817 members had been involuntarily removed. The present membership of the party (including candidates) is 1,382,860, which represents 9.4 percent of the total population. They are organized into 43,506 basic units.

Party membership is a requisite for most leadership positions, as stated earlier. Nonparty members can be found in important technical positions in many segments of economic activity but their influence within the system is minimal. The party is a path to elite status, a fact which can be readily surmised by the present occupational structure of party members. The working-class component within the KSC has been declining since the 1960s. In 1961, factory workers comprised 36 percent of the membership; by 1969 this proportion had sunk to 26.1 percent. However, of the 333,952 candidates enrolled between the Fourteenth and Fifteenth Party Congresses, 62 percent were workers. Thus, for the first time in 20 years, the decline of the workers' share in the party had been arrested. In 1961, the party contained 9.6 percent old-age pensioners; by 1969 this had increased to almost 16 percent. The proportions of members in professional occupations, such as physicians, public employees, engineers, artists, etc., rose to 33.1 percent.[43] From the aforementioned figures it can be argued that before the Fourteenth Party Congress in 1971, the party was an aging organization. Fully one-third of its members were fathers of families.[44] When considering the female percentage of the party, it becomes evident that the KSC was dominated by more mature elements who obviously had the welfare of their families in mind. The percentage of members in the 18–40 age group showed a marked decline, while the percentage of Communists in the 40–80 age group increased.[45] After 1971, however, this trend was reversed. Ninety percent of the candidates enrolled between the Fourteenth and Fifteenth Party Congresses were under 35 years of age and 50 percent under 25. Women constitute, on the basis of 1962 statistics, 27.2 percent of party membership, which does not speak well for the enthusiastic claims of equality made by many Communist spokesmen.[46]

Access to higher education is also closely regulated by the Czechoslovak Communist party. The cadre reports (*kadrovy posudek*) are the decisive factors in admission to institutions of higher learning or for promotion to higher positions in any line of work. Under the impact of the income leveling policies of the KSC, there were, until 1967 and again since 1969, no great material incentives for individuals to commence the process of higher education, particularly since the rewards of party membership were likely to be higher than those gained from the educational process. Yet one has to be cautious in labeling the KSC an elite because of the vast discrepancies in status and income among party members themselves. The available figures indicate that the KSC has a pyramid structure and that the working class members are a minority at its base. Jaroslav Krejci, who studied social stratification in postwar Czechoslovakia, points out that at varying times different groupings have held preeminence. During the late 1940s, it was the personnel manipulating the threat systems, i.e., the secret police, who held prominence. These were supplanted by army elites as international tensions grew, and these in turn were supplanted by technocrats and intellectuals as the party faced increased economic difficulties and a dearth of ideas to cope with them.[47]

As the mass expulsions after 1968 demonstrate, the party is not only a source of upward mobility but can be a source of downward mobility as well. Lower-ranking positions frequently presented their incumbents with far more security than those which were highly visible and demanded a level of political activity for which they could be held accountable. The post-1968 downfall of the liberalizing elements struck KSC members much harder than nonmembers. The party is the ultimate arbiter of everybody's status within the society. The best illustrations of this are the hundreds of thousands who have been expelled in the wake of 1968 and reduced to menial positions despite their high qualifications.

Party Leadership

The dominant personality in any ruling Communist party is the leader who controls the party apparat. The leading personality in the party may be titled Chairman, First Secretary, or Secretary-General, but his control of the Secretariat and Politburo (in the case of Czechoslovakia, the Presidium) ensures a large measure of personal control over party and state. In the immediate postwar period, an anomaly existed in which the most prestigous leader of the KSC, Klement Gottwald, held the chairmanship while Rudold Slansky was the Secretary-General. This as well as other reasons placed the two party leaders in a conflict which was resolved through Slansky's purge in 1961. The purges of the early 1950s had a cohesive effect on the leadership of the KSC. Those who benefited from these purges shared a strong interest in preserving the stability of the party's leadership. Thus, members of the party apparat after the purges can be characterized by their proven loyalty to the central party leadership.[48] While elsewhere in the wake of the Twentieth Party Congress of the Communist Party of the USSR and the subsequent Polish and Hungarian uprisings in 1956 there was a renewed emphasis on collective leadership as a corrective to the cult of personality, in Czechoslovakia the office of secretary-general and titular head of state were vested in the same person, Antonin Novotny. The Novotny leadership remained essentially unchanged between 1954 and 1963. Most of the leaders were Czechs raised in lower-middle-class working families. All of them rose to their positions through trade-union or parliamentary politics during the First Republic. The majority of them had only a minimum of formal education but years of experience in illegal underground activities and subversion. All could be characterized as "Kremlin-oriented," with several (e.g., Siroky, Kopecky, and Koehler) having spent considerable time in the Soviet Union. Others (like Novotny, J. Dolansky, and G. Kliment) were not of working-class origin and spent the war years in Nazi concentration camps. Still others (e.g., V. Nosek, A. Hodinova-Spurna, J. Valo, Kreibich, and B. Vrbensky) were members of the Czechoslovak government-in-exile in London. This leadership was known to be well disciplined, resolute, and revolutionary. It is interesting to note, however, that when compared to Bulgaria, Poland, and Hungary, the KSC leadership shows the lowest number of persons active in revolutionary involvement before and during World War II.[49]

In 1963, changes in the top party leadership were finally made. Bacilek and Koehler were removed from power in April 1963, and Premier Siroky, Vice-Premier Dolansky and a number of less prominent Gottwald associtees lost their positions. All the leading figures of the period of the cult of personality were removed from power except Novotny himself. The new leaders which Novotny appointed owed their positions to him and were prepared to defend Novotny against opponents, at least for some time. However, the grip of the old guard, bound together by common responsibility for the repression of the past, was finally broken in 1963.

During the second phase of the Novotny period, from 1963 to 1968, the main concern of the party leadership was to maintain its dominant role against forces which it could no longer fully control. As the opposition in Czechoslovakia gained momentum, the party steadily lost the initiative in determining the course of events and found itself more and more in the role of either yielding to pressures for change or of taking measures to keep the forces of change under control. The history of the "new economic system" first proposed in late 1963 provides an excellent example of this. Other reform measures initiated during the second period of the Novotny administration suggest a similar halfheartedness; a step forward followed by a step backward. Nevertheless, whether by intent of the Party or by default, many important reforms were instituted during this period.[50]

While the process of reform continued, the party leadership kept up a steady barrage of criticism and warnings to dissident groups, occasionally backing these up with administrative measures. The last attempt of the Novotny leadership to check the forces which threatened its hold on power came in the fall of 1967. After the stormy Writers' Congress of June 1967, at which criticism of unprecedented boldness had been heard, administrative measures were taken against several of the dissident writers who had spoken, and the newspaper *Literarni noviny* was taken from the Czechoslovak Union of Writers and placed under party control. In addition, new accusations of Slovak nationalism were made. It was at this point, at the end of 1967, that the opposition to the Novotny leadership within the Central Committee succeeded in ousting Novotny from his post as First Secretary of the party, and in proceeding to an elimination of the old guard from positions of power. The victory of the anti-Novotny faction was not a victory based on any solid program of reform, but on hatred of Novotny himself together with the growing awareness that the party's position really was disastrous. Alexander Dubček's election to the post of secretary-general was indicative of the fragile nature of the victory. Dubček seems to have been elected as much for his moderation and lack of militancy as for the fact that he was acceptable to all factions. His Slovak and Soviet loyalty was never in doubt.[51]

The new party leadership under Alexander Dubček followed a short-lived policy of "democratization" of Czechoslovak society. It pledged to uphold the principles of socialist democracy and to rehabilitate all those who suffered from the violations of socialist law during the 1949–54 period.

In 1968, under the leadership of Dubček, Cernik, Smrkovsky, and Svoboda, there was no clear-cut national program and the ends and means of the movement were obscure to both the leadership and the followers. Consequently, the Prague Spring did not become a model for state-building, and "socialism with a human face" turned out to be only a label affixed to a social movement. Yet, the Soviet leaders and their followers branded the 1968 events in Czechoslovakia as being as counterrevolutionary as those in Hungary in 1956. Their aims, according to Jozef Lenart, Secretary of the Slovak Communist party and a member of the KSC Central Committee Presidium, were the same, i.e., "to defeat socialism and restore capitalism."[52]

Alexander Dubček and Gustav Husak represent a new generation of leaders. Neither of them was a part of the top leadership before the war; neither spent the war years in Moscow, and both participated in the Slovak National Uprising of 1944. In the immediate postwar era they were not included in the top leadership of the national party; on the contrary, Husak was the victim of the 1951 purges and in 1954 was sentenced to life imprisonment. During the same period, Dubček was a second-level apparatchik.

The present members of the Presidium of the KSC and the Central Committee are on the whole better educated than the party leaders who preceded them. The preponderant majority of the leaders joined the KSC between 1945 and 1948; they represent a generation which came to maturity during the war and made their careers under the present system. The present leadership falls into two types of ideological attributes: those who successfully made the post-1968 transition and those who consistently opposed the 1968 reforms and came into the leadership only as the result of Soviet intervention. In the first group are Lubomir Strougal (first Czech graduate of the KGB school in Moscow in 1951), federal Prime Minister and member of the party Presidium; Gustav Husak, Secretary-General, member of the party Presidium, and president of the republic; Peter Colotka, Slovak Premier and member of the party Presidium; and Jozef Lenart, First Secretary of the KSS and member of the party Presidium. In the second group are Vasil Bilak, Central Committee secretary and member of the party Presidium; Miroslav Capka, chairman of the party Control and Auditing

Commission; Antonin Kapek, member of the party Presidium; Alois Indra, chairman of the Federal Assembly and member of the party Presidium; and Josef Korcak, Czech premier and member of the party Presidium. The latter represent the group of hardliners who remained in opposition throughout the Prague

Table 3.3. Leadership of the Czechoslovak Communist Party (KSC)

PRESIDIUM	
Full Members:	Gustav Husak
	Vasil Bilak
	Peter Colotka
	Karel Hoffman
	Vaclav Hula
	Alois Indra
	Antonin Kapek
	Josef Kempny
	Josef Korcak
	Jozef Lenart
	Lubomir Strougal
Candidate Members:	Miloslav Hruskovic
	Milos Jakes
CENTRAL COMMITTEE SECRETARIAT	
Secretary-General:	Gustav Husak
Secretaries:	Mikulas Beno
	Vasil Bilak
	Jan Fojtik
	Josef Havlin
	Milos Jakes
	Josef Kempny
	Jindrich Polednik
	Jaroslav Haman[a]
Members:	Antonin Brabec
	Marie Kabrhelova
	Cestmir Lovetinsky[b]
	Frantisek Pitra
	Oldrich Svestka
PARTY CONTROL AND AUDITING COMMISSION	
Chairman:	Miroslav Capka

SOURCE: *Rude Pravo,* December 2, 1977.
[a]Elected at the Eleventh KSC Central Committee Plenum on March 16, 1978.
[b]Relieved of membership on March 16, 1978.

Spring.[53] It is said that some of these hardliners favored a punitive purge against the principal liberalizers but were restrained by Husak, himself a one-time victim of Stalinist purges.

Other party leaders, such as Karel Hoffman, Vaclav Hula, and Josef Kempny (all members of the party Presidium), or Milos Jakes and Miloslav Hruskovic (both candidate members of the party Presidium), as well as Mikulas Beno, Antonin Brabec, Miroslav Capka, Jan Fojtik, Josef Havlin, Oldrich Svestka, Marie Kabrhelova, Jaroslav Haman, Jindrich Polednik and Frantisek Pitra, (all members of the Central Committee Secretariat) moved into positions of power only after the fall of the Dubček regime in 1969.

The present leadership gives every appearance of stability, never diverging from the Soviet line. The stability of the leading cadre, however, must be interpreted as symptomatic of political stagnation and immobility. An outward sign of the present political immobility is the practically unchanged composition of top party bodies, of the Presidium, and of the Central Committee Secretariat. The party has made hardly any headway in reconciling itself with the masses, which remain largely passive and addicted to "consumerism." Fundamental reforms remain anathema, and the economic field, despite some tangible improvements, continues to be hampered by centralist controls. The only bright spot since the Fifteenth Party Congress (April 12–16, 1976) is the promise, however vague, to allow individual reentry into the party of members expelled or struck off the lists.

Concurrently with the increase in membership in the party, the number of full Central Committee members was raised in 1976 from 115 to 121 and that of the candidates from 45 to 52; the number of members of the Central Control and Auditing Commission remained unchanged at 51. The overall composition of the 1976 Central Committee was not substantially different from the previous one elected in 1971. Now as before, the full members include the members of the party Presidium, all secretaries and members of the Central Committee Secretariat, all leading regional party secretaries, the mayors of the three largest cities (Prague, Brno, and Bratislava), heads of the more important Central Committee departments, prime ministers and heads of important ministries, chairmen of representative bodies, heads of the most important mass organizations, chairmen of the academies of sciences, several factory managers, a couple of generals, and a sprinkling of outstanding workers, farmers, and members of the intelligentsia.

Although the KSS has been manifestly treated as a territorial organization of the KSC, the Slovak party's top bodies are a little more than transmission belts between the Prague center and the three Slovak regional party organizations.[54] Therefore, it is appropriate to include in this section at least a brief analysis of the Slovak party leadership.

As of March 1, 1976, the KSS reached the greatest numerical strength in its history, with 319,606 registered members and candidates.[55] The social structure of the newly admitted party members and candidates appears better in Slovakia than is true of the state-wide average. Over two-thirds of those newly admitted were workers and collective farmers (the state-wide average in 1976 was 62.6 percent). The age distribution in Slovakia conforms to the state-wide average, with over 90 percent of the new arrivals being under 35 years of age.[56]

The Slovak Central Committee, elected at the 1976 Party Congress in Bratislava, consists of 91 full members—10 more than was elected at the 1971 Slovak Party Congress. Of the old Central Committee, 57 members were reelected and 24 were dropped. There are 34 new arrivals. The reshuffle remained within the normal limits of about one-third. The representation of women was slightly raised, from 13.6 to 15 percent. Six women were relieved of membership and nine were added, bringing their number to 14. The reshuffle among Central Committee candidates was far more radical. Of the original 27, only 2 were retained; 8 were promoted to full membership and the rest were sacked. The number of women in this body was doubled, from 3 to 6. The overall numerical strength was raised from 27 to 30.[57]

There were no personnel changes in the top party bodies. All

Table 3.4. Top Leadership of the Slovak Communist Party (KSS)

PRESIDIUM	
Members:	Ladislav Abraham
	Peter Colotka
	Herbert Durkovic
	Miloslav Hruskovic
	Jan Janik
	Jozef Lenart
	Elena Litvajova
	Ludovit Pezlar
	Viliam Salgovic
	Gejza Slapka
	Miroslav Valek
CENTRAL COMMITTEE SECRETARIAT	
First Secretary:	Jozef Lenart
Secretaries:	Miloslav Hruskovic
	Jan Janik
	Ludovit Pezlar
Member:	Bohus Travnicek
CONTROL AND AUDITING COMMISSION	
Chairman:	Miloslav Boda

As of January 1, 1977.

members of the Presidium and the Secretariat of the KSS Central Committee were returned to office—an obvious reflection of the desire to maintain the outward forms of stability. Thus the uneasy coalition between the more circumspect forces and the dogmatists is likely to continue in regard to the composition of the top bodies. The salient reason for this may well be that the Soviet Union is unwilling to upset the cart in a difficult international situation when "détente" is under scrutiny. Perhaps the greatest threat to stability in the KSS leadership is presented by the fact that Slovakia's privileged position as the less developed part of the country appears to be drawing to an end. This is most clearly indicated by the fact that for the next five years investments are to be distributed proportionally. Any further "catching up" to the Czech Lands will depend mainly on Slovakia's own resourcefulness. Should this new economic policy, dictated from Prague, create undue pressure on the Slovak "policy makers," a rupture between the procentrists and anticentrists in the Slovak top party bodies may become inevitable.

Level of Support

The working class support which the KSC enjoyed in 1948 has waned considerably since if measured by occupation as a guidepost. In 1946, for example, the proportion of active workers within the KSC was 57 percent; by 1956 it had dropped to 36 percent; in 1966 to 33 percent.[58] After the 1968 purges it dropped to an estimated 30 percent—the lowest level during the postwar period. Only recently has there been a reversal in this trend. Nevertheless, the present working-class support of the KSC gives the party a social composition profile similar to that of the USSR in which the workers are also a distinct minority and the party is increasingly composed of functionaries.

With the decline of working-class participation in the KSC another phenomenon which manifests itself is the increasing age of the membership. In 1949, for example, 14.5 percent of the party members were under 25 years of age, but in 1966 only 9 percent.[59] It is interesting to note that in 1966 students constituted only 6.4 percent of the total party membership. Similarly, despite heroic efforts in which those applicants for university admission who were of working-class origin obtained preferential treatment, the proportion of working-class students at Czechoslovak universities fluctuated between 27.6 percent and 37.9 percent.[60]

Under the Dubček regime, while the support for the new leadership was genuine and enthusiastic, there were no major attacks on the institutions of socialism themselves.[61] Most of the effort was directed at instilling a measure of democracy into the activities of deliberative bodies, both party and governmental, and opening up input channels for nonparty members. However, it cannot be authoratatively stated that this effort resulted from a sophisticated understanding of the art of the possible or from a genuine devotion to socialist norms. In a number of questionnaire studies commissioned during Dubček's incumbency, the response of the public to the reform initiatives was remarkably positive.[62] These studies demonstrate little difference in the opinions of party and nonparty members on a number of key issues on which both groups were questioned. Similarly, there were few differences based on sex, age, occupation, and education. On the basis of the available data, it is fair to conclude that the Dubček regime might have won an open election by a wide margin.

In a highly industralized society, only a minority responded to the appeals of egalitarian doctrinaire communism. The rank-and-file membership, by and large, responded enthusiastically to the Dubček reforms. Yet, there were many to whom the reforms represented a major threat because the economic reformers intended to weed out those who were not qualified for managerial or other leadership positions. Since 43 percent of the Czechoslovak managers are not formally qualified for the positions they hold, many favored the retention of the old system which assured them of continuation in their prestige positions.[63] When one adds to this all the university students who were admitted on the basis of class origin rather than qualifications, faculty members whose chief qualification was representing the correct political line, and the factory militia who derived a psychological superiority from their position, one arrives at a substantial block of people who had a stake in the maintenance of the status quo. These elements feared the dilution of the egalitarianism of Czechoslovak communism and they protested those measures which would have differentiated rewards. They constituted the bedrock on which the post-1968 party could be founded.

Since the great purge of 1970, the KSC, with its present 1,216,745 members and 166,115 candidates organized in 43,506 basic units, has changed drastically. The party has lost credibility. It lost the bulk of the members who joined the party before the 1948 coup. In 1970, for example, only 90 out of the 500 Communists still living who had participated in the international brigades in Spain were members of the KSC, and only 3,000 out of the 12,000 who joined the party before World War II remained. The purged KSC is composed of cynical bureaucrats, army and police officers, senior citizens, and some workers kept on the rolls to improve its proletarian composition.[64] According to one paper prepared by a group of "former sociologists," active supporters of the occupation regime constitute about 10 to 15 percent of the population.[65] This group includes: (1) persons involved in Stalinist crimes after 1948 who fear that if things become too liberal again they will have to account both for their new and their old crimes; (2) paid party bureaucrats, usually unskilled, who are being rewarded generously for their loyalty; (3) old-age pensioners, who have devoted their whole life to communism and who do not want to admit they have been deceived; (4) careerists and parasites who would serve any regime; and finally, (5) a small handful of fanatic extremists, closer to the Marxist brand of communism, who are clinging to the only permissible fountain of wisdom, the Soviet Union.

About 70 percent of the population, according to the sociologists, is passive and deliberately apolitical. They seek self-fulfillment in material goods, a full education for their children, and the distractions of sports and light entertainment. Active dissidents constitute 15 to 20 percent of the population. These are mostly intellectuals but also former party workers, military men, and civil servants, i.e., the idealist founders of the Communist system purged for their attitudes during the Prague Spring.

Charisma and Bureaucracy in the Party Leadership

Since 1948, when the Communists took power, the KSC has produced only one charismatic leader: Alexander Dubček. Gottwald, Zapotocky, Novotny, and Husak all achieved leadership positions by tilling the vineyards of the party apparat. They were not borne into office on the shoulders of their enthusiastic fellow countrymen. Even Dubček lacked the attributes of a typical charismatic leader; he was elected to the post of first secretary as much for his moderation and lack of militancy as for the fact that he was acceptable to all factions. His Slovak and Soviet loyalties were never in doubt. Dubček genuinely wanted to do what the people wanted, what the rank-and-file party members wanted. His natural inclination was to try to see everybody's point of view; Dubček tried to reconcile the differences within the party leadership, and his modest speeches were aimed at uniting the widest possible front in support of the democratization process. Dubček's vacillation or his willingness to compromise could have been responsible for his poor judgment of people. For example, he supported Oldrich Svestka, the editor-in-chief of *Rude Pravo*, who later turned against Dubček; he helped Viliam Salgovic, who was put in charge of the secret police and promptly prepared the ground for the invasion. Dubček was too ready to believe in people's good qualities. His humanism, however, was a vital part of the Czechoslovak moral regeneration.[66]

Gottwald, no doubt, had a substantial following within the party due to his long stewardship in the prewar years. Still, the period of the forties and fifties involved such national divisions that it would be difficult to say that Gottwald had great personal popularity. He presided over Czechoslovakia in the period now called the cult of personality. The positions the leadership occupied could be attributed to ascribed status rather than charisma. It is difficult to assess Gottwald's leadership qualities because the cult of personality obscured the process of selection in politics. The subordination of the KSC to the Soviet leadership did not promote the development of native charismatic leadership. After the assault on the cult of personality in 1956, the emphasis on collective leadership precluded the rise of dynamic personalities whose appeal was based on charisma.

Although Gustav Husak is officially the most powerful man in Prague and the historical equivalent of such personalities as Klement Gottwald and Antonin Novotny, he is still not the undisputed leader that his predecessors were. His hand has been strengthened by becoming president of the republic in May 1975, but Husak has not risen, and probably will not do so in the future, above his real function as a glorified coalition leader. Ever since his election as party leader in April 1969, Husak has been treading a course between his moderate-conservative policies and the hardline criticism coming from his opponents. Himself a victim of the show trials of the 1950s, a champion of Slovak rights, and a moderate reformer during the Prague Spring, Husak's approach to normalization has concentrated on strengthening the leading role of the party in all essential areas with the least amount of disruption and recrimination.

It would seem that Husak's position within the party has been strengthened by small steps, but never to the point where he could not be blocked by his opponents. The differences between the factions in the leadership were quite apparent in 1972, a fact highlighted by Husak's reluctance to hold political trials of dissidents. Again, in late 1977, Husak was subjected to criticism by spokesmen of both the presumed orthodox and pragmatic groups within the party leadership. The critics reportedly voiced dissatisfaction with Husak's alleged weak hand in dealing with political opponents such as Charterists, and also found fault with the country's economic situation. The orthodox elements around Vasil Bilak apparently were pressing for a separation of the offices of the party secretary-general and of the president of the republic. These reports have been nourished by allegations that Husak had transferred his supervision of two important Central Committee departments, administration and security, to his political associate, Presidium member and CC secretary Josef Kempny. The control of these two departments has traditionally been considered the real stronghold, if not the power base, of the party leader. But no matter how severe the criticism, Husak has always enjoyed the advantage of Soviet support and the fact that his opponents have not possessed all the qualifications to carry out the process of normalization.[67]

The present leaders of the KSC have deliberately assumed a low profile and justify their existence in pragmatic terms. During the most of its existence, the KSC leadership has been remarkably bureaucratized. This has been partially due to Soviet pressure, and largely due to the deliberate choice of the KSC leaders themselves. Since Czechoslovakia had not had any negative historical experiences with the USSR, the KSC leadership tended to equate the utopian dimensions of communism with the Soviet experience. Due to the law-abiding nature of the population and its historical experience with the Austro-Hungarian *Rechtstaat*, the KSC developed into a tightly hierarchial organization which practiced Soviet-style democratic centralism. This tight bureaucratization was scarcely conducive to producing glamorous leaders. Thus, Husak carried on in the established traditions of the party.

Aspirations and Results

The KSC rode into power on a platform of vastly exaggerated promises which stimulated equally high expectations. The idealized image of the USSR painted through party propaganda, coupled with a substantial amount of enthusiasm among the youth of the country, conspired to produce utopian expectations which even the most effective of governments would be hard put to fulfill. In the aftermath of the 1948 takeover, the Czechoslovak Communist party was scarcely in a position to provide the best of anything. The country was still recovering from the severe dislocations of population and resources resulting from World War II. The chaos was compounded by the loss of thousands of people from skilled and managerial positions, people who either left the country in protest of the KSC takeover or were purged due to "undesirable backgrounds." By 1950, it was abundantly clear that Czechoslovakia would not become a workers' paradise overnight. The purge trials of the early fifties were at least partially the result of the economic failures and the party's search for scapegoats. The KSC faced a formidable task in satisfying the aspirations of a population which had lost its democratic institutions without obtaining overwhelming material benefits in return. The compulsive economic leveling of the regime created a wide range of dissatisfactions in the middle and working classes who traditionally did not compare their levels of living with Eastern Europe but rather with the more advanced countries of the West. This dissatisfaction was an underlying theme of all the crises which faced the KSC from 1948 to 1968.

In 1968, the party sought to break out of the vicious circle of egalitarianism by emulating many lessons of the Yugoslav experiment. The structure of rewards benefited those groups with the least aspirations, paying them in excess of what their labor would bring on the open market. To this may be added the thousands of apparatchiks occupying positions beyond their capabilities. These groups had a vested interest in the continuation of an equalizing regime, and they no doubt provide the backbone of Husak's support. On the other hand, those groups who aspired to economic and social mobility, and who form a majority in an industrialized state, opted for change.

Although Czechoslovakia came under military occupation in the summer of 1968, political persecution did not reach full force until the spring of 1969. Accordingly, attitudes toward values, which had held steady from 1967 to 1968, changed drastically in 1969. "Freedom"—now more than ever out of reach—was chosen as the most important value by 2,217 people interviewed in Czechoslovakia.[68] Only 7 percent of those interviewed chose the concept of "getting ahead"—now implying that one would have to kowtow to the new rulers.

Another index for measuring the performance of the regime revealed that during the Prague Spring, the Czechoslovak radio and television began to assume the functions of effective communications media. Of the 2,952 adults in Czechoslovakia interviewed in 1968, only 37 percent were Radio Free Europe (RFE) listeners. As the Czechoslovak media became more informative and more heedful of issues Czechoslovak audiences wished to hear discussed, the need for RFE diminished. However, with the invasion of the country, the situation was dramatically reversed. Confidence in the domestic communications media was shattered and RFE's audience shot up to 71 percent, remaining at an exceptionally high level of 65 percent well into 1969.

Interviews conducted in Czechoslovakia since 1969 indicate that the greatest desire of the people is still for "a truly democartic, freely elected government" and "more freedom under the present system." On the international level, they aspire to "a genuine rapprochement between East and West" and "greater Western influence in the East."

THE NATIONAL ENVIRONMENT

Czechoslovakia is a country with an area of 49,373 square miles, including Slovakia's 18,924 square miles. Its 1972 population was 14,435,613, of which 4,580,667 were Slovaks. Expressed in percentages, 65 percent of the population are Czech, 30 percent Slovak, and the remaining 5 percent Hungarian, German, Polish, and Ukrainian. The capital city of Prague has a population estimated at 1,083,717.[69] Most of the Czech population is urban and industrial; during the First Republic, the majority of Slovakia's population was rural and agricultural. One of the achievements of the communist system in Czechoslovakia is the greater equalization of the income differences which separated Bohemia-Moravia from Slovakia before the war. Slovakia is no longer a pastoral agricultural setting; about 70 percent of its present population is engaged in industrial pursuits.[70] The only area in Eastern Europe which compares remotely with Czechoslovakia's rate of industrialization is East Germany. However, East Germany's industries are new compared to those of Czechoslovakia because of the devastation it suffered during World War II and because the East Germans were forced to build a new complex in agricultural areas after the loss of the Silesian complex in Poland. One of the banes of prewar Czechoslovak industry was that they produced too many items in too small series; the production ranged from steel and heavy machinery, aircraft, and automobiles, to glassware and musical instruments. Czechoslovakia possessed ample coal resources, on which it could base heavy industry. The country needed an active foreign trade to maintain the living standard of its population. Its large textile industires depended on imported natural fibers and its people on agricultural imports which were necessary to maintain an adequate diet. Since 1948, however, Czechoslovakia has become dependent on trade with Eastern Europe and the USSR. Its fuel oil needs must be met almost entirely from Soviet imports. In this it is not significantly different from other industrialized Eastern European states. Czechoslovakia's economy is closely tied to the COMECON partners, and therefore she is highly vulnerable to Soviet political pressure.

The Economic System

Since 1948, Czechoslovakia has had a centrally planned economy. The economic system closely emulates the Soviet model inasmuch as the planners placed primary emphasis on heavy industry and neglected investment in Czechoslovakia's well-developed lighter industries and the agricultural sector. In 1960, when the socialist republic was established, Czechoslovakia had a greater proportion of its economy in the public sector than did any other bloc state.

By 1962, the entire system was facing a profound crisis because of faltering growth rates in almost every sector of the economy. These could be attributed to a wide variety of factors, ranging from an emphasis on heavy industry (which had partially lost its export markets due to a build-up of capacity in the same fields in neighboring East European states) to underinvestment in such key fields as agriculture. In 1962, *Rude Pravo* admitted that agricultural production (87 percent of which was in the "socialist sector") had not yet exceeded the 1938 levels.[71] In 1963, Czechoslovakia was the only socialist country which had achieved negative economic growth.[72] The country was compelled to accept increased food imports, which further damaged its balance of trade.

These circumstances forced the entire situation onto the attention of the Twelfth Party Congress in December 1962, and which provided the reformers with their first access to the levers of power, eventually causing the ouster of Novotny. Their demands did not solely concern the economy but extended to issues which vitally affected the political system itself, such as the reopening of that Pandora's box, the purge trials, This was the Congress which saw the birth of the coalition of Slovak and Czech liberals which came into increasing ascendance over the next six years.[73]

Czechoslovakia is a highly developed industrial state. Close to 90 percent of its population derives its livelihood from nonagricultural pursuits.[74] This high level of industrialization, as stated earlier, has been a constant source of difficulty for an economic model which has been borrowed from a semi-developed setting. One of the persistent problems which has confronted the Czechoslovak economy is efficiency in the utilization of labor. The two main causes that have contributed to this problem are the relatively low wages paid the labor force and the dislocations brought about by heavy and rapid investments. The economic model was better suited to an underdeveloped setting than to the allocation of human and capital resources in a highly industrialized area. Accordingly, the results were, on a relative scale, far more impressive in Slovakia than in the Czech Lands. During the Communist era, Slovakia has been the recipient of substantial investment, while the Czech industries have been actively recruiting Slovak labor to compensate for chronic shortages. Over a twenty-five year period, this has led to a radical shift in the occupational structure of Slovakia. In 1948, 60 percent of the Slovak population derived its livelihood from agriculture. Today the percentage involved in agriculture has been halved, and Slovakia has almost acheived economic parity with the Czech Lands.[75] With the growing prosperity, the Slovak party leaders have resolutely condemned the export of Slovak labor to the Czech Lands as the first step of their denationalization. The leaders of the KSC have taken justifiable pride in the development of Slovakia.

Apart from the international consideration of the Czechoslovak economy, the system has wrought great changes in the status of workers. Prewar Czechoslovakia was a country which retained many feudal aspects in the relationships between its classes. Any white-collar worker felt superior to his blue-collar brethren. Regardless of how low the skill or education level of the white-collar worker, he was in a position of social and economic superiority to the most highly skilled manual worker. The regime has reduced these social distances and contributed greatly to the workers' self-identification with socialism in general and with the regime in particular. The working class has obtained opportunity for vertical mobility that it lacked under prewar conditions by access to administrative positions, to the military officer corps, and to higher education. This has provided a substantial number of people with increased self-esteem.

The leveling policy of the Communist system has also alienated diverse groups. It has proved socially and economically harrowing to the former upper and middle classes, and earned the regime their hostility. It has also frustrated those with ambition. Highly qualified people with negative cadre reports have been forced into menial positions. This has profoundly affected the traditional class structure, and created a state of tension between the new and old elites.

When the threat system was removed in 1968, the Czechoslovak economy began traveling in the direction of greater differentiation of economic rewards. The Prague Spring constituted a revolt by the upward mobility both in and out of the party. The economists, who were the main protagonists of the reforms, proposed to revitalize the system by introducing the Yugoslav model of market socialism. In Yugoslavia, this system has created substantial distances in both social status and income; there is no reason to suppose that the effects of this system would have been different in Czechoslovakia. If the issue had been submitted to a democartic vote, it is doubtful that the Czechoslovaks would have opted for further leveling.[76] The trend during the spring of 1968 was toward the opposite direction: a host of special interest groups came into existence, ranging from the Boy Scouts to churches. The Soviet entry in 1968, however, removed from debate the issue of income differentiation in the Czechoslovak economy. A government decree in the summer of 1971 reaffirmed the importance of state planning as the basis for economic management.

Although industrial production improved during the immediate postinvasion period, inflationary panic-buying continued, and worker productivity fell as demoralization spread. A series of price increases and wage contorls implemented under Husak's leadership reduced inflationary pressures and, to some extent, increased productivity but failed to resolve chronic economic problems such as the overcentralization of heavy industry, the failure to modernize, and the inferior quality of goods. In addition, a high rate of absenteeism continued to plague the economy. Yet, Czechoslovakia has virtually no unemployment in a total labor force of 7.5 million people, 59 percent of which are women. The capita gross national product (GNP) in 1973 was approximately $2,704, which represents a standard of living somewhat higher than the prewar level. About 70 percent of Czechoslovakia's foreign trade is with other Communist countries. Half of this is with the USSR which provides 40 percent of all Czechoslovakia's raw materials, including 99 percent of its oil and 84 percent of its iron ore.[77]

Nationality and Religion

The value systems of the citizens of Czechoslovakia differ widely. Since the state is multinational, there are few universally shared values. Vast differences exist between the Czechs and Slovaks on such issues as equality, autonomy, and religion.

The Czechs share a tradition of anticlerical skepticism and egalitarianism which is deeply embedded in the folklore. However, one must sharply distinguish between the rural and urban areas. In the rural areas during the prewar period, the church and the village priest occupied an esteemed position, and from eyewitness observation, this continues to be the case even now, if to a lesser degree. These traditions of egalitarianism and democracy conflict with the traditional patterns of stratification within the society. The form of Catholicism which was foisted upon the Czech peoples after the Battle of the White Mountain in 1620 reintroducted feudalistic patterns. Most Czechs are somewhat schizophrenic in their attitude toward the Roman Catholic church and their socialization has furthered this sense of schizophrenia. Midnight mass on Christmas Eve, Easter church attendance, the tales of the glories of the Hussite wars, the Taborites, and the Czech nobles martyred after the Battle of the White Mountain are part and parcel of the political socialization of every Czech child. To this can be added an irreverent literature created by rebels against church and state, ranging from the nineteenth-century poet Karel Havlicek-Borovsky to Jaroslav Hasek. In the Czech Lands, church attendance was largely ritualistic; before the war the most frequent communicants were elderly women in kerchiefs. The church became a vital social and political force only in times of stress when attendance became a way of manifesting protest.

The Slovak tradition was quite different. As in Poland, the Slovaks had a far more intimate relationship to the church. The church was seen as the guardian of national tradition. It was always strongest in rural areas, and in Slovakia most of the population was rural. Before World War II, Slovakia did not possess a large intelligentsia which could instill a spirit of skepticism in the urban masses. However, after the Communist takeover in 1948, the pressure on believers, especially the young, and the widespread atheistic propaganda campaigns made religion in Slovakia an ancillary instrument of coercion. Religion served the interests of the ruling elite in the persecution of both real and imaginary enemies of the socialist system. Since the party leadership under Gottwald, Zapotocky, and Novotny was ill-equipped to deal with functional differentiation and social complexities, coercion coupled with "persuasion" was given priority over rewards, and the religious organization felt the impact of this quest. No dramatic changes were made in the diverse patterns of coercive behavior until the Dubček era when it was discovered that the participatory thrust of the various interests in Czechoslovakia—including the religious interests—could produce the positive results necessary for reforms. Since April 1969, however, the party elite has once again been preoccupied with the problem of legitimacy, and has reverted to the instruments of coercion and "persuasion" in an attempt to resolve the problem of religious-political interaction.[78]

In 1948, the Roman Catholic church claimed 75 percent of 12,339,000 inhabitants. There were approximately 8.5 percent Protestants; about 7.5 percent were members of the Czechoslovak (Hussite) church. The remaining 9 percent of the population made up a complex mosaic of several smaller denominations led by the Czech Catholics of Slovakia which in 1950 were forced to merge with the Orthodox Catholics—a religious group under the Moscow patriarchate.

From October 14, 1949, when the Czechoslovak National Assembly created a Government Bureau for Church Affairs, to May 2, 1968, when the Dubček regime declared that churches and religious societies had full rights to participate in the solution of all problems of the socialist republic, the will of the church was broken and its influence subdued. During the Prague Spring, thousands of clerics were rehabilitated, monasteries and cloisters rebuilt, and parishes brought to life again. But religious freedom in Czechoslovakia was short-lived. The postinvasion leadership instituted new socialization methods which were aimed at the eradication of any "alien influences" exerted upon the Czech and Slovak people during the Dubček era, including the influence of the church. The clergy and schools were made once again responsible to party directives.

Although in September, 1977, negotiations with the Vatican led to a partial agreement, the situation of the Roman Catholic church in Czechoslovakia remains very difficult. For instance, seven students of the Bratislava Theological Faculty who qualified in 1975 were denied permission to be ordained as priests because they had refused to attend the Slovak *Pacem in terris* Congress. Ten bishoprics in Czechoslovakia are still vacant, and of 3,500 priests, 500 are forbidden to engage in any kind of pastoral activity.[79]

While freedom of religion is controlled, atheistic propaganda is an integral part of the educational program. Young people, students, and the Socialist Youth Union are the principal targets of the atheistic campaign waged in the monthly *Vysoka Skola*

(High School), *Tvorba* (Creation), and other magazines designed to influence students. Still, the religious situation in Czechoslovakia is not yet entirely "normalized." Although the Czechoslovak government does not publish religious statistics, there is no question that the church still represents a force in the state, yet not as in Poland, where it enjoys the power to significantly challenge state policy.[80]

Since the 1930s, one of the most commonly shared values has been the fear of Germany and German culture. The Czechs, as a small nationality, have always felt under attack by an imperialistic German nation. After the establishment of the Czechoslovak Republic in 1918, the majority of Czech Germans refused to acknowledge the legitimacy of the new state and became its citizens only grudgingly. During the 1930s the leader of the Sudeten German Party, Konrad Heinlein, obviously took his inspiration from Nazi Germany. The conduct of the German occupation forces in Czechoslovak territories during World War II only deepened hatred and strengthened the conviction that the country would never enjoy security unless the German minority were expelled. Yet the expulsion of about two and a half million Germans in 1945 reinforced the continuing fear of Czechoslovakia's German neighbors. The existence of refugees' political parties in West Germany since the war, coupled with the unwillingness of the German Federal Republic to accept the de facto situation in Eastern Europe, lent the German threat an aura of plausibility. The Czechoslovak mass media reinforce this image by all means at their disposal. It is only the *Ostpolitik* of Willy Brandt which revised the image of Germany as a revanchist continuation of the earlier order.

Czechoslovak foreign policy in the Communist era utilized this traditional fear of Germany to promote the image of the party as the protector of traditional national interests. This was not difficult in view of the increasing importance of Germany as a full-fledged NATO partner. The Soviet Union was consistently depicted as the only state which could underwrite the current Czechoslovak territorial status. German refugee politics played directly into the hands of the KSC by their strident demands for revision.

According to the latest statistical data, only 78,000 citizens living in Czechoslovakia at the end of 1973 declared their nationality to be German, compared with 140,000 in 1961.[81] This exceptionally large decline had been caused by emigration (between 1955 and 1974, 68,224 ethnic Germans were permitted to resettle in West Germany) and by the relatively high average age of the group. The 1961 census showed that the Germans were statistically the oldest national group in the state. The average age of the Slovaks was 26 and that of the Czechs 32; the Germans averaged 46, almost half of them over 50. The German minority has the lowest birth rate and highest death rate of all ethnic groups in Czechoslovakia.[82] In Western Bohemia, where about a quarter of all ethnic Germans reside, only 371 children of German origin were enrolled in German language courses in 1975. Pupil interest in German continues to decline; authorities attribute this lack of enthusiasm to the fact that children who want a higher education prefer to master Czech or Slovak. The cultural centers are mostly used by members of the older generation, which suits the official policy of achieving gradual assimilation of the younger generation of ethnic Germans.

The largest minority group in Czechoslovakia is the Hungarians. Since Hungary is not a great power in Europe, the Hungarian question in Czechoslovakia never carried the emotional impact of the German problem. Due to Hungary's role as an active partner in the Axis Alliance, there were efforts by the Beneš regime to resettle the Hungarian population immediately after the war. Between 1945 and 1948, hundreds of thousands ethnic Hungarians were forced to leave the country for Hungary, and about as many others were subjected to an assimilation process. However, after the coup of February 1948, the policy of reslovakization—which aimed at converting individuals of the Hungarian culture into Slovaks—was halted, and the Hungarian minority has enjoyed tranquillity ever since. By the time of the 1970 census, there were 541,000 ethnic Hungarians in Czechoslovakia—among them many who were repatriated from Hungay under Communist rule.[83] Apparently, the Hungarian Communists, because of their loyalty to the Bolshevik cause under Bela Kun in 1919, had much greater influence on the Soviet policymakers who decided resettlement issues than did the Czechoslovak Communists, whose loyalty to the Bolsheviks during the same period was questionable. For the past thirty years, ethnic Hungarians have been permitted to perpetuate their culture through schools and other agencies of acculturation.

The other minorities in Czechoslovakia, with the exception of about 250,000 Gypsies, are not politically or numerically significant. The Slansky case, and to a certain extent the events of 1968, revived the question of the Jews. The fact is that the Jewish community, which at one time numbered 360,000, has been reduced to about 18,000. Most of those who remained live in mixed marriages and follow Czech culture, so that they are rapidly losing all identity as a distinct community.[84] There are also Poles and Ukrainians, totaling 0.6 percent and 0.3 percent respectively of the population; neither of these groups constitutes a viable political entity.[85] As the result of World War II, Czechoslovakia has become a truly Slavic state. Thus, international anxieties have to a great extent replaced domestic ones.

THE PARTY AND THE CZECHOSLOVAK POLITICAL CULTURE

The peoples of Czechoslovakia have a long and continuing experience of living with regimes of dubious popularity. A great deal of the popular culture of Czechoslovakia subjects the establishment to critical scrutiny; government is traditionally viewed with skepticism. Hasek's *Good Soldier Schweik* is such a good citizen of Austria-Hungary that his loyalty and enthusiasms manage to disrupt and defeat the best-laid plans of constituted authority. Schweik expresses a national tradition which is far from dead. The Soviet presence in Czechoslovakia is widely resented, even though the Soviet military deliberately maintains a low profile to minimize provocation. They have achieved this by isolating Soviet troops in a few garrison towns and by permitting little communication with the local populace. The KSC is the recipient of much negative support. The post-1968 sentiments in many quarters are that things could have been much worse, that people are making the best of the present situation. There was a sigh of relief because so few people were persecuted for activities stemming from the Prague Spring. Husak is generally credited with this state of affairs, which flowed from his own experience as a political prisoner during the fifties. Apart from some foot-dragging bordering on economic sabotage, there is little evidence of any active resistance.[86]

The present political system is a continuation of the Novotny era in that economic and political experimentation have been largely discarded in favor of the tested verities of the past. Censorship and controls have been reimposed on all aspects of public life and Czechoslovakia remains carefully in step with the Soviet Union.

The Political System

The present Czechoslovak constitution was promulgated on July 11, 1960. Sections of the constitution were revised by a 1968 law (before the invasion) which attempted to establish more equitable representation between Czech and Slovaks in federal bodies and in economic development. The law canceled the preferential treatment of the Czech Lands by increasing the autonomy of national organizations in the formation, administration, and operation of the economy. In practice, however, the exercise of political power in Czechoslovakia more resembles a unitary than a federal system. Despite a federal constitution and a multiplicity of governmental institutions, all policy-making powers lie with the Czechoslovak Communist party, and the governmental organs serve merely as agencies of implementation.

In theory, Czechoslovakia is a multiparty system. The six

parties represented in the bicameral Federal Assembly are part of the National Front coalition established in 1945; now, under Communist rule, they present a single-candidate list for confirmation by the voters.[87] Below the federal structure there is a hierarchy of regional and local governmental organs consisting of national committees (*Narodni vybory*) in which regional national committees (*Krajske narodni vybory*) are superior to the district committees (*Okresni narodni vybory*) which, in turn, are under the jurisdiction of national governments. There are two such governments, one for the Czech Lands and one for Slovakia.

The present political system of Czechoslovakia is greatly different from that of October 1968. Fifty-eight of the 112 articles of the 1960 Czechoslovak constitution have been amended to create a federal state. Before October 1968, Czechoslovakia was a unitary state with a unicameral legislature. The Prague Spring brought Slovak agitation for the reform of the system. As a result, on January 1, 1969, Czechoslovakia became a federal state with a bicameral legislature. The Chamber of the People is comprised of 200 deputies elected by districts based on population; the Chamber of Nations consists of 150 deputies of whom 75 are elected by the Czech National Council and 75 by the Slovak National Council. The two bodies are bridged by the chairman of the Federal Assembly and his two deputies who are the chairmen of the chambers.

The consent of both chambers is required for the passage of a law. The number of majority votes needed to pass a bill depends on the kind of bill under consideration and on the chamber voting. The candidates for election to the Chamber of the People are nominated by the National Front. Members of the Chamber of Nations are selected by the National Councils, which are the legislative bodies of the Czech and Slovak Republics.[88]

As in other Communist states, the business of the legislature is carried out by its Presidium which sits in almost continuous session; it has 40 members, 20 selected by the Chamber of the People and 20 (10 Czechs and 10 Slovaks) by the Chamber of Nations. The Presidium carries out the legislative function while the Federal Assembly is not in formal session, which is most of the time.

The executive branch has been federalized, as well. The country now has two seats of government, Prague and Bratislava. Administrative and executive governmental power resides with the Cabinet and the president of the republic. The president (chief of state) is elected by the Federal Assembly for a five-year term. The president, with the approval of the Federal Assembly, appoints a Cabinet, including a premier as head of government. Before April 1969, there was a tacit agreement that for every ministry held by a Czech there would be a Slovak state

Table 3.5. Leadership of Czechoslovak Government, December 7, 1976

President of the Republic	Gustav Husak*
Federal Assembly, Chairman	Alois Indra
Prime Minister	Lubomir Strougal
Deputy Prime Ministers:	Peter Colotka*
	Vaclav Hula
	Josef Korcak
	Karol Laco*
	Matej Lucan
	Rudolf Rohlicek
	Josef Simon
	Jindrich Zahradnik
	2 vacancies
Ministers:	
Agriculture and Nutrition	Josef Nagr
Finance	Leopold Ler
Foreign Affairs	Bohuslav Chnoupek
Foreign Trade	Andrej Barcak*
Fuel and Power	Vlastimil Ehrenberger
General Engineering	Pavol Bahyl*
Interior	Jaromir Obzina
Labor and Social Welfare	Michal Stancel*
Metallurgy and Heavy Engineering	Zdenek Pucek
National Defense	Martin Dzur*
Technical and Investment Development	Ladislav Supka
Telecommunications	Vlastimil Chalupa
Transport	Vladimir Blazek*
Minister in Charge, Federal Price Office	Michal Sabolcik*
Minister-Chairman, People's Control Board	Frantisek Ondrich
Minister and Vice-Chairman of State Planning Commission	Vladimir Janza

*Represents Slovak nationality.

secretary, and vice versa.[89] That agreement, like so many others since 1969, has been ignored. In reality, the Czechoslovak Communist party remains dominant and controls the skein of both federal and local governments. The nominal federal arrangements are the most visible surviving products of the Spring of 1968. The post-1968 emphasis on the leading role of the party has again relegated government to the level of an executive organ. It remains to be seen whether federalism in Czechoslovakia will ever amount to more than lip service. One goal of the Federal constitution was to bring many Slovaks into top leadership positions and thus to satisfy past Slovak demands for equal representation at the national level. With Gustav Husak occupying both the top party and state positions, there have been certain rumblings among Czech Communist leaders concerning a Slovak usurpation of power.

The Czechoslovak judiciary consists of a multitude of People's Courts, usually made up of one professional judge and two lay assessors, which serve as courts of original jurisdiction. In addition, there is hierarchy of courts of appeal culminating in the Supreme Court (*Nejvyssi soud*) which is the highest court of appeal, elected by and responsible to the Federal Assembly. There is also a Constitutional Court which determines constitutional questions among the several branches of government and between the two regional assemblies. Prosecution rests in the hands of the Procuracy, which has the obligations for the maintenance of legality even above the duties of prosecuting.

Government is provided by the Cabinet which has, in effect, branch administrations with the national committees. The Cabinet is not noted for the political potency of the figures who sit on it, but rather, as in the USSR, is a body of administrators who exhibit competence in running their respective departments.

Socialization

In Communist societies, the overt behavior of the populace must conform to certain norms. These norms usually include participation in organized political activities, maximization of production efforts, and support for government policies. Moreover, members of the polity must profess belief in certain values which are desired by the elite. In general, the inculcation of these values, and of the entire ideology, is the goal of political education and of the socialization efforts of any Communist government, including that of Czechoslovakia. The inculcation of the desired values may occur through various processes. The two most common ones used in Czechoslovakia after 1948 were political education of youngsters and resocialization of the adult population.

The Communist regime was committed to changing the social composition of the university-educated elite. Essentially, their aim was to change the class origins of those who entered the university, placing an emphasis on the working-class background and deemphasizing the education of those who belonged to the erstwhile bourgeoisie. In order to achieve this, the regime created elaborate schemes for quotas which discriminated against students of "tainted" class origins and weighted admission procedures in favor of those with the proper background, even though their test scores might be lower. In the process, the regime politicized the educational system, devalued the prevailing educational standards and diminished the general high regard in which academic degrees had been held. The all-pervasive economic leveling within the society also removed the economic distances between career rewards, thus higher education was no longer necessarily the pathway to higher levels of income. On the contrary, at least in the early years of the program, academic qualifications were not particularly well rewarded. With economic leveling there came social leveling, and academic degrees were no longer the source of either economic or social status which they had been in the First Republic. This changed situation served as a disincentive for self-improvement and was reflected in the relatively low rate of applications to universities in relationship to the availability of places. Moreover, the number of places in any faculty was determined by the central economic plan, which did not make them responsive to student demands or societal needs. The main emphasis was placed on technology, and the proportion of people with this type of training was much higher than in any other industrially developed society.[90] This led to a general lethargy reflected in the low morale among the very generation which the system most needed in order to implement its reforms. It provided the sons of the former bourgeoisie with a sense of discrimination but it did not endear itself to those whom the discriminations were designed to benefit. While the overall number of students in higher education climbed quite dramatically due to greatly expanded facilities, an even more dramatic expansion could have easily accommodated both the old and new elites.[91] The system also discriminated against those with an interest in the social sciences, a discipline which became acceptable only during the 1960s.

The schools became politicized because they were a prime agent for the socialization of youth into the values of a Marxist-Leninist society. In addition, the system was changed to instill a positive orientation toward all influences emanating from the USSR while downgrading traditional Western influences. Russian was the sole modern language taught at the primary level and all texts were liberally larded with messages reflecting the values of the prevailing system. This was not unusual; even prewar texts attempted to stimulate positive attitudes toward the institutions of the republic, a practice which was then seen as teaching good citizenship. However, the prewar values were not tied to one specific philosophy or party. Under the present system the students do not receive overt political instruction until the sixth year. The subject matter of civics courses deals not only with the Czechoslovak system but with Soviet institutions as well. The stress on the Soviet model and its relevance to a Czechoslovak socialist extended even to the adoption of Soviet degrees, such as Candidate of Sciences, in favor of the traditional Czechoslovak doctorate.[92] This imposition of foreign values rendered the task of socialization into new values even more difficult.

In addition to formal educational institutions, Czechoslovakia also possessed the the usual plethora of Communist youth organizations associated with such systems. These subsumed the prewar voluntary organizations such as the *Sokol*, tne *Junak* (Boy Scouts), and others. They were replaced by the *Jiskry*, which organized children six to nine years old; the Pioneer Organization, for those between nine and fifteen; and the CSM, the *Ceskoslovensky Svaz Mladeze*, for those above fifteen. The membership of the CSM was intended to serve as a preliminary to full-fledged membership in the party and was meant for those who identified with the goals of the system and who desired a career within its framework. The active membership was confined to a minority of those eligible. The CSM was a highly centralized institution roughly equivalent to the Soviet Komsomol, and it enrolled its members without regard to occupational, geographic, or age differences. As in the Soviet practice, the leadership was provided by the party officialdom; it included neither the most talented nor the youngest party bureaucrats. As a result, a generation gap developed between the leaders and the membership. Moreover, young people who worked in factories or on farms had very little in common with university students. By the 1960s, voices were raised which favored the federalization and decentralization of the CSM. These proposals were beaten back and the university proponents expelled from both the CSM and the university. This foreshadowed the complete collapse of the CSM during the Prague Spring. The organization disintegrated into a variety of suborganizations which were more like Western voluntary associations based on the special interests of the participants. The Young Pioneers survived the Spring of 1968 far better, partially because of a more capable leadership and because the Pioneer activities, such as camping, were far more attractive to the young.

Normalization in post-1968 Czechoslovakia called for the reestablishment of the practices which were rejected during the Prague Spring. In March of 1969, the Leninist Youth Union was established as a reincarnation of the CSM; in 1970 it was renamed the Socialist Youth Union of Czechoslovakia (SYU). It retains this title to the present time. As before, it is highly centralized, and it is doubtful that it will prove to be any more attractive than its predecessor.

Between 1948 and 1968, the Czechoslovak Communist party was proportionately the largest within the entire bloc. As previously stated, practically all of its membership was of postwar vintage. The party's bloated ranks confronted its leadership with a massive task not only of socializing the young generation into its values but also of resocializing those whose ideological commitment was slight and whose knowledge of Marxism-Leninism was even less.[93] The party launched a massive educational effort for its rank and file and placed special emphasis on those functionaries who were better educated in the party's aims and values. There was an effort to draw everyone into discussion groups at their place of employment, where they were forced to espouse opinions which many did not hold and which some despised. The result was often Svejkian evasion, and the traditional dichotomy between the private and public Czech person reasserted itself as a continuation of Czech political tradition. These experiences imbued a new generation with a measure of cynicism toward all officially proclaimed verities. This skepticism came into full flower in the sixties when it could be expressed with a degree of freedom. Moreover, the multitude of secondary groupings which were officially sponsored by the party and which were designed to diminish or supplant the role of the family met with only limited success. These associations were run by older party members who, like parental authority figures, were to be rejected. Therefore, the generation gap in a socialist society remained a dysfunctional influence from the point of view of the leadership.

The early post-invasion attempts to reach Czechoslovak society by means of the news media bore little success. The Soviet News Agency started to publish a Czech language weekly, *Tydenik Aktualit*, with a circulation of 100,000. Yet Prague, the largest single consumer of the printed word in the country, had only 33 subscribers to this journal.[94] The Society of Czechoslovak-Soviet Friendship also registered a decline in membership, once as high as 2.5 million. The Society's 8,000 local organizations shrank to some 1,500 by early 1969. A poll taken in 1969 among the army draftees showed 75 percent of the respondents opposed the restoration of friendship with the Soviet Union.[95]

One of the repeated demands by the party since April 1969 has been that the working people should participate to a greater extent in the direction of society through the agency of the National Front and voluntary social organizations.[96] These voluntary social organizations fulfill a dual purpose in the socialist political system. On the one hand, they increase the participation of the working people in the administration of the state, and on the other, they look out for the special interests of their members. However, at no time or under any circumstances are these social organizations permitted to compete with the socialist state, oppose the policy of the party, or be autonomous or even semiautonomous and thus create the dangers of "pluralism" so closely identified with the "evils" of 1968. Hence, greater participation in voluntary social organizations in Czechoslovakia has only one chief purpose, i.e., to enable the political socialization process to become more effective.

To this day, strenuous attempts are made by the Husak regime to mold the "new socialist man" in Czechoslovakia. The school, radio and television, the press, books and libraries, movies and the theater, the church and social organizations are all instruments of political socialization. All are scrutinized by the party and government so as to forestall harmful ideological messages and to allow for the publication and circulation of positive propaganda. The evidence offered in the present study, however, suggests that the degree of success has been negligible.

PARTY BEHAVIOR

The KSC passed through several phases after it achieved power in 1948. During his five years in office, Gottwald was essentially concerned with consolidating the hold of the party over the country. The years between 1953 and 1963 were essentially a period of normalizing a bureaucratized regime. The structure withstood the many internal and external shocks—internally, the depression of 1962–63; externally, the Polish and Hungarian uprisings—without any overt crises. Nevertheless, the negative economic growth rate of 1963 brought forth a new era of experimentation which divided the councils of the party and culminated in the quasi-revolutionary Spring of 1968, a period which came on the heels of many reforms in which the nature of the ruling elite changed and its cohesion was lost.[97]

The crisis of 1968 presented Husak with a task which would challenge even the most imaginative leader. Husak succeeded Dubček on April 17, 1969, under the impact of the Soviet presence in the country. The Soviet leadership preferred Husak when it became clear that Dubček was incapable of providing the appropriate style of leadership. Nevertheless, Husak carries on his shoulders the opprobium of being the first to break the solidarity of the reform movement and to deal with the Soviets separately.[98] Husak is viewed by the populace as a man of some intelligence and given personal credit for the relative mildness of the post-1968 regime. He generates little enthusiasm, even among his followers. It is generally believed in Czechoslovakia that the present leadership represents the best obtainable under the given circumstances. There is a hope that Husak will be able to keep the hardliners from inflicting their will, and that he might yet develop into another Kadar. This will in great degree depend on the measure of trust which he might develop within the Soviet leadership and on the Soviet domestic situation itself. To be truly popular, any national leadership has to develop a measure of domestic indepenence. It remains to be seen to what extent Husak will be able to achieve this. So far, the present leaders of the KSC have been very unwilling to tread any path which might bring them into conflict with Soviet interests. This can be ascertained from the regime's response to the "Charter 77" movement.

"Charter 77" revolves around some specific events which occurred in Czechoslovakia during the summer and fall of 1976. The heart of the issue was the persecution and prosecution of a group of young rock musicians who called themselves "The Plastic People of the Universe." They were sentenced in Prague to eighteen months in jail for the dissemination of decadent and anarchist ideas. On September 25, 1976, the party organ, *Rude Pravo,* attacked three personalities of the 1968 era, Vaclav Havel, Zedenek Mlynar, and Frantisek Kriegel for seeking the support of Heinrich Böll, the Nobel Prize-winning German author, in behalf of the "Plastic People." From that moment on, the protest broadened to include major segments of Czechoslovak life. The court of appeals acknowledged that the sentences against the musicians were protested from many segments of public life, including reputable jurists and political leaders. Dr. Milan Huebl, a historian and former rector of Prague Party College, charged that inhuman conditions in Czechoslovak jails and reprisals against family members were the rule of the day. The Czech dramatist, Pavel Kohout, attacked the practice of "apartheid" against intellectuals.

This atmosphere led to the organization of the "Charter 77" declaration, uniting many disparate elements, ranging from conscientious Communists, such as the historian Karel Bartosek, to the late philosopher Jan Patocka. To quote Ladislav Hajdanek, one of the earliest signers of the Charter, "The important thing is to throw light, to find out what sort of society we live in. If the goverment cannot keep its declarations, it must not make them. The Charter is a legalistic action based on morality. It is not a political action for me. It is not even a technically political action structured as a non-political action. It is a moral action."[99]

The document was promptly confiscated by the secret police after the Czechoslovak government discovered that *Le Monde* was to run a story about a human rights manifesto to be released in Prague. State security then proceeded with the confiscation of the original "Charter 77" which bore the signatures of 241 signers. Despite the government's use of direct harrassment, arrest, and campaigns designed to intimidate the signers into desisting from any further activity, the list of signers grew to 750 by June of 1977. Many of the signers were workers and nonintellectuals who had not been victimized by the purge of Dubček supporters. They signed merely as an act of conscience. The

Charter had a chilling impact on the regime because of the potential landslide of hundreds of thousands of signers who would be deprived of their positions or subjected to other penalties. This is what induced the government to utilize extreme threat methods which had not been in force since the early 1950s. The Charterists issued three documents all together. The first consisted of the Charter itself. Documents Two and Three detailed the actions taken by the security organs against the signers. The last document was signed by such dissidents as Professor Jan Patocka, playwright Vaclav Havel, and Professor Jiri Hajak.[100] About 100 signatories have lost their jobs, and Lt. Gen. Vilem Sacher, the highest-ranking military signer, was demoted to a private in the reserves on March 24, 1977, by a presidential decree issued by Husak. Others were charged with various infractions of the law; their cases are now winding their way through the bureaucratized judicial machinery.

The Charter 77 movement is of importance both within Czechoslovakia and in other countries. At home, it shows that the ideas and ideals of the Prague Spring remain, that a courageous group of reformers maintains the Czech tradition of passive resistance, and that the Husak leadership may be divided and, in any event, has yet to legitimize itself. Abroad the Charter likewise causes problems; it provides Eurocommunists with a point of reference on which to commit themselves for or against many practices of Soviet bloc ruling parties, and it serves as a source of encouragement for other East European dissidents.[101]

The road to popularity and general acceptance for the post-1968 regime will be long and arduous. The loss of half a million party members is a serious blow to the KSC. Yet it may well be that with a more compact, better disciplined party, Husak's leadership will have an easier time implementing its policy objectives, but this will not necessarily increase its popularity. The hardliners within the Husak leadership, symbolized by Oldrich Svestka, Vasil Bilak, Alois Indra, and Antonin Kapek, will not stir the public imagination. Ultimately, any approach to strengthening the system will have to rest on continued Soviet support. The very fact that the hardliners are not in full power attests to the Soviet awareness of their problems and to a willingness to give the moderates a chance to stabilize the system.

The stabilization of the post-1968 situation has been well served by a significant increase in the supply of consumer goods. The economic devices utilized to achieve this improvement are not easily described, since the government complains about lagging economic performance and a general lack of labor discipline.[102] Yet, there is general agreement that the availability of consumer goods has been improved. This may result from significant Soviet loans or from more favorable trade arrangements with the COMECON countries. Whatever the reasons, the fairly satisfactory economic situation takes the edge off much of the remaining discontent. In order to discredit the economists of the Prague Spring, led by Ota Sik, the Husak leadership is trying to demonstrate that the country is viable under the present system of economic planning. Most of the bold proposals of the liberal economists have been scrapped, and all that remains is some increased managerial autonomy within the individual enterprises, particularly in the consumer goods sector.

The current economic situation in Czechoslovakia leaves the country dependent on the goodwill of the USSR and the other COMECON countries. About 70 percent of Czechoslovakia's exports are tied to the Soviet Union and the bloc countries on the basis of long-term contracts, a problem which the Dubček leadership tried to solve through increased trade with the West. This was, however, a long-range objective. It can be surmised that Czechoslovakia still needs the highly sophisticated technology avilable in the West but the Husak leadership will not be able to move as fast in opening up contacts with the West as the other block states, with the exception of Poland, Romania, and possibly Hungary, which appear to be charting a more independent course. The majority no doubt preferred the proposed reforms because they envisioned a measure of economic independence, but the planned economy has become more palatable with improved performance. As in politics, the populace is grateful that the Soviet presence has not been economically punitive.

The outcome of Czechoslovakia's internal policies will be determined by the limits of tolerance set by the Soviet leadership. Since the Hungarian new economic mechanism has met with some opposition from the Soviet leaders, the Czechoslovaks will probably have enough sense to postpone experimentation with economic reforms. The Soviet Union itself had scrapped Sovnarkhoz and Libermanism in 1965, and its leaders show no interest in bold experimentation. The heart of the Czechoslovak reforms of 1968 was a transition to a socialist market economy. This orientation has been thoroughly stymied by the post-1968 leadership, which has openly ridiculed the ideas of Ota Sik and his associates.[103] As in other policy matters, the ultimate limit of Czechoslovak reforms will depend on what is considered permissible by the Soviet leadership. As long as the Soviets maintain their hegemony, the present leaders of the KSC will not move again into the avant-garde of change.

The Spring of 1968 found the Czechoslovak leaders groping for a new identity, both in terms of the party's domestic foreign policies. The economic policies of Ota Sik presupposed a much improved economic relationship with the West, geared to an expectation of expanded economic contact with those countries which could provide the Czechoslovak economy with sorely needed technology. Some of these policy aims have survived; Czechoslovakia has continued to improve its relations with West Germany, resulting in an attendant upswing in trade with the GFR. In this policy the Czechoslovak leaders have not departed too far from what was considered permissible for the bloc as a whole. Since the Soviet Union is also bidding for expanded commercial contact with the West, it is difficult to deny this to Czechoslovakia. The visit of Willy Brandt to Prague no doubt had the effect of improving economic relations at levels consistent with the Soviet desire for détente with the West in general.

Unlike Romania, Czechoslovakia is at present one of the strongest backers of all Soviet policies. Whether it concerns the

People's Republic of China, détente, the world Communist movement, the Middle East, or Africa, the Czechoslovak leaders formulate policy statements that are a mirror reflection of Soviet interests.

In 1968, Czechoslovakia's experiment was welcomed by the major West European Communist parties, many of whose leaders saw the Czechoslovak reforms as a pathway to the revitalization of their own causes. The Czechoslovak experiment stirred enthusiasm among the intellectuals and the young, and it was viewed as a vehicle for the Europeanization of the Communist movement. The Soviet intervention hit the West European parties particularly hard and led to splits and a demoralization of their leadership. Major sectors within the French and Italian parties decried the Soviet intervention and have not yet been reconciled to the Soviet course of action. This constitutes one more of the many divergences which divide the Communist parties of the bloc from the nonruling Communist parties of Western Europe. The repression of the many cultural organizations which contributed to the making of the Prague Spring has strained relationships between the new leadership of the KSC and the West European Communist parties. Nevertheless, the Czechoslovak leadership will maintain its present course because the political leaders of the Soviet Union have become at least as important a constituency as domestic public opinion.

CONCLUSIONS

The principal difference between Czechoslovakia and the other states of the Soviet bloc lies in the presence of a semielitist Communist party which, until August 1968, drew substantial support from the working class. Since that time, however, the Czech working class has become one of the antisocialist elements in the state. In addition, a substantial portion of the entire populace, probably constituting a majority, had profound sentimental ties to socialism and left-wing thought. In the working class there existed a spirit of egalitarianism which was hostile to the entire middle class and its privileges. This dislike for the titles and prerogatives of the middle class could, under propitious circumstances, be translated into antiintellectualism. This latent working-class dislike constituted a weapon against the Communists of bourgeois or intellectual background. If the working class seemed prejudiced, so were the middle classes which frequently shunned all manual work as degrading to their status. This class antagonism was hospitable to Stalinist sentiments which put a premium on conformity and which became manifest during the Slansky trial, when only too many party members were willing to believe the worst of those who were Jews, Slovaks, or intellectuals.

In Czechoslovakia, the KSC has faced no strong counterforce. The Polish United Workers party (Communist party) must continually contend with a strong Roman Catholic church which, at times, has been an effective supporter of the party and, at other times, a powerful challenger. The KSC has had no such serious challenge to its hegemony. In Yugoslavia the leadership must contend with an extremely complex multinational situation, so that the League of Communists of Yugoslavia could not demand the degree of domestic consistency or harmony which the KSC obtained. The Yugoslav nationalities form veto groups and can thwart specific policies of the federal party. In Czechoslovakia, the Czechs form a decisive majority in the state; the church has not been a potent force, and the Czechoslovak Communist party, due to the sheer weight of its numbers, could rule without effective countervailing force. After 1948, the alienated bourgeoisie was far too splintered to constitute a plausible threat and, in addition, many of their numbers were coopted by the system. In many ways this situation resulted in both the excesses and the repressiveness which prevailed until the nascent reforms of 1963. It also led to a system of all-pervasive leveling in which higher qualifications were not appropriately rewarded. This is the general atmosphere of conformity which ultimately bred resentment among both party intellectuals and among the vast nonparty multitudes which longed for advancement. Moreover, the imposed egalitarianism struck many as corrupt in as far as party membership and loyalty to the system were rewarded materially by better positions. The rewarding of loyalty rather than professional performance was criticized in and out of the party because it was widely considered as unfair and a handicap to economic performance. While in the 1950s the drive for equality gave the KSC a special edge, in the 1960s it became a major handicap. However, any retreat from this enforced egalitarianism raised anxieties in the thousands of faithful members and brought the party to its particular position of *immobilisme* during the early 1960s. The reforming intellectual wing of the KSC prevailed only after the economy encountered a major crisis.

Czechoslovakia also possessed a very lively intellectual community which developed within the party itself, particularly because many intellectuals espoused Marxist principles. Their views were fully aired for the first time during 1968. While many members of the intellectual community were Communists, most of them claimed a Western political heritage and believed in free expression, untrammeled by censorship or state supervision. In the period before the Soviet entry, this community provided a remarkable outpouring of literary activity. The Slavophile tendencies of the intelligentsia were always based on illusions and little actual knowledge of conditions either in Tsarist Russia or in the USSR. Therefore, many of the intellectual members of the KSC could easily delude themselves that the Prague Spring would become tolerable to the Soviets. They revived the historical delusion that the Czechoslovaks would again serve as a "civilizing" influence for all Slavdom. The Communist intellectuals believed that they could alter the praxis of Marxism-Leninism imported from Moscow into the Marxist humanism espoused by such philosophers as Gajo Petrovic in Yugoslavia, Lesek Kolakowski in Poland, and Ladislav Mnacko, Karel Kosik, Ivan Svitak, and Milan Prucha in Czechoslovakia, who all have attempted, in Vladimir Kusin's words, to Europeanize Marxism. Their goal was not only the reform of basic philosophic doctrines but the change of concrete realities as they found them in Czechoslovakia. Their aim was to restore the country to its tradition as a society of laws and freedom of expression. Furthermore, the philosophers were seeking a social pluralism which would have reestablished the ties to Western traditions.

In retrospect, the reactions of the USSR to the Czechoslovak experiment were quite predictable. The liberalization in Czechoslovakia threatened to unleash similar forces latent in all of the Communist parties. The main motivating force behind the Warsaw Treaty intervention came from the Soviet Union. The demands of the dissenting Soviet intellectuals were not so different from those articulated by the Czechoslovak intellectuals. Their attack was not primarily against the party or communism but rather against the monopoly of power exercised by an omnipotent bureaucracy. The principal difference between the USSR and Czechoslovakia was that in the Soviet Union the intellectuals did not enjoy the mass support which was given to the Czechoslovak reformers. For a brief moment, the Czechoslovak intellectuals triumphed and managed to convert a ruling Communist party to their point of view, a role which the Soviet leaders scarcely intended to duplicate. Moreover, a glance at the map will disclose that Czechoslovakia's exit from the Warsaw Pact, which the Dubček regime never considered, would have considerably weakened the Soviet position in central Europe. The KSC reform leadership leaned over backwards not to convey this possibility to the Soviet Union, but the Soviets could not be sure to what extent the KSC was practicing the art of the possible rather than manifesting sincere adherence to the principles of socialist internationalism. The other ruling Communist parties consented to the "entry" into Czechoslovakia with varying degrees of enthusiasm. Romania, a Warsaw Pact member, was left out of the deliberations and the military action. At the other end of the spectrum, East Germany was the most enthusiastic in welcoming the Soviet initiative. Whatever the degree of enthusiasm or reluctance, all ultimately participated in the termination of the Prague Spring.

Once the invasion was completed, time was on the side of the Soviet leaders. They knew that if they would wait long enough, inevitable fissures would develop among the leaders of the KSC, and that they held the power to promote their chosen factions to a position of dominance. In this expectation they were not disappointed. As time pressed on, the Soviet presence in Czechoslovakia became an accepted phenomenon both at home and abroad. Since any viable leadership would have to learn to live with this humiliation, the present KSC leadership is merely conforming to the facts of life.

In the present situation in Czechoslovakia there are few unique domestic solutions. The leadership has acknowledged the Soviet thesis that the USSR intervened in order to preserve socialism in Czechoslovakia. This self-criticism has muted some of the bitterness the Soviet Union reaped from West European Communist parties and has stilled many domestic voices. The KSC is in no position to introduce bold initiatives or to further unique policies and programs. Consequently, recent articles in journals and newspapers in Czechoslovakia have put increasing emphasis on consolidation within the socialist community and defense of common interests and achievements within the Communist movement. Its leaders understand that they must remain safely within the fold.

NOTES

1. Giovanni Sartori, *Parties and Party Systems: A Framework for Analysis* (London: Cambridge University Press, 1976), p. 221.

2. *Ibid.* Emphasis added.

3. *Ustava Ceskoslovenskej Socialistickej Republiky* (Constitution of the Czechoslovak Socialist Republic) (Bratislava: Vydavatelstvo politickej literatury, 1967), article 4, p. 9.

4. See *Zastupitelska soustava Ceskoslovenske socialisticke republiky* (The Representative System of the Czechoslovak Socialist Republic) (Prague: Svoboda, 1974), p. 117.

5. See John Albert White, *The Siberian Intervention* (Princeton, N.J.: Princeton University Press, 1950); Gerburg Thunig-Nittner, *Die Tschechoslowakische Legion in Russland* (Wiesbaden: Otto Harrassowitz, 1970), pp. 30–31; and Adam B. Ulam, *The Bolsheviks* (New York: Collier Books, 1965), pp. 431–34.

6. See Peter A. Toma, "The Slovak Soviet Republic of 1919," *The American Slavic and East European Review* (1958), 17(2):203–15.

7. Karol Medvecky, *Slovensky prevrat* (The Slovak Revolution) (Bratislava: Komensky, 1931), 4:271.

8. It is interesting to note that during the struggle for national independence, Smeral sided with the Hapsburgs, and therefore after the war he found himself isolated and in dire need for support. Although he was to the right of the socialist movement and an antirevolutionary, nevertheless Smeral found it expedient to turn towards the Comintern. Zinoviev, who was just as expedient to regard revolutionary purity as less essential than obedience, used Smeral as a tool of the Comintern.

9. See Jindrich Vesely, *O vzniku a zalozeni KSC* (About the Origin and Foundation of the Communist Party of Czechoslovakia) (Prague: Svoboda, 1953).

10. *Dejiny Komunisticke strany Ceskoslovenska* (The History of the Communist Party of Czechoslovakia) (Prague: Statni nakladatelstvi politicke literatury, 1961), pp. 164–65.

11. Paul E. Zinner, *Communist Strategy and Tactics in Czechoslovakia, 1918–1948* (New York and London: Frederick A. Praeger, 1963), p. 250, citing *Internationale Presse Korrespondenz* (June 30, 1931), 11:63. 1934.

12. See *Imprecorr*, no. 63, 1931.

13. *Dejiny KSC*, p. 221.

14. John A. Lukacs, *The Great Powers and Eastern Europe* (New York: American Book Company, 1953), pp. 188–89. Keith Eubank, "Czechoslovakia and the Origins of World War II," in Miloslav Rechcigl, Jr., ed., *Czechoslovakia Past and Present* (The Hague and Paris: Mouton, 1968), pp. 208–9, citing Litvinov to Alexandrovsky, March 25, 1938, *New Documents on the History of Munich* (Prague: Svoboda, 1958), pp. 39–43 and 62–63.

15. For further details, see Peter A. Toma, "Soviet Strategy in the Slovak Uprising of 1944," *Journal of Central European Affairs* (October 1959), 19(3):290–98.

16. The official history of the KSC, *Dejiny KSC*, states (p. 458): "The Kosice government program integrated the whole of our revolution. The provisions of the program aimed in a national and democratic spirit to mobilize the masses of our people and open the road to the further evolution of our revolution. The securing of this program was a splendid victory for the KSC, the proof of its theoretical maturity, and established its right to stand at the head of national and state life. The Kosice Program saw the exemplary application of Leninist teachings about the advance of the proletariat in a democratic revolution. It expressed the experience which our people gained in the years of our struggle for national liberation. The Kosice Program solidified the hegemony of the working class led by the KSC and its ties with the other members of the working class."

17. Zinner, *Communist Strategy and Tactics in Czechoslovakia*, pp. 254–58.

18. See Vaclav Kral, ed., *Vznik a vyvoj lidove demokratickeho Ceskoslovenska* (The Origin and Development of People's Democratic Czechoslovakia) (Prague: Ceskoslovenska akademie ved, 1961), p. 176.

19. See Peter A. Toma, "The Political Role of the Coup of February 1948 in the History of Socialist Revolutions," in Miloslav Rechcigl, Jr., ed., *Czechoslovakia Past and Present* (The Hague and Paris: Mouton, 1968), pp. 269–95.

20. Otto Ulc, "The Communist Party of Czechoslovakia," *East European Quarterly* (June 1972), 6(2):206, citing *Rude Pravo*, Nov. 20, 1948, and Feb. 27, 1951; *Zpravodaj KSC*, no. 16, a supplement to *Zivot Strany*, April 29, 1969.

21. *Prispevek k dejinam KSC* (Vienna: Europa-Verlag, 1970), p. 12.

22. *Ibid.*

23. Individuals forced to depart from their positions of power in 1963 included Bruno Koehler, head of the Cadre Department of the Central Committee; Alexej Cepicka, Gottwald's son-in-law who had served as Justice and Defense Minister; Karol Bacilek, First Secretary of the Slovak Communist party, and Josef Urvalek, president of the Supreme Court and chief prosecutor at the Slansky trial. See also Peter A. Toma, "The Czecho-Slovak Question under Communism," *East European Quarterly* (March 1969), 3(1):15–30.

24. The KSS came into being in May 1939, when the KSC leadership under Klement Gottwald left Czechoslovakia for Moscow and the Slovak Communist leaders Ludovit Benada, Julius Duris, Jan Osoha, and others went underground to organize an independent Communist organization for Slovakia. However, the KSS had not become a member of the Comintern—its ties with the Third International were carried out by the KSC—and therefore all political decisions of the KSS were coordinated with the illegal Central Committee of the KSC in Prague. See *Dejiny Komunisticke strany Ceskoslovenska*, p. 399 ff.

25. Jaroslav Krejci, *Social Change and Stratification in Postwar Czechoslovakia* (New York: Columbia University Press, 1972).

26. In effect, all segments of party life had excluded themselves from central direction. This was most evident in the instance of "cultural workers" over whom the party lost control, and could be extended to youth organizations, trade unions, and the army itself. See Vladimir Kusin, *Political Groupings in the Czechoslovak Reform Movement* (New York: Columbia University Press, 1972).

27. The secret Fourteenth Congress met at Vysocany, August 22–24, 1968, in the immediate aftermath of the Soviet occupation. Attendance was somewhat sporadic and the Slovak contingent largely stayed away. The Vysocany Congress was subsequently declared illegal and its work replaced by the official Congress held May 25–29, 1971. For the proceedings of the Vysocany Congress, see Jiri Pelikan, ed., *The Secret Vysocany Congress* (London: The Penguin Press, 1971). Proceedings of the "legal" Fourteenth Congress are contained in *XIV. sjezd Komunisticke strany Ceskoslovenska* (The 14th Congress of the Communist Party of Czechoslovakia) (Prague: Svoboda, 1971).

28. *Zivot strany*, August 10, 1969.

29. While no comprehensive membership statistics have been published in the aftermath of the expulsions, *Rude Pravo* (December 15, 1969) stated that overall membership had declined by 473,731. The estimates are that overall party membership declined by 27.8 percent. Richard F. Staar, ed., *Yearbook on International Communist Affairs 1971* (Stanford, Calif.: Hoover Institution Press, 1971), p. 27.

30. "A Letter From Prague," *New Politics* (Spring 1973), 10(3):66–70.

31. See supplement to *Rude Pravo*, August 10, 1968.

32. Radio Bratislava, April 30, 1969.

33. *Rude Pravo*, June 2, 1969.

34. *Ibid.*, July 16, 1969.

35. *Ibid.*, January 31, 1970.

36. Supplement to *Rude Pravo*, June 1, 1971.

37. See D. Hanes, "Pet let socialisticke federace" (Five Years of Socialist Federation), *Tribuna*, January 2, 1974.

38. Ulc, "The Communist Party of Czechoslovakia," p. 209.

39. In Slovakia, a recent survey discloses that of 420,000 posts requiring secondary or higher education, only 230,000 (55 percent) were held by those who had these requisites. *Nove Slovo*, October 26, 1972, pp. 1 and 3.

40. Ulc, "The Communist Party of Czechoslovakia," p. 207.

41. See Gustav Husak's report to the Fifteenth Congress of the KSC in *Rude Pravo*, April 13, 1976.

42. *Yearbook on International Communist Affairs 1971*, p. 27.

43. *Zivot strany*, June 22, 1970.

44. Krejci, *Social Change*, pp. 103–4.

45. *Tribuna*, July 15, 1970.

46. Barbara Wolfe Jancar, *Czechoslovakia and the Absolute Monopoly of Power: A Study of Political Power in a Communist System* (New York, Washington, and London: Praeger, 1971), p. 111.

47. Krejci, *Social Change*, pp. 143–44.

48. Elias Zdenek and Jaromir Netik, "Czechoslovakia," in William E. Griffith, ed., *Communism in Europe* (Cambridge, Mass.: MIT Press, 1966), 2:217.

49. See Carl Beck et al., *Comparative Communist Political Leadership* (New York: David McKay, 1973), pp. 122–23.

50. For details, see Robert F. Lamberg, "Revision und Beharrung in der Tschechoslowakei," *Osteuropa* (May/June 1966), 16(5/6):289–99; J. M. Montias, "Economic Reform in Perspective," *Survey* (April 1966), no. 59, pp. 48–60; H. Gordon Skilling, "Interest Groups and Communist Politics," *World Politics* (April 1966), 18(3):435–51; and Peter A. Toma, "The Czecho-Slovak Question under Communism," *East European Quarterly* (March 1969), 3(1):15–30.

51. For a representative reading of the literature dealing with the Dubcek era, see Andrew Oxley et al., *Czechoslovakia: the Party and the People* (New York: St. Martin's Press, 1973) and V. V. Kusin, ed., *The*

Czechoslovak Reform Movement, 1968 (Santa Barbara, Calif.: ABC-Clio, 1973).

52. *Pravda*, May 21, 1974.

53. *Radio Free Europe Research*, September 30, 1970, p. 14.

54. According to Party Statutes, the KSS merely "carries out in Slovakia the resolutions of the KSC Central Committee" and must consult the Prague center in all important questions. See Statutes of the KSC as published in *Rude Pravo*, June 1, 1971.

55. *Pravda* (Bratislava), March 27, 1976.

56. *Zivot strany*, March 1, 1976.

57. *Pravda* (Bratislava), March 29, 1976.

58. Ulc, "The Communist Party of Czechoslovakia," pp. 207–8.

59. *Ibid.*, p. 209.

60. Kusin, *Political Groupings*, p. 132, citing M. Chlupac, "Student a jeho vychozi socialni pozice" (The Student and His Exit into Social Position), *Nova Mysl*, December 1966.

61. See Jaroslav Piekalkiewicz, *Public Opinion Polling in Czechoslovakia, 1968–69: Results of Surveys Conducted During the Dubcek Era* (New York: Praeger, 1972), pp. 226–45.

62. *Ibid.*, pp. 78–112.

63. Krejci, *Social Change*, p. 113.

64. A. H. Brown, "Changes in the Levels of Membership and Social Composition of the Communist Party of Czechoslovakia, 1945–1973," *Soviet Studies* (July 1975), 27(3):416.

65. See *The Christian Science Monitor*, second section, January 7, 1975.

66. See Andrew Oxley et al., *Czechoslovakia: The Party and the People* (New York: St. Martin's Press, 1973).

67. See Adolf Mueller, "Zur Lage in der Tschechoslowakei" (The Situation in Czechoslovakia), *Osteuropa*, (August 1973), 23(8):599–617.

68. Radio Free Europe, Audience and Public Opinion Research Department, *Some of APOR's Findings in Terms of the Problem of Analytical and Direct or Indirect Verification by Subsequent Developments* (Munich: RFE, April 1976). Mimeo.

69. *1973 Britannica Book of the Year* (Chicago: Encyclopaedia Brittanica, 1973), p. 208.

70. Krejci, *Social Change*, p. 29.

71. Galia Golan, *The Czechoslovak Reform Movement: Communism in Crisis* (Cambridge, England: Cambridge University Press, 1971), p. 13, citing *Rude Pravo*, December 5, 1962.

72. *Ibid.*, p. 12, citing *Rude Pravo*, February 11, 1964.

73. For a thorough discussion of this problem, see Peter A. Toma, "The Czecho-Slovak Question under Communism," *East European Quarterly* (March 1969), 3(1):15–30.

74. Krejci, *Social Change*, p. 43.

75. *Ibid.*, pp. 28–30. Krejci states between 1948 and 1968 the Slovak contribution to per capita income rose from 61.2 percent to 80.1 percent.

76. Piekalkiewicz, *Public Opinion Polling*, pp. 93–95. Only one-fifth of the respondents in a questionnaire study had a reservation about democratic reforms because they would only benefit the intelligentsia. Another 19 percent states that the new process of democratization had changed nothing. A majority of 53 percent believed that the democratic reforms were beneficial to all.

77. See V. Cap and S. Dubsky, *Statistical Survey of Czechoslovakia 1974* (Prague: Orbis, 1975).

78. See Peter A. Toma and M. J. Reban, "Church-State Schism in Czechoslovakia," in Bohdan R. Bociurkiw and John W. Strong, eds., *Religion and Atheism in the USSR and Eastern Europe* (London: Macmillan, 1975), pp. 273–91.

79. For further restrictions, some of which are of a police character, see the *Frankfurter Allgemeine Zeitung* (Germany), May 31, 1975.

80. In Poland, Stefan Cardinal Wyszynski remained a political power, while in Czechoslovakia the Church fared far worse without any mass outcry in its defense. The Czechoslovak prelate, Cardinal Josef Beran, was sentenced to a fourteen-year term, which he served in full.

81. *Demografie*, no. 2, June 1974.

82. *Rude Pravo*, June 5, 1969.

83. George Schöpflin, ed., *The Soviet Union and Eastern Europe: A Handbook*, (New York: Praeger, 1970), p. 32.

84. See Malcolm Browne writing from Prague, *International Herald Tribune* (Paris), August 25, 1975.

85. Krejci, *Social Change*, p. 8.

86. *Ukoly odboru pri upevnovani socialisticke zakonnosti: materialy z celostatniho aktivu k ukolum odboru pri upevnovani socialisticke zakonnosti, konaneho v Praze dne 3. rijna 1972* (Trade Union Tasks for the Strengthening of Socialist Legality: Materials from the All-State Meeting on the Tasks of the Trade Unions for the Strengthening of Socialist Legality, Held in Prague on October 3, 1972) (Prague: Vydalo Oddeleni propagandy a vychovy uro, 1973).

87. The National Front is theoretically a coalition of five parties dominated by the KSC. These include the Socialist party, the People's party (Catholic), the Slovak Revival party, and the Slovak Freedom party.

88. The new election law of July 1971 changed the terms of office from four to five years to coincide with the party congress, which convenes every five years. Although multiple candidates for the Federal Assembly had been under consideration in 1968, the new electoral law enforced the exclusive power of the National Front to nominate a single list of candidates for elective office.

89. However, this measure, like many others, has not been implemented and there has been substantial retrenchment. See *Radio Free Europe Research*, December 17, 1970, pp. 4–6.

90. Otto Ulc, "The Communist Party of Czechoslovakia and the Young Generation," *East European Quarterly*, (June 1972), 6(2):212, cit-

ing Maria Hulakova, *Nova Mysl*, no. 14, July 11, 1967, pp. 8–12; *Statisticka rocenka CCSR 1968* (Prague: SNTL, 1968), p. 491.

91. The total university enrollment for 1967–68 was 137,497; not quite 1 percent of the total population. *Ibid.*, p. 212.

92. Peter A. Toma, *The Educational System of Czechoslovakia* (Washington, D.C.: HEW No. (OE) 76-19126, 1976) and Stanislav Vodinsky, *Czechoslovakia: Education* (Prague: Orbis, 1963), p. 22.

93. Ivan Volgyes, "Political Socialization in Eastern Europe," *Problems of Communism* (January–February 1974), 23:47.

94. *Svobodne Slovo*, December 3, 1968.

95. Jan Kozic in *Tribuna*, July 9, 1969, no. 26.

96. See Milos Rehurek in *Nova Mysl*, February 1974.

97. For a monumental study of the Prague Spring, see H. Gordon Skilling, *Czechoslovakia's Interrupted Revolution* (Princeton, N.J.: Princeton University Press, 1976).

98. Of the 1,192 delegates who attended the Vysocany Congress, only 50 were Slovak. On August 26–29, 1968, the Slovak Congress met, and on the first day, declared the Vysocany Congress was valid. Upon Husak's return from Moscow the Slovak Congress reversed its stand on Vysocany and on August 26 declared it illegal, in line with the Soviet leadership's declaration.

99. Tom Stoppard, "Prague, The Story of the Chartists," *The New York Review of Books,* August 4, 1977.

100. Peter Millard, *Prager Winter* (Vienna: Herold Druck, 1977).

101. Josef Havlin, "Vyznam Rijnove Revoluce pro svetove dejiny" (Importance of the October Revolution for World History), *Zivot strany*, October 24, 1977, no. 22.

102. *Ukoly odboru pri upevnovani socialisticke zakonnosti*, pp. 26–30.

103. See Thomas E. Heneghan, "Czechoslovakia: The Economic Discussion Continues," *Radio Free Europe Research,* Background Report no. 51, March 19, 1975.

Manfred Grote

4. The Socialist Unity Party of Germany

The preeminent political force in the German Democratic Republic (DDR) is the Socialist Unity Party of Germany (SED). It is a mass party with a core of committed cadres and a hierarchically organized apparatus. The SED's control over East Germany is pervasive; it goes beyond the government to include the communications media and all economic, social, and cultural affairs. The ideology determines the binding goals and values of the society. In short, the SED is a totalitarian party. Certain changes in scope and methods of control—to be dealt with below—are suggestive of a gradual transformation into a "milder" form, say, authoritarianism. But at this time the essential characteristics of the totalitarian conception are still present.

A noteworthy feature of the East German political system is the so-called National Front. It is an expression of "popular front" policies, comparable in many aspects to the practices in other East European countries. Four political parties continue to exist in the DDR. They are the Christian Democratic Union (CDU), the Liberal Democratic Party of Germany (LDPD), the National Democratic Party of Germany (NDPD), and the Democratic Peasants' Party of Germany (DBD). The CDU and the LDPD were established in 1945, drawing support from the middle-class elements of the then Soviet Occupied Zone. But the parties' independence was short-lived; their survival depended on strict collaboration with the Communists. The NDPD and the DBD—both led by Communists—were established in 1948. Their purpose was to weaken the support for the Liberals and the Christian Democrats. These tactics were designed as a temporary expedient, but eventually evolved into an integral part of the system of the SED.[1]

All parties are aligned under the National Front, which is an outgrowth of the earlier Antifascist Democratic Bloc. It also includes the several important mass organizations, the Free German Trade Union Federation (FDGB), the Free German Youth (FDJ), the Democratic Women's Federation of Germany (DFD), and the Cultural League (KB). The National Front is completely controlled by the SED. All parties and the aforementioned mass organizations are assigned blocs of seats in the People's Chamber (*Volkskammer*) and in the representative bodies on lower levels. The proportion of seats remains fixed. At election time the voters are presented with a so-called unity list, which provides only for the elimination of candidates, whenever more than one is listed for a given office. Otherwise the list must be accepted or rejected as a whole. It takes some courage to use the private voting booth and to reject the ticket or to stay away from the polls altogether. The usual practice is to go as a group from the place of work and to cast the ballot openly. The elections are primarily intended to mobilize the masses. They are, at best, akin to a ratification process. The election on November 14, 1971, had the amazing turnout of 98.48 percent. The single slate of the National Front claimed 99.85 percent of the votes in its favor and only 0.15 percent against it.[2] The fixed distribution of the 500 seats of the People's Chamber—according to the election results of October 17, 1976—assigns to the SED 127 (25.4 percent); the DBD, the NDPD, the CDU, and the LDPD each 52 (10.4 percent); the FDGB 68 (13.6 percent); the FDJ 40 (8.0 percent); the DFD 35 (7.0 percent); and the KB 22 (4.4 percent).[3]

The SED is in absolute control, making the DDR—in effect—a uniparty state. The SED finds it advantageous to maintain the appearance of a multiparty system. It hopes to project a democratic image toward the West. Furthermore, the parties and the mass organizations outside the SED continue to serve a very useful function of integrating those citizens who have reservations about a specifically Communist party. Such persons can join a bourgeois party, albeit a party fully engaged in furthering the objectives of the SED. The latter denies ruling the other parties and insists on merely pursuing a policy of "comradely cooperation."[4] Nevertheless, the utilization of the National Front has enabled the SED to be a mass party without actually broadening its own base; it can thereby sustain a high degree of cohesiveness and discipline as a Communist cadre party.

The leading role of the SED is formally established by the constitution of the DDR, which states: "The German Democratic Republic is a socialist state of workers and peasants. It is the political organization of the working people in town and countryside under the leadership of the working class and its Marxist-Leninist party" (Article 1). Regarding the National Front, it states: "The alliance of all forces of the people finds its organized expression in the National Front of the German Democratic Republic." (Article 3).[5] In the following pages we will (1) review the SED's development to its present status, (2) examine the party's organization, (3) analyze its leadership capacity and problems, and (4) attempt to assess the role of the party in East German society.

THE SOCIALIST UNITY PARTY

Foundation and Development

German communism has undergone dramatic changes during its history of over half a century. Its beginnings as a revolutionary opposition party date back to the birth of the Weimar Republic in 1919. At this time, extremely radical elements of the Social Democratic Party of Germany (SPD) broke away to form the Communist Party of Germany (KPD), under the leadership of Rosa Luxemburg and Karl Liebknecht. The KPD evolved into a formidable radical-leftist party, which stood uncompromisingly opposed to the Weimar system.[6] Blindly devoted to the destruction of the Social Democrats in Germany, the KPD followed a strategy of incredible shortsightedness in cooperating with the Nazis. When the Nazis seized power in

January 1933, the KPD was promptly banned and large numbers of its members were arrested and murdered. Most of the leaders either went underground or left Germany in the face of the intensifying Nazi terror. A sizable group of functionaries went to Paris and from there to Moscow, where they remained for the duration of World War II. During this period Stalin exacted total subservience to his policies from the German Communists. Those leaders who disagreed with the "popular front" policies of that time were among the first victims of the great purge. Indeed, the impact of Stalin's purges on the German Communist emigration was devastating; the KPD lost hundreds of functionaries in the Soviet Union.[7]

Two notable survivors were Wilhelm Pieck and Walter Ulbricht. Ulbricht headed the group of German Communists who returned to Germany on April 30, 1945. His group functioned as an executive organ of the Soviet Military Administration. The latter permitted the formation of political parties and trade unions in the Soviet Occupied Zone on June 10, 1945. On the following day the KPD was reestablished, making it the first postwar political party in Germany. The party's political program was fully the work of the "Muscovites."[8] Ulbricht took charge of the key positions, while the 70-year-old Pieck was responsible for general policy and representing the KPD to the outside world. At this stage, Stalin's policies respecting Germany were flexible and adaptable. Initially, they were designed to gain influence in all of Germany, despite the divisions into the four occupation zones. The Soviets, therefore, agreed to certain concessions, which they were unwilling to grant the other East European countries under their control. This flexible posture was clearly reflected in the founding proclamation of the KPD. It departed significantly from orthodox Stalinism in openly courting the support of the relatively strong social democratic elements. The Soviet system was not to be forced on Germany, it proclaimed. Instead, an antifascist democratic system was to be established, including parliamentary democracy, individual rights, and free enterprise.

The KPD sought close cooperation with the other parties in

the Soviet Occupied Zone. However, an early proposal to create a unified workers' party, offered by the leadership of the reestablished SPD, was not accepted immediately. Ulbricht had determined that the time for an organizational union with the SPD had not yet come. The Communists did not wish to take this step until a strong and loyal corps of functionaries was available, one which could assume the key positions in the future unity party. Also, certain internal divisions had to be overcome. Many of the old cadres still harbored a deep hostility toward the Social Democrats, and the very idea of collaboration was unacceptable to them. There was also some opposition to Ulbricht's policy of complete and unconditional identification with the Soviet occupation forces. Ulbricht and his associates were able to isolate their political opponents, and unify the party and consolidate their control over it. Enjoying the special favor of the occupation forces, the KPD soon dominated political life in the Soviet Zone.

However, being the preferred organ of the occupation power did not improve the KPD's standing with the people. It remained remote and unpopular, while the SPD expanded its influence over the population. Such developments, entailing the very real prospect of a humiliating defeat, if the then anticipated free elections were actually held, caused the KPD to make a sudden about-face on the question of unity with the SPD. Now the SPD had second thoughts about the idea. To make the process of unity more palatable for the SPD, the KPD advocated the thesis of the "special German way," a unique German road to socialism. Although SPD leader Otto Grotewohl was won over by the KPD, other Social Democrats worriedly saw unity as the device through which the Communists would eliminate the SPD as an independent political force.[9] However, attempts to gain time were unsuccessful. A conference of thirty representatives each from the SPD and the KPD was convened on December 20, 1945, and the decision to prepare for unity was taken. The SPD insisted at this time that unity should be based on the free decision of the party membership and should be taken within an all-German framework. As it turned out, only in West Berlin was the SPD able to conduct a referendum on the question, with the majority expressing opposition. The formal merger of the two parties into the SED was accomplished on Easter, 1946.

In its initial phase, the SED was a typical leftist mass party. Within two years its membership increased from about 1.3 million to nearly 2 million.[10] This constituted approximately 16 percent of the adult population.[11] The First Party Congress had stipulated a distribution of leadership posts on the basis of parity. However, tensions between Communists and Social Democrats occurred from the beginning and the latter were gradually pushed aside. Nevertheless, during this period of the "special German way," the SED incorporated certain democratic features. The party saw itself as the leading political force in all of Germany, its propaganda placing it in the forefront of the struggle for German unity.

The phase of the "special German way" ended abruptly in 1948, a year prior to the founding of the DDR. The intensification of the cold war and the conflict between the Soviet Union and Yugoslavia caused Moscow to revise its posture respecting Germany. Different roads to socialism were no longer tolerated; Stalinism was the only valid model. The Soviet Occupied Zone was to be tied closely to the Eastern bloc. To help implement this policy, the SED was transformed into a "party of the New Type." Far from being a truly new type, this simply meant the strict application of the Soviet pattern of party organization and leadership as developed by Lenin and Stalin. "To learn from the Soviet Union is to learn how to win," was the SED's slogan for this process of Sovietization.[12] Party ideologist Anton Ackermann was obliged to proclaim that his thesis of the "special German way" had been "absolutely false and dangerous."[13] The study of the history of the Communist Party of the Soviet Union was made the foundation of all party schooling.[14]

The creation of a cadre party after the Soviet model called for a cleansing process, the purging of all "hostile" elements. For this purpose Ulbricht fashioned his own purge instrument, the Central Party Control Commission. The restructuring did not eliminate the features of the mass party completely; for the membership—although substantially reduced—remained relatively high.[15] A clearer distinction between the rank-and-file members and the party activists was drawn. A new probationary membership category, the candidate status, was introduced. On all party levels reliable and loyal cadres took charge, guaranteeing absolute power to the central party apparatus. With the foundation of the DDR in October 1949, the SED became the ruling party, assuming complete control over state and society. In 1950 the Third Party Congress adopted a new Party Statute, calling for an intensified struggle against the remnants of social democracy. Pervasive administrative changes and social reforms were implemented, such as the dissolution of the five *Länder* (provinces) and the creation of fifteen (including East Berlin) administrative districts in their place, the forced collectivization of agriculture, the socialization of industry and commerce, and the establishment of armed forces.

The brutal expropriations, the persecution of peasants unwilling to join collective farms, the widespread use of terror by the newly established State Security Service—all of these generated strong hostility against the regime. The first serious test for the SED came with the death of Stalin on March 6, 1953. Under Ulbricht's leadership, the cult of Stalin had been most eagerly pursued. Ulbricht had proclaimed: "We will succeed, for the great Stalin leads us."[16] His death shocked the SED leaders and caused a temporary state of confusion and disorientation. Conversely, it raised hopes among the citizenry for a mitigation of repression and some liberalization. In the face of mounting discontent in the country and Soviet pressure to adopt a new course, the SED leadership reluctantly proclaimed a softer line. The party promised improved living conditions and a strengthening of individual rights. The steps taken, however, came too late and were too small to prevent the uprising of June 17, 1953. It was precipitated when higher work quotas—fixed in May of that year—were not withdrawn as the new course was introduced. The workers gave vent to their acute discontent by staging strikes and mass demonstrations. They were joined by other segments of the population, and strikes and demonstrations were staged all over the DDR in spontaneous fashion. The uprising was crushed with the assistance of Soviet tanks, but it was not altogether without consequence.[17]

A faction within the Central Committee of the SED called for major reform and the removal of Ulbricht. It was led by Wilhelm Zaisser, member of the Politburo and minister of state security, and Rudolf Herrnstadt, Politburo candidate and editor-in-chief of *Neues Deutschland.* But in view of the recent challenges to the East German regime, the new leadership in Moscow was unwilling to accept the risk of replacing Ulbricht. With Moscow's help, Ulbricht was able to reassert himself and remove or censure his opponents. No shortcomings were officially admitted to and the uprising itself was portrayed as a fascist putsch.[18] The Fourth Party Congress in 1954 gave clear indication that the SED was not going along fully with the general thaw in the Soviet Union. Ulbricht considered the softer line a mistake. With great tactical skill he approved only unavoidable changes and weathered successfully one of the more difficult periods for postwar communism: the process of de-Stalinization, declared by Khrushchev at the Twentieth Party Congress of the Soviet Communist Party in 1956. Although officially revising his judgment about Stalin's importance, Ulbricht prevented serious discussion about the problems of Stalinism within the SED. He ordered the party members to think less about the past and more about the economy.

But attacks against Stalinism and criticism of Ulbricht's despotic methods from within the party increased. Intellectual circles saw de-Stalinization as an opportunity to move against the primitive leadership methods of the party apparatus. In connection with the events in Poland and Hungary in the latter part of 1956, numerous groups within the SED pressed for an unequivocal rejection of Stalinist principles. Once again Ulbricht proved his supreme mastery in out maneuvering opponents. Since 1953 he had pursued a policy designed to prevent an alliance between the workers and the intelligentsia. Thus, the workers did not protest when he moved against leading intellectuals and top party officials who had criticized him. Moreover, the tragic events in Hungary proved Ulbricht correct in the eyes of the Soviets and raised their respect for him. He had effectively stamped out all those elements aspiring to implement liberalizing reforms, which had caused so much trouble for Moscow in other areas of its bloc. Ulbricht kept winning the internal power struggles, and his dominant position was fully confirmed by the Fifth Party Congress in July 1958. The more notable opponents who lost their posts at the time were Karl Schirdewan, Ulbricht's deputy in the Politburo, Fred Oelssner, the party ideologist, and Ernst Wollweber, the minister for state security. Ulbricht prevailed by successfully playing people off against each other, by nailing down the support of the majority of the Politburo members, and by raising accusations loudly and publicly, while effecting unavoidable rehabilitations discreetly and quietly.[19]

Conceding severe shortages in consumer goods, the party promised major increases in per capita consumption. To increase productivity and shore up support for the regime, the political indoctrination programs were expanded and intensified. Ulbricht proclaimed the great goal of the creation of a new man embracing a socialist morality.[20] But efforts toward these ends seemed to have the opposite effect, for the number of refugees increased dramatically. The SED's answer to the mass flight of East Germans was the construction of the Berlin Wall in August 1961. The enormous loss of productive labor had been threatening the very existence of the DDR. From that perspective, the sealing of the frontiers and the building of the Berlin Wall were essential for survival. From September 1949, when refugees from the DDR were first registered, until August 15, 1961, a total of nearly 2.7 million persons fled to West Germany. This figure does not include an estimated one million who left East Germany but who did not move through the emergency reception camps (*Notaufnahmelager*).[21]

The Wall marks another phase in the development of the SED. The period of renewed terror abated within a year, and the SED at last commenced a cautious program of de-Stalinization. The Wall had brought an end to the vicious downward spiral for the DDR. Now the East Germans applied themselves trying to make the best of the given circumstances. As productivity increased, the standard of living improved. This in turn lessened the public's resentment of the regime. As the trends were reversed, the DDR experienced impressive economic growth during this period. Further, the SED, recognizing the need to bridge the gap between itself and the general public, launched a program of "social pacification."[22] Particularly noteworthy were the concessions made to the young, who were subjected to a little less regimentation and received more opportunity to structure their own private lives according to personal preferences. Substantial legal reforms were implemented in 1962, making sentences for first offenses more lenient, emphasizing educational methods and rehabilitation rather than purely punitive measures. In 1963 the New Economic System (NES), a comprehensive new system of planning and directing the people's economy, was launched. It was supplemented in 1964 by an ambitious program to modernize industry.[23] The SED endeavored to combine modern industrial methods and a degree of self-regulation with a centrally planned economy. Decisions were to be made at the level where they could be made most expertly. The leadership recognized that the DDR's opportunities would lie chiefly in scientific and technological modernization, for work force and industrial capacity would be relatively constant. This meant greater reliance on scientific direction of the economy and more material incentives for the workers. The NES would seek to apply the performance principle, and it would be under the guidance of the pragmatically oriented technocrats and experts.

The adoption of reforms in the economy and in other areas, such as the local election reform of 1965 which made possible a process of selection from a number of candidates exceeding the number to be elected in a given district, produced a noticeable change in the general atmosphere. The DDR's impressive economic surge, placing it in eighth place in world industrial production in 1967 and second only to the Soviet Union in the

Communist East, gave the regime increased self-confidence and stature. East Germans were beginning to take pride in the accomplishments of their state. The marked improvement of the general living conditions, coupled with the years of intense efforts for political reeducation and indoctrination of the people, generated a somewhat broader acceptance of the regime. But the society has not, as yet, been transformed by the SED to the point where it has become fully supportive and loyal.[24]

In the area of foreign affairs the SED was able to achieve a major objective: the de jure diplomatic recognition of the DDR outside the socialist camp as a separate sovereign German state. The general acceptance of the two-state theory of Germany and had been fervently sought by the DDR. Over the years the East German position on the German question had undergone basic change. In the past, Ulbricht had spoken consistently in terms of a cohesive German nation, as shown in his proposal for a German Confederation.[25] The preamble of the 1968 constitution still referred to the DDR as a socialist state of the German nation. But when the West German government, under Chancellor Willy Brandt, advanced its Eastern policy initiatives and its new concept of "two German states within one German nation," the SED leadership declared the concept of the all-German nation to be dead. With increasing vehemence it was insisted that the DDR is a totally separate nation-state, a "socialist nation" which differed fundamentally from the "bourgeois nation" of West Germany. As a détente policy toward the Federal Republic became inescapable for the DDR, every effort was made toward the strictest demarcation. The Bonn policy of increased contacts between the people was rejected as a device designed to undermine the SED system and demarcation was set as a precondition for responding to Bonn's initiatives.[26] The Treaty on the Basis of Relations between the Federal Republic of Germany and the DDR was concluded in 1973, clearing the way for entry of both German states into the United Nations and full recognition of the DDR in the Western world.[27]

As for the conflicts within the world of communism, the SED has unwaveringly and consistently identified with the Soviet

Union. SED leaders have proclaimed that Maoism constitutes a complete break with Marxism-Leninism. More recently, Peking is being condemned for supporting the concept of all the all-German nation, which is interpreted as an attack on the DDR.[28] The DDR is seen as being "linked in fraternal friendship with the USSR by everlasting bonds."[29] Not only on the ideological level, but economically as well, a close partnership exists. The Soviet Union and the DDR are each other's most important trading partners.[30]

A review of the SED's several development phases shows that it is not a static and monolithic organization. Orthodox Stalinism has been abandoned. There are contradictions between what is practiced and what is preached. The ideological exhortations emanating from the Seventh and Eighth Party Congresses (1967 and 1971, respectively) are difficult to reconcile with the practices of a modern industrial state. The SED continues to see itself as a Marxist-Leninist revolutionary party. But in the day-to-day practices of governing a modern industrial state, the principles of Marxism-Leninism appear to be more important as justification and camouflage for existing power relationships than as guidelines for policies.

Organizational Structure

The SED's organizational structure follows closely that of the Soviet Communist party. Its guiding concept is known as "democratic centralism." This Leninist principle means that (1) the leading party organs are to be democratically elected and are accountable to those who have elected them, and that (2) all decisions of the higher party organs are binding on the subordinate levels and must be implemented through strict party discipline. The democratic component of the principle exists in theory only. In practice, a severely hierarchical system prevails. The superior organs compile the lists of candidates and control the elections. The process is one of appointment from the top, rather than election from below. Reports are presented, but the membership has little or no opportunity to discuss these, not to speak of any participation in the decision-making.

According to the SED's statute, the Party Congress is its highest organ. It is to be convened every five years. During the intervals, the Central Committee (CC) is considered the highest authority, responsible for the implementation of Congress resolutions. The CC has 145 members and 57 candidates.[31] It normally convenes four times a year and works through a number of standing and ad hoc commissions.[32] Neither the Party Congress nor the CC is a deliberative body which is engaged in decision-making and policy formulation. Their primary function is the affirmation of decisions presented to them.

The most powerful body is the Politburo. Formally, its function is to assume the political leadership between the plenary sessions of the CC. It meets about once a week and makes all the major decisions. The 19 members and 9 candidates are elected by the CC from its own membership. The party's executive body is the Secretariat. It incorporates eleven secretaries, elected by the CC, who are responsible for the various departments. The general secretary chairs both the Secretariat and Politburo. He is the head of the party and as such the most powerful man in the political system of the DDR. The departments of the Secretariat include those required to manage the party and those to oversee the administrative departments of the government. Generally, for each state organ there exists an equivalent party organ which exerts indirect authority through the overlap in personnel and frequent joint meetings with the respective state organ. Some 2,000 (out of approximately 70,000) functionaries are active in the apparatus of the CC.[33]

Under the CC apparatus are the district party organizations for the fifteen administrative districts of the DDR. An annual delegates' conference formally heads these organizations. In charge are the district directorates through their bureaus, commissions, and the secretariat. Heading the sizable district secretariats are the first district secretaries, who are typically among the top-level party leadership. As a rule they are members of the CC and some even of the Politburo. Thus they are in frequent and close consultation with the Politburo—mostly through special liaison members—and the Secretariat of the CC. Special CC "instructors" may also be employed to inform the district organizations of the latest party decisions and tasks.[34]

The level below the district party organizations is formed by the *Kreis* (county or borough) party organizations. A biannual delegates' conference is the highest organ on this level. The executive body is formed by a *Kreis* secretariat, headed by a first *Kreis* secretary. There are 252 such organizations. Of these, 215 (including 6 city party organizations) oversee the local party organizations within the counties of the DDR. The remaining 37 are established for the larger factories, universities, and certain other corporate entities.[35] This reflects the party's practice of basing its organization not only on territorial divisions, but also on functional and production lines.

The local party organizations oversee the several base organizations of a particular locale, factory, or administrative establishment. The base organizations constitute the smallest party units; they are the equivalents of the cell. Over 50,000 exist throughout the DDR. They are organized at places of work, such as factories, offices, schools, and within the framework of residential associations. They are also organized in the armed forces, but here they are part of a separate organizational scheme. The base organizations are considered the link between the party and the people. Their purpose is to realize the SED's goals in all areas of life and to impress upon the average citizen the pervasive presence of the party. It is generally a small, easily supervised unit. A minimum number of three persons may form such a group. The average size is 26 members and three candidates.[36] However, in some plants, membership may be in the hundreds, requiring subdivision into several so-called party groups. The base organizations are expected to be a close community which can provide extensive personal contact. The leader, who is elected by the members, is responsible for generating a high degree of acceptance of and submission to the superior party organs. The party is interested in all facets of the individual party member's life. It wants to embrace the total individual; to achieve this goal it does not distinguish between party member and private citizen.

Through this generally well-functioning network of organizations on all levels, the SED assures its dominant position. The leadership has adopted changes in its organizational structure whenever it has seemed necessary to improve effectiveness and efficiency. More recently special attention has been focused on the problems arising from the party's efforts to consolidate its dominant position in all areas of society, without causing an estrangement between the bureaucratic apparatus and the mass of its members. The demands imposed on the lower level of functionaries can be exacting. This is especially true for those in the production sector who must cope not only with obstinate central planning bureaucracies and frequent jurisdictional confusion, but also with the problems of critical shortages of various consumer commodities, not to mention the various other responsibilities they may have. A typical functionary may belong to four or five organizations, councils, or boards, which take up most of his spare time. The directives of the CC reach him by way of a veritable flood of papers. For such reasons certain changes and adjustments have been made. Although centralism has by no means been abandoned, steps have been taken to increase the responsibility and effectiveness of the individual functionary. More decision-making has been transferred to the local levels.

The Leadership

The SED presents itself as the party of the working class. Its membership promotion continues to concentrate on workers and peasants. But it is no longer a workers' party in the strict sense of that term. Men and women with higher education and professional training constitute a growing proportion of the total membership and assume increasingly the leading positions. SED membership has climbed to a total of 1.9 million.[37] This amounts to over 11 percent of the population of slightly under

17 million. The membership conditions have been eased, enabling an applicant to become a member after one year of candidacy and the recommendation of two party members with a minimum of two years' standing.[38] A breakdown of the membership into socioeconomic groups reveals that 45 percent are workers, 28 percent are white-collar workers, and 6.4 percent are peasants.[39] Almost one-half of the white-collar workers may be classified as belonging to the intelligentsia. In terms of the social structure of the DDR as a whole, it can be said that the workers are presently underrepresented and the intelligentsia overrepresented. Quite naturally, this shift reflects the party's effort to meet the need for a more highly trained personnel to help run a complex, modern industrial society. The presence of academically trained party members is especially noticeable in the middle ranges of the hierarchy. Obviously, the leadership does not feel that the SED's image as a workers' party is adversely affected by these developments. Indeed, it takes pride in what it considers the general upgrading of the qualifications of its functionaries.

The SED has throughout its existence maintained extensive training programs for cadres. The considerable efforts and expenditures in this area are, no doubt, an excellent investment for the party. They are rightly recognized as a key to the success of the system. A special emphasis has been placed on the improvement of management and planning skills.[40] Generally, the objective of the training programs is to provide the functionary with the necessary specialized knowledge in his field of responsibility and an adequate grounding in the basics of sociology and human relations. For this purpose the party is making special training courses available to some 35,000 students in about 450 schools, which are attached to the *Kreis* organizations. A higher level of training is provided for up to 3,000 students in 25 "special schools," attached to district organizations.[41] In these schools, one-year courses and intensive three-month courses are offered for the leading functionaries on the district level. The highest level of party schooling is provided by the "Karl Marx" Party Academy and by the Institute for Social Sciences. The Academy offers three-year programs, leading to a degree in the social sciences. It is open to the members of the CC, the secretaries of the district and *Kreis* organizations, and the leading functionaries in government, the economy, and the mass organizations. The Institute is comparable to a graduate school, offering four-year programs, which may lead to a doctorate. Admission is highly selective and restricted to future "leaders."[42] Generally, the schooling programs have proved to be beneficial, raising the functionaries' productivity and usefulness to the party.

Great importance is attached to ideological work. It still ranks highest on the list of the functionaries' responsibilities. As a dutiful cadre, one must be ever mindful to instill a socialist consciousness in the people.[43] Cadres are further expected to provide effective leadership through appropriate resolutions, directives, and guidelines to subordinate levels. The implementation of party policies is to proceed in all areas of government, the production sector, and the cultural and educational institutions. It is a total effort. The effective mobilization of the rank and file is essential, placing a premium on good organizational work. Another very important concern is the selection and training of politically and professionally promising party members. The satellite parties and the mass organizations are, of course, tied into this effort and play a significant supplementary role.

With the adoption of the NES, the SED leadership set into motion a process of modernization and rationalization. At its inception, it was a truly innovative approach, designed to move the planned economy out of chaos and stagnation. The program incorporated the reforms formulated by the Soviet economist J. G. Liberman, seeking to apply concepts of price, profit, interest, and value to the planned economy. The whole process of planning was revised, calling for the abandonment of the multiyear plan in favor of so-called "perspective" planning, which would provide only broad guidelines. The burden of the specific planning would fall on the Associations of People's Industries. These associations and the individual plant managers were to be judged on the basis of cost and efficiency per unit, rather than the fulfillment of quotas in terms of numbers or tonnage. All bonuses and advantages were contingent on efficiency. Interest was charged on all capital advanced to plants in order to stimulate prudent use. The novel concept of the socialist market was proclaimed. It required the managers to sell their products, either in a domestic market with more selective consumers, or in a highly competitive world market. The implementation of the program involved a much heavier reliance on the managerial-technocratic elites. Their expanded role has been formidable, especially in the production sector. However, whether it will lead to liberalization and fundamental change in the DDR remains speculative at this time.

When the graduates of the technical and economic colleges took charge, new and different operating procedures were introduced. This has led to a certain amount of tension between the older group of leaders, with a more dogmatic Marxist-Leninist orientation, and this younger group of technocrats, with its bend toward pragmatism. The principal command posts are still in the hands of the older generation, whose outlook has been significantly shaped by the era of Stalinism. Inevitably, of course, a younger generation will gradually assume the ranks of power. A comparative analysis of the membership of the CC shows that the average age of the members has decreased to below fifty years.[44] Their professional backgrounds are increasingly in the fields of technology and management, as well as academia.[45] A widely recognized study of the SED party elite identifying these trends concludes that the CC has changed from a mere sounding board of the Politburo to a group involved in genuine consultation and deliberation.[46] This study goes on to suggest that the transformation occurring in the CC represents a trend toward "consultative authoritarianism" in the DDR.[47]

The top leadership group, the Politburo, is a relatively stable and solidified body. It has had remarkably little turnover in membership due to power struggles. For twenty-five years the dominant figure in the Politburo was Walter Ulbricht. The end of his tenure as the head of the party came in 1971, when he was eased out of the position of First Secretary. The changeover was troublefree and involved relatively little loss of face for Ulbricht.

He was made the honorary chairman of the SED and retained his two other positions, chairman of the National Defense Council (until his resignation in 1972) and chairman of the Council of State (until his death in 1973). Ulbricht was succeeded by Erich Honecker, an all-round party leader and for years Ulbricht's deputy. Honecker was clearly in line for the top position; his takeover represented continuity and stability.

Honecker was born in 1912 in the Saar region as the son of a coal miner. By 1930 he was a member of the KPD and prominently active in the party's youth movement. In 1935 he was arrested by the Nazis and subsequently sentenced to ten years incarceration for conspiring to commit treason. Freed in 1945 from the Brandenburg penitentiary by the Soviet armed forces, he became immediately active in the reestablished KPD. He entered the Politburo of the SED as a candidate member in 1950 and became a full member in 1958. He reached the center of power as the leader of the FDJ, the Communist youth organization he founded and headed from 1946 to 1955. He then spent about one year in the Soviet Union for further political studies and training. In 1958 he advanced to the powerful post of CC Secretary for Security, Military, Organizational, and Cadre Affairs.[48] He has been described as a sober, methodical, and energetic apparatchik. But there also seems to be a gregarious and fun-loving side to his nature, reflecting his un-Prussian roots in the Saar region. Over the years he carefully expanded his power base by placing his supporters in key positions within the party. His reputation has been that of a hardliner who has been adamant on the strict demarcation between the two German states. Reportedly it was Honecker who was responsible for the planning and execution of the construction of the Wall. In general, he seems to typify the tough and hard-working generation of party functionaries which has matured in the DDR and is dedicated to make both party and state stronger and more efficient. More recently—following Leonid Brezhnev's example—he also became the formal chief of state by assuming the chairmanship of the Council of state.

Since the Ninth Party Congress of the SED, held in May

1976, the Politburo membership has consisted of the following persons: Honecker, General Secretary and chairman of the Council of State; Hermann Axen, CC secretary for international ties; Friedrich Ebert, vice-chairman of the Council of State and vice-president of the People's Chamber; Werner Felfe, first secretary of the Halle district; Gerhard Grüneberg, CC secretary for agricultural economics; Prof. Kurt Hager, CC secretary for culture and science and chief ideologist; Gen. Heinz Hoffmann, minister of national defense; Werner Krolikowski, first deputy chairman of the Council of Ministers; Werner Lamberz, CC secretary for agitation (killed in helicopter crash in Libya in March 1978); Erich Mielke, minister of state security; Dr. Günter Mittag, CC secretary for economics; Erich Mückenberger, chairman of the Central Party Control Commission; Konrad Naumann, first secretary of the Berlin district; Alfred Neumann, first deputy chairman of the Council of Ministers; Prof. Albert Norden, CC secretary for propaganda; Horst Sindermann, president of the People's Chamber; Willi Stoph, chairman of the Council of Ministers; Harry Tisch, chairman of the FDGB National Executive; and Paul Verner, CC secretary for security. The candidate membership has included Horst Dohlus, CC secretary for party organs; Joachim Herrmann, CC secretary and editor-in-chief of *Neues Deutschland;* Dr. Werner Jarowinsky, CC secretary for trade and distribution; Güunter Kleiber, minister of machine and transport manufactures; Egon Krenz, head of the FDJ; Ingeburg Lange, CC secretary for women's affairs; Margarete Müller, Council of State member; Gerhard Schürer, chief of the State Planning Commission; and Werner Walde, first secretary of the Potsdam district.[49]

A comparison of this group with the Politburo membership announced at the Eighth Party Congress in 1971 reveals relatively insignificant changes. The vacancy created by the death of Herbert Warnke, head of the FDGB, was filled by Warnke's successor Tisch, who moved from candidate to full membership status. Three other candidates—Felfe, Mielke, and Naumann—were also promoted, thus expanding the full membership from sixteen to nineteen. A small turnover occurred among the candidates, two were dropped and two—Krenz and Walde—were newly admitted.[50]

The dominant faction and Honecker's principal support base in the Politburo is made up of conservative, but flexible, functionaries, who have considerable experience in party work, government, and the military. It favors a continuation of the closest possible links with the Soviet Union in all fields. The members of this faction include such men as Axen, Felfe, Hager, Hoffmann, Mielke, Naumann, and Verner. Another identifiable faction is made up of several of the younger technocrats, who look to Stoph for leadership. This group includes such men as Grüneberg, Jarowinsky, Kleiber, Mittag, and Schürer. They are all accomplished specialists in their respective fields of responsibility. A third faction consists of the rather orthodox and dogmatic older members, such as Ebert, Müller, Neumann, Norden, and Mückenberger.

At the time of this writing there is indication that Stoph is Honecker's major rival and a possible severe power struggle cannot be ruled out. Claims have been flourishing that the Politburo is seriously split and that confidence in Honecker's leadership ability is eroding.[51] Ironically, Honecker's problems are in good measure attributable to his policy of expanding the consumer goods sector to create a German version of "goulash communism." This necessitated a greater economic orientation toward the West, especially West Germany, all of which had a considerable destabilizing effect. The appearance in early 1978 of an opposition manifesto, issued by an organized opposition within the SED, is tangible evidence of a leadership crisis.[52]

A full assessment of these developments is not yet possible. But it is useful to keep in mind that the SED has been a tough and cohesive organization, and thus far these features were present in the Politburo. The men at the top continue to identify with the principles of Marxism-Leninism. They see themselves as leaders of the "bastion" of socialism, most exposed and threatened by the West. Their belief in the validity of the ideology is quite possibly enhanced by the possession of considerable privileges and the awareness of belonging to the chosen few who think and decide for the masses. Moreover, even the functionary who initially joined the SED for purely opportunistic reasons comes to realize—as he had made his way to the top—that he has no future without the SED. The fact that his own well-being and that of the party are linked is likely to make him a "believer."

The pressure to conform to the precepts of Marxism-Leninism is formidable. The pragmatically oriented technocrat can escape it only if he is willing to forego or abdicate a political role. To gain access to the centers of power, to participate in the decision-making process rather than merely to carry out the decisions, requires faithful, unquestioning adherence to the official party line. The prevailing atmosphere is one of stern intolerance of deviating opinions. It appears that not even on the highest level does an opportunity for plain and open talk exist. This state of affairs reduces the SED leaders occasionally to prisoners of their own ideology. The surprisingly inaccurate assessments of Western political affairs and some woefully unrealistic economic policies may serve as cases in point. They are the consequence of considerable loss of objectivity and misperception due to ideological blinders. When the influence of the sober-minded technocrats is discussed, it must be kept in mind that it is largely confined to new methods and approaches, without questioning the basic goals. The managerial-technocratic elites are largely apolitical. They are consulted, and they participate regularly in the decision-making. But their conceptions for modernization and rationalization are designed—in the final analysis—to strengthen the system, to make it more effective and efficient. However, they may have a long-range impact, which can lead to basic change. Modernization and rationalization have meant, for instance, that individual performance is properly recognized and awarded. One consequence has been that upward mobility no longer takes place exclusively within the party hierarchy.[53] Indeed, the expert managers, the functional elites from economy, science, and academic institutions, whose skills are in high demand, can afford to ignore the party and still expect to pursue a career as professionals. However, if such a person is ambitious and in search of real political power, he must engage himself politically and ideologically; he must be a committed party member.

The SED under Honecker has been open to new experiences. It has identified what is required for the consolidation of power and acted accordingly. In the process, important new reform measures and policies were adopted. These may have significant long-range consequences; but they have not, as yet, brought about basic changes in the party. It is probably more accurate to refer to them as new tactics and expedients in the pursuit of the established goals. The two fundamental goals are the creation of the "socialist man" and the industrial expansion and economic growth of the DDR. From the SED perspective, these two goals—the first being essentially ideological, the second essentially economic in nature—are interrelated, and each is supportive of the other. Inescapable political and economic necessities led to the adoption of the NES and the subsequent reforms and policy revisions. This has enormously expanded the role of the expert; but it has also created conditions for the commitment of the expert to the prevailing political and ideological positions. The contrast between the dogmatists and the pragmatists has become blurred. The changes this development has wrought, including the substantial changes in the social structure of the SED, have not meant fundamental political changes. The regime itself has directed the efforts to raise the general level of education and training. It has seen to the recruitment and integration of the managerial-technocratic elites. The experts, rising in status, do not question the basic principles. As they have been trained in the DDR, they accept the top leaders and the basic political goals. The political leadership and the experts emerge as partners, not rivals.[54] As experts they are interested in the rational implementation of policies and objectives within the framework of their responsibilities and the given dominant system.

A fundamental change away from totalitarianism would have occurred only if ideological alternatives were tolerated. Thus far, anyone espousing an alternative to Marxism-Leninism is not seen as a mere political rival: he is considered an existential enemy.[55] There have been very few open dissidents, and they all seem to be effectively neutralized or imprisoned. During the sixties, rallying points for some dissent were the universities, notably Humboldt University in Berlin. Here, Prof. Robert Havemann formulated a theory of "dialectics without dogma," advocating reform of the SED to allow internal opposition and constitutional reform to provide for a formal parliamentary opposition. Charged with having advocated an alternative to the existing political order in the DDR, Havemann was expelled from the party, dismissed from his chair in 1964, and had his name struck from the German Academy of Sciences. He succeeded in forming and leading something like a dissident movement, made possible by the protective mantle of extensive publicity in the West. This "protection" did not, of course, cover his followers. More recently—again typically following the lead of the Soviet Union—troublesome dissenters or critics of the regime were forced into exile, as in the case of the noted Marxist songwriter and singer, Wolf Biermann.

The technocrats have been well integrated; their increased role has not led to liberalization. The NES itself has not been brought to full realization. Subsequent measures narrowed the scope and intent of the original design. The leadership reversed some of the steps taken toward decentralization in planning. In the fall of 1965 it was already apparent, also, that policies designed to realize fully the DDR's potential in the world market could not be pursued because of the constraints imposed by COMECON and the renewal of the mutual trade agreement with the Soviet Union. Erich Apel, a principal architect of the NES, committed suicide at that time, and it is alleged that it was caused by his despondency over these developments. The SED is concerned about the technocrats' potential impact on the ideology. To counteract detrimental influences, it strives to keep alive revolutionary values. The young, well-trained functionaries are indoctrinated to be "fighters" who throw all their energies into their occupation, who seek to excel professionally, and who provide exemplary initiative.[56] They do not want to change the system, they want to make it work better. They may be frustrated over the old-style apparatchiks, who in turn are apprehensive about their status. But such rivalries are kept within tolerable bounds and do not seem to represent a danger to the party.

The SED And East German Society

The SED is firmly entrenched in East German society. No area of national life escapes its control. In its practices and general frame of reference it is an archetypical postrevolutionary Communist party.[57] Its outstanding features are rational management of the government and economy, extensive bureaucratization, and acute intolerance of dissent. To further its objectives, the party maintains a huge propaganda apparatus; it has its own newspapers and periodicals and has subjected all radio, television, and other communications media to its control.[58] The party keeps a watchful eye on the Protestant and Catholic churches, which have avoided conflict by steering clear of politics and by not contravening any party objectives. The cultural life of the DDR is, of course, carefully supervised and controlled. The fine arts and literature are considered an integral part of the ideology. Contemporary literature has, on occasion, been effectively coordinated with major party programs, notably in connection with the forced collectivization of agriculture.[59]

No effort is spared to enhance the party and to build socialism. Nevertheless, a large proportion of the population remains unconvinced. It is simply resigned to the rule of the SED. East German attitudes toward the regime reflect more indifference than hostility. A more substantial commitment can be found among young persons. The DDR's youth organization is relatively effective in its indoctrination efforts; it has the highest "socialization potential" among East European youth leagues.[60] But the average citizen doubts the validity of Marxism-Leninism. He is aware of the inconsistencies between theory and practice, and he realizes that socialization has not provided for him the benefits generally enjoyed by West Germans. He resents the incessant indoctrination efforts. But he prefers to conform, for the person who doubts the claims of the party and contests its absolute supremacy forfeits his rights under the socialist system. The shadow of the Gulag Archipelago will accompany him until he falls in line and shows the proper understanding.[61] The people's acquiescence should not, therefore, be interpreted as constituting support for the regime. The DDR is not, as yet, a consolidated and contented society. There is a developing sense of nationhood and a genuine pride in the achievements of the DDR. But for the most part the sentiment seems to be that some great things were accomplished despite communism, not because of it.

Among the genuine achievements of which the DDR can be justly proud is the high degree of social equality and mobility. The educational system is excellent, and there is a wide access to higher education and career advancement. Another achievement, probably the one most often noted with approval, is the relatively high material well-being of the people. The DDR has the highest standard of living in the Communist world. In its quest for legitimacy, the SED regime has had to rely chiefly on economic success. Other states in Eastern Europe could appeal to nationalistic feelings or even experiment with liberalization measures in order to broaden popular support. These means were not available to the SED; the improvement of the material standards of the individual citizen was the only way for the SED to consolidate its domestic position.[62] The party has attempted to augment the factor of economic success with some carefully controlled public participation in societal affairs. However, the fostering of popular involvement in various areas of public life, a process known as "manipulative participation," has enjoyed only limited success.[63]

Nevertheless, the DDR must be considered a viable political and social entity which has made impressive advances. But reform and progress have been of an essentially economic and technological nature. There has been no commensurate ideological adaptation and relaxation.[64] Undoubtedly, the marked improvements in living conditions have gained the regime a somewhat broader acceptance. But this has evidently not reached the stage where the SED can be assured of the people's loyalty. It continues to isolate the East Germans from international life and denies them a freer exchange with West Germany, fearing the possible eroding and unsettling impact of contacts with the West. The SED is conscious of the gap between itself and the general populace. The truth is that the Wall and the death strips cannot be relied upon forever; an eventual reconciliation with the people must be achieved. The recently demonstrated greater political flexibility and the responsiveness to consumer expectations are indicative of an increased effort to bridge the gap.

When Honecker assumed the position of general secretary in 1971, an ambitious social program was launched. It has brought such single improvements as wage and pension increases and the easing of working conditions for mothers. But the complete fulfillment of this program was predicated on the continuation of the economic momentum of the sixties. However, the DDR economy would also be affected by the recession and inflation plaguing most of the world by the mid-seventies. No further impressive growth rates could be registered. The dramatic increase in real income, along with a greater availability of certain consumer commodities which the public had been led to expect, did not materialize. To counter inflation, the SED leadership has promised stable prices. It faces mounting difficulties keeping that promise. Often, steady prices are maintained at the expense of quality and quantity. Shortages in various categories, especially clothing, are becoming more acute. The DDR economy has been facing an ominous deterioration of its terms of trade. From 1970 to 1974, the world market prices for the kind of goods the DDR exports have risen by 65 percent; the prices for the raw materials it must import have risen during this period by 170 percent.[65] The leadership has attempted to match the trade losses through increased productivity. Still, huge deficits were incurred in trade with the West. Thus, no further substantial improvements of the standard of living can be expected in the immediate future. The increases in national income are being absorbed by the price increases for imports.

The first five years of Honecker's leadership were celebrated by the SED's Ninth Party Congress as a period of triumphant achievement. The consolidation of strength and the future success of the regime were seen in the continued improvement of the standard of living, the maintenance of internal political calm, and wide external recognition. In general, the Congress endorsed the continuity of the old policies. However, the leadership was obliged to renege on the 40-hour work week, suggesting that productivity must be significantly raised before it can be uniformly adopted.[66] The economic pressures dictate more cooperation with the West, especially West Germany. The DDR needs trade agreements and credits badly. Generally speaking, Bonn has been ready to accommodate this need. But in return the DDR is expected to make concessions for the easing of human conditions, closer contacts between the people of the two German states, and freer exchanges of ideas and information. The negotiations between West and East Germany have been tough and hard-nosed. Honecker has extracted high prices for the softening of his previous position on the issue of human contacts and exchanges.

As noted earlier, the exposure of East Germany to Western influences is a matter of grave concern and presents a dilemma for the SED. Ever since Bonn's successful Eastern policy initiatives, the SED has been beset by a formidable problem. It has had to be responsible to détente, or it would suffer isolation and economic deterioration. But in responding, the party risked—according to its own assessment—an erosion of its power base. Bonn's Eastern policy was denounced as a device to undermine the regime; strictest demarcation was insisted upon as a precondition for normalized relations between the two German states. But as Honecker endeavored to alleviate the DDR's economic problems and to continue to improve living conditions, as he had promised, he had to relax his posture. During the meetings with West German Chancellor Helmut Schmidt at the culmination of the European Security Conference in Helsinki in July 1975, Honecker gave indication that he would open up. But this flexibility has undermined Honecker's position. Concern about the erosion of the SED regime and an always possible massive Soviet intervention has cast some doubt on Honecker. He seems to be walking a delicate tightrope. Thus far there has been a total unwillingness to tolerate even a modest measure of freedom of thought and criticism. Several open dissidents were expelled to the West. But the notable Marxist regime critic Rudolf Bahro, who sought a Communist alternative, was arrested on charges of spying for West Germany.[67] He has been compared with the Yugoslav Milovan Djilas. His case is indicative of how dangerous the SED leadership considers those critics who dwell on the differences between the practices and the ideals of Marxism-Leninism.

The regime's legal status abroad is fully established, especially since the European Security Conference, which reaffirmed the sovereign existence and territorial integrity of the DDR. But to fully consolidate its rule, much more must be done to increase popular satisfaction at home. The likelihood of another uprising is very remote, as long as the factors behind the uprising of 1953—severe economic deprivation and a high degree of insecurity and organizational weakness within the SED—are not present. Today the SED is strong and self-confident. Thus, even a recurrence of economic hard times is not likely to shake it. It is possible, however, that another ideological crisis, like the de-Stalinization process touched off by the Kremlin in 1956, might occur. Such a development might precipitate fundamental changes, for it would entail the potential emergence of a strong intraparty opposition. Therein lies the promise for a transformation of the SED.

NOTES

1. See Roderich Kulbach and Helmut Weber, *Parteien im Blocksystem der DDR* (Cologne: Wissenschaft und Politik, 1969); and James H.

Wolfe, "Minor Parties in the German Democratic Republic," *East European Quarterly*, 4(1):457–78.

2. U.S. Department of State, Bureau of Intelligence and Research, *World Strength of the Communist Party Organizations*, 25th Annual Report (Washington, D.C.: Government Printing Office, 1973), p. 50.

3. *Statistisches Jahrbuch der DDR 1977* (Berlin: Staatsverlag der DDR, 1977), p. 427. The elections are for 434 seats; the remaining 66 seats are filled by East Berlin members, who are elected by the East Berlin City Assembly. In the 1971 elections, 584 candidates were listed for the 434 seats, providing for the elimination of 150. See Eberhard Schneider, "Die Volksvertretungen in der DDR," *Zeitschrift für Politik* (July 1975), 22(2):183–201.

4. See Rudolf Stöckigt, "Co-operation of the SED and the Other Parties of the National Front," *German Foreign Policy* (1974), 13(2):174–88.

5. On October 7, 1974, coinciding with the twenty-fifth anniversary of the DDR, the law for the revision of the constitution of the DDR was promulgated. All references to the concept of the German nation were eliminated and many important provisions were changed. The changes were so extensive that one may justifiably refer to it as a *new* constitution. See Dietrich Müller-Römer, *Die Neue Verfassung der DDR* (Cologne: Wissenschaft und Politik, 1974).

6. In November 1932 the KPD had over 300,000 members and nearly 6 million voters, placing it third in strength, after the Nazi party (NSDAP) and the SPD. Carola Stern, "East Germany," in William E. Griffith ed., *Communism in Europe* (Cambridge: MIT Press, 1966), vol. 2, p. 54.

7. *Ibid.*, p. 58.

8. The representatives of the German communist underground had next to no influence. With only two exceptions, the 16-member Central Committee was filled by functionaries who had lived in Moscow. See Carola Stern, *Ulbricht: A Political Biography* (New York: Praeger, 1965), pp. 101–4.

9. See Erich W. Gniffke, *Jahre mit Ulbricht* (Cologne: Wissenschaft und Politik, 1966), pp. 95–170.

10. The SED began with 1,298,415 members; 53 percent came from the SPD and 47 percent from the KPD. Carola Stern, *Porträt einer bolschewistischen Partei* (Cologne: Wissenschaft und Politik, 1957), p. 51.

11. Hermann Weber, *Die Sozialistische Einheitspartei Deutschlands 1946–1971* (Hanover: Literatur und Zeitgeschenhen, 1971), p. 11.

12. Stern, "East Germany," p. 67.

13. Stern, *Porträt*, p. 85.

14. Stern, *Ulbricht*, p. 111.

15. In April 1950, membership was down to 1,750,000; in September 1953, it was 1,230,000. Stern, "East Germany," p. 68n.

16. Quoted by Weber, *Die Sozialistische Einheitspartei*, p. 17.

17. See Arnulf Baring, *Uprising in East Germany: June 17,1953* (Ithaca: Cornell University Press, 1972), esp. pp. 89–113.

18. See the Resolution of the Central Committee of the SED of June 21, 1953. *Ibid.*, pp. 160–73.

19. See Stern, *Ulbricht*, pp. 170–72.

20. See Ulbricht's "Ten Commandments of Socialist Morality." Text in John Dornberg, *The Other Germany* (Garden City, N.Y.: Doubleday, 1968), pp. 228–29.

21. About 3.6 to 3.7 million Germans have left the DDR since 1945, according to Ernst Deuerlein, ed., *DDR 1945–1970: Geschichte und Bestandaufnahme* (Munich: Deutscher Taschenbuch Verlag, 1971), pp. 236–37. An additional factor in respect to East German economic losses is the reparations payments extracted by the Soviet Union, which never wavered in her demand for $10 billion at prewar prices. See Heinz Köhler, *Economic Integration in the Soviet Bloc* (New York: Praeger, 1965), pp. 10–43. Estimates of the total economic losses through reparations and refugee outflow run as high as $26,750,000,000. Dornberg, *The Other Germany*, p. 17.

22. Stern, "East Germany," p. 80.

23. Robert W. Dean, *West German Trade with the East* (New York: Praeger, 1974), p. 74.

24. See Hermann Rudolph, *Die Gesellschaft der DDR—eine deutsche Möglichkeit?* (Munich: Piper, 1972).

25. See Walter Ulbricht, *Whither Germany* (Dresden: Zeit im Bild, 1966), esp. pp. 413–22.

26. Bernd Weber, "SED Ideology: Rapprochement and Demarcation," *Aussenpolitik* (1972), 23(1):41–48.

27. For background and subsequent developments see Karl E. Birnbaum, *East and West Germany: A Modus Vivendi* (Lexington, Mass.: D.C. Heath, 1973) and Franz-Christoph Zeitler, "Perspektiven der Folgeverträge mit der DDR," *Zeitschrift für Politik*, (July 1975), 22(2):140–64.

28. Manfred Steinkühler, "Globale und gesamteuropäische KP-Konferenz," *Aussenpolitik* (1975), (2):169.

29. Kurt Hager, "The Rout of Hitler Fascism and the Formation of two German States," *International Affairs*, 1975, no. 6 (June), p. 12.

30. See Eberhard Schulz and Hans Dieter Schulz, *Braucht der Osten die DDR?* (Opladen: Laske, 1968).

31. Rüdiger Thomas, *Modell DDR* (Munich: Hanser, 1977), p. 30.

32. Of these, the Central Party Control Commission is especially noteworthy. It is charged with maintaining "purity" and unity among party ranks. In seeking out and eliminating internal opposition and deviation, it has full disciplinary powers over all party members without accountability to other organs. Equivalent control commissions operate on the district and county levels. Joachim Schultz, *Der Funktionär in der Einheitspartei* (Stuttgart: Ring, 1956), p. 17.

33. Peter Christian Ludz, *The German Democratic Republic From the Sixties to the Seventies* (Cambridge: Harvard University Press, 1970), p. 33. For a detailed survey of the Central Committee apparatus see Stern, *Porträt*, pp. 338–56.

34. Stern, *Porträt*, p. 278.

35. Eckart Förtsch, *Die SED* (Stuttgart: W. Kohlhammer Verlag, 1969), pp. 49–50.

36. Schultz, *Der Funktionär*, p. 12.

37. Thomas, *Modell DDR*, p. 30.

38. Ludz, *The German Democratic Republic*, p. 34.

39. Kurt Sontheimer and Wilhelm Bleek, *Die DDR: Politik, Gesellschaft, Wirtschaft* (Hamburg: Hoffmann und Campe, 1972), pp. 88.

40. SED, *Directive of the VIII. Party Congress of the SED for the Development of the National Economy of the DDR for the Period 1971–1975* (Dresden: Zeit im Bild, 1971), pp. 20–25.

41. Ludz, *The German Democratic Republic*, p. 38.

42. *Ibid.*, p. 39.

43. Richard Herber and Herbert Jung, *Kaderarbeit im System sozialistischer Führungstätigkeit* (Berlin: Staatsverlag der DDR, 1968), pp. 45–112.

44. Peter Christian Ludz, *Parteielite im Wandel* (Cologne: Westdeutscher, 1968), pp. 163–223.

45. *Ibid.*, p. 183.

46. *Ibid.*, p. 55.

47. *Ibid.*, p. 258.

48. See Heinz Lippmann, *Honecker and the New Politics of Europe* (New York: Macmillan, 1972).

49. *Europa Year Book 1977;* Günter Buch, ed., *Namen und Daten: Biographien wichtiger Personen der DDR* (Berlin: Dietz, 1973); and Thomas, *Modell DDR*, pp. 294 and 351–61.

50. SED, *Protokoll der Verhandlungen des VIII. Parteitages der Sozialistischen Einheitspartei Deutschlands*, (Berlin: Dietz, 1971), p. 255.

51. See *Der Spiegel*, January 16, 1978, pp. 21–27.

52. DDR: Das Manifest der Opposition (Munich: Goldmann Verlag, 1978). First published in *Der Spiegel*, January 2 and 9, 1978.

53. Ludz, *The German Democratic Republic*, pp. 40–45. Ludz has studied representative careers of Politburo members; the typical advancement patterns include (1) advancement solely within the SED, (2) advancement solely within the state apparatus, (3) advancement first in the party and then in the state apparatus, and (4) advancement first in the state apparatus and then in the party.

54. Förtsch, *Die SED*, pp. 124–25.

55. *Ibid.*, pp. 9–17.

56. *Ibid.*, p. 125.

57. Robert G. Livingston, "East Germany Between Moscow and Bonn," *Foreign Affairs* (January 1972), pp. 301–2.

58. See Burton Paulu, *Radio and Television Broadcasting in Eastern Europe* (Minneapolis: University of Minnesota Press, 1974), ch. 6.

59. See the massive compilation of documents regarding the SED's cultural policies by Elimar Schubbe (ed.), *Dokumente zur Kunst-, Literatur- und Kulturpolitik der SED* (Stuttgart: Seewald, 1972).

60. Ivan Volgyes, "Political Socialization in Eastern Europe," *Problems of Communism* (January-February 1974), pp. 46–55.

61. Manfred Spieker, "Mensch und Gesellschaft im Sozialismus," *Politische Studien*, no. 221 (May–June 1975), p. 273.

62. Birnbaum, *East and West Germany*, p. 54.

63. Thomas A. Baylis, "In Quest of Legitimacy," *Problems of Communism* (March–April 1972), pp. 46–55.

64. Peter Christian Ludz, *Deutschlands doppelte Zukunft* (Munich: Hanser, 1974), p. 91.

65. *Die Zeit* (Hamburg), September 19, 1975, p. 8.

66. Erich Honecker, "Current Aspects of our Domestic and Foreign Policy after the 9th Party Congress," *Panorama DDR*, no. 5 (1976).

67. See Rudolf Bahro, *Die Alternative: Zur Kritik des real existierenden Sozialismus* (Cologne: Europäische Verlagsanstalt, 1977).

Selected Bibliography

Baring, Arnulf. *Uprising in East Germany: June 17, 1953*. Ithaca: Cornell University Press, 1972.

An excellent analysis of the riots, strikes, and massive public demonstrations challenging the SED regime. Included are the SED version of the events and many relevant documents.

Deuerlein, Ernst, ed. *DDR 1945–1970: Geschichte und Bestandaufnahme*. Munich: Deutscher Taschenbuch, 1971.

A useful compilation of documents pertaining to the DDR political system and major policy decisions of the SED.

Förtsch, Eckart. *Die SED*. Stuttgart: W. Kohlhammer, 1969.

A detailed anlysis of the internal development and structure of the SED. A focal point is the SED's perception of its role in highly industrialized East German society. The heuristic model is that of a totalitarian party.

Gniffke, Erich W. *Jahre mit Ulbricht*. Cologne: Wissenschaft and Politik, 1966.

A former SPD member writes about his experiences in the first Central Committee of the SED. Of particular interest is his account of the unification of the SPD and KPD.

Lippmann, Heinz. *Honecker and the New politics of Europe*. New York: Macmillan, 1972.

A sympathetic political biography of Erich Honecker.

Ludz, Peter Christian. *Parteielite im Wandel*. Cologne: Westdeutscher, 1968.

An empirical study of the SED Central Committee membership, focusing on the transformation of the social structure of the party leadership and its impact on the party in general. Available in English under the title, *Changing Party Elite in East Germany*. Cambridge: MIT Press, 1972.

Ludz, Peter Christian. *The German Democratic Republic From the Sixties to the Seventies.* Cambridge: Harvard University Press, 1970.

An analysis of social and political change in the DDR. It is drawn from a series of lectures given in a seminar of the German Research Program 1968, at Harvard. It incorporates the findings of his earlier study of the SED elite.

Rudolph, Hermann. *Die Gesellschaft der DDR–eine deutsche Möglichkeit?* Munich: Piper, 1972.

An interesting case study of the possibilities and limitations of political indoctrination. It concludes that society has not been transformed by the SED to the point where it is fully supportive of the regime.

Schultz, Joachim. *Der Funktionär in der Einheitspartei.* Stuttgart: Ring, 1956.

A valuable early study of the SED's policies respecting cadres and its bureaucratization.

SED. *Programm der Sozialistischen Einheitspartei Deutschlands.* Berlin: Dietz, 1976.

The complete official platform of the SED, as unanimously adopted by the Ninth Party Congress in May 1976.

Sontheimer, Kurt and Wilhelm Bleek. *Die DDR: Politik, Gesellschaft, Wirtschaft.* Hamburg: Hoffmann and Campe, 1972.

A helpful survey of the DDR in general, including a chapter on the SED. An English version appeared under the title, *The Government and Politics of East Germany.* New York: St. Martin's Press, 1975.

Stern, Carola. *Porträt einer bolschewistischen Partei.* Cologne: Wissenschaft and Politik, 1957.

The first comprehensive study by a widely recognized authority of the development and functioning of the SED. Although dated in many respects, it is still very informative and useful.

Stern, Carola. *Ulbricht: A Political Biography.* New York: Praeger, 1965.

Inasmuch as the history of the SED is the story of Walter Ulbricht, this biography includes important material for the study of the SED.

Stern, Carola. "East Germany." In William E. Griffith, ed. *Communism in Europe*, vol. 2. Cambridge: MIT Press, 1966.

Good background material on the history and policies of the SED from 1945–65. A particular emphasis is placed on the relations between the DDR and the People's Republic of China.

Thomas, Rüdiger. *Modell DDR.* Munich: Hanser, 1977.

A handbook full of facts, figures, and documents on the political system, the economy, foreign policy, education, and culture of the DDR.

Weber, Hermann. *Die Sozialistische Einheitspartei Deutschlands 1946–1971.* Hanover: Verlag Für Literatur und Zeitgeschen, 1971.

A good general study of the history and politics of the SED.

Miklós Molnár

5. The Communist Party of Hungary

Only a tiny proportion of the Communist militants who had spent the war years in the USSR returned to Hungary in 1945; the Stalinist purges had decimated their ranks more than the police and the courts of the Horthy regime had. Some of them went back to Hungary by parachute. In fact, a handful of courageous militants came back to form guerrilla units behind the German lines. Among the many who perished were Richard Rózsa and György Kilián. Others survived, such as Zoltán Fodor and Sándor Nógrádi. Another group of Hungarians came back in the ranks of the Soviet army and its services: the writer Béla Illés, a colonel; and the editorial staff of *Uj Szó* (New Word), the Hungarian paper of the Soviet Army. The political leaders returned in several waves, the first of which included Ernö Gerö, József Révai, Mihály Farkas, and Imre Nagy. Mátyás Rákosi himself came back only in 1945, followed by others.

By whom and how was this general staff formed? After he returned to the USSR from the prisons of Horthy, Rákosi was recognized as leader of the Hungarian faction of Moscow, and he kept his important post with the personal assent of Stalin, perhaps even under his command. But Ernö Gerö, an old hand of the Comintern and probably of the secret service, also had solid connections. According to certain rumors, he had as much power as Mátyás Rákosi, the top-ranking official, if not more. Mihály Farkas was probably promoted by the influential circles of the Komsomol, and Imre Nagy, it appears, had free access to Molotov. Apart from the struggles for influence, which organ or what person chose this staff and solved the delicate question of hierarchy? Documents we have do not tell us.

In any case, the four from Moscow who arrived first set themselves up as a Provisional Central Committee as early as November 5, 1944, in Szeged. They moved to Debrecen in December and remained there until March 1945. In the meantime, on January 19, another Central Committee had been formed in Budapest by Antal Apró, Bertalan Barta, Márton, Horváth, János Kádár, Gyula Kállai, Károly Kiss, István Kossa, István Kovács, Gábór Peter, and Zoltán Vas. With the exception of Vas, they all were militants from within Hungary who were coming out of hiding. The secretary of the HCP, László Rajk, who had been arrested in December 1944, was still in prison. The two Central Committees united on February 23, and Rákosi became the secretary of the new committee.

The number of members belonging to the Hungarian Communist Party (HCP) after it emerged from the underground is uncertain: 3,000, according to a speech by Rákosi; a hundred or less, according to others. The membership certainly increased with an incredible speed. At the end of 1945, the HCP already had 500,000 members. But its real strength lay elsewhere, in Soviet power, i.e., in the Red Army and in the international political authority of the Allied Control Commission, presided over by Marshal Voroshilov. The HCP, however weak it was numerically, was the agent of this immense power. But it would be a serious error to underestimate other elements, namely the force of the organization, propaganda, and operation of the HCP itself. It was the only political party that knew what it wanted, that had a program, an ideology, and a model of organization and operation. In the general confusion of the period, these could only be assets.

From 1945 to 1947, even to the beginning of 1948, the HCP, like the other Communist parties of Central and Eastern Europe, followed a popular front policy and took part in a governmental coalition composed of four democratic parties. The HCP held three ministerial posts. In subsequent administrations, it had five, in addition to the chairmanship of the High Council for Economics. Its internal history was marked by the National Conference of May 20, 1945, and later by the Third

Congress of the party which was held from September 28 to October 1, 1946, under the banner of the struggle against the reaction—which meant against the troublesome elements of the other parties in the governmental coalition, including the Social Democratic party. From 1947, the unification of the two parties was on the agenda, despite opposition from most socialist leaders.

Incapable of resisting the HCP's pressure, the Social Democratic party (SDP) eventually yielded. Its so-called rightist leaders resigned. On June 12, 1948, the congresses of the two parties agreed to the union. On the same day they met in a united congress. The new party was formed, and until the events of 1956 it carried the name of Magyar Dolgozók Pártja, the Hungarian Workers' party (MDP).

Until the unification of the two parties, the direction of the HCP had changed little from its composition in 1945, except that part of the 1945 Central Committee constituted itself in 1946 as a Politburo of nine members, while the others remained members of an enlarged Central Committee. In the Politburo, elected at the close of the Third Congress of the HCP, the Moscow group held five positions out of nine; it also dominated the General Secretariat as well as the Committee for Organization charged with directing the apparatus. In fact, it was not the entire Moscow team, but the quadrumvirate of Rákosi-Gerö-Révai-Farkas that controlled the party—with the help of a dedicated and strictly led apparatus.

In the unified party, a few former so-called leftist Social Democrats held a certain number of high posts, but the principles of organization and the true power hierarchy remained unchanged.

Practically alone in the possession of power, the HCP shifted toward openly Stalinist policies from the beginning of 1948. Nationalizations, projects for forced industrialization, the beginnings of agricultural collectivization, massive purges and arrests, the *Gleichschaltung* of intellectuals—we see the same characteristics in Hungary as in the other people's democracies. Hungary, too, became a people's democracy. The political turn went hand in hand with an ideological reinterpretation of the new society and the new state. The issue no longer was, as before, to construct a "new democracy," but rather to construct a "people's democracy," erecting socialism with the help of the dictatorship of the proletariat and its vanguard, the Communist party. One year later, in 1949, when nearly all the former leftist socialist leaders who had adhered to the unified party had already rejoined the former leaders of the democratic parties in the prisons or in the cemeteries, those Communists who were judged dangerous or cumbersome began to be eliminated. The Rajk trial of October 1949 opened a long period of liquidations within the HCP itself.

After Stalin's death, the HCP again went through a period that, in more than one respect, distinguished it from the other Communist parties. In June 1953, the HCP leaders were summoned to Moscow in the company of one of their disgraced comrades, Imre Nagy. The Hungarian delegation was received in the Kremlin by the complete Soviet Party Presidium: Beria, Khrushchev, Malenkov, Mikoyan, Molotov. This was the collapse of the whole system that Rákosi and his companions had constructed. The Soviet comrades heaped criticism on those who were most responsible for Stalinist policies and compelled them to "correct their mistakes" in every respect and to share power with Imre Nagy. Rákosi kept his post as secretary general of the party, but Nagy took his place at the head of the government.

Thus the era of reforms began. It was marked by the amelioration of the economic and political situation in the country, by the release of thousands of political prisoners, and by the relentless fight between the Stalinist faction and the liberal faction led by Nagy. Eighteen months later, in the spring of 1955, Nagy was relieved of his duties, sweeping away with his fall the politics of reform as well as a great number of his collaborators. This neo-Stalinist interlude was not to last. After the Twentieth Congress of the Soviet Communist party, the liberal wing of the party slowly regained ascendancy at the same time that unrest was increasing among the population. The October events in Poland were the catalyst. On October 23, 1956, Budapest experienced the greatest mass demonstration in its history. During the night, arms reigned supreme. The battle raged for six days. In the meantime, Gerö, who had replaced Rákosi the preceding June, in turn yielded his post to János Kádár. Imre Nagy, suddenly reinstated in the Politburo of the party, was again appointed president of the Council of Ministers. During the truce of barely six days, Nagy reestablished the former governmental coalition with the democratic parties, won over the insurgents to his program, restored order, and negotiated the retreat of the Soviet troops. But after these few days of precarious independence, the Soviet tanks again moved out to attack the capital. The desperate resistance of a few thousand insurgents and of some units of the Hungarian army could not stop them. The Soviet intervention of November 4 marked the end of the revolution.

The HCP, as an organization, vanished in the first hours of combat on the night of October 23. Of its powerful apparatus, only a few officials remained, barricaded behind the doors of the Central Committee headquarters, which was guarded by Soviet tanks. It was the same in the provinces. Once more, the HCP was dissolved, and from its ashes a new Communist party was formed: the Magyar Szocialista Munkáspárt, the Hungarian Socialist Workers' party (MSzMP), a name it still retains today. The new party, under Kádár, would have great difficulties in imposing itself as the sole governing party, as the repository of socialism and the national destiny.

The initial decrease in the number of adherents was a consequence of yet other difficulties. The party had lost its credit and its authority not only with the great majority of the population, but also among its former members. Besides, Kádár and his team inspired little confidence among the former Stalinists and even less among the partisans of Imre Nagy, who felt betrayed. However, the main body of the apparatus resumed its place, with some new departmental heads here and there.

A popular personality in spite of the role he played in November 1956, the architect of a new liberal policy, and a skillful politician, Kádár has until now survived, but at the price, it appears, of numerous concessions. Since 1972, the HCP has had to curb the development of the "new economic mechanism" and restrict cultural liberties. A group of sociologists, headed by Rákosi's former prime minister, András Hegedüs, was dismissed; writers were reprimanded and, for the first time in almost fifteen years, arraigned in court.

The Eleventh Party Congress, which met from March 17 to 22, 1975, and the policy pursued since this date, finally dissipated these fears. Still, a muffled opposition to the Kádár policy expressed itself during this Congress, and it is probable that some of the potential leaders of a harder line might have speculated on his fall.

Owing to its economic achievements, Hungary has become, after East Germany, the most prosperous socialist country and has a more or less satisfied population. Its system of agriculture is unique in Eastern Europe: collective agriculture no longer encounters peasant opposition, and owing to the extraordinary flourishing of the Hungarian kolkhozes, there is enough food on the market. All this produces a relatively serene political climate, unlike that of all the other countries of the socialist bloc. If Kádár were disavowed or, even worse, removed from his functions, it would be tantamount to the disavowal of the only somewhat successful Communist experiment.

THE ROLE AND ORGANIZATION OF THE PARTY

Status

The strength of the HCP has never been its popularity among the voters. After it came to power in 1919, general elections with secret ballots and universal suffrage were held. Even at that time, however, single lists were used. Consequently, the official lists prevailed without difficulty. Thus Hungary elected its councils, or soviets, at all the lower levels: villages, towns, precincts, and districts. The local councils then elected delegates to the councils of the counties and of the major cities, which in turn sent their delegates to the National Assembly of Councils, the "parliament" of the dictatorship of the proletariat. For the next quarter of a century, the minuscule, illegal HCP did not think for a moment of appealing to the voters—except to dissuade them from voting Social Democratic. The attempts of the crypto-Communist MSzMP to stand in elections failed.

In 1945, for the first and only time in its history, the HCP participated in free elections: municipal elections in October, general elections in November. In the first, Communists and Socialists presented single lists and carried off 43 percent of the vote in Budapest. In the second, held in the whole country and on separate lists, the Communists got 17.4 percent of the votes, the Social Democrats nearly as many. The big winner, the party of the Smallholders, won convincingly with more than 57 percent of the votes. The votes obtained by the party of the Smallholders included the specific votes for the party—as a member of the governmental coalition—as well as those of the opposition, which could express itself only by voting neither Communist nor Socialist. In 1947, Communist electoral tactics were to admit other political parties to the elections precisely in order to divide the enormous bloc of the Smallholders.

These facts have a certain importance: they provide the only way to measure the electoral influence of the HCP in the new Hungary, one year after its emergence from the underground. They show an influence certainly not negligible, but extremely limited. All things considered, the result of the 1945 elections probably reflected the real relation of political forces: the HCP was at the head of the medium-sized parties, but it was far from having a truly national audience. It represented certain social categories and groups more than it did vast social classes; that is, it represented a part of the urban proletariat (but a smaller part than the SDP represented), the poor peasantry of certain traditionally radical regions, and finally, an important part of the Jewish electorate. Of the 800,000 votes it obtained, less than a quarter came from Budapest, which illustrates at once the HCP's weakness in the only great workers' stronghold, the capital, and its relative popularity in the provinces.

The elections after 1945 do not allow us to draw any conclusions. Already in 1947 they were not entirely falsified, but they were distorted by the use of "blue" ballots, enabling a certain number of Communist voters—carefully selected—to vote twice. In the end, the HCP benefited little by this, because the fraud produced very few additional votes but in turn deprived the HCP of an important part of the credit and the confidence that it had previously held. After this date, Hungary has had only fictitious elections bearing no relation whatsoever to public opinion.

What then is the HCP? It is impossible to define its "status" according to the norms and notions of Western political science. The last indications about its electoral bases date from thirty years ago. It is not a revolutionary party: on the one hand, it is the sole holder of power, and on the other hand, its organization, its roots, and its operation are highly bureaucratic. From the sociocultural point of view, it is likewise impossible to define it with precision. Is it really a party of the proletariat, as ideological tradition has it? It has never been such in the past, and nothing indicates that its recent evolution has made it the authentic representative of a working class that is utterly different from the prewar proletariat. The HCP's constant concern to justify itself at least by means of a preponderance of workers among its followers continues to clash with this indifference—or with this dissatisfaction—even today, as its social composition shows. Does it exist, then, primarily for the sake of the party apparatus itself? Does it attempt to conduct state affairs as best it can to the extent that circumstances permit? Until we have more information with which to work, we have to be content with this summary definition.

At no time in its history has the HCP been tolerated. Even in the brief period between its formation in November 1918 and its accession to power in March 1919, it suffered from acts of intolerance, even repression. The HCP had never had any alternative other than illegality or power. Its political aspirations certainly changed according to circumstances, but even when it supported antifascist tendencies, as between 1941 and 1944, or "advanced" democratic tendencies, as between 1945 and 1948, its fundamental aspiration remained the same: power, either undivided or partial.

Membership

At its lowest ebb, the HCP had no more than several hundred adherents. This was true in the mid-twenties, when repression had practically annihilated its organizations. It was true in 1936, when the Comintern dissolved the party. It was true, finally, after the successive losses of the 1940s, before the end of the war. The 3,000 members at the end of 1944 given in the official history of the HCP is a maximum estimate and cannot be relied upon. But even if this estimate were accurate, the HCP would remain an entirely insignificant party from the point of view of its membership while underground: 0.05 percent of the adult population.

At its highest level, before the influx of the Social Democrats, the party had 743,836 members (August 1947). In the summer of 1948, just before the unification, it had 887,472 members (the already emaciated SDP then numbered 240,658). Finally, the unified party (the MDP) had 1,128,130 members, that is, 12 percent of the entire population of Hungary. The HCP then undertook a vast review of its membership, which resulted in 179,000 exclusions, to which must be added some 130,000 who had failed to present themselves to the review commission. More than 100,000 of those admitted were at the same time qualified as candidates. In all, 756,588 persons were admitted as full members and 124,156 as candidates—a total of 880,744.[1] According to the same official sources, between the reviews of the summer of 1948 and the fall of 1950, the unified HCP recorded another decrease of about 70,000 members, due, besides deaths, to new exclusions as well as to the fact that a certain number of admitted members and candidates (about 30,000) had not presented themselves to pick up their membership books.[2] After all these fluctuations, the membership has become stable at around 850,000–900,000 members and candidates.

After the HCP almost disappeared during the revolution of 1956, its membership increased abruptly between 1957 and 1959. Thereafter, the rate of increase was slower. The exclusions, which were rare before 1948, became massive (178,850) when the unified party was "purified" in 1949. Between 1948 and 1956, more than 350,000 members were excluded from the party, some 40,000 between 1954 and 1956. There have been relatively few exclusions in the new Communist party, the MSzMP.

Since Hungary has about 10.5 million inhabitants, it is easy to calculate the percentages: 1–12 percent (with an average of 6–8 percent) of the entire population belonged to the HCP in power, as opposed to 0.05 percent in the darkest underground years before the war.

In 1948, in order to overcome the inherent disadvantages of a mass party, the HCP introduced a special category of members, that of activists called "party workers." Their number reached 106,859 in 1948, 20 percent of whom were women, according to the registers; but according to another estimate, their actual number amounted to some 125,000. This corresponded roughly to the party apparatus with its paid officials plus a certain number of Communist activists who worked for the state: army officers, company directors, presidents of cooperatives. The category of activist (provided with a special card) was eventually abolished. There remained the apparatus proper, comprising the officials of the Central Committee as well as of the committees of the towns, of the counties, of the districts, and of the large companies. At its zenith, the MDP numbered some 20,000 organizations. It is impossible to draw conclusions from this concerning the number of paid officials. All the secretaries of cells are not "independent" officials, that is, paid by the party. In the small factory or neighborhood cells, the members of the bureau are, in general, workers who perform their function in the party organization as volunteers. Besides, the party requires its members to do a certain amount of "social work" voluntarily. The paid officials are destined for the more important organizations at the level of the precincts in cities, at the level of the municipal administration in the villages, and at the level of the ministries in the state apparatus. The greatest concentration of paid officials is found, except for the central apparatus, at the middle level, i.e., in the county committees and the large cities. The apparatus of the Budapest committee, for example, has always been a kind of second municipality. Many officials of the HCP are also destined for propaganda work and especially for the party schools. They collectively constitute "the apparatus," that is, the army of paid officials, the "permanents." In order to measure, if only by approximation, the numerical importance of this army, it is necessary, however, to take into account the "false" volunteer activists: secretaries of middle-level organizations (cells) who are carried on the payroll of their respective companies but who work practically full-time for the party. Thus about one Communist in seven or eight is probably a party official.

The age groups of members differ from one period to the next, and the facts are not available for all periods. In 1948, before unification with the SDP, 18.9 percent of the members were under 24, 63.3 percent were between 24 and 50, and the rest—roughly 18 percent—were older. Except for some minor fluctuations, these proportions have hardly changed. But the tendency is now toward rejuvenation. Among the 200,000 new members admitted between 1970 and 1975, 44.1 percent are under 26, 44.9 percent between 27 and 39, that is, 178,000 members on the whole, as compared to 12,000 members of more than 40 years of age.

The MDP, under the direction of Rákosi, emphasized the adherence of women to the party. In fact, in 1948, 30 percent of the members were women, which probably represents a world record not only in the Communist movement but also in the life of political parties in general. The MSzMP has had to be content with less: women make up only 26 percent of its membership. This decrease corresponded to a certain political "demobilization" of women who had returned to their homes since 1956.

Above all a workers' party and the repository of the dictatorship of the proletariat, the HCP always made great efforts to form a solid foundation among the working class. In 1919, its foundation was the social agitation that reigned in Hungary as in the rest of Europe. By that date it had merged with the SDP, which brought all the unionized workers with it. During the long period of its illegality, between 1919 and 1945, it was among the workers of the large factories that the HCP obtained certain successes.

Immediately after the war, the HCP gained much ground at the expense of the SDP. Certainly, part of this increase resulted from successive mergers with the HCP; another part resulted from the increase in the total number of workers. Nevertheless, the Social Democratic factor was indeed becoming weaker, though it was still powerful.

There is another significant point: in the purges after the unification of the two parties, an astonishingly high number of workers were excluded from the party—51,600, no less than 28.8 percent of all those excluded. More than 50,000 others were demoted to candidates.

The result was a paradoxical situation. The HCP before unification counted 34.7 percent factory workers and 6.6 percent agricultural workers; the unified HCP-MDP counted slightly less.

The statistics given in HCP publications show a strong proportional increase (59.2 percent) of worker members for the years 1950–53. In reality, however, those numbers were calculated by taking into consideration not only the professions that the counted members actually practiced, but also their social origins. The Communist worker who had become a minister of state or a general carried the same statistical value as a former minister or a general turned worker. Owing to statistical checking, these official sources eventually admitted that by taking into account only the professional distribution, the proportion of workers, instead of growing, actually diminished in the party:

41.2 percent in 1951, 40 percent in 1952, 38 percent in 1953, 38.6 percent in 1954, 37.4 percent in 1955, and 37.3 percent in 1956.

The massive promotion of former workers to administrative posts and directorships (party, state, army, police, companies) was not solely responsible for this. The decline in the standard of living, the rise in work norms, an oppressive political climate, and disillusion and discouragement also played a role in it.

The HCP, reorganized after the events of 1956, seems to have shown a rather strong increase in the proportion of the miscellaneous categories, employees, peasants, and others, at the expense of the worker element. It was 6–8 percent of the membership of the MDP before 1956 and has remained 18–20 percent of the members of the MSzMP, without significant change, from 1957 until today. This rise is partially explained by the adoption of new census methods that are closer to reality.

The proportion of peasants is 14–15 percent according to social origin, about 12 percent according to profession in the years 1950–53, and about 10.5 percent between 1954 and 1956—a percentage that further decreases slightly in the following years. From 29.5 percent in 1957, the proportion of workers increased to 34.6 in 1962 (177,315) and 35.1 percent in 1966 (204,731). Workers and peasants together represented 46.8 percent in 1970 and 45.5 percent in 1975.

The MSzMP has separately enumerated its members serving in the armed forces, retired people, and other miscellaneous categories, groups which previously had been disguised in the statistics under more general headings.

As has always been the case, the category of employees, along with the workers, constitutes the main body of HCP membership: 34–39 percent in the 1950s, 28.7 percent in 1962, 26.1 percent in 1966—a progressive decrease probably due to changes in the statistical headings as well as to withdrawals.

The available facts concerning the composition of the HCP according to age, profession, and social composition are incomplete and contradictory. They are also based on changing and imprecise criteria. What becomes evident is the tendency toward aging and at the same time the decreasing proportion of manual workers and peasants. Party officials, officers, retired persons, intellectuals, and the undefined miscellaneous categories constitute by far the majority of the membership: about 60 percent. The aging of the party cadres may be natural, given the factors that have contributed to it, but there are political factors here, as well. That is, they are a matter of policy, much like the massive promotion of Communist workers to administrative posts and directorships.

Certainly, the present HCP, with its some 700,000 members, again resembles the party before 1956 more than it does the MSzMP of the first years after its reorganization. Purely existential motives must, therefore, have brought it a certain proportion of its present adherents. Nevertheless, the HCP-MSzMP is based on an important core of members who are devoted to its cause and who support it to a man. The relations between the leadership of the party and the mass of its members seem more intimate and closer than under Rákosi's Stalinist regime. At the same time, loyalty to the leadership requires less constraint today than previously. A Hungarian Communist expresses himself more freely now than twenty years ago; he does not feel followed and watched even in his private life, and he allows himself a life-style that conforms to his personal tastes. To be sure, standards remain strict. But disciplinary punishments—to the point of exclusion in serious cases—also reflect a certain laxity, which the Communists of Rákosi's era avoided lest even more draconian measures be imposed.

Structure and Leadership

Apart from a few minor differences, the HCP is based on structures that are identical to those of other Communist parties in power: basic cells in companies, administrative units, institutions, villages, or neighborhoods. The cells are part of broader territorial organizations, which are themselves placed under the authority of county committees in the provinces and city committees in urban areas. With the exception of the neighborhood or village cells, the basic organizations are found at the place of work; on the higher levels, though, the distribution is territorial and geographic. The basic organizations, in the factories of Budapest, for instance, are placed under the authority of provinces; the county committees are responsible for all the party organizations in their respective administrative units.

With the exception of political and electoral campaigns, demonstrations, and the like, the neighborhood cells have had neither great importance nor many tasks to fulfill. The cells in factories, ministries, and companies have had more, since they exercise a "leadership" function—always poorly defined—in the conduct of affairs at the institution itself: production, work discipline, salaries, moral climate, political information and propaganda. They have an identical role in the local union organizations as well as in the so-called mass transmission organizations, such as the councils of women and cultural organizations. The Young Communists, although they have a certain autonomy, also work under the direction of the party organization.

The committees of five major cities and of the nineteen counties enjoy true political autonomy and power. Yet they, too, are subordinate to the Central Committee, the superior party organ between congresses. At times, especially from 1945 to 1953, the autonomy of the provincial committees alarmed even the central leadership. Certain county secretaries played the role of the petty prince, behaving as if they were new nobles and allowing themselves to take no notice of the instructions sent out by the Central Committee. Today, this problem seems resolved, but the decision-making power of the city and county committees remains rather important with respect to local affairs.

The real political power is concentrated in the hands of the Central Committee and its apparatus, which is divided into departments (economy, propaganda, etc.). Elected by the Party Congress, which convenes every four years, the Central Committee is theoretically the embodiment of all members of the party and the executor of their collective will. In practice, however, it is something else again.

At present, the delegates are elected to the Congress according to the rules in effect since 1966. The Central Committee determines the number of delegates, and the conferences of the nineteen counties and the Budapest conference elect them. According to custom, the delegates are elected from lists presented by the territorial committee. Theoretically, the "great electors," assembled in conference, are free to modify the list, even to reject it and choose other candidates. In practice, however, they simply approve the list. Under these conditions, the mass of the members has no influence whatsoever on the composition of the congress.

The delegates thus assembled every four years as the general Party Congress amount to some 500–600 persons, selected according to a clever formula for age, sex, seniority, and geographical, social, and professional distribution. The party congress is essentially a voting machine. It passes everything the leadership proposes: program regulations, special resolutions, and, lastly, the new central committee. Consequently, the election of the latter is a matter of routine. The list is established in advance by the Politburo and the Central Secretariat and is approved by an ad hoc Bureau for Candidacies. The voting is done without challenges. The official candidates are all elected, without exception. Whatever conflicts there might be among tendencies, clienteles, or persons—they do exist, all the same—take place behind the scenes, never in front of the congress, never in public. Those in power have, with the help of this system, a whole series of safety valves. They control the selection process at all levels. From the delegates of the conferences to the delegates to the congress, all electors are carefully selected, and at the same time, owing to the system of official lists, any surprise is practically eliminated in advance. Divergences from the wishes of the leading group—to say nothing of reversals—can only occur in two ways: either with the help of a genuine revolution within the party or with "help" from abroad. The first has only happened once: in the summer of 1956, four months before the revolution, the discontent of the "base" forced the Central Committee to get rid of Rákosi with, it is true, the assent of the

Kremlin. The second has been more frequent. In 1953–54, for example, first the Politburo and then the Central Committee were rather profoundly reorganized on the pressing "recommendations" of the Presidium of the Soviet Communist party, anxious to weaken the preponderant influence of Rákosi's group.

Apart from this kind of reorganization, the team in power is sole master of the situation. It never relinquishes its power, which, in principle, it exercises by delegation, and it is jealously on the watch to ensure that the statutory renewal of the Central Committee by the Congress—theoretically the highest organ—is done according to what has been decided in advance.

Thus elected by the Congress, the Central Committee in turn elects its Politburo as well as the members of the other central organs: the Secretariat, commissions for propaganda, economy, and the like. In the 1950s, the members of the Organization Bureau (which no longer exists) were also nominated by the Central Committee; in contrast, the department heads of the party apparatus, who previously were simply appointed, are now elected by the Central Committee.

It would be easy to spell out these procedures in detail. But it is more difficult to answer the fundamental question of what is the actual power of the Central Committee. In theory, it is and has always been the party's highest decision-making organ between Congresses. In reality, since the party came out of the underground, the Central Committee has never held the power nor played the role that the party constitution gives it. Since 1945, the Politburo has monopolized the seat of power, and the Central Committee has confined itself to approving the Politburo's decisions.

This situation has subtly changed since 1953. Even if certain political adjustments and personal changes were imposed by Moscow, the Central Committee has become a battleground for fights over different views and has thereby assumed a certain importance.

Certainly the Central Committee's inclinations toward independence have never had an altogether autonomous character. Moscow has always had a hand in it. On the other hand, the

Central Committee expresses primarily the climate of opinion that reigns among the apparatus. The Central Committee has about twenty-five ministers and deputy ministers, as many if not more high party functionaries, about twenty other high state and company officials, roughly fifteen officials from unions and other mass organizations, and about ten workers and intellectuals. It is, then, a body representing essentially the three great bureaucracies: the party, the state, and the mass organizations. It is not surprising that the Central Committee is sensitive to the mood of the apparatus and that it tries to make the latter's opinion prevail.

On the other hand, however, the Politburo is in a position to control all these bodies, as well as the Central Committee itself. It relies essentially upon the same party apparatus, which occupies a predominant place in the Central Committee and which, through the subtle play of the hierarchies, also dominates the state and union bureaucracies.

One can affirm, without great risk of being wrong, that—as opposed to the Party Congress, which practically never exercises its authority—the Central Committee can play an almost autonomous leading role, but only under extraordinary circumstances. But in "normal" times, and as long as it fulfills "heaven's mandate," the leading team of the party unquestionably has the real decison-making power.

Have the modifications and the personal rearrangements that occurred after 1953 really changed the power structures within the HCP? As for the Politburo and the Secretariat, they seem to have acquired—just as the Central Committee did—greater authority between 1953 and 1956. The partial retreat of Rákosi's group, imposed by the Presidium of the Soviet CP, gave free play to the confrontation of the "Rákosist" and "Nagyist" tendencies while favoring the appearance of a third, "centrist" tendency. This group was to find its leader in the person of János Kádár after his reinstatement into the Politburo in July 1953, when Gerö replaced Rákosi at the head of the Central Secretariat. In a general way, the numerous adjustments of the leading party line, together with personal reshuffling, favored the renewal of the Politburo's importance. Of the quadrumvirate, which the Kremlin practically dismissed in June 1953, Rákosi was to remain only until July 1956, and Gerö until the October revolution of the same year; Farkas surfaced for a short period in the meantime. All disappeared after the 1956 revolution. No other group was able to constitute itself, as had these four, as a restricted leading group. For a time, the Politburo shared power with the Central Committee, within the limits that have already been indicated.

The astonishingly copious and broad-minded information furnished by the official publications has depicted a Communist party that is shallowly rooted among the factory workers and even more shallowly among the peasantry. In order to prove that the party belongs to the working class—which is theoretically in power—party statistics refer us to the category of manual workers promoted to leading positions or, in the words of Djilas, to the bureaucratic "new class." In fact, most members of the leading organs are recruited there—Politburo, Secretariat, Control Commission, Commission for Revision, and Central Committee.

As for the operation of the party, the MSzMP, while providing a new format for its activities, does not formally differ from its predecessor. Likewise, its services resemble those of other Communist parties in power. In theory, the Party Congress fulfills the role of legislator; the Central Committe directs the organization and activities between Party Congresses; the Politburo, which is responsible to the Central Committee, is the permanent executive; at its side are the Central Secretariat and, if necessary, other bureaus charged with such sectors as agitation and propaganda, and the economy. The commissions of control and of revision fulfill special functions, particularly in the area of discipline and in the inspection of finances. Recently, they have been reunited into a single Control Commission, elected not by the Central Committee, but directly by the Party Congress.

According to the new party rules, the leadership is collegial, and the elected members are removable in the case of a grave fault. Decisions are transmitted on the principle of "democratic centralism," that is, resolutions taken by the higher organs are obligatory and executory for the lower organs. Likewise, each elected organ is responsible to the higher organ and must account for its activities. Discussion and criticism are authorized, even encouraged, as long as the majority has not come to decision on the matter. However, the fundamental party statutes and resolutions no longer encourage, as they did in 1957–60, members to participate in the elaboration of party politics. Likewise, the 1957 rules considered criticism a duty of each member and the stifling of criticism a punishable offense, but the new rules make this duty a simple right.

The Mass Organizations

According to a tradition that goes back to the party's origins, the HCP has always made great efforts to create "mass organizations of transmission": organizations for the young, for women, for peasants, for cultural, sporting, and patriotic associations, and others. In addition, Communist activity in the unions has always had capital importance. The nature of these organizations and their function, however, varied considerably from period to period.

During the underground phase between the two wars, the numerous organizations had above all to disguise HCP activities. Since the HCP was prohibited under the Horthy regime, the Communists organized themselves and spread their propaganda among the unions, peasant associations, unemployed intellectuals, choral societies, athletic and nature clubs, and the like. The Young Communists have always had a particular twofold status: as a mass organization and as a semiautonomous organization of the party.

The politics of the popular fronts led to the creation of another kind of organization, e.g., the Committee for Historical Commemoration, or the Hungarian Front (embryo of the 1945 National Front for Independence). The March Front, which was created by the leftist populist intellectuals in 1937, remained essentially populist, and finally was to terminate in the formation of the National Peasant party, which was rather close to the Communists, but nevertheless independent. The Hungarian Front, founded later, deserves more attention from the point of view of HCP tactics. Through the Hungarian Front, the HCP in fact aimed at two more ambitious and more distant objectives than merely using the front as a cover organization. From 1941 on, especially from 1942–43, the HCP concentrated on the formation of an antifascist democratic bloc. In 1943, after the dissolution of the HCP, the Békepárt (Peace party) pursued this policy with perhaps more élan and success, if only because of the reversal of the military situation on the Russian front. The Hungarian Front was born after the German army occupied Hungary on March 19, 1944—with the participation of the Social Democrats, the left wing of the Smallholders, the Communists of the Peace party, and an antifascist religious organization, the League of Lorrainese Cross. The National Peasant party was admitted later.

As the Red Army advanced, the political goal of this formation took shape. The question was no longer merely to organize resistance—which had a certain importance but which remained nevertheless a militarily negligible factor—but to prepare the postwar period. This period, certainly, was seen differently by different people. But they had points in common, especially the desire to participate actively in the postwar reconstruction.

On December 2, 1944, the Communist general staff that had come from Moscow formed another front—the National Front for Independence (of Hungary); its composition was rather similar to that of the Hungarian Front.

At the end of 1944, then, there were two National Fronts in Hungary, just as there were two Central Committees of the HCP. Urged on by the necessity to organize the postwar period—as early as possible and without waiting for the liberation of the capital—but also prompted by other considerations, the Muscovite Communists, who had been parachuted into Hungary after an emigration that had lasted a quarter of a century, intended to organize the country according to the instructions they had received. But in Hungary, as in the other countries of the region, the fronts were to play the same central political role. They were to constitute the vast framework for a political reconstruction; they allowed the HCP to exclude not only the rightist elements but also the liberal anti-Communists and to assure the HCP itself of a position of strength. Thus, the Yalta accords were respected to the letter while at the same time arrangements were made with a view to eventual changes.

The front still exists under the name of the Patriotic Popular Front. During the past three decades, it has been reorganized and renamed several times. At a brief moment in its history, in 1954, Imre Nagy attempted to restore its original function of assembling the democratic forces, but he was not successful. The front, considered as a pluralistic organization, belongs to the era of the "beginning" of the people's democracies.

The other mass organizations have, to the same extent, lost the little autonomy that they had in the transition period of 1945–48. They are numerous: the National Association of Cooperatives, the National Council of Hungarian Women, the Society for the Propagation of Scientific Knowledge, the National Peace Council, the Hungarian-Soviet Society, and others, not to mention the Young Communists, who remain, at the same time, the most important organization and the reservoir of the party. As "transmission belts," their task is to spread the Communist word in the circles they reach, then to "educate" as well as "mobilize" these circles, if necessary.

Sluggish and bureaucratic, the unions have found a renewed relative strength since the Kádárist reconstruction of 1957. However, their activities run counter to the inherent limits of the state-as-employer system. Besides, they have probably lost their credit among the workers. In this respect, the events of 1956 are revealing. In this short period during which free organizations blossomed, the unions did not play a great part. The workers were instead trying to form workers' councils, simultaneously organs of production management and of local political power.

In order to understand the HCP's attitude toward the council movement, it is necessary to state at once that the latter has appeared and reappeared for half a century under different names, and not just under the label of councils or soviets. In imitation of the Russian soviets, the Hungarians formed workers', peasants', and soldiers' councils in 1918. But in the bourgeois-democratic revolution of the end of October, as in the Republic of the Councils in 1919, the political parties—first Democratic, then Social-Communist—got the upper hand, leaving to the councils only a limited local field of action.

At the end of 1944 and in 1945, Hungary was again the scene of a council movement. Encouraged by the Communists, national committees were formed in various localities as people's organs of power and administration. Simultaneously, factory committees were formed in various factories. Both were to disappear.

The factory committees survived the national committees. They were never organs of power; in the beginning, they served as support for the politics of the HCP, not only against the employers but also against Social Democratic influence. After the nationalization of the factories and the absorption of the SDP, the HCP no longer needed them. From the summer of 1947, the unions assumed control of the direction of the factory committees, which in 1948 were finally converted into union committees.

The HCP's attitude had not changed by the council movement of 1956. It looked on the emergence of the council movement with poorly disguised hostility, and, after the Soviet intervention, Kádár's reconstructed HCP did likewise. For a brief time, Kádár still negotiated with the Central Workers' Council of Greater Budapest, but he did so only in order to gain time. As soon as the strength of his government was sufficiently consolidated, the workers' councils and the national councils were dissolved and their leaders thrown into prison.[3]

Before concluding this discussion of the structure, operation, and organization of the party, it is necessary to recall the role of the party apparatus in the administration of the state, the economy, and cultural life. Under one heading or another, all sectors of the state and even of society are crowned by the departments or divisions of the central apparatus. At present, there are six: the departments for party affairs, propaganda, science and culture, economic affairs, public administration, and foreign affairs, not to mention the bureaus charged with the affairs of the Central Committee itself. These are the "superministries," controlling, either through direct intervention or through the intermediary of powerful Communists, the state, union, and cultural bureaucracies. The intervention and control of the party apparatus is not always practiced at the same level or with the same intensity. Kádár's party was undoubtedly allowed the relations between the party appartus and the state apparatus to become looser while conferring on the latter greater independence than during Rákosi's time. One must not, however, lose sight of the fact that the leading organs of the state—ministries, offices, and councils of every kind—are obliged to carry out the instructions of the party, i.e., the instructions of the Central Committee and Politburo. Consequently, the party maintains its command over the state through the various channels of control and transmission, even though the system has become more relaxed and less centralized than in the past.

The HCP and Its National Environment

With a total area of 93,030 square kilometers and a population of 10.5 million inhabitants, Hungary is one of the smallest of the medium-sized states of Central and Eastern Europe. It is also one of the oldest. The history of the Hungarian people and state goes back over a thousand years with some centuries of greatness and of power. Long linked to Austria through the personal union of the Habsburg sovereigns, Hungary before World War I was three times larger than today and had a population of about twenty million inhabitants, almost half of whom were Slavs and Romanians. After the Peace Conference and the Treaty of Trianon, all this changed completely. In post-Trianon Hungary, only insignificant pockets of nationalities could be found, with the exception of the German minority of Transdanubia. Most of the latter, however, were exiled after World War II. Consequently, present-day Hungary is not confronted with the problem of national minorities. On the other hand, more than three million Hungarians remained, after 1919, in the "successor states," Czechoslovakia, Yugoslavia, and Romania (enlarged by Transylvania). Here is the origin of Hungarian revisionism under Horthy between the two wars, a revisionism attenuated today, but probably not entirely resorbed.

Nearly two-thirds of the population belong to the Roman Catholic church and some 30 percent to the Protestant churches. The Orthodox and Jews are numerically of little importance. In prewar Hungary the Jews made up about 5–6 percent of the population (6.2 percent after World War I, 5.1 percent in 1930 not counting converted Jews). According to a recent book, only some 140,000 survived the Nazi persecutions, although its author estimates the present number at 100,000.[4] Actually, figures on religion in postwar Hungary must be taken with caution because individuals no longer declare their confession. On our estimate, at least half the 500,000 Jews of prewar Hungary are still in the country. The antagonism between Catholics and Protestants has long been a thing of the past. On the other hand, there is still a "Jewish question"—a latent anti-Semitism, especially directed toward the Jewish component of the HCP.

The population density is very high in the capital, which has almost two million inhabitants, and in some other urban centers. It varies between forty and one hundred per square kilometer in the agricultural regions.

An agricultural country in the past, Hungary is poor in minerals and energy resources. Yet certain sectors—machinery and transportation, mechanics, optics, food, chemical products, and textiles—experienced rapid development even between the two wars. But about 56 percent of the population still lived from agriculture.

The destruction during the war has been estimated at five times the annual revenue. Therefore, the first economic plan essentially aimed at reconstruction. In 1949–50 the politics of industrialization began. In the meantime, two socioeconomic changes upset the countryside. In 1945, the new government, under pressure from Communists and Agrarians of the New Left, carried out land reform that had long been awaited by the agricultural workers and the poor peasants. Exactly 642,342 people were allotted 4,875,000 hectares of land—2.92 hectares per person on the average. Simultaneously, the new state expropriated more than 1.3 million hectares of woodland, pastures, and uncultivated land. On the whole, in round numbers, 3,200,000 hectares of cultivable land were affected. With one blow, seignorial, or semifeudal, Hungary disappeared, giving way to the new agrarian structures of small and medium landowners. These new agrarian structures disappeared in the wake of the second great change: the collectivization of agriculture after 1949.

The combined effects of industrialization, urbanization, and agrarian transformation have thoroughly changed the structure of the population and of the economy. About 23 percent of the population continues to live from agriculture, which provides some 18 percent of the national gross revenue. The share of industry has risen to 55 percent and that of commerce and transportation to 22 percent. Besides Budapest, five cities have over 100,000 inhabitants (Miskolc, Debrecen, Pécs, Szeged, and Győr), and twelve more have over 50,000.[5]

It is impossible here to trace the development of all the different sectors of the Hungarian economy. According to all available information, the prewar level was reached around 1949–1950 and is said to have increased five times over by 1968 (the beginning of the economic reforms). It has grown since then at an average yearly rate of 6.3 percent. Agricultural production, too, is claimed to have achieved a high growth rate in proportion to the other socialist countries, namely, 5 percent yearly.[6]

The standard of living of the workers, as well as that of the peasants, artisans, and intellectuals, has improved, particularly since the introduction of economic reforms in 1968, although it remains inferior to that of East Germany and far below that of the Western countries.

The stratification of Hungarian society has been constantly changing since 1945 and, with still more reason, since the HCP was established as the only party in power. With the collapse of the prewar regime, a whole political and economic class disappeared, one that had been firmly entrenched as the leading class. It is wrong to view it as an essentially aristocratic class based on great landed properties, even though these survived until 1945 and extended over half of the cultivated land. In reality, these high aristocratic classes and the nobility were retreating before the bourgeoisie or, very often, were intermingled with it. If the descendants of the great established families still dominated the Upper House of Parliament, the diplomacy, the army, and perhaps a few other privileged functions, they did not dominate economic and cultural life, public administration, or even political life. In all these vital domains, the "Christian and seignorial" upper middle class ruled as masters—with an assimilated Jewish bourgeoisie at its side.

For some time after the war, it could still have been possible to follow this formerly dominant middle class as it went into full decline. The land reform uprooted one of its layers, the nationalization of the companies uprooted another, the purge of public administration a third, and so on. The political retreat of this class kept pace with its economic and social retreat. It was still an opposition during 1945–48, but then disintegrated. The particularly odious police and administrative measures that the Rákosi regime took against its survivors between 1950 and 1953—suppression of retirement pensions, eviction, banishment from Budapest, and deportations—only affected elements that had become inoffensive and, in general, aged. In any case, the alleged "reaction" during the revolution of 1956 would not have had a social basis worthy of the name. Since then, the remnants of the formerly leading middle classes have disappeared, either because of the assimilation of the young, or by the death of the elderly, or even by the exodus of 200,000 Hungarians to the West in 1956.

Communist societies have a special character and it is not easy to define their new social structures. The peasantry also disintegrated in the wake of the collectivization of agriculture. Modernization did the rest by reducing the agricultural population as a whole. The peasantry was formerly dispersed over the countryside on small plots of land; at the same time it was divided according to wealth. But today it is a more or less cohesive class concentrated in 2,800 agricultural cooperatives and 150 state farms. It forms only about 23 percent of the population, including what remains of the individual farms and the wage earners of the state farms.

The rural exodus will soon have involved one million active workers. About 700,000 farmers left the soil between 1949 and 1968, some tens of thousands had already left it before, and more than 100,000 have done so since then. They have reappeared in other sectors of the economy, just as the individual artisans, who are now reduced to about 50,000, joined together with 200,000 artisans in cooperatives.[7]

The vast majority of the active population are wage earners: officials of the administration, company employees, teachers, workers, and the like. The liberal professions are practically nonexistent, since almost all scholars, physicians, architects, lawyers, actors, journalists, and even writers work in state institutes, state hospitals, state offices, and state publishing firms. On the whole, they represent three and a half million wage earners, according to the latest available figures.

Hungary's ethnic composition, as already noted, is remarkably homogenous. Owing to a generous policy toward the small groups of national minorities—Germans, Serbians, Croats, Romanians—the authorities' relations with them do not present any problem (except those that are specific to the social groups to which they at the same time belong).

It seems more difficult to gauge the importance of religion in the relations between the population and the authorities. The latter's policy toward the churches is actually very tolerant, in contrast with the anticlerical and antireligious violence of the 1950s. This tolerance is rewarded by a kind of political consensus, provided by the Protestant churches as well as by the Catholics and Jews. To what degree does this consensus extend to the congregation of these churches? This we cannot answer: we do not know the proportion of those who attend church and, with still more reason, we do not know how many believe but do not attend church. Whatever the answer, it is clear that religious faith has ceased to be an important political factor. Even the invisible barrier between the Christian and Jewish faith on the one side and the Communist doctrine on the other side is becoming less insurmountable. As the practice of religion is free, a believer today can approve of the regime without coming into conflict with his own conscience. Moreover, if only in order to conform to social custom, many registered Communists have their children baptized, even though they do not later send them for religious training. Party newspapers and pamphlets condemn such behavior, but it does not entail disciplinary measures for the culprits. Since the party uses only ideological means against the religions, the opposition stops at that; as before, neither side assumes a properly political character.

The domain of political feelings, sympathies, and antagonisms as well as the scale of values are, if that is possible, even more impenetrable than the problem of religious behavior. In the absence of free elections, an independent press and other mass media, impartial sociological investigations, and public opinion polls on a large scale, it is impossible to go beyond general estimates. It is especially difficult to determine the changes that have occurred since the 1956 revolution. This event demonstrated the extent of the hostility of the population, if not toward socialism and some of its economic and social accomplishments, then toward the Communist political system. Certainly, there were no elections in October 1956 that could give any indication about the political preferences of the population. In any case, very few could have voted Communist: some 5–6 percent perhaps, in the estimate of such well-placed personalities as János Kádár and George Lukács.[8] The vast majority was divided between the political parties that had risen again, including the Catholic parties, and the council movement. This does not at all mean that cultural and moral feelings and values in favor of the past, conservative or reactionary, would have prevailed in Hungary in 1956. The deepest convictions of the population were expressed essentially in the rejection of the Communist system, in its negation, not in the positive affirmation of other values and convictions. This was a negation of the monolithic system, a negation of the methods of totalitarian dictatorship, a negation above all of foreign influence, that is, of Soviet domination. This negation to a certain extent implies the affirmation of opposite values such as nationalism, pluralism, and attachment to individual liberties. But for us to maintain that in revolution the Hungarian people had "voted" either for a parliamentary regime of the Western type, or for a system of councils and of self-government, would be pure speculation. The "plebiscite through revolt" of 1956 allows one to affirm only three things: (1) Hungarian nationalism manifested itself with extreme vigor against the Soviets; (2) the Communist system was clearly rejected on the political level without necessarily implying the rejection of the new economic and social structures; and (3) ten years of Communist indoctrination had by no means erased the attachment of the population to liberal-democratic values.

More than twenty years after the events of 1956, it is difficult to measure present feelings. It remains unlikely, however, that either time or the undoubtedly more flexible and more liberal policy of the Kádár regime has changed the deepest convictions of the population. The positive consensus that the present regime enjoys rests, it seems, on well-defined economic and political bases, but by no means on new values and feelings. Hungarians follow Kádár's HCP, even support it to a certain extent, as a lesser evil than the Stalinist past, and as a lesser evil than the other Communist regimes. They support the new economic policy, they support the sensible alleviation of the police system, they support the relative freedom the intellectuals enjoy, and they support the rather easy granting of passports. But they remain opposed to the single-party system, to the Warsaw Pact and the presence of the Soviets in Hungary, to the disadvantages of trade with COMECON countries, and to many other things. In a word, the attachment to the nation, to pluralism, and to liberal values remains intact, according to all available signs.

The Hungarian attitude toward imperialism—according to the same signs and uncertain estimations—is ambiguous. The ardent antiimperialism that Communist papers report is probably found only in a thin layer of the population close to the HCP: members of the apparatus, privileged members of the state bureaucracy and the mass organizations, the political police—the army being already less certain on this point. On the other hand, the image of the West—of a liberating West, in any case—has tarnished considerably since 1956. Hungarians no longer are too optimistic about the Western powers, including the United States, as "champions of freedom." At the same time, the crusades, wars, and interventions of these powers in Asia and Latin America seem to have provoked mixed feelings. Hungarians certainly did not applaud the Vietnam War, especially not the human suffering it caused, but at the same time they saw it as another proof of the absence of determination in American policy.

If Hungarian opinion seemed indifferent to Vietnam (just as it is toward Cuba and Chile), the same does not apply to the conflict in the Middle East. Everything seems to indicate that public opinion sympathizes with Israel. One cannot explain these sympathies solely by Jewish influence in Hungary itself; after all, Hungary has a solid anti-Semitic tradition. Nor can one explain them by anti-Arab racism. The principal factor in the Hungarians' pro-Israel feeling lies in the fact that they regard the conflict as a small people's struggle for existence against the Arab countries supported by the Soviet Union.

The Soviet element, then, appears to be omnipresent in the formation of public opinion. It determines behavior and modifies even the scale of values. To understand its impact, one has to understand the importance of the Soviet presence for thirty years, Moscow's direct role in the Communist seizure of power and in the crushing of the revolution, the effect of "russification," as well as the difference between the two cultures. The

Hungarian perceives himself as eminently European in his history, his religion, and his civilization. The Soviet domination, consequently, is alien to him in this respect, as well.

Here, too, one must mention the dislike for the Romanians. If Hungarian nationalism has weakened toward its other neighbors, the Yugoslavs and the Czechoslovaks, the same is not true for its neighbors to the east. Hungarian public opinion has always resented the separation of Transylvania, more than it resented the loss of regions in the north and in the south given to Czechoslovakia and Yugoslavia, respectively. This resentment has remained alive even after World War II, particularly because of Romanian policy toward the Hungarian minority.

Strategies and Tactics

The strategy and tactics of the HCP compared to those of other political parties have this peculiarity: "conflict" has an infinitely more important place than "integration." This does not mean that the HCP turns up its nose at the aspirations specific to its national environment. It took them into consideration before as well as after the seizure of power. The national factor was of prime importance in Nagy's experiment in 1953–54 as well as in the more recent and more enduring one of János Kádár.

During the long underground period after the failure of the Republic of the Councils in 1919, the HCP did not change its strategic line until the later 1930s. It remained fixed on the final objective: the seizure of power by means of a proletarian revolution and, at the close of this revolution, the establishment of the dictatorship of the proletariat. Its main slogan was: "For the second Republic of the Councils!" Considering the HCP's extremely limited audience, such a program was, at one and the same time, chimerical and laden with threat. It appealed to forces that could not even qualify as political minority groups, much less as social groups. The HCP simply tried to reach, through its propaganda and its organizations, the most disadvantaged, the most desperate, the most radical, the most exalted—but also the most idealistic people, those most ready to sacrifice themselves—in all social groups: workers, poor peasants, the unemployed, the sick, those on the fringes of society, disillusioned sons of the upper bourgeoisie, artists, students, and Jews. In the same spirit, it tried to enlarge this circle during the crises, which hit precisely the most wretched the hardest. Thus, while its program remained a chimera in interwar Hungary, the HCP envisaged the use of violence by small groups that would attempt to impose their will on the majority of the population. In short, it envisaged the repetition of Lenin's coup of November 1917, but under entirely different conditions.

The violent and desperate character of these tactics and of the strategic objective at which they aimed was accentuated by other elements. First, the HCP did not represent any social class or any true social stratum. Consequently, it was not coherent enough to lead a struggle both social and political. Perhaps organized but by no means structured, the HCP called to the struggle groups that were even less structured, groups that changed at the whim of circumstances, amorphous and ephemeral.

Another factor that provoked the reckless violence of the HCP was its illegality and the police repression directed against it. The dynamics specific to small groups and small minority units also acted in favor of violence in tactics.

The appeal to active and determined small groups has proved to be more efficient, although still in a very limited way, since the middle of the 1930s. Owing to the tactics of the popular fronts, all Communist parties, whether less or more important, were able to associate themselves with popular movements and more widely held, though minority, antifascist ideas. Ever since then, the call for violence has had a goal other than the repetition of Lenin's achievement; it has assumed a national character. All the same, it took almost ten years for the HCP to benefit from this change in tactics, which was of course imposed by the Comintern. The first obstacle was the very character of the HCP: its past, its traditions, its leaders, its composition. More than its brother parties, the CP of Hungary was imbued with its exalted past of 1919: it could not conceive of adopting a tactic "inferior" to the one that had been its glory at the time of the Republic of the Councils, a dictatorship of the proletariat. After this past, to fight for a democratic republic of the 1918 type was to fall back an entire historical stage. Besides, the most prestigious of its leaders, Béla Kun, was also the least prepared to do it.

Despite some progress between 1937 and 1939, only after 1941 did the HCP really start to advance on the new path. A resolution of September 1, 1941, stated: "the Central Committee invites the leadership of the party to establish contact with the important bourgeois parties of Hungary, among others with the leadership of the government party in power, in the interest of the accomplishment of anti-German national unity." It also invited the bourgeois parties "not to treat the Communist party as an enemy but on the contrary as an ally." In return, the HCP promised not to transgress, for as long as the proposed alliance lasted, "the limits of the constitution" nor to attempt "to change by the use of violence the existing state and social order." "The Party of the Communists of Hungary," one further reads, "will use all its activity, its influence among the masses, and its organizational strength exclusively against the common enemy as long as the common national objectives have not been reached."[9]

The politics of the fronts took its "definitive" form for the transition years 1945–48. The relation of forces was constantly modified in favor of the HCP owing to the "salami tactic," which consisted in eliminating adversaries slice by slice. The framework, however, remained unchanged; on the surface, tactics and strategy overlapped: the HCP affirmed, during all these years, that its only objective was a "free, democratic, and independent Hungary," in other words, a "new democracy" or a "people's democracy" headed by a government of all the united democratic forces. The HCP thus seemed to be a loyal partner in the realization of a far-reaching national project, but one not at all revolutionary in the proletarian Marxist-Leninist sense.

For three years the words "dictatorship of the proletariat" were not even pronounced, and party spokesmen, especially Mátyás Rákosi, did not cease to criticize severely the "former sectarian comrades" who were nostalgic for the Republic of the Councils of 1919.

From the point of view of tactics, the HCP took other measures to polish its new image. As promoter of the land reform, it gave the illusion of a definitive democratic solution for the agrarian problem with the slogan, "the land to the peasants." Whoever talked of collectivization or nationalization of the land was immediately accused of being leftist or sectarian. On the cultural level, Georg Lukács was brought forward. The party let him play the "pope" of literature, a pope who was certainly rather dogmatic in the eyes of writers living in their own poetic universe and thereby insensitive to the appeals for the construction of a new society, but a pope who was astonishingly liberal and comprehensive in comparison to the Zhdanovs or even the Bertolt Brechts. Lukács' cultural "platform"—thoroughly supported by József Révai—admirably complemented the general politics of the HCP and, in fact, was an integral part of it.

As for national traditions, no one exalted them as much (no one would have dared to exalt them in the presence of the Soviet Army, the heroes of the fight for Hungarian independence), as did the leaders of the HCP. The "new Hungary" and its "new democracy" appeared in their writings and their speeches as the direct continuation of the national insurrection of Prince Rákóczi and of Kossuth's war of independence.

This national frontist policy—tinged with a bit of genuine nationalism—also included the HCP's great, original project for the formation of new elites. That is, it set up a system of people's colleges to favor the promotion not only of young worker and peasant cadres but also those of bourgeois origins—all in an essentially democratic and national spirit. In these colleges, crowned by the NEKOSz (National League of People's Colleges) and patronized by the Communist minister of the interior, László Rajk, nothing was criticized with as much vigor as sectarianism and all other "leftist" deviationism.

It is neither possible nor desirable to survey the application of the HCP's new tactics in all areas of national life. The political police extended its operation beyond the pursuit of war criminals, fascists, and harmful reactionaries. It became the HCP's political instrument against its own allies, if only by virtue of the threat—often carried out—it made to politicians little inclined to yield to the demands of the Communists. Officials not protected by parliamentary immunity quickly became acquainted with the prisons of the AVO and later of the AVH (State Security Section, later State Security Authority) as well as with its notorious methods of interrogation. But in extreme cases, the HCP did not hesitate to appeal to the Soviet occupation authorities.

Apart from pressure and intimidation, the HCP also made use of the masses. With the help of its disciplined and perfectly efficient organization, it succeeded in mobilizing many people, especially in Budapest. In the demonstrations against the "speculators and stockjobbers," and in the demonstrations against "the reaction" there were easily 100,000 persons, if not more.

The HCP's policies toward the churches were also marked by a combination of moderation and violence. At first, the HCP energetically resisted the anticlerical and atheistic traditions of the old days. However, the HCP was not ready to compromise with the churches. First, it refused any compromise with regard to the exemption from expropriation of church land, especially that of the Catholic church, which had been one of the greatest landowners. Likewise the tolerance toward parish schools did not last long. The measures for the dissolution of the religious orders affected, with a few exceptions, the teaching orders, as well. The secularization of education, which most democratic parties approved, was not long in coming. Finally, if the HCP curbed the atheistic and anticlerical zeal of its most radical followers, the same was not true for the "clerical reaction." Such a reaction undoubtedly existed. In the minds of certain prelates, the defense of the church was confounded with the defense of the politics of the past. This was true of Cardinal Mindszenty and other, less-known ecclesiastics. The hostility of these clergymen, however, furnished the HCP with a pretext for attacking all too assertive ecclesiastics and thus prepared the way for the police repression that was not long in coming.

Returning to the analysis of the strategy and of the tactics of the HCP in the first years after the war, a conclusion is evident. The element of violence reappears indisputably and probably inevitably. Contrary to appearances, tactics and strategy actually do not overlap. If the HCP had not had designs other than those it proclaimed it could have given up violence and waited peacefully for its "national" and reformist politics to produce their effect and win favor with the voters again. But the partial success or partial failure of the free elections radicalized it, leading it to take a harder line. This became more evident as relations among the wartime allies deteriorated. Thus, violence recovered its place in HCP tactics, with one difference: the party now had the means to employ it. These coercive means were all the more formidable as they were based on the support of the Soviet Army. But it also had political means: the masses and the party organization. Certainly, the HCP did not succeed in becoming a class party, the party of the proletariat it so ardently wanted to be. It has remained after 1945 as before: an anomalous party without real social cohesion. But organization and discipline, the famous "party spirit," superseded the lack of social cohesion. The party, henceforth, no longer consisted of small groups that appealed to other small groups. It was a massive, dynamic, and disciplined political force, a force that mobilized the masses and succeeded in imposing its will on the majority of the population and on the other parties.

After the absorption of the SDP, the HCP had sole power. Was this seen in advance, prepared and drafted from Moscow, as the partisans of the "blueprint theory" affirm? Or was the HCP in 1945 itself in the unknown, ready to play the game of the democratic fronts? Or did the favorable circumstances begin the process of the seizure of power? In the specific case of Hungary, there is an element that makes the author of this study as well as other historians lean toward the second version.

In 1948, the leading team of the HCP seems itself to have been taken unawares by the turn of events. Proof of this lies in the self-criticism expressed by Rákosi and even more explicitly, by Révai, about the concept of the "people's democracy." We have made a mistake, they declared in essence, by considering the new democracy as something durable and as a form of state and society fundamentally different from that of the Soviet Union. In fact, the people's democracy is nothing other than a "relatively peaceful passage" to socialism. Finally, the people's democracy, descended from the people's democratic revolution, is a "special form of the dictatorship of the proletariat"; were it not for the absence of the soviets, nothing would distinguish it from the one in the Soviet Union.

If the politics and methods of the Hungarian CP prior to 1948 presented some special characteristics distinguishing it from the other Communist parties, this was not the case in the following period. But yet again, since 1953, the ways of the HCP have branched off from the normal path of the people's democracies. Foremost in the anti-Titoist crusade and in the sovietization of the country during the years when Stalinism predominated, the HCP effected a most spectacular turnabout in June 1953. As for its tactics, the "reform era" of 1953–55 was until then an unprecedented variant of "enlightened communism" (according to François Fejtö). Certainly, the isolated and almost solitary moving spirit and promoter of the "June politics," Imre Nagy, attempted to introduce "frontist" elements into it by seeking especially the support of populist and nonparty writers as well as by trying to reinvigorate the front, which still existed on paper. But this does not constitute his true originality. His unique experiment was to humanize the system, as Dubček's group was to do twelve years later in Czechoslovakia. To redress wrongs, to release and rehabilitate the victims of police arbitrariness, to loosen the screws of economic constraints and like measures—these were only the material goals. Even at that, because of the hostility of Rákosi and Gerö and of the apparatus in general, the changes were kept to a minimum. What Nagy wanted was to recreate—or rather create—a climate of confidence and to reestablish communication between the party and the people. The other original feature of his experiment was precisely the hostility on the part of the other Communist leaders and of the apparatus. For the first time in the history of communism, a miniscule group, reduced practically to Nagy and his personal collaborators, attempted to reverse the engine in the face of a suspicious, even hostile, apparatus. In the later experiment of the Prague Spring, the situation was more favorable because the party almost completely rallied to Dubček's line. In the case of Nagy and his friends, one can not really speak of new tactics employed by the party but only by a group within the party. In this sense, the experiment of Hungary only reveals potential tactics, tactics that can prevail only under exceptional conditions. In the first place, it was necessary to have Moscow's support—even its initial encouragement—in order to attempt this experiment in humanization. Second, in order to pursue it, an appeal had to be made to the moral conscience, which had long been anaesthetized, of the Communist elite. There was still another original aspect of the reform era of 1953–55. It was only through a genuine crisis of conscience among the Communists that the resistance of the bureaucratic apparatus could be at least neutralized, even shaken, for a certain period. There was too little time, however, to see the experiment through; it finally ran aground on the rock of this same bureaucracy, on the one hand, and on a temporary stiffening in Khrushchev's politics of de-Stalinization on the other.

Let us here pass over the turmoil of the revolution of 1956 as well as the first years of Kádár's regime, which, after the collapse of the previous regime, assumed control.

Kádár's politics go even further than those of the June 1953 program. On the economic level, especially, there can be no comparison between the hasty improvisations of the reform era and the "new economic mechanism" which was put into place after several years of studies and which is based today on long experience. As for "socialist legality," the successes are also undeniable and even more extensive, if only because the present HCP has spent a great deal of time making its police less arbitrary and its justice worthier of the name. One of the most spectacular successes has come in the most difficult field: agriculture. The HCP has been able, after a long and prudent wait followed by a violent attack on the peasantry, to carry out an almost total collectivization without endangering production. Furthermore, Hungarian agriculture has become profitable, the cooperatives prosper or at the very least function well, their activity is becoming diversified, and the rural standard of living rises constantly.

A complete inventory of the accomplishments would be as long as an inventory of the failures and weaknesses. But the balance is positive in the sense that the tactics of the regime have eventually overcome popular resistance and have rallied public opinion. For its part, the Kádár regime enjoys a certain popularity, which allows it to maintain a serene political climate and to advance with circumspection down the path of enlightened reform. What it lacks compared to the reform era as well as to the feverish summer of 1956 is the élan and the enthusiasm of great expectations. Hungarian public opinion does not expect wonders; it contents itself with its relative freedom and slow improvement and hopes above all that this may last. Kádár's popularity rests, in fact, on the fear of something worse.

FOREIGN RELATIONS

The relations of the HCP with the other people's democracies have never departed from routine. The only exception to this rule was the crisis of Prague in 1968. As a consequence of Kádár's attitude, the hard-line Communist parties of the Soviet camp, that is, those of Czechoslovakia and East Germany, have looked unfavorably upon the liberal experiment developing in Hungary. Above all, the German CP was probably implicated in the pressures that the "Communist community" exerted on the leadership of the Hungarian CP, which it considered rather too liberal. Too little information has leaked out to allow us to know enough about it, but the affair is probably far from over and Kádár and his already decimated team will probably have to face other attempts to "bring them into line."

The HCP's attitude toward the Western countries has always been and remains extremely cautious. Hitler's last satellite, Hungary, was in an awkward position after the war; as in 1920, moreover, it was treated without consideration by the Allies. During the Rákosi era, the foreign policy of the HCP consisted of "supporting" the antiimperialistic campaign of the Soviet Union. Détente was not to bring great innovations. It only liquidated certain minor affairs in litigation and allowed the normalization of diplomatic relations with some Western countries. On this level, the behavior of Kádár's regime has hardly changed anything. Although eager, for obvious economic reasons, to draw nearer to the Federal Republic of Germany, Hungary was one of the last countries to resume diplomatic relations with it.

Prudence and moderation also prevail with regard to the Western Communist parties. The HCP takes care not to get involved in the polemics that often enough divide the fraternal parties, especially the Italian and French. The party press, though aligning itself with Moscow's position, avoids as best it can such controversial issues as China or Cuba.

For one reason or another and despite the explosion of 1956, Hungary has proved to be the most obedient satellite of the Soviet Union. Shortly after the war, it made heavy sacrifices in order to satisfy Moscow's most excessive economic demands. It was the first to comply to the letter with the sovietization of its economy, its politics, and its culture. The Hungarian CP hurled the rudest insults against Tito (when it was instructed to do so) and against the United States during the cold war. If the tone has changed since 1957, the content has not. Moscow can always count on the "support" of the Hungarian CP.

Budapest's practically unconditional alignment with Moscow has made it difficult to understand the audacious experiments to make its regime viable. It is difficult to judge whether that is good or bad. But only at this price can the HCP pursue—until further notice—its politics of prudent reforms in the rather hostile, or at the very least suspicious, milieu of the Communist bloc that surrounds it.

Besides, circumstances are responsible for the fact that the Hungarian party will never be able to loosen the vise of the Soviet party's tutelage, not even to the modest extent that the Romanians and the Poles have. The reasons for this are diverse, although in essence it is only a question of variations on two themes: the internal weakness of the HCP, which always made it dependent on Moscow, and Hungary's vulnerability as a small country without resources.

The history and the organization of the HCP have shown the various aspects of this dependence. Theoretically, the party of the first and only Republic of the Councils in Central Europe was well placed to resume its avant-garde role after World War II. In principle at least, it also had the necessary cadres because of the number and the quality of its Muscovite emigration. If such was not the case, it was primarily because these same cadres were progressively thinned out. Certainly, time also accomplished its work. The Communist militants of Béla Kun's commune had been relatively young, but twenty-five years later their average age was between 50 and 60. Rákosi was 53 in 1945, Gerö and Révai 47, Imre Nagy 49, Georg Lukács 60. Others died a natural death (Jenö Landler), still others perished on the Spanish front (Máté Zalka [General Lukács]) or in active service in Hungary or even during the war. Nevertheless, neither the war nor Horthy's prisons and tribunals created such a holocaust as Stalin's purges. The proportion of leaders purged was extremely high: fifty-three executions and disappearances in seventy to eighty arrests. That is, there were only about twenty survivors among the notables listed in a biographical dictionary of the HCP. In addition, the survivors have often not been allowed to go back to Hungary or received permission to do so only several years after the liberation.

In 1945, a group of subordinate Communist officials assumed the leadership of the HCP, officials who had neither the international reputation of Kun and Landler, nor the experience of Szántó and Vági, nor the ideological fame of a Lukács, nor the artistic reputation of a Béla Uitz. They could not but comply to the letter with the orders of the Kremlin; they had to be overzealous in order to prove their absolute loyalty.

In addition, a complex system of Soviet agents was established in the first hours of the Soviet occupation. These were not only the Soviet occupation authorities, to whom the armistice convention gave political, military, economic, police, and censorship powers, an event without precedent in European history. Other Soviet agencies were established to control domains as varied as the operation of the numerous so-called mixed economic societies (e.g., shipping, civil aviation, mining of various minerals) and the distribution of films.

The Hungarian CP is still militarily and politically dependent on the Kremlin as well as on the various control channels of the Soviets—from bilateral relations to political instruments, such as the Warsaw Pact, as well as the presence of advisers and of the Soviet Army on Hungarian territory. In short, the sovereignty of the HCP is, essentially, as fictitious as is that of the country itself. On the other hand, inside this iron collar, the HCP has relative freedom of movement, which probably goes together with a more polite tone in Soviet-Hungarian relations. For reasons of international prestige and because of changes inside the Soviet CP itself, the leaders of the Kremlin would not easily resort again to force against one or the other of their rebellious satellites. Thus, the Soviets must listen to them, to discuss, to bargain if necessary. This is happening more and more often, especially on the level of economic relations, as several COMECON meetings and especially the case of Romania prove. Without going that far, the leaders of the Hungarian CP, too, are more determined than ever to refuse to sacrifice the interests of their own country for the benefit of the mother country of international communism. All this is part of an evolution that characterizes all Communist parties in power, but especially that of Hungary. Established with the help of Soviet power and dependent on it on more than one level, the HCP has become, through the natural process of interaction and interdependency with the population, a responsible government.

NOTES

1. We have drawn all this statistical data from the official publication *Legyözhetetlen erö* (Budapest: Kossuth, 1968), except for the last total, which results from our addition (instead of the figure 880,717 furnished in the cited source).

2. *Legyözhetetlen erö*, p. 197.

3. Miklós Molnár, *Budapest 1956: A History of the Hungarian Revolution* (London: Allen and Unwin, 1971), pp. 174–80, 246–50.

4. Paul Lendvai, *L'Antisémitisme sans juifs* (Paris: Fayard, 1971), pp. 34, 321, 347.

5. *Képes politikai és gazdasági világatlasz* (Illustrated Political and Economic World Atlas) (Budapest: Kartográfiai vállalat, 1966); *Magyar statisztikai zaebleinyv* (Statistical Handbook of Hungary) (Budapest: Kossuth, 1976).

6. *A népi Magyarország negyedszázada*, pp. 35–37; *L'Europe de l'Est in 1970*, étude réalisée par Thomas Schreiber. La documentation française. Notes et études documentaires. No. 3, pp. 781–83 (Paris, 1971).

7. Emil Gulyás, "A magyar mezogazdaság fejlödése nemzetközi összehasonlitasban mezögazdaságunk szocialista átszervezése óta" (The Development of Hungarian Agriculture since its Socialist Transformation as Compared International Study), in *A népi Magyarország negyedszázada* (A Quarter of a Century of People's Democracy in Hungary), p. 367. See also in the same volume Sándor Orbán, "A parasztság osztálytagozódásának alakulása a felszabadulás után" (Evolution of the Social Stratification of the Peasantry since the Liberation), pp 335–46, as well as by the same author, *Két agrarforradalom Magyarországon: Demokratikus es szocialista agrárátalakulás 1945–1961* (Two Agrarian Revolutions in Hungary: Democratic and Socialist Agrarian Transformations 1945–1961) (Budapest: Akademiai, 1972). See also Statistical Handbook (1975).

8. Molnár, *Budapest 1956*, p. 182.

9. *Dokumentumok a magyar párttörténet tanulmányozásához* (Documents for the Study of the History of the Hungarian Party) (Budapest: Szikra, 1955), 5:58–60.

M. K. Dziewanowski

6. The Communist Party of Poland

No other single issue has affected the Communist movement of Poland more than the struggle over the national problem. Prior to 1918, in a country that had been partitioned for well over a century, the controversy involved not only the attitude of the entire Marxist movement toward the task of rebuilding native statehood, but also the relationship with the Great Powers dominating the Polish lands, chiefly Russia, which up to 1915–1916 controlled the bulk of historic Poland, while being, at the same time, the matrix of the nascent social revolution.

From the very beginning, the two leftist groups of the Polish Socialist movement, which in December 1918 formed the Communist Workers' Party of Poland, were torn between two tendencies: one nationalistic, another cosmopolitan. Initially, the cosmopolitan trend was much stronger. Both parent organizations of the Communist Workers' Party of Poland, the Social Democratic Party of Poland and Lithuania, and the Polish Socialist Party-Left, were dominated by the people who, like Rosa Luxemburg, Karol Radek, or Feliks Dzierżńyski, emphatically rejected Poland's independence as harmful to the interests of the Polish proletariat. All of them, but especially Rosa Luxemburg, treated nationalism as a survival of a bourgeois past, and aimed at the "organic incorporation" of Poland into Russia.

It was under the influence of the "Luxemburgist" trend that, in 1918, the Communist Workers' Party of Poland refused to accept the country's newly won independence, and for almost five years fought against the existence of the Polish Republic, urging amalgamation with the USSR. It was only in 1923 that the party formally and reluctantly accepted the Polish State as a fact of life. For about two decades, from the close of the nineteenth century to the early 1920s, many of the most heated debates of the Socialist and/or Communist movement were focused around the dilemma of organic incorporation versus national independence.

At the same time, however, an undercurrent of nationalism always existed in the leftist working class movement of Poland. The movement always harbored a small group of people who cherished, often only half-consciously, their independence from the Bolshevik-oriented Marxist groups in Russia; this group stressed less the international perspectives of the social revolution and was more preoccupied with domestic aspects of the class struggle and with the distinctness of Polish socioeconomic conditions, proudly emphasizing the revolutionary seniority as well as greater maturity of the Polish proletariat. Already in 1879, the Russian revolutionary Stepniak-Kravchinskii wondered why the early Polish Socialists were at the bottom of their hearts patriots, although they insisted on calling themselves cosmopolitans. Stepniak-Kravchinskii made a perceptive and in a way prophetic statement, anticipating the events of 1944:

> We could hardly take a hundred steps without my companions calling before my imagination some deed of valor or self-sacrifice of martyrdom. A sense of dread overpowered me. There is not a city in the world whose soil is as bloody as Warsaw. It seemed as if every stone of the pavement we trod, under the dirt and snow covering it, must have its stains of martyrs' blood. I understand then why Warsaw has been and will always be the site of revolution. Until it is burnt to ashes and destroyed . . . and its citizens not allowed to settle within a score of miles, as with old Carthage—till then Warsaw may be reduced to gloomy silence, but never subdued by despotism; and at the first call of liberty they will rise in arms to one man.[1]

The vague and initially rather amorphous undercurrent of patriotism flowing under the cosmopolitan crust of Polish communism was brought to the surface only some eight years after the proclamation of national independence. In 1924, a young Communist writer, Juliusz Brun-Bronowicz, published a series of essays entitled *Stefana Żeromskiego tragedia pomyłek* (*Stephen*

Żeromski's Tragedy of Errors). Analyzing critically a novel by a leading Polish writer, the hero of which brings Bolshevik ideas with him from Communist Russia to Poland, Brun-Bronowicz preached the necessity of a *native* revolution similar to, but not identical with the Communist upheaval in Russia. Writing during the early 1920s, Brun-Bronowicz made an observation (one then very unfashionable in leftist Marxist circles) that the Bolshevik revolution had been essentially a "Russian national upheaval." Poland, argued Brun-Bronowicz, should follow its example in essence but not in all details, certainly not in methods which were often alien to the Polish mentality and tradition. By this, Brun-Bronowicz implicitly rejected the universality of the Soviet experience, especially its applicability to Polish conditions, and asserted that there was a peculiar native way to achieve socialism-communism in Poland. His reasoning also implied that cooperation, not subordination, would be the most proper relationship between the revolutionary movements of the two countries. He argued that by rejecting the Polish state, the party had created the impression that it represented the working class against the nation, and not the nation against capitalism.

The conflict between these trends in the Communist movement of Poland, cosmopolitan versus nationalistic, has been one of the most persistent and important themes of the party's history. The ideological conflict has had numerous practical implications. It has affected, first of all, the character of the party's relationship with the CPSU by raising the issue: should the Polish comrades obediently follow Moscow's dictates in every respect, or should they act on their own and thereby adopt the Bolshevik experience to the specific, local conditions of their native country? Would, for instance, the style and methods of the Soviet party work if rigidly applied by the Polish Communists?

The "National Communist" concept of the proletarian revolution was repeatedly condemned by Moscow and consequently by the largely leftist leadership of the CP of Poland. The "Luxemburgist heritage," mixed with the Stalinist approach to the style of the party work, dominated the mainstream of its life up to the war and was still strong until the years 1955–56. Nevertheless, the "nationalistic deviation" struck roots in the party's rank and file. Despite frequent denunciations, despite ruthless purges, "the nationalistic deviation" was never completely eradicated from the party. Suppressed during the 1930s, the trend resurfaced during and after the war.

In order to comprehend more fully the post–World War II Polish Communists one has also to bear in mind the tragic end of the old CP of Poland. Briefly, the story of the party's liquidation is this. From the early thirties the CPP became the scene of a series of witch hunts, most of them reflecting the zigzags of Stalin's policies. First, there came the purges of the suspected "Trotskyites." Then the line was shifted and the party was accused of hiding "nationalistic deviations," of harboring a bunch of "provocateurs, spies, and diversionists" allegedly planted in the CPP by the "agents of Piłsudski."[2]

The decisive blow to the party was struck during the Great Purge which affected the CPP more than any other section of the Comintern. Several hundred Polish Communists who were then on Soviet territory were either shot or sent to various concentration camps. Those who happened to be abroad were lured back under one pretext or another and then liquidated. This included such prominent leaders as Adolf Warski-Warszawski, Julian Leński-Leszczyński, Wera Kostrzewa (Maria Koszucka), and the poet and writer, Bruno Jasieński, author of the popular novel, *I am Burning Paris.* As a result, by the middle of 1938, the CPP ceased to exist as an organized political movement.

No official announcement of its liquidation was ever published. Several hundred Polish Communists were liquidated and no more than seventy or eighty of those who survived the war were released and returned to Poland after 1946. It is worthwhile stressing that most survivors of the purge, other than those who were either too insignificant to be purged or who served the Stalinist apparatus, owed their salvation to the fact that they were in Polish prisons. One of them was Władysław Gomułka. A well-informed member of the CPP writes that some of the Polish Communists were so deeply disillusioned

> that they were even ready to get into Polish prisons. They did not yet know what was in store for them, but they felt that the dark road was coming to an end, that they were being strangled, and they wanted to get back. They wanted to be in Poland: there they worked enthusiastically as Communists and of course many of them were arrested.[3]

Thus, the CPP was destroyed by the end of the "Great Purge." Due to the weighty nature of the matter, the decision must certainly have been undertaken by Stalin himself. The exact date of the decision may be only guessed; it probably took place sometime after May 1, 1938.[4] The only official Soviet pronouncement on the subject of the dissolution of the CPP is a report by Dimitri Manuilsky at the Eighteenth Congress of the Bolshevik Party of March 1939.[5] According to him, the CPP was penetrated to the core by Trotskyite as well as Polish nationalistic subversive elements.

In order to understand the real reasons behind the dissolution of the CPP one has to start with considerations of a general nature. By 1937–38 the possibility of revolution in Poland seemed fainter than ever. Piłsudski's successors had consolidated their hold on the country, and, following the disastrous great depression, a period of considerable economic progress had ensued. Consequently, Stalin probably came to the conclusion that in the event of another "revolutionary situation" arising in Poland, the Red Army would do a better job than the CPP. One has also to stress that the CPP had never been a factor of great importance in Comintern calculations, except as a Soviet "transmission belt" to Germany. But with Hitler's triumph, the Soviet hopes for a German upheaval had evaporated. As a result, there was little reason for maintaining the party since it was an ineffective instrument. By the time of the dissolution, Stalin had apparently decided to reshape his strategy completely and to build his own bridge to the Third Reich.

Stalin knew, of course, that any deal with Hitler would provoke strong opposition within CPP ranks. The Polish party, with its gradually decreasing yet still large Jewish membership, on the one hand, and with its growing undercurrent of Polish nationalism, on the other, could hardly accept such a deal without a dramatic protest. Thus it may be said that the CPP, one of the last major victims of the Great Purges, was, at the same time, one of the first victims of the Stalin-Hitler agreement.

The present essay is not the place to speculate why "the God that failed" still retained the allegiance of some of the Polish survivors of the Great Purge. There is no doubt, however, that the liquidation of the party was a traumatic experience and was bound to leave a deep scar in the minds of its surviving members who reorganized the movement during World War II.

Since Władysław Gomułka has been the man who influenced the postwar Polish Communist movement perhaps more than anybody else, it would be in order to say a few words about him. Born in 1905 in Eastern Galicia, son of a worker, he played only a minor role prior to World War II in the work of the old CPP. After the Nazi-Soviet partition of Poland in September 1939, Gomułka and a group of his friends who shared his mistrust of Stalin, yet remained faithful to communism, refused to go to Moscow. Instead, they stayed in German-occupied territory and appealed for Comintern support in organizing a Communist resistance movement against the Nazis on Polish soil. The appeal went unheeded, but after the German attack on the Soviet Union in June 1941 Moscow allowed the surviving party members in Poland to reorganize in 1942. Since the word "communism" had been thoroughly discredited by the Stalin-Hitler pact and the behavior of the Soviet authorities in eastern Poland, the new group was to be called the Polish Workers' party (PWP).[6]

It is interesting to note that at the beginning, the new party followed a cleverly devised strategy of concealment, and tried to manipulate its image. The words "communism" or "Communist" were carefully avoided, and patriotic slogans were frequently used instead of the Old Marxist battle cries. Initial contact between the PWP and Moscow was tenuous. Evidently Gomułka's election to the secretary-generalship by the PWP

Central Committee in November 1943 was without Soviet knowledge or concurrence because of ruptured communications with the Kremlin. To remedy the shaky domestic position of the PWP, Gomułka considered it essential to broaden its exceedingly narrow political base. He therefore made repeated attempts to reach an understanding with the Polish Socialist party (PPS) and other leftist groups, and even established some contacts with the Polish government-in-exile in London. Following this strategy, Gomułka gained the support of people like Marian Spychalski, Władysław Bieńkowski, Władysław Kowalski, Zenon Kliszko, and Ignacy Loga-Sowiński—all men without any significant Moscow background. They maintained that the native weakness and political isolation of the PWP dictated a strategy of compromise, and that the party, in particular, must reject the outdated "Luxemburgist nihilism" regarding the national issue in favor of a stand placing greater stress on patriotism, and certain measure of domestic autonomy.

On this basic policy question, Gomułka and his supporters were opposed by the Moscow-trained group of Stalinists led by Bolesław Bierut, Hilary Mints, Jakób Berman, and Roman Zambrowski. The tougher line of the Muscovites demanded that the party go it alone and shun any compromise with the other leftist groups, relying upon Soviet support to place them in power over any opposition. Again the old issues of the interwar period flared up—should the Soviet methods be transplanted to Poland? Should the Stalinist style of party work be introduced? Gomułka and his followers argued for a "mild revolution," especially in the countryside, while Bierut and his supporters insisted on orthodox "Bolshevik" methods and policies, including collectivization of the land. The "Muscovites" accused the "Natives" of being "radishes," that is, red outside but white inside, where they themselves were "beetroots" or "tomatoes"—red all the way through. The "Natives," on the other hand, in their confidential conversations, berated the slavish dependence of their rivals on the Soviet authorities, while envying their more intimate contacts with them.

After the establishment of the Communist-dominated Provisional Government in 1944–45, the two rival groups continued their competition for control of the new party, as well as of the state political apparatus. Although the "Muscovites," owing to their closer ties with the Soviet apparat, were in ascendancy, the "Natives" were still doing fairly well. Gomułka remained in his commanding position as party Secretary-General, concurrently becoming Vice-Premier and Minister of recovered Territories; Spychalski became Defense Vice-Minister in charge of army political education; Kowalski headed the Communist youth movement, and Bieńkowski the party's educational program.

From the beginning, the "Natives" tried to soften somewhat the harsh effects of the Soviet military occupation, to restrict looting by the Red Army, and to proceed cautiously with collectivization. They maintained that the new regime in Poland should be Communist, but it need not necessarily be a carbon copy of the Soviet model. This emphasis upon that was later termed the "Polish way to socialism" did not mean that Gomułka and his followers were not loyal Communists fully dedicated to establishing the rule of the party. While their policies in the early years gave an impression of relative moderation, they were both uncompromising and unscrupulous when it came to crushing those who stood in the way of full Communist political mastery. The Polish Peasant party of Stanisław Mikołajczyk, which was the chief center of resistance and remnant of the underground "Home Army," was suppressed during Gomułka's leadership by methods that were fully in accord with Stalinist practice.

Indeed, while the nationalistic coloration of Gomułka's policies stemmed in part from his mental and temperamental makeup, it also derived from his tactical goal: the facilitation of the Communist take-over. Nor was the concept of a Polish road to socialism outwardly opposed at this stage by the Soviet leaders in Moscow. They apparently calculated that tolerance of nationalistic slogans would help to weaken Polish popular opposition to communism during the crucial take-over period. The ideal of "building socialism" by maximum domestic effort through methods in accordance with the native tradition had a considerable appeal to the rank and file of the PWP, then rapidly expanding its thin cadres after 1945. This became especially true after December 1948 and the forced merger of the PWP with the main representative of native radicalism, the Polish Socialist party. This merger more than doubled the membership of the party, now renamed the United Polish Workers' party (UPWP). The fusion profoundly affected the nature of the new party: it now represented an amalgamation of various elements among whom genuinely patriotic Poles, largely former Socialists, were quite numerous.

After effective political opposition had been silenced, however, Moscow's attitude underwent a sudden change. To understand the shift one has to remember the contemporary international scene. In September of 1947, the Cominform was established with the primary objective of tightening Soviet control over the nascent "People's Democracies," including their domestic as well as foreign policies. At the first meeting of the Cominform, Gomułka could not help expressing some misgivings to his colleagues in the Polish Politburo concerning Moscow's intention to enforce more strictly its control over other Communist parties, as had been the case of the dissolved Comintern. He was also preoccupied with Poland's long-range national interests, and with the possibility of a Soviet-German deal at Poland's expense. At the Cominform conference, Gomułka indirectly pointed to "the question of the western territories" as a touchy issue in Poland's relations with the Soviet Union.[7] On June 3, 1948, only three weeks before the Soviet-Yugoslav dispute reached its climax with the Cominform denunciation of Tito, Gomułka assailed the "Luxemburgist nihilism" of the old CPP at a plenary session of the PWP Central Committee and expressly eulogized the Polish Socialist party for its stand on the issue of national independence. He declared that "both for the PPS and for the PWP the independence of Poland is a supreme consideration, to which all others are subordinated."[8] Both statements implied a certain mistrust towards Moscow, a suspicion of its possible future intentions toward Poland's territorial integrity and state sovereignty.

Following the break with Tito, the "Muscovite" wing of the Party leadership took Gomułka to task, at a Central Committee meeting from August 31 to September 3, 1948, for his reiteration of the national independence theme at the June Plenum. His past attempts to compromise with other parties and his emphasis on a Polish way to socialism were now scornfully denounced as a symptom of nationalism. He was accused of favoring a conciliatory attitude toward Tito while taking a defiant stand vis-à-vis the Soviet Union and of trying to negotiate with Moscow on a level of equality; he was, moreover, charged with slowing down the tempo of collectivization, and with "prematurely" dismissing some Soviet experts.

Instead of meekly admitting his guilt, Gomułka defended himself courageously and even tried to counterattack. His "errors" in the realm of ideology had, after all, been shared to some extent by practically all his colleagues in the Polish party leadership, as well as by most of the party bosses in the other "People's Democracies." But his condemnation had obviously been decided beforehand: the Central Committee was merely acting out a morality play carefully contrived by the Stalinist faction, upon orders from Moscow, for the benefit of the rest of the party. After a prolonged and bitter debate, the Politburo found Gomułka guilty of "nationalist deviation" and suspended him from his post as secretary-general.

In 1949, Gomułka was obliged to confess his cardinal sin in these revealing words:

> The core of my rightist, nationalist complex must have been my attitude to the Soviet Union—to the CPSU(b). . . . My attitude should be reduced not so much to . . . the relationship between the CPSU(b) and the Polish Workers' party as to the relationship between Poland and the USSR as states. . . . It never entered my head that Poland could progress along the way to socialism without being supported by the Soviet Union, but . . . it was difficult for me to shift my attitude as regards the Soviet Union to the ideological party plane.[9]

Between September 1948 and December 1949, three sweeping purges were carried out in the UPWP to eliminate those who shared or sympathized with Gomułka's views. The purges affected practically one-fourth of the party membership, their scope and intensity clearly reflecting Moscow's conviction that the resurgence of nationalism represented a dangerous force in the Polish party. Obviously, Gomułka's concept of a Polish way to socialism, which Moscow had tolerated as helpful during the take-over period for tactical reasons, had now become dangerous in view of the Yugoslav experience.

On August 2, 1951, Gomułka was arrested and spent the next three years under house arrest in an isolated villa on the outskirts of Warsaw. On several occasions the Soviet leaders, including Stalin himself, sought to ascertain from the new bosses of the UPWP when Gomułka would be brought to trial—and presumably liquidated, in the manner of László Rajk, Traicho Kostov, and Rudolf Slansky. The standard answer from Gomułka's comrades was that preparatory investigations were not yet completed. This was only part of the truth: in reality the investigators had failed to the end to break Gomułka and make him admit his guilt. Moreover, if placed on trial, he had threatened to bare some wartime party secrets.

Stalin's death and the "thaw" that followed paved the way for Gomułka's ultimate rehabilitation in the wake of the Twentieth CPSU Congress, repudiating Stalinist policies. At the same time the party's hold over the country was undermined by the growing ferment among Polish workers, students, and intellectuals. The workers' insurrection that took place in Poznań, in June 1956, was a new factor in the annals of communism and represented a most serious challenge to the regime.[10] By going on strike, staging a massive demonstration, and fighting even tanks sent against them, the workers of Poznań disregarded the grim precedent of the suppression of a similar affair in Berlin three years earlier, in June 1953. By this challenge, the workers of Poland reasserted themselves, and became a new force to be reckoned with. Mounting ferment among youth and intellectuals gave a further push to the elements within the Polish party that recognized the wrath of increasingly broad strata of the population and that realized the necessity of liberalizing somewhat the Stalinist system.

The Poznań uprising gave the final push toward the significant reform of the regime usually referred to as the Polish October. At the historic Eighth Plenum of the Central Committee of October 20, 1956, Gomułka, now elected again first secretary, against Khrushchev's protestations, made a programmatic speech. He condemned the political repression of the Stalin period in Poland, and concluded:

> Socialism is a system eliminating man's exploitation and oppression by man. . . . The roads to . . . as well as the models of socialism may differ. . . . Only through experience and through study of accomplishments of the various countries building socialism can a model of socialism be created that best fits given conditions.[11]

This was an emphatic restatement of his slogan of "Polish way to Socialism". The bloodless "October revolution" of 1956, which swept Gomułka back into power against the Soviet opposition, was a reformation achieved within the Communist framework. Despite these limitations, the triumph of Gomułka was, under the circumstances, a positive development. For the first time in the history of any Communist party, the spontaneous pressure of public opinion brought about a change of the ruling team as well as an improvement of its operative methods. Mass terror was finally abandoned, most collective farms dissolved, cultural and religious policies liberalized. Gomułka's victory was, therefore, a crucial event in the history of Polish communism, a movement away from Stalinist objectives and practices, an attempt at humanizing the system and making it more amenable to the wishes of the people. In Hungary, the Polish upheaval inspired a revolt which failed, but eventually paid off in a retarded but significant liberalization of the regime. To the rest of Soviet-dominated Eastern Europe, the Polish October was an inspiration and an encouragement, an example to emulate, a beacon to follow.

One must stress, however, that soon after Gomułka's return to power, the shock of the Poznan uprising and the events of October 1956 began to wear off. After paying lip service for a couple of years to the principles of political and economic reform Gomułka gradually lost his drive and daring, and developed a crippling inflexibility and narrow-mindedness. During the 1960s, all former plans for an extensive economic reform were abandoned. Against warnings of many of his advisers, Gomułka returned to the policy of pursuing the goal of very rapid industrial growth, regardless of obstacles and human sacrifices. This was impossible without tightening political controls and tight censorship. Yet, despite renewed use of "administrative pressures," Gomułka never restored the Stalinist mass terror.

All this does not diminish the historic importance of the "Polish October." To the Polish people it gave several years of badly needed respite, and inspired them with badly needed self-assurance. The stagnation of Poland's economy during the 1960s should not obscure the fact that, during the years 1955–57, the Poles spearheaded the movement for economic as well as political reform within the Soviet bloc, despite constant attacks not only by Moscow, but also by their Czech, Romanian and East German comrades. During those years, Poland made a significant contribution to the revision of Marxist political as well as economic theory. Thanks to the Poles, the methods as well as the objectives of the Stalinist system were submitted to a severe, searching criticism, its priorities revised, and new options outlined and gradually accepted by many other parties throughout the world.[12] The Polish rejection of the universality of the Soviet experience was soon taken up by many other parties, for instance, the Italian, and contributed to the spread of what is generally known as "Eurocommunism."

Many explanations have been advanced as to why the hero of those days lost his early courage and gradually jettisoned most of the gains of the Polish October; some reasons were of a domestic nature, some were motivated by the rapidly changing international scene, some may be attributed to his mental limitations, as well as to his failing health. One of the main reasons for Gomułka's restrictive and stern behavior during the 1960s is to be found in his native cautiousness and his perception of Poland's *raison d'état*. Preoccupation with the pervading specter of a Russo-German rapprochement at Poland's expense was constantly with him. The danger was dramatized by Adzubey's mission to Bonn in 1964, which alarmed Gomułka as a possible first step toward German reunification. Nicholas Bethell, in his biography of Gomułka, stresses that he saw in Adzubey's planned journey a confirmation of his worst fears of a Russo-German bargain at Poland's expense.[13] Gomułka's role in the overthrow of Khrushchev is not yet fully known, but there is enough evidence to say that the Polish party leadership threw whatever limited influence vassals could exercise at the center of power on the side of Khrushchev's enemies.

While the year 1956 marked Gomułka's great triumph, the years 1968–70 were his darkest days. The suppression of the youth manifestations protesting the loss of academic rights and cultural freedom, the "anti-Zionist" campaign, and the participation in the invasion of Czechoslovakia constitute some of the most controversial pages of his declining years. Since a detailed analysis of Gomułka's evolution is necessarily outside the scope of the present short essay, one must dwell only on the points which are vital for comprehending the nature of Polish Communism.

In order to understand his attitude toward the Czechoslovak crisis, one must bear in mind that the core of Gomułka's strategy had been the consolidation of the Polish-Soviet alliance. He considered it the cornerstone of Poland's policy, a precondition of her survival as a state. Gomułka had assumed a convergence of basic interests between Poland and the Soviet Union: good relations with Moscow were the only safeguard of the country's security, stability, and very existence. Hence, throughout his fourteen years of rule he tried not to obtain maximum independence from the Soviet Union, but rather tried to act within permissible limits of autonomy, often equating coordination within subordination. Gomułka remained suspicious of the far-reaching objectives of the *Ostpolitik*, despite the Czech, as well as West German, protestations that the rapprochement between Prague and Bonn was merely an innocent case of convergence of economic interests. All the Czech assurances of loyalty to the Warsaw Pact and the CEMA notwithstanding, he, as a man schooled in Marxist logic, must have interpreted Prague's "economic opening to the West" as the first step in a broader cooperation between Czechslovakia and the strongest of the NATO European countries. Like Brezhnev, Gomułka probably understood Czechoslovakia's evolution as representing not only a danger of "revisionist infection," but also as a potential threat to the existence of the East European Communist system, especially to the East German state, the survival of which he regarded as vital to Poland's security.

Throughout the Czechoslovak crisis of 1968, Gomułka tried, by acting consistently along lines parallel to Moscow, to reverse one of the persistent patterns of East European history, that of recurring Russo-Polish enmity. This was the key to Poland's participation in the occupation of Czechoslovakia by the Warsaw Pact troops in August 1968. By supporting the intervention, Gomułka tried to convince the Russians that it was possible to count on the Poles as Moscow's loyal allies. The first precedent was set up in October 1956, when he prevented a seemingly imminent violent outburst of protest against Soviet domination, pacified the country, and then stuck to the bargain by limiting Poland's domestic autonomy to tolerable limits. The second precedent was established in August 1968 when, against the overwhelmingly pro-Dubček sentiments of his people, he ordered Polish troops to march along with their Warsaw Pact partners. Thus Gomułka, while trying to safeguard what he perceived as his country's fundamental interests, lost no opportunity to prove his loyalty to Russia. In this respect he was a follower of Roman Dmowski and his National Democratic party policies during the period 1904–14. The residue of National Democratic thinking was still rather strong in Poland and Gomułka knew it: he often quoted Dmowski whenever the fundamentals of Russo-Polish relations were discussed.[14]

Another factor which enhanced Poland's position within the Communist camp has been the Sino-Soviet split. Czechoslovakia's unreliability, in addition to the intensification of the Moscow-Peking quarrel, had made Poland's loyalty so much more important to the Center. Again following in the footsteps of Dmowski, Gomułka firmly ranged Poland in the Russian camp.[15] After China's defection from the Soviet camp, Poland became Moscow's largest and most important ally. Thus, the Czechoslovak crisis and the Sino-Soviet split catapulted Gomułka to a new position of prominence and prestige: the place in the Soviet system previously occupied by Czechoslovakia was taken, at least partially, by Poland.

Soviet gratitude for his role in the Czechoslovak crisis and for his support against China was displayed at the Fifth Congress of the United Polish Workers' party held in Warsaw in November 1968. There, faced by the provincial party apparat—largely penetrated by his antagonist, the leader of the partisans, Mieczysław Moczar—Gomułka won with flying colors. Once more he had been elected first secretary of the Central Committee, while his rival was not even made a full member of the Politburo.

The peak of Gomułka's career was reached in December 1970 when, together with West German Chancellor Willy Brandt, he put his signature on the Polish-German treaty acknowledging the Oder-Neisse lines. Despite the striking limitations of the treaty, it represented a personal achievement of considerable importance. Having muddled through the events of 1967–68, the "anti-Zionist" campaign, the student revolt, the Czechoslovak crisis, and having legitimized Poland's new Western frontiers, Gomułka was at his peak. Apparently he could now look with considerable confidence on some sort of "small stabilization." He was, however, overtaken by the events of December 1970. These have to be discussed in connection with the "anti-Zionist" crisis and with the youth demonstrations of March 1968.

In order to set the event in a historic perspective, one has to understand the nature of Polish-Jewish relations during the last half century or so. It seems beyond doubt that many Polish Jews saw in communism an ideology of universal brotherhood and looked upon the CP of Poland as an instrument of transplanting to their adopted country the idealized Soviet model. In the early 1930s the Jews, who constituted some 10 percent of the country's population, accounted at least for some 26 percent of the CP of Poland. In the 1920s the percentage was still higher.[16] On the other hand, since the party was really a tiny sect, its Jewish component constituted merely a fraction of the total Jewish population. Yet, in a country as anti-Russian and anti-Communist as prewar Poland, the pro-Communist sentiments of some Jews were eagerly exploited by native anti-Semites.

Following the Soviet occupation of Eastern Poland in 1939, many Jews living there found themselves forcibly incorporated into the USSR. Most of the Polish-Jewish Communists, as well as some fellow travelers, eagerly offered their services to Moscow, and spent the war years on Soviet soil working for the USSR. In 1943, when Stalin took up the idea of extending Soviet power over Eastern Europe, they participated in the implementation of his plans for postwar Poland. Among the "Muscovites," as opposed to the "Natives," the Jews formed a large group, and their actual influence went far beyond their numerical strength owing to the group's superior educational background. The number of Jews among the "Natives" was much smaller. After the war, when the two groups merged and formed the ruling elite of the Stalinist Polish People's Republic, these differences and antagonisms never completely disappeared.

Meanwhile, in the German-occupied parts of Poland, Hitler proceeded with his "final solution" to the Jewish question, while applying an almost equally cruel policy toward the educated stratum of Polish society. As a result of the Nazi policy, over six million Polish citizens were annihilated; half of them were Jews, while the other half were ethnic Poles.[17]

The Soviet take-over of Eastern Europe after World War II brought large numbers of Jews to high places, and Poland was no exception. According to Richard V. Burks:

> In Poland there was . . . a balance [between ethnic Poles and Communists of Jewish extraction]. Berman, who controlled the secret policy, and Minc, who ran the economy, shared power with the gentiles Bierut, who was liaison with Moscow, and Gomułka, who domi-

> nated both the recovered lands and the cadre office. Just below the summit of power, the party Jews tended to concentrate in certain ministries and functions. They congregated in the foreign ministry and the ministry of foreign trade, because they were almost the only ones whom the party could trust who had the requisite knowledge of foreign languages and high finance. They also flooded into the central committee and the security police, perhaps because they felt safer near the centers of decision-making. In Bucharest, Budapest, and Warsaw virtually every important police official was Jewish. . . . Often these police officials were survivors of Nazi extermination camps, and they did not let mercy or other humanitarian considerations stand in their way when it came to dealing with the class enemy. Indeed, many Jews were publicly associated with the extremist policy followed by the satellite regimes. . . .[18]

The immediate postwar years saw the emergence in the USSR of a new phenomenon—an official Communist anti-Semitism disguised as anti-Zionism. The years 1948–49 saw a purge of most leading Soviet intellectuals of Jewish origin (as a rule described as "rootless cosmopolitans") and the removal from sensitive military as well as civilian posts of a great majority of people of Jewish background. The wave of "anti-Zionism" spread to Romania, Hungary, and Czechoslovakia, but as late as the 1950s had no significant echo in Poland. The UPWP did not have on its conscience either the cruel extermination of the Jewish cultural elite, like that conducted by Stalin in 1948–49, or the Slansky trial, or the brutal liquidation of the overwhelmingly Jewish Ana Pauker faction.

Meanwhile, a far-reaching realignment of political forces took place throughout the Soviet orbit. In Poland, the inner circle of the "Muscovites," which contained a high percentage of people of Jewish extraction, or the so-called "Puławy faction," abandoned their previous Stalinist attitude, and sought alliance with the more moderate forces of the party. In 1956, after the Poznań uprising, the "Puławy faction" threw their support to the "liberals" favoring the return of Gomułka to power and the loosening of Soviet controls over Poland.[19]

The parting of the ways took place during the early and middle 1960s. The Polish party's and Gomułka's past record as far as anti-Semitism was concerned had been rather good. When, after the Poznań uprising, Khrushchev suggested that the Polish party try Minc and Berman as scapegoats responsible for the sorry state of the Polish economy, the Poles refused to do so.[20] Later on, Khrushchev frequently insisted that there were too many Jews at the top echelons of the Polish party, but again this was not followed by any reprisals or purges. The showdown came only with the outbreak of the Arab-Israeli clash of June 1967.

The start of the Six-Day War found the Polish media engaged in condemning "the growing threat of Israeli aggression," but without the vehemence characteristic of the Soviet press or radio. The overwhelmingly favorable response of the Polish public to the Israeli victory obviously shocked the party. The reaction was most embarrassing to the leaders of the country who had tried so consistently to align its foreign policy with that of its protector, and thus consolidate the position of a most loyal partner of Moscow.

Events rapidly followed one other. On June 12, 1967, Warsaw broke off diplomatic relations with Israel. A week or so later a vigorous anti-Zionist drive was launched by Gomułka himself, who, to stay in power, had to reaffirm his solidarity with Moscow's anti-Israeli line. In a speech of June 19, he issued a solemn warning to those who "applauded the Israeli aggression," and stressed that the People's Poland would not tolerate a "fifth column" in its midst.[21] Soon, emulating Gomułka's zeal, similar speeches were made by other party leaders, eager to outbid the First Secretary. Thus, the "anti-Zionist" drive was dramatically stepped up. By December 1967, the campaign included a purge of high officials who had been compromised by their pro-Israeli stand. Some of them were ethnic Poles sympathetic to Israel, but the Jews predominated.

The antigovernmental student demonstrations of March 1968 were partly influenced by the events in Czechoslovakia, partly caused by the mounting dissatisfaction of the young educated people with the increasingly inefficient regime of Gomułka. The mass media immediately spotted the fact that among the leaders of the demonstrations, the Jews, as it happened, were rather numerous. Moreover, it was stressed that the fathers of several demonstrators held important state as well as party posts. These facts were seized upon by the opponents of Gomułka, mainly the "partisans." They accused him of tolerating the existence of a widespread "Zionist-Revisionist plot" eager to push Poland toward an "irresponsible, anti-Soviet adventure" at the time of the Middle Eastern crisis, in which Moscow had taken a determined pro-Arab stand.[22] Now, despite Gomułka's initial reluctance, the purge of the Jewish element in Poland's political, economic and cultural life was intensified.

On March 19, seeing that the "Anti-Zionist" drive was assuming undesirable proportions, Gomułka delivered a speech addressed to party activists in which he tried to tone down the campaign. He emphasized that Zionism was not a major threat to Poland. He stressed that the party's anti-Zionist drive "may have been misunderstood by some in the past," and condemned both anti-Semitism as well as Zionism. He declined to put the responsibility for the disturbances solely at "Zionist" doors. Gomułka classified the Jews in Poland in three groups: first, the Zionists with open allegiance to Israel; second, the "cosmopolitans" with allegiance divided between Israel and Poland; third, the "most numerous group, the true native sons." He suggested that the first group should leave Poland, while he advised the secondary category to "avoid the fields of work in which national affirmation is crucial." The third group was warmly praised for its loyalty.

Despite Gomułka's speech, a further intensification of the purge of Jews from most top-level party and state positions took place. The purge was paralleled by a mass exodus of Jews from Poland. About half of the Jewish population left the country. Since Gomułka's and the Polish party's credentials, as far as the Jewish problem was concerned, had been rather good, the question arises as to how to explain the "anti-Zionist" campaign. In his analysis of the Polish scene of 1967–68, one political scientist has thus summarized the situation:

First, the generally negative reaction of official policy on the Arab-Israeli war, from a population which could hardly be considered pro-Semitic, was an unmistakable sign of the regime's past failure to win political consensus. This rude awakening was further aggravated by the uninhibited display of pro-Israel sentiments on the part of some of the Jewish members of the communist elites, which dramatized the flimsiness of loyalties even among the party's most trusted members. Moreover, the First Secretary may have been subjected on this occasion to pressures from the "native" (that is, those who spent the war years in the Communist underground in Poland) party members who had been known for a long time to resent the prominence of the "Muscovites," in high party councils. Under these circumstances and in view of Gomułka's firm pro-Soviet commitment, which may have become a *sine qua non* of his own survival as a leader, it was natural for him to issue a strong warning to those who openly defied the major premise of the party credo and threatened his precarious grip over the body politic.[23]

Soon the purge assumed the character of a witch hunt, and developed a dynamic force of its own. While further analyzing its causes, the same observer of the Polish scene stresses the connection between the campaign and the intraparty factional struggle:

> The Polish Ides of March demonstrated beyond any doubt that the majority of Jewish party leaders, irrespective of their individual political pasts, had become the core of the liberal faction. These "revisionists" had to go. The intensity of the purge was aggravated by the now openly anti-Semitic machinations of the "native" party faction, whose leaders saw, at last a chance of gaining ascendance.[24]

To these considerations one should add another aspect of the "anti-Zionist" campaign. The events of 1968–69 cannot be fully understood unless one takes also into account the generational conflict within the party. During the 1960s, the aspirations of the young apparatchiks (mostly ethnic Poles of proletarian or peasant background) for better opportunities and fast promotion grew more rapidly than the party's ability to satisfy them. There was much less room at the top than the number of young candidates. Only an upheaval which would fundamentally shake the existing power relationship could make new openings available.

The changing structure and composition of the party should be viewed against a broad background. One of the most important of the socioeconomic changes that have taken place in Poland during the post–World War II years has been the urbanization of the country, resulting in a dramatic shift of the rural masses into the cities, and their slow but sure influx into the party. The prewar Communist Party of Poland had been run largely by intellectuals of Jewish background. The Polish Workers' party and its successor, the United Polish Workers' party, initially were strongly influenced by the survivors of this prewar Communist elite, largely of Jewish extraction. But postwar socioeconomic changes, followed by the events of 1967–69, eroded the initially preponderant position of this small group.

Any careful observer of the Polish scene during the late 1960s was bound to notice this increasing pressure of the impatient, intolerant, ruthless young men of peasant origin eager to get rid of the usually better educated old-timers, many of them of middle-class Jewish background, and to take their place. In a way, what happened in Poland in 1967–69 was similar to the process of replacement of the old Bolshevik cadres of the CPSU under Stalin. One has to bear in mind, however, that the Polish purge involved no bloodshed, tortures, or deportation to concentration camps.

The process has brought about a further "domestication" of the party, or the development of "a domestic perspective" which "is inevitably acquired even by the most loyal Soviet functionaries when they are assigned to specific tasks within the framework of more loosely defined ideological conceptions." The perspective, which involves a "frequently unconscious preoccupation with local, domestic Communist objectives, at the expense of broader, international Soviet goals," cannot be completely identified with "national communism" of the Yugoslav type.[25]

The events of December 1970, which resulted in the fall of Gomułka, cannot be analyzed here in detail. The immediate cause of the workers' uprising in the Baltic coast cities of Gdansk, Gdynia, Sopot, and Szczecin, was the increase in food prices by up to 30 percent, and the introduction of a new industrial wage scale, ordered just on the eve of Christmas. The fact that the party undertook a series of such sudden and drastic measures, so deeply affecting the lives of every citizen, at such an inappropriate moment, revealed the amazing unresponsiveness of the party's leadership to the needs and moods of the masses, and its separation from the population.[26] Like the Poznań riots, the Baltic workers' revolt was ruthlessly suppressed with the help of the armed forces; according to official publications, 45 were killed and 1,165 wounded. The crisis brought to power Edward Gierek, a former party boss in Silesia. The internal upheaval was primarily the result of the workers' uprising, but it was immediately taken advantage of by a party "counterelite" of Gomułka's rivals. The opposition was headed by Edward Gierek, Mieczysław Moczar, and Piotr Jaroszewicz. All three of them, for a long time, had been critical of Gomułka's rigidity and growing incompetence, especially in the economic field, and only waited for an opportunity to overthrow and replace him.

Despite the fact that the revolt had been suppressed, the workers gained a series of concessions in the form of relief for their worst grievances. They forced the withdrawal of a wage payment system that would have inflicted hardships; they formed workers' committees and even, temporarily, their own workers' militia. Finally, it was also the workers' pressure that compelled the party to reshape its leadership and revise somewhat its methods of exercising power. Thus, for the second time in the history of postwar Poland, a workers' uprising forced a change which, without being fundamental, was significant.[27] The Soviet Union, unlike during the October 1956 crisis, kept its hands off, and did not attempt, at least openly, to influence the events in Poland.

After the suppression of the open revolt, the workers of Szczecin scored yet another telling victory. On Sunday, January 24, 1971, they compelled a group of top party leaders to travel in person from Warsaw to Szczecin to hear the workers' grievances. The First Secretary of the Central Committee, the Prime Minister, the Minister of the Interior, the commander-in-chief of the armed forces, all of them had to come to the docks, spend some ten hours, from 4:00 P.M. to 2:00 A.M. the next morning, negotiating with the workers in a free and often most outspoken dialogue. What was even more significant, the party leaders had to give in to most of the workers' demands.[28] A similar dialogue lasting some seven hours also took place in Gdańsk. No history of any other Communist regime knows a similar case of the dictatorship of the proletariat put into practice, at least momentarily.

The events of December 1970 in Poland, like the Polish October of 1956, have had considerable repercussions throughout the Communist camp. This includes the Soviet Union, where the current Five-Year Plan for 1971–75 was hastily revised to provide for more consumer goods, and East Germany, where higher pensions and lower prices were immediately decreed. For the second time, Poland set an example for others to follow, and acted as a harbinger of limited but liberalizing trends in the Soviet orbit.

Thus, the whirlwind that swept the Baltic cities has profoundly shaken the party and has propelled into power a new ruling team. Gierek, a former coal miner with Polish as well as French and Belgian experience, a man with a pragmatic bent, has seen the roots of the malaise in the lack of adequate rewards which would provide the needed incentives for better work, and in the gap separating the party from the broad masses of the people, alienated from it by its insensitivity to their vital needs and sentiments. The first moves of the triumvirate were to rescind price increases, suspend the new wage scales, and boost the minimum pay rates, family allowances, and pensions. The current economic plans were revised to emphasize agriculture and consumer goods. A new agricultural policy was outlined and put into practice. The 10 million peasants who live on 3.6 million private farms have also won significant concessions from the state. Compulsory delivery quotas which the peasants had to supply at low fixed prices were abolished, and private ownership of land consolidated. The hitherto negative attitude toward some 200,000 private enterprises in retail trade and services has been toned down. More housing and a cheap, small car has been promised to Polish consumers. At the same time, efforts were undertaken to improve relations with intellectuals by relaxing the censorship somewhat, and by making foreign travel easier. Permission was given to rebuild the royal Castle of Warsaw, the concession stubbornly refused by Gomułka. After the initial liberalization, the new leadership has gradually returned to some of the restrictive and harassing practices, reminiscent of the last years of the Gomułka regime.

Gierek has also made a conciliatory gesture to satisfy, at least partially, some of the Catholic hierarchy's more pressing grievances: some 7,000 sequestered church buildings, chapels, monasteries, and parish halls in the Western territories were restored to the Church's ownership, and heavy taxation, imposed on the Church by Gomułka, was annulled. Nevertheless, Gierek's attempts to come to an agreement with the Church did not produce significant results. The problems of youth education, freedom of Catholic publications and associations have remained too difficult to surmount. The elevation of Cardinal Karol Wojtyła to the papacy in October 1978 has only made the party's task more difficult by inspiring the Polish Catholics with new self-confidence.

Parallel with these liberalizing gestures, an attempt at altering the style of the party work has been undertaken by Gierek. Frightened by the events of December 1970, trying to imitate Kadar, he has tried to establish some sort of a dialogue with the people and break down the wall of persistent mistrust between the party and the masses. The food riots of June 1976 and the rapid spread of the political and intellectual dissent movement have indicated that the dialogue has not been a lasting success. His overambitious policy of speeded-up modernization of Polish industry, largely by means of large foreign loans, began to boomerang, creating new tensions, and has given birth to an outspoken dissent movement. The attempts at suppressing the dissent by "administrative measures" failed. By the close of the 1970s Poland has found itself again in a potentially explosive situation, pregnant with all sorts of possibilities.

Having telescopically examined the party's turbulent history, focusing on the most dramatic and controversial issues, one has now to analyze briefly its present structure and character as well as its role in the life of contemporary Poland.

As has been already mentioned, the party considers itself as the agent of the country's modernization, as well as the guardian of the country's integrity and even its very existence. This was stressed in Gomułka's preelectoral speech of January 19, 1957. On the eve of the polling, he warned his countrymen that a failure to support him and the ruling party would result in Poland's disappearance from the map of the world.

The party's self image does not quite, to put it mildly, correspond to its reflection in the minds of the people at large. The role of the party in the forcible transformation of Polish society, the methods used, as well as the tempo of the process of modernization have been subjects of numerous and bitter criticism. The Polish press and other publications are merely a pale reflection of the running, and often vitriolic, private debates on the subject. Here underground publications, which have multiplied during the late 1970s, would, probably, be a more reliable source of information.[29]

Nevertheless, there are a few crucial issues on which the regime enjoys a measure of popular support. Here one should mention the following: the necessity of further economic growth (though not necessarily all the methods of achieving it), medical care and welfare policies, further development of the educational system, and last but not least, the crucial need of not offending the powerful Eastern neighbor, the guarantor of the Oder-Neisse frontier.

The list of issues on which the country's public opinion is at odds with the ruling party is certainly longer than the one just enumerated. The people of Poland, while reluctantly trying to reconcile themselves to the role in the international arena to which the outcome of World War II had relegated their country, are critical as to the manner in which the hegemonic role of the Center has been exercised and the way it is being implemented by the party. Many Poles would accept the need of some sort of alliance with Soviet Russia on geopolitical but not on ideological grounds. Here the Finnish model is regarded as more appropriate also for other western neighbors of the USSR, including Poland.

The slavish dependence of Poland's rulers on Moscow is generally considered to be unwarranted. To this one should add the widespread suspicion that Moscow takes advantage of its political ascendancy to exploit Poland economically. Criticism is also leveled against the condescending attitude of the minority in power ("the owners of People's Poland") toward the non-Communist majority. The often high-handed and arbitrary methods of the public administration and its security organs are profoundly resented. The events of 1956, 1970, and 1976 were the most striking manifestations of these sentiments.

An integral part of the party's self-image is its working-class character. But an analysis of the party's social composition only partly confirms this view. While in 1956 the number of workers constituted 42.8 percent,[30] in March 1959, according to Zenon Kliszko's report, they formed 41.8 percent, and in June 1964 only 39.5 percent of the party's membership.[31] According to the figures published in December 1971, during the Sixth Congress of the UPWP, from among 2,270,000 members and candidates, only some 40 percent are actually blue-collar workers and 12 percent are peasants. The *Statistical Yearbook* of 1977 shows that the party numbered 2,568,366 members of which 40.3 percent were workers (including 4.3 percent of agrarian workers), and 11.8 percent farmers. The number of professional people has been, all the time, oscillating around thirty percent.[32] It appears that the party has been largely controlled by the last group, a new bureaucratic intelligentsia, mostly of worker and peasant origin, but rapidly losing its contacts with its original background, as the events of 1970 and 1976 have revealed.

The organizational structure of the UPWP is similar to that of other Communist parties. It is based on a combination of territorial and functional principles. While the territorial organization corresponds to the administrative divisions of the country, the functional one is determined by the place of employment. The supreme party organ is supposed to be its congress, characterized by a careful selection of delegates, well orchestrated and rehearsed speeches, and unanimous decisions. The "rubber-stamp" function of the congress is beyond doubt. This has not always been the case with the two other vital bodies: the Central Committee and its Political Bureau. It was in these two bodies that, during the critical periods of 1948–49, 1956, and 1970, the real factional struggles were resolved. The Politburo is, as in other Communist systems, the hub of the party structure, the real locus of power.

The party has been trying to reshape not only Poland's social and economic structure but also the traditional cultural patterns. The immediate postwar period witnessed an attempt at carrying out a minor "cultural revolution" in Poland by promoting massive expansion of the educational system, and a vigorous attempt at its reorientation from humanistic to technological goals, with emphasis on Marxist secularism and rationalism. The post-World War II period also witnessed a determined drive to alter the structure of the educated classes by making all levels of education accessible to all strata of society, and thus to alter the ethos and the structure of the intelligentsia. Yet, it is an open question as to what extent the model of the Polish intelligentsia has been successfully changed, as a leading Polish sociologist, Jan Szczepanski, claims, from "broad nonprofessional, amateurish, dilettante, cultivated intellectualism," to scientific, technically-minded professionalism.[33] It seems that the pattern of thinking of the new intelligentsia is still permeated largely by the values developed by the old gentry. What is more significant, the old patterns of behavior and values have proven overwhelmingly attractive not only to the new intelligentsia, but also to the top echelons of the party.[34]

The Polish party is theoretically patterned on the CPSU. Yet, operating in a different social environment, the UPWP is far from duplicating the character of its original model, while often paying lip service to its universality. The totalitarian tendencies of the Polish party are balanced by the existence of a number of countervailing forces, absent in the USSR. The most important among them has been the Roman Catholic church, which still can claim allegiance of the majority of Poles. Even many nonbelievers respect and support the church as the main guardian of the traditional national values, attend religious services and contribute to the upkeep of the clergy. One of the symptoms of the stubborn opposition to the Communist ideology has been the existence of those "practicing non-believers," or people who go to church just to manifest their opposition to Communism. Among the less organized, more amorphous groups one should mention such interest groups as private farmers (controlling some 80 percent of the land), over 200,000 entrepreneurs, and such influential strata as intellectuals and professionals—groups which are still much stronger than in the USSR.

To the countervailing forces one must also add some 8–10 million Polish emigrés living in the West. Through their constant visits, through the parcels and money they send to help their family and friends in Poland, through their publications, like the Paris monthly *Kultura*, and through the Western radio stations they staff, they affect not only the material well-being of their former fellow countrymen, but also the political climate prevailing in Poland.[35]

Theoretically, among the countervailing forces one could count the two existing political parties: the United Peasant party and the Democratic party, the setting up of which is, in itself, a tribute to the principles of political plurality. Any closer examination of the nature of both parties and their relationship with the UPWP does not, however, warrant such a supposition. These two so-called "allied parties" are not really independent political entities but mere instruments of the hegemonic party, "transmission belts" to the peasants and the small professional-entrepreneurial strata respectively. The Communists have admitted this repeatedly and often quite frankly.[36]

The party's situation is ambivalent: it is torn between the necessity to placate the powerful protector, and the need to keep domestic dissatisfaction from assuming the explosive forms it reached in June 1956, December 1970, and June 1976. Because of mounting political and sociocultural pressure, and because of the progressive erosion of the official ideology, officially called "Marxism-Leninism," there has been less commitment to it among the party members. By avoiding the quicksands of Marxist dialectics, by expressing its policies in less ideologic terms, and occasionally by catering to popular sentiments, the party has been trying to bridge the gap separating it from the largely still traditionalist, nationalistic, sulking and rebellious masses. The explosion of the great expectations, partly caused by Gierek's exaggerated promises in 1971/2, have contributed to the spread of consumerism, which makes control of the volatile society still more hazardous.

In the Communist movement of Poland, as in other leftist formations of this type, there has never been an absolute dichotomy between the Marxist current and the nationalistic undercurrent. Each has fed the theories and actions of the other. The domestic evolution of Soviet Russia, as well as the recent infusion of Third World "national liberation" slogans into Soviet foreign policy, have made it somewhat easier for the Polish comrades to redraw their own history, as well as their current goals, in these terms. Nevertheless, their task is far from simple, and pitfalls abound at each turn of the twisted uphill road.

NOTES

1. Stepniak-Kravchinskii, "The Young Poland and Russian Revolution," *The Russian Storm-Cloud: or, Russia in her Relations to Neighboring Countries* (London: Swanson, 1886), pp. 143–44. For a collection of documents on the history of the Social Democratic party of Poland and Lithuania, 1893–1918, see O. B. Szmidt, ed., *Social-Demokracja Krolestwa Polskiego i Litwy . . .*, 2 vols., vol. 1, 1893–1904, vol. 2, 1914–1918 (Moscow: 1934 and 1936, respectively). For a basic treatment of the origins of Polish communism in English see M. K. Dziewanowski, *The Communist Party of Poland: An Outline of His-*

tory (Cambridge, Mass.: Harvard University Press, 1959 and 1976), esp. chaps. 1–6. For a pertinent collection of documents see Georg W. Strobel, ed., *Quellen zur Geschichte des Kommunismus in Polen, 1878–1918* (Cologne: Wisseschaft und Politik, 1968). See also: Georg W. Strobel, *Die Partei Rosa Luxemburgs*, (Wiesbaden: F. Steiner, 1974), for the most important resolutions of the SDKPiL congresses and conferences see *Z pola walki*, no. 16 (Moscow: 1934).

2. For a disappointing treatment of the subject by a party historian, see J. Kowalski, *Zarys Historii Polskiego Ruchu Robotniczego w Latach 1918–1939* (An Outline of the History of the Polish Workers' Movement in the Years 1918–1939) (Warsaw: Ksiazka i Wiedza, 1962). For an attempt at a treatment by an outsider of the liquidation of the CPP see M. K. Dziewanowski, *The Communist Party of Poland*, 2d ed. For a brilliant yet unconvincing explanation of the dissolution of the party by a former leader of its Trotskyite faction, see I. Deutscher's article, "La tragédie du Communisme Polonais entre les deux guerres," in *Les Temps Modernes*, March 1958.

3. See "Interview with an Ex-Insider: The Party that Vanished," *Les Temps Modernes*, March 1958. N. S. Khrushchev admitted that: "It was easy for Stalin to destroy the leaders of the Polish Party because most of them lived and worked in the Comintern in Moscow. The only reason Bierut and Gomułka stayed alive was that they were relatively unknown in the Party circles." *Khrushchev Remembers*, 2 vols. (Boston and Toronto: Little Brown, 1970), 1:107.

4. *Kommunisticheskii International*, 1939, no. 4 (April), p. 119.

5. "The Eighteenth Congress of the Communist Party of the Soviet Union(B). Report . . . given by Comrade D. Manuilsky," *World News and Views*, April 6, 1939, p. 382; compare this statement with the statement of the five parties and the official commentary published in *Trybuna ludu* of February 19, 1956. During the present writer's visit to Poland in 1958 he had a chance to discuss the problem with two leading party historians: both of them admitted that they had no chance of seeing the pertinent documents, that the communiqué of the five parties rehabilitating the CPP was issued without examination of the "evidence faked by a gang of saboteurs and provocateurs."

6. For an analysis of the transition period between the liquidation of the CP of Poland and the formation of the PWP see Andrzej Korbonski's article, "The Polish Communist Party, 1938–1942," *Slavic Review*, September 1967.

7. For his speech: *For a Lasting Peace, For a People's Democracy*, Bucharest, No. XI, november 10, 1947, pp. 18–24.

8. Though not published at the time, this statement and other details of the June Plenum were later brought out at the Central Committee session at the end of August and reported in the PZPR theoretical organ *Nowe Drogi* (Warsaw), September–October 1948. Commenting on Gomułka's alleged "Titoism," N. S. Khrushchev writes in his memoirs: "Now, you might ask, how did Gomułka get mixed up in the Yugoslav problem? How could he be accused of having a pro-Yugoslav

position? Gomułka had led a Polish delegation to Yugoslavia before the final break between Stalin and Tito but after a black cat had already crossed the road between them. While in Yugoslavia, Gomułka made some speeches in which, naturally enough, he said some things calculated not to offend his hosts, but rather to praise Tito for what he was doing. Later, when conflict arose inside the Polish leadership, Gomułka's opponents used those speeches against him, saying he had sympathized with Titoist positions. This was enough for Stalin. He considered anyone who had close contacts with Tito to be little better than Tito himself. This was typical of Stalin: anyone associated with his enemies was treated as an enemy." *Khrushchev Remembers* 2:181–82. For Khruschev's and Stalin's attitudes toward Gomułka, *ibid.*, 2:170–83.

9. *Nowe Drogi*, November 1949.

10. Georges Mond, "Les échos et les conséquences du XXième Congrès de P. C. de l'U.R.S.S. en Pologne," in Rene Girault, ed., *Mythes et réalités de l'Europe de l'est en 1956*," (Paris: Institut National d'Etudes Slaves, 1977).

11. For the text of the speech see *Trybuna ludu*, October 21, 1956. The Polish October has a large literature; among useful background works one should mention: Flora Lewis, *A Polish Volcano: A Case History of Hope* (London: Secker & Wartburg, 1959) Konrad Syrop, *Spring in October* (London: Weinfeld and Nicholson, 1956); Frank Gibney, *The Frozen Revolution* (New York: Farrar, Strauss and Cudahy, 1959); and S. L. Shneiderman, *The Warsaw Heresy* (New York: Horizon Press, 1959). For analysis of the events: M. K. Dziewanowski, *Communist Party*, pp. 267–80; Z. Brzezinski, *The Soviet Bloc: Unity and Conflict* (Cambridge, Mass.: Harvard University Press, 1960), pp. 333–39; for a selection of documents edited by Jerzy Mond, see *6 Lat temu* [Six Years Ago] (Paris: the Literary Institute *Kultura* 1962); for an interesting interpretation of the events of a participant, Witold Jedlicki, "Chamy i 'Zydy" [The Bumpkins and the Jews], *Kultura* (Paris), December 1962; the author was close to the Puławy faction, then supporting Gomułka; see also Jerzy Mond's report about Gomułka's discussion with Polish journalists soon after his return to power in October 1956 in *Zeszyty Historyczne Kultury* (Paris), 1963, no. 4.

12. For a discussion of Poland's contribution to the loosening of the Soviet bloc, see Andrzej Brzeski, "Poland as a Catalyst of Change in the Communist Economic System," *The Polish Review*, spring 1971.

13. "Gomułka's greatest complaint against his political opponents is that they take Poland's existence for granted, that they act as if Poland were a self-sufficient island. He sees such men as totally unrealistic and does not hesitate to accuse them of being ready to sacrifice Poland's vital interest for the sake of such luxuries as freedom of expression." Nicholas Bethell, *Gomułka, His Poland and His Communism* (New York, Chicago, San Francisco: Holt, Rinehart and Winston 1969), pp. 244–45. While granting a limited scope to non-Communist groups, Gomułka firmly opposed a multiparty system. Those who favor reestablishment of several political parties, he declared in 1957, "would

perhaps suggest that we change the geographic and political situation of Poland, that it be moved to another part of the globe or another planet." Quoted in *East Europe*, 1957, no. 3, p. 4. See also: Jerzy Mond's essay on Gomułka, *Kultura* (Paris), July 1965.

14. For an attempt to draw a parallel between Dmowski's and Gomułka's policies of cooperation with Russia, see Adam Bromke, *Poland's Politics: Idealism vs. Realism*, (Cambridge, Mass.: Harvard University Press, 1967). Hansjakob Stehle's book, *The Independnt Satellite* (New York: Praeger, 1965), also contains many perceptive observations about Gomułka as a historic personality; see also Georges Mond, "La Pologne et l'Europe Orientale face au différence Sino-Soviétique," *Notes et Études Documentaires*, Paris, Documentation Françcaise, no. 3238, Paris, Novembre 20, 1965.

15. Only one generation ago, Roman Dmowski bluntly warned his countrymen against getting involved in a conflict with Russia and prophesied: "the time may come when those who are now dreaming about partitioning Russia will anxiously ask whether she is strong enough to withstand the pressure of China. . . . this moment may not be very far away." *Świat powejenny a Polska* (the Postwar World and Poland) (Warsaw: 1931), p. 186.

16. "According to an official Communist source, in 1933 some 26 percent of party members were Jewish. This figure seems on the low side. Perhaps it covers only those activists who were willing to admit that they came from Jewish families. An anti-Communist source estimates the proportion of Jews in the party in 1931 at about half and there are indications that in 1940 the percentage of Jews in the Communist party of neighboring Lithuania was 53.8. In any case, it is clear that the bulk of the Communist youth organization was Jewish. In the Polish population as a whole Jews amounted to 10.5 per cent (in 1924). . . . The proportion of Jewish activists in the Polish party varied with time and place. During the middle twenties, when the party was at its apogee, the proportion declined notably, owing to the vast (if largely temporary) influx of Ukrainian and Belorussian peasants." R. V. Burks, *The Dynamics of Communism in Eastern Europe* (Princeton, N.J.: Princeton University Press, 1961), p. 160. "The influence of Jews on party life, moreover, was generally greater than the percentages would suggest. Jewish activists were probably better educated than the average, and more likely to achieve the level of leading cadre. Many Jewish Members of the Polish party were former rabbinical students."*Ibid.*, p. 161.

17. Polish-Jewish relations under the Nazi rule have been a subject of numerous controversies; for the background of these relations see: F. Friedman, *Their Brothers' Keepers*, (New York: Crown, 1957); K. Iranek-Osmecki, *He Who Saves One Life* (London, Orbis, 1970); W. Bartoszewicz and Z. Lewin, *Righteous Among Nations* (London: Orbis, 1969); or, in the U.S. edition, *The Samaritans—Heroes of the Holocaust* (New York: Twayne, 1970); and W. Bartoszewicz, *The Blood Shed Unites Us* (Warsaw: Interpress, 1970); For a short summary of the problem, see S. Korbonski, *The Polish Underground State: A Guide to the Underground,*

1939–1945, (East European Quarterly, Boulder and Columbia University Press, 1978), pp. 120–39, 253–56.

18. R. V. Burks, *Dynamics*, p. 166. "Early in 1949 the Hungarian and Rumanian governments, on whose territories 90 per cent of surviving East European Jewry was domiciled, outlawed Zionist organizations and deported Zionist missions. Local Zionist leaders were secretly tried and given long prison terms. Israeli diplomats were accused of espionage and expelled. In September 1949, on the occasion of the trial of L. Rajk, the leader of the nationalist wing in the Hungarian party, almost the entire body of Hungarian Jewish Communists who had spent the war years in Switzerland was executed. In the summer of 1952, three top-drawer Rumanian Communists of Jewish origin—Pauker, Georgescu, and Luca—were purged. In December 1952, the *éminence grisé* of the Czech party, R. Slansky, was placed in the dock, along with a dozen other Jewish leading cadres. Slansky and his fellow accused were condemned in December 1952." *Ibid.*, pp. 167–68.

19. The complex intraparty intrigues involved in the process and motivation of various factions are outside the scope of this short essay. For an interesting analysis of the situation in Poland in 1953–56 see Jedlicki, "Chamy i Zydy," pp. 3–41. Gomułka's British biographer, Nicholas Bethell, shows sympathetic understanding of Gomułka's difficulties in 1967–68 without subscribing to his views or excusing some of his obnoxious methods. Nevertheless the author stresses that "Gomułka is no anti-Semite" and that he "was dragged along by events, by a situation he did not control." He tried to limit the so-called "anti-Zionist campaign" (p. 264). His speech of March 14, 1968, had this very purpose. For a perceptive reappraisal of Gomułka's rule, see Adam Bromke, "Beyond the Gomułka Era," *Foreign Affairs*, April 1971.

20. Jedlicki, "Chamy i Zydy" p. 169.

21. Situation "Report-Polad," *Radio Free Europe Situation Reports*, June 22, 1967.

22. *Trybuna ludu*, March 20, 1968.

23. Stanislaw Staroń, "Political Developments in Poland: The Party Reacts to Challenge," *Orbis*, winter 1970; see also A. Ross Johnson's article "Poland: End of an Era?" in *Problems of Communism*, January-February 1970.

24. Staroń, "Political Developments." To the best knowledge of this author there has been no adequate, up-to-date analysis of the role of the Communists of Jewish descent in the Soviet empire-building in Eastern Europe after World War II. While Stalin was suppressing Jewish life and culture in the USSR and even indulging in the annihilation of the Jewish intellectual elite, he still was using East European Jewish Communists to carry out his designs on the periphery of the Empire. There is here some analogy with the use of the Greek *phanariotes* by the Ottoman sultans: in both cases an oppressed minority was used by the empire-builders for their own purposes. The problem of transition of many Jewish party members from devout "Muscovites" and Stalinists

to "liberals" and "revisionists" is another fascinating subject worthy of scholarly investigation. For a brilliant analysis of the complex, ambivalent relations betwen Jewishness and communism see Leopold Tyrmand's essay on "How to be a Jew under Communism" in his *Cywilizacia Komunizmu* [Communist Civilisation] (London: 1972).

25. Brzezinski, *The Soviet Bloc* p. 52.

26. These increases in food prices, explained the deputy chairman of the Planning Commission, Professor J. Pajestka, on December 12, 1970, were due to the difficult situation in Polish agriculture and foreign trade and to the necessity of achieving "a correct structure of consumption," by which he meant a shift in popular consumption from foodstuffs to industrial goods, allegedly necessary because domestic consumption had a negative effect on the export of meat products. *Trybuna ludu* of December 13, 1970 stated in its editorial that "further reduction in the export of meat products is inadmissible" because of Poland's need for hard currency. For the best presentation of the subject see Leopold Labedź, "From Poznań to Gdańsk," *Interplay* (London), March 1971; for a broad analysis of Gomułka's failure, see W. Bieńkowski, *Sociologia kleski* (Sociology of Disaster) (Paris: The Literary Instytute Kultura, 1971).

27. For a collection of documents pertaining to the December 1970 events, see *Dokumenty Poznań 1956—Grudzien 1970* (Paris: The Literary Institute Kultura, 1971); for a *post mortem* of the Gomułka regime, conducted by the Party Committee on February 6–7, 1971, see the special issue of *Nowe Drogi*, 1971. The weekly *Poliyka* of December 30, 1970 admitted: "Although there are various degrees of responsibility, the party is responsible for the causes that gave rise to the tragic events. Elements of stagnation were growing in the economy. The picture presented by propaganda was far from reality."

28. *Glos Szczećinski*, January 26, 1971; see also E. Wacowska, ed., *Rewolta szczećinski i jej znaczenie* (The Szczecin Revolt and Its Significance The Literary Instytute Kultura, 1971).

29. For some voices of the underground opposition published abroad, see publications of the Literary Institute in Paris (*Kultura*); J. Kuron and K. Modzelewski, *List Otwarthy do Partii* (an Open Letter to the Party) (Paris: The Literary Institute Kultura, 1966); W. Bieńkowski, *Motory i Hamulce Socializmu* (Driving Forces and Breaks of Socialism) (Paris: The Literary Instytute Kultura, 1969); and J. Szpotanski, ed., *Satyra Podziemna* (Underground Satire) (Paris: The Literary Institute Kultura, 1971).

30. *Nowe Drogi*, no. 6, 1956.

31. *Trybuna ludu*, June 20, 1964, *Rocznik Statystyczny 1977 (Warsaw, P.W. 1977), p. 21.*

32. *"Report of the CC of the UPWP for the period betwen the Vth and VIth Congresses," Trybuna ludu*, December 5, 1971. According to the report, the party numbers 910,000 workers 250,000 peasants, and 980,000 white-collar workers. "Among 980,000 white-collar workers belonging to the UPWP there are approximately 190,000 engineers and

technicians, over 140,000 teachers, nearly 120,000 economists, 28,000 agricultural and forestry experts, and 12,000 medical doctors." *Ibid.* It is worth bearing in mind that the sectors of the economy under direct state control employ some 10 million workers and employees and that Poland has some 34 million inhabitants. For an analysis of the party structure by a Communist sociologist see M. Sadowski, *Przemiany społeczne a system partyjny* (Social Changes and the Party System (Warsaw: diw 1969), pp. 198–204. For interesting data available on the UPWP see the article on the party's dynamics in *Życie partii*, 1974, no. 8 (267).

33. Jan Szczepański, "The Polish Intelligentsia: Past and Present," *World Politics* (April 1962), 14(3):419; as the sociologist put it, the political leaders of Poland "are to some degree interpenetrated by traditional intellectuals, but the latter have rather limited influence on political decisions"; see also Alexander Gella, "The Life and Death of the Old Polish Intelligentsia," *Slavic Review* (March 1971), 30(1):17, and a revealing study by a senior Polish sociologist, Josef Chałasiński, in his book *Prseszlość i przyszlość inteligencji polskiej* (The Past and Future of the Polish Intelligentsia) (Warsaw: Ludowa Spótdzielnia Wydawnicza, 1958).

34. For a symposium covering several key aspects of social changes brought about by the Communist seizure of power, see Adam Sarpata, ed., *Przemiany spoleczne w Polsce Ludowej* (Social Changes in People's Poland) (Warsaw: PIW 1965); for a study in interconnections between the post–World War II political system and social changes, see Sadowski, *Przemiany społeczne a system partyjny, passim.* See also J. J. Wiatr, "Polityczne nastepstwa premian strktury spolecznej" (Political Consequences of the Changing Social Structure), *Nowe Drogi*, January 1971.

35. The Polish diaspora in the West is a large, significant factor, yet until 1956 the emigres were ostracized, criticized, and practically ignored by the ruling party as representing mostly backward and reactionary forces. Betwen 1956 and 1971, the old policy alternated with halfhearted attempts at making an occasional friendly gesture. The change of mind in this respect on the part of Gierek's team has been in itself a tribute to the strength of the countervailing force. The fact that the main purpose of the new course toward the Polish emigration has been to channel and eventually politically neutralize it does not completely affect the significance of the policy.

36. For instance on February 18, 1971, the official party paper, *Trybuna Ludu*, discussing a recent *Sejm* session, stated that both the "allied parties" ideologically fully agree with the UPWP and act under its guidance; for the confirmation of this opinion see *Przemiany spoleczne a system partyjny*, pp. 59 and 71.

Also, the Polish one-chamber parliament, the *Sejm*, cannot be considered as a countervailing force. As one of its few independent, Catholic deputies put it melancholically: "Our Sejm is not the type of parliament one finds in Western democracies. . . . Our parliament is not a battlefield on which social forces fight for power," (Dr. Stanislaw Stomma, chairman of the Catholic parliamentary club). *Znak*, March 26, 1961; quoted by Stehle, *The Independent Satellite*, p. 177.

Trond Gilberg

7. The Communist Party of Romania

The Romanian Communist party (RCP) has been one of the least examined parties in the East European socialist states. As compared to the massive outpourings of research on the Czechoslovak, Polish, and Yugoslav parties, the number of works devoted to the RCP is small, although some of these volumes contain a considerable amount of information and penetrating analysis.[1] The relative dearth of material on this party is somewhat puzzling, for the RCP has become one of the most influential elements in the relationships between the ruling regimes in the so-called "socialist commonwealth," and Romanian foreign policy has attracted wide attention in official circles in the West, perhaps especially in Washington, where both President Nixon and President Ford have spoken of a "special relationship" with Bucharest. Domestically, the RCP has conducted a massive nation-building campaign whose social and economic results, at least, have been very impressive. Against this kind of background, it behooves us to examine more closely the structural features of the RCP, its main policy goals, the strategies and tactics for achieving such goals, and the main successes and failures of these Communist-led policies.

THE HISTORICAL DIMENSION

The development of Romania since World War II and the position of the RCP in Romanian society have usually been examined in terms of fairly clear periods or eras. During the period 1944–48 (a period covering the liberation of the country from German domination in August 1944 and the abandonment of the various coalition governments which had been in charge since the war, as well as the abdication of the king in 1947), the RCP was primarily engaged in consolidating its organization and expanding its membership while maintaining a high profile in the coalition government, gradually pushing aside the "bourgeois" parties and the Social Democrats. In this period, important elements of the RCP economic program were also enacted, such as nationalization of the banks and parts of industry, and a land reform which split up the old estates and produced a class of smallholders. In this period, "collaborationist elements" were also ruthlessly persecuted, and this meant that fascist organizations, such as the Iron Guard, were effectively destroyed and removed from any possible contention for power.[2]

During the second period, 1948–53, Romania underwent an experience similar to that of all the other people's democracies in Eastern Europe: the domestic and foreign policies of the country were ruthlessly subordinated to the interests of Moscow; the RCP became a full-fledged satellite party, unquestioningly obeying commands from the Kremlin, and the party carried out a series of purges designed to root out "domesticists," "nationalists," "cosmopolitanists," "Zionists," and "Titoists." The RCP moved decisively to destroy all remnants of bourgeois power, influence, and organizational ability, and the Social Democrats were forcibly "joined" with the Communists in a common party. Rapid modernization, with primary emphasis on heavy industrialization, produced severe dislocation for the population. This manifested itself in a significant lowering of the standard of living and a series of major problems usually associated with rapid urbanization without the economic and service infrastructure necessary to accommodate the masses of people crowding into the cities.[3]

After Stalin's death, most of the regimes of Eastern Europe underwent a protracted period of uncertainty over Moscow's position vis-à-vis the area, coupled with a process of de-Stalinization which engulfed many of the top cadres of the preceding period. It is in this period, too, that the struggle between the so-called "Muscovites" and their leaders who had spent the war years in their own countries ("domesticists") took place.

In Romania, no significant de-Stalinization process took place. There were several reasons for this internal peculiarity. First of all, the leadership struggle between Muscovites and domesticists had *preceded* Stalin's death in Romania; Ana Pauker had already been toppled from her position in 1952, to be replaced by Gheorghe Gheorghiu-Dej.[4] Second, the party was still only weakly established in the population, relying upon a considerable amount of real or threatened terror to stay in power after years of harsh policies, and the leadership probably felt that a major shake-up along the lines of Hungary would produce a situation which might get out of hand.[5] Third, there were no real anti-Stalinists among the top contenders for Ana Pauker's position; any meaningful alternative simply included other officials, who were at the same time nationalists, whereas "liberals" of the character of an Imre Nagy could not be found among the top echelons of the RCP.[6] Thus, the successor to Ana Pauker was Gheorghe Gheorghiu-Dej, an individual whose views on the party's position in society, as well as the basic economic policies to be followed, were quite similar to the deposed leader, except that Gheorghiu-Dej was a domesticist and a Romanian nationalist.[7] And fourth, there was even at this time a hint of the future quest for autonomy from Moscow: the fact that de-Stalinization was afoot in the Soviet Union and most of the other former satellites was not seen as a reason for Romania to follow suit.

The combination of factors outlined above ensured that even in the post-Stalinist era, the RCP continued its harsh regime, with tight political controls and an economic policy which emphasized rapid industrialization and now also collectivization of agriculture at the expense of consumer goods and the standard of living.

Although the Stalinist traits of the RCP's domestic policies were maintained, an increasingly nationalistic approach became discernible after 1960. An important element in the party's position in society was this nationally oriented policy which produced an element of genuine support in the masses of the population, despite the economic hardships which had to be endured. In fact, the consolidation of the RCP in society, which had been buttressed by coercion and organizational expansion in the period 1952–60, was further enhanced by the increasing emphasis on the RCP as a *national* party, closely tied in with Romanian history and traditions, a party which would lead Romania to a more elevated position in the world, denied the country for centuries by foreign invaders. The RCP made several foreign policy moves which exhibited this nationalistic vision, the most celebrated of which is the so-called "declaration of independence" in early 1963, when the Romanian leadership pointedly stated that each socialist state has the right to develop according to its own specific conditions, and that relations among such states must be based on the principles of "mutual advantage," noninterference in internal affairs, and equality.[8] In domestic politics, the sources of RCP authority also changed; in preceding periods, it had been based on the threat of coercion and also on the actual achievements of the regime in building an industrial base which would result in significant improvements in people's lives in future generations; now, the regime clearly demanded allegiance on the basis of its *nationalistic* achievements as well. The combination was established of a strict internal political regime, with a party which clearly emphasized its absolute authority in all walks of life, ruling under the auspices of traditional Romanian nationalism, and a maverick foreign policy which rearranged political ties and trade patterns toward the West, a combination that continues to this day as a hallmark of the unique position and policy of the RCP.

The Quest for the "Multilaterally Developed Society"

With the advent of Nicolae Ceausescu to power in 1965, the RCP's self-proclaimed role in society was expanded and somewhat altered, although many elements of previous policies remain. Several objectives have been most strenuously emphasized as primary party goals during the last decade.

1. *The expansion of the party's position in society.* In numerous statements by Nicolae Ceausescu and other prominent leaders of the RCP, the point has been repeatedly made that the party must expand its organizational framework and intensify its activities in order to reach ever-increasing members and strata of the population. Such increased activity is necessary because the RCP has become even more important in an era which is officially defined as "the creation of the multilaterally developed society." In such a stage (to be described in detail below), the supreme force of society takes on added tasks and responsibilities, chiefly the process of intensified mobilization of the population for the fulfillment of the extremely ambitious economic, social, and political goals established by the party leadership. The party under these circumstances must become even more active than was the case in previous epochs, especially in the fields of conscience-building and of political socialization and indoctrination. Thus, while many of the Communist parties in Eastern Europe seem to be adjusting to a changed situation of increased social and economic pluralism in which the profile of the party will become somewhat lower, the RCP is in the midst of a political-ideological offensive which is designed to maintain party control in all areas of human activity and indeed to expand it.[9]

The implementation of the ideological campaign has been manifested in several ways. First of all, the ideological element in party work has been intensified, both for top echelon members and for cadres at the county (*judet*) and local levels. Seminars and ideological programs have also been instituted in larger numbers than earlier in economic institutes, factories, and in academic institutions. The political element at all levels of education has been significantly increased, even in purely technical fields and the hard sciences. Short courses at the Stefan Gheorghiu Academy, which is an institution attached to the RCP Central Committee for training party and administrative cadres in political matters, have increased in number during this period.[10]

The intensive ideological activity among party cadres and administrative personnel at all levels has been matched by increased control over the arts and literature, as well as in other areas of cultural activity. There have been purges in the Writers' Union, in the party and government institutions primarily responsible for supervising the arts, and at the Bucharest Opera and other theaters in the capital. Political themes and positive descriptions of "nation-building" now abound where ten years ago writers focused on some of the social ills resulting from contradictions in socialist society. In sculputre, the themes emphasized are also increasingly political, and this medium is being utilized as a vehicle of criticism against mismanagement and "bourgeois tendencies" in all walks of life. Similar themes abound in the theater and the cinema. Common to all these art forms is the suppression of the image of individuals "opting out" of society in order to pursue individualistic notions and views.[11]

Among the masses of the population, ideological work has picked up considerably during the last three to four years. There are constant campaigns at places of employment, in residence areas, and in the "houses of culture" which dot the countryside and city sections. The frequency of political meetings and "voluntary weekend work," which is usually heavily infused with political indoctrination, has also increased in the 1970s.

This massive campaign is designed to accomplish two major objectives. First of all, ideological mobilization is seen as a crucial element in the ambitious economic program of the regime; material incentives, still rather meager in many fields, are supplemented by more symbolic payoffs such as special titles, medals, and the many honors bestowed upon "outstanding achievers" in the production process. At the same time, the political education campaign is aimed at the long-range transformation of values, whereby "socialist outlooks" are instilled in the population, thus vastly increasing their willingness to work and also their capabilities for a successful completion of the task before them.[12]

Second (and of more immediate concern), the campaign is designed to combat the manifestations of "old values" still admittedly present in the population, and also to remove the "socialist contradictions" which have developed during the years of Communist rule. Nicolae Ceausescu has repeatedly castigated the party for its failure to combat such manifestations effectively, and as late as the Eleventh Party Congress (November 1974) he hammered home the message by once again focusing on the following problem areas:

a) Remnants of "bourgeois-landowner" mentality, chief among which are greed, egotism, concern with one's own immediate family rather than the society as a whole, corruption, sloppiness at work, and inefficiency. According to the RCP leader, the continuaton of such behavior patterns and values constitutes a very serious impediment both to the economic development of the country and to the efforts to create a new "socialist consciousness" among the people. Ceausescu has defined "socialist consciousness" as dedication to work, concern for one's fellow man and society as a whole, honesty, truthfulness, reliability, and punctuality; all these character traits are to be matched by commitment to socialism and communism and to the RCP as the supreme force in society. It is clear from the frequent campaigns initiated by the party that this goal of conscience-building is indeed quite far from fulfillment at the present time, but the perceived need for it ensures that the heavy ideological hand of the leadership will continue its grip on Romania.[13]

b) Problems arising from the development of society in the period of socialist development. *Era Socialista* and other theoretical and political journals frequently discuss problems arising from the rapid development of society under Communist rule, and the general secretary often returns to this theme, as well. According to Marxism-Leninism (as well as the current version of it in the RCP), the social strata under socialism are not antagonistic toward one another because conscious exploitation is impossible under Communist rule. Unfortunately, the actual *practices* of "certain elements" in the political and administrative elite at various levels create real contradictions and antagonisms. The most important aspects of such "antisocial" behavior are unjust accumulations of wealth, favoritism, *bakshish* (a marvelous Romanian word which describes the many practices of corruption and favoritism which traditionally played such an important part in Romanian society), and "elitisim." There have been scandals in which fairly high officials have been dismissed or even prosecuted for amassing wealth beyond the legally established salary figures. Favoritism is apparently a rather frequent practice in the assignment of scarce housing space or places in institutions of higher education. (Nowadays, there are occasional rumors about nepotism at the very top, where Ceausescu's wife, Elena, holds an important position in the party and several other relatives are in high posts of the government.) Most observers agree that *bakshish* remains a major problem at virtually all levels of society. As for "elitism," Ceausescu and others have repeatedly said that many party cadres and bureaucrats behave in such a way that they are out of touch with the people, and in fact relate to the masses only in terms of empty slogans and ritualistic incantations of Marxism-Leninism, while they have no interest in the solution of real problems. Both in 1971–72 and since June 1973 several high and medium-level party leaders have been dismissed for "elitism" and "sloganeering."[14]

The ideological campaign increased in intensity during 1976 and 1977, in preparation for the celebration of the centennial of Romanian independence. An important ideological conference of cadres in the party and government (as well as the artistic and literary world) was held in the summer of 1976, and the goals of the "cultural revolution" were reiterated, indeed expanded.[15] Following the conference, the Romanian media and the intelligentsia were mobilized to drive home the message of the continued need for ideological education and indoctrination. A further impetus for this campaign was provided by the festival "Hymn to Romania," which was an attempt to mobilize amateur talent for a song and dance competition throughout the country in 1976 and 1977; its goals was to inspire the masses through patriotic and "socially engaged" musical activities which could further be utilized to drive the ideological message home. Since only "deserving" workers and peasants were allowed to participate in the festival, this campaign presumbly served as a stimulant to increased material production as well.[16]

By all accounts, the ideological offensive of the last two years has further restricted individuals' ability to express themselves in fields such as the arts, literature, or politics, and the level of economic control has also been increased. This process of accelerated mobilization has apparently failed to produce major political results, however. At the end of 1977, Ceausescu was still complaining about the lack of commitment and the continued existence of "retrograde values" in the population.

Part of the problem for the general secretary was the development of a small but rather vocal dissident movement in Romania. In the spring of 1977, the well-known author Paul Goma became the leading figure in a group of dissidents who claimed the need for considerable change in social and political matters in the country, based upon Ceausescu's acceptance (in principle) of the Helsinki agreements. After an initially flexible response from the regime, which included a private conversation between Goma and Cornel Burtica, head of the RCP's top ideological section, Ceausescu became increasingly irritated with the dissidents' demands, and throughout the spring and summer he repeatedly lashed out against them, on occasion strongly hinting that their activities were tantamount to treason.[17]

The dissident movement was a nuisance which attracted some international attention, but it did not have the impact of the movements in Poland, Czechoslovakia, or East Germany. Of greater importance, at least potentially, was the growing disenchantment of Romanian workers with the continuation of economic mobilization without corresponding rewards. During the summer and fall of 1977, there were repeated strikes in Bucharest and elsewhere, and on some occasions the militia had to be called out to quell disturbances.[18] Of particular worry to the regime was the fact that the strike movement had gathered much sympathy and active support among the young—certainly a bad omen for a regime in pursuit of the "new socialist man and woman." It is likely that the existence of such tendencies, officially categorized as "retrograde" by the regime, will produce further emphasis on ideological controls and indoctrination.

2. *The gradual reorganization of the political machinery, which will decisively implement the principles of "rotation of cadres" and the "removal of duplication of positions."* In conformity with the emphasis on greater party activity in Romanian society is the attempt to simplify the organizational structures of governmental ministries and economic organizations, a plan which will remove many individuals from "desk jobs" to "jobs in the production process." This policy reflects a somewhat belated realization that both the economic and the political administration structures of Romania are extremely top-heavy, encompassing large numbers of people with considerable skills in engineering and other crucial fields who are occupied in purely administrative positions. A removal of some of these cadres to industry and other areas of the economy will presumaly have a beneficial effect on production. At the same time, Ceausescu has been supervising a massive transfer of top party leaders to positions outside of the RCP inner circles, ostensibly for the purpose of "sharing talent" with other institutions and structures, especially the governmental bureaucracy, but certainly also for the purpose of preventing any development of powerful counterelites or groups of individuals with political and administrative power concentrations even remotely comparable to that of the general secretary. Thus, Nicolae Ceausescu is the only individual who maintains multiple memberships in the top organs of the party, the state, and the many commissions and "working groups" which are established to oversee all aspects of political, cultural, and socioeconomic life. This massive offensive of administrative reorganization has been particularly pronounced during the last three years (since the spring of 1973) and has already made Ceausescu so powerful (in structural terms) that he may in fact provide the closest example of "Stalinist" centralization currently available in Eastern Europe.[19]

The increasing concentration of the top political positions in Romania can be illustrated by an examination of the line-up of memberships in the RCP's leading bodies. At the Tenth RCP

Congress in August 1969, the party had a Presidium, an Executive Committee, a Party Collegium, and a Secretariat. The membership of these bodies was as follows:

Permanent Presidum:

Nicolae Ceausescu, Emil Bodnaras, Paul Niculescu-Mizil, Gheorghe Pana, Dumitru Petrescu, Gheorghe Radulescu, Virgil Trofin, Ilie Verdet.

The Secretariat:

Nicolae Ceausescu, General Secretary; Mihai Gere, Paul Niculescu-Mizil, Gheorghe Pana, Vasile Patilinet, Dumitru Popescu, Virgil Trofin.

The Executive Committee:

Full members: Nicolae Ceausescu, Ion Gheorghe Maurer, Maxim Berghianu, Emil Bodnaras, Florian Danalache, Constantin Dragan, Emil Draganescu, Janos Fazekas, Petre Lupu, Manea Manescu, Paul Niculescu-Mizil, Gheorghe Pana, Dumitru Petrescu, Dumitru Popescu, Gheorghe Radulescu, Leonte Rautu, Gheorghe Stoica, Virgil Trofin, Ilie Verdet, Vasile Vilcu, and Stefan Voitec.

Candidate members:

Iosif Banc, Petre Blajovici, Miu Dobrescu, Aurel Duca, Mihai Gere, Ion Iliescu, Ion Ionita, Carol Kiraly, Vasile Patilinet, Dumitru Popa, and Ion Stanescu.

Central Party Collegium:

Mihai Dalea, president; Simion Bughici, vice-president; Dumitru Ivanovici, Ioan Gluvacov, Andrei Cervencovici, Stefan Duduman, Gheorghe Ionescu, Ion Medrea, and Alexandru Sencovici.[20]

During the period 1969–73, numerous personnel changes were effected in the RCP, and new bodies, the so-called "joint councils," were created with a mixed membership of individuals from both top party bodies and leading governmental ministries. The Presidium in 1973 consisted of Nicolae Ceausescu, Emil Bodnaras, Manea Manescu, Ion Gheorghe Maurer, Paul Niculescu-Mizil, Gheorghe Pana, Gheorghe Radulescu, Virgil Trofin, and Ilie Verdet. In the Executive Committee, all of the Presidium members occupied a post, supplemented by Maxim Berghianu, Gheorghe Cioara, Constantin Dragan, Emil Draganescu, Janos Fazekas, Petre Lupu, Dumitru Popescu, Leonte

Rautu, Chivu Stoica, Vasile Vilcu, Stefan Voitec, and Florian Danalache. The candidate members included Constantin Babalau, Iosif Banc, Petre Blajovici, Cornel Burtica, Miron Constantinescu, Mihai Dalea, Miu Dobrescu, Laurel Duca, Mihai Gere, Ion Iliescu, Ion Ionita, Ion Patan, Vasile Patilinet, Ion Stanescu, Mihai Telescu, Iosif Uglar, and Richard Winter.[21]

In the secretariat could be found Nicolae Ceausescu, Stefan Andrei, Iosif Banc, Cornel Burtica, Miron Constantinescu, Ion Dinca, Mihai Gere, Gheorghe Pana, and Dumitru Popescu.

Between 1973 and the Eleventh RCP Congress in November 1974, a series of personnel changes took place. Ion Dinca and Iosif Banc were removed from the Secretariat. Aurel Duca was removed from his position as candidate member of the Executive Committee, while Elena Ceausescu, wife of the general secretary, became a full member of that body, as did Lina Ciobanu. Miron Constantinescu died in the summer of 1974. Ion Gheorghe Maurer retired in 1974.

At the Eleventh Congress a considerable simplification of the top RCP structures was undertaken. The Presidium was abolished altogether, and there was some rearrangement of the Executive Committee, which now had the following membership: Nicolae Ceausescu, Emil Bobu, Emil Bodnaras, Cornel Burtica, Elena Ceausescu, Gheorghe Cioara, Lina Ciobanu, Emil Draganescu, Janos Fazekas, Petre Lupu, Manea Manescu, Paul Niculescu-Mizil, Gheorghe Oprea, Gheorghe Pana, Ion Patan, Dumitru Popescu, Gheorghe Radulescu, Leonte Rautu, Virgil Trofin, Iosif Uglar, Ilie Verdet, Vasile Vilcu, Stefan Voitec. The candidate members were: Stefan Andrei, Iosif Banc, Chivu Stoica (now deceased),[22] Mihai Dalea, Miu Dobrescu, Mihai Gere, Nicolae Giosan, Ion Iliescu, Ion Ionita, Vasile Patilinet, Mihai Telescu, Ivan Ursu, Richard Winter.*

In the Secretariat, Nicolae Ceausescu was joined by Stefan Andrei, Cornel Burtica, Gheorghe Pana, Dumitru Popescu, Iosif Uglar, and Ilie Verdet. The Central Collegium had several lesser leaders as members; Chivu Stoica was the president of this

*This body was now called the Political Executive Committee.

body, which otherwise included no member of the Executive Committee or the Secretariat.[23]

During the last two to three years, the number of joint councils or commissions has been significantly expanded, and these structures have all included staffing with Ceausescu's close associates in the top positions. The most important of these bodies is the Supreme Council for Socioeconomic Development, of which body Ceausescu is the chairman. Another such body, established in 1973, is the Council on Economic and Social Organizations (whose main task it is to supervise the administrative functions of party bodies and state structures); it is headed by Gheorghe Pana, a trusted follower of Ceausescu and one of the Central Committee secretaries.[24]

While the ideological campaign was stepped up, personnel changes continued apace. There was, first of all, the continued movement of individuals from Bucharest to the provinces, as part of the "cadre rotation" which had first assumed major proportions in 1973. But even at the top of the RCP organization there were several changes. In late January 1977, a major shake-up took place, first and foremost in the RCP, but subsequently also in the government apparatus. The party development centered around the expansion of the Permanent Bureau of the Political Executive Committee, which had been established after the abolition of the Presidium at the Eleventh RCP Congress. The Permanent Bureau originally had five members, as follows:

Nicolae Ceausescu (RCP general secretary)
Manea Manescu (prime minister)
Gheorghe Oprea (deputy prime minister)
Ion Patan (deputy prime minister)
Stefan Andrei (RCP Central Committee secretary).

In January 1977, the following individuals were added to the Permanent Bureau:

Cornel Burtica (RCP Central Committee secretary)
Gheorghe Radulescu (deputy prime minister)

Ilie Verdet (RCP Central Committee secretary)
Elena Ceausescu (member, Political Executive Committee).[25]

The functional specialities of the Bureau members give strong indications of the party's major policy priorities at the present time. Ceausescu is both head of state and party leader; Manescu, as prime minister, is the primary overseer of economic performance; Oprea is in charge of joint economic ventures with foreign firms; Patan has the official title of minister of foreign trade and international economic cooperation, and Andrei has headed up the party's international relations section for some time. Among the new members, Burtica is responsible for ideology (and thus the main overseer of the ideological campaign), while Verdet has been associated with cadre policies. Radulescu is the primary link to the COMECON.

In contradistinction to the other newcomers, Elena Ceausescu lacks high administrative credentials (she is head of the Chemical Research Institute). Mrs. Ceausescu's elevation to the top RCP body is primarily a function of the general secretary's tendency to promote relatives to important posts. At the same time, the inclusion of a woman in this august body is consistent with the campaign to expand the recruitment of women into the party.[26]

In addition to the party reshuffle, there were several personnel changes in the government apparatus, and in several cases this involved drawing county first party secretaries into the central administration.[27] Such a move serves to enhance Ceausescu's position and control in several ways. First of all, most of the county first secretaries are staunch supporters of the general secretary, and all of them owe their appointments to the important regional party bodies to him; drawing such men to the political center is bound to increase Ceausescu's leverage there. Secondly, vacated positions require replacements, and this established the opportunity for the general secretary to promote yet another group of individuals, thus increasing the latter's loyalty to him.

As can be seen from the lists above, Nicolae Ceausescu is the only individual who holds top positions in all of the main party bodies. The reorganization in 1974 removed some of the individuals who had been members of the important Presidium in the period 1965–74, while other members of that august body were moved to the numerically expanded Executive Committee. Some of the members of the Secretariat, on the other hand, obtained only candidate memberships in the Executive Committee (e.g. Stefan Andrei), and this undoubtedly reduced their power in the RCP and made them less likely contenders for power at the very top.

Nicolae Ceausescu also holds the most important state position, head of the State Council, and thus president of the republic. Top party leaders occupy all the most important governmental positions in a pattern of overlapping memberships so familiar in the Communist political systems in Eastern Europe, and similar control is extended to all mass organizations in society.

Ceausescu's control of the party apparat and the RCP's hold over all major organizations in society are buttressed by the continuous expansion of the membership of the party within the masses of the population. According to the general secretary's report at the Eleventh Party Congress in November 1974, the total membership at that time stood at 2,480,000, an increase of 500,000 since the Tenth Congress in 1969. The social composition was as follows: workers, 48.4 percent; collective farmers, 22 percent; intellectuals, 21 percent. More than 71 percent of the total membership was said to be engaged in "material production." The figures presented also showed that 25 percent of the total membership was made up of women, and of the nationalities, Romanians constituted 89 percent of the total membership, while Hungarians made up 8 percent, roughly the concentration found in the general population. The general secretary called for more women and young people to be recruited into the party.[28]

In comparison with the 1969 congress, there had indeed been an expansion in the importance of workers in the rank and file of the RCP; in 1969, this social category constituted 43.0 percent; peasants, however, were 28 percent of the total then, and the intelligentsia 22.8 percent. Thus, both peasants and intelligentsia had dropped slightly in the period between the two congresses.

It should be pointed out, however, that the intelligentsia had reached its lowest percentage of total membership in December 1972—only 18.8 percent, which represented a rather drastic drop since the 1972 RCP National Conference, when this category represented 22.8 percent of all members. The intelligentsia may thus be staging a comeback at this time. The peasants, on the other hand, have experienced a continuous decline (24.0 percent in July 1972, and 23.1 percent in December of that year).[29]

The nationality composition of the RCP has remained steady for a long time, and considerable efforts are made to ensure that the distribution in this area matches that of the general population. This equity is less noticeable at the intermediate and higher levels of the RCP, however; here, Romanians are overrepresented, and Hungarians and Germans relatively underrepresented.[30]

The expansion of the RCP continued in 1975. At the end of that year, there were 2,577,434 members; of these, roughly 50 percent were workers, while 20 percent were peasants; the category "intellectuals" made up 22 percent. The thrust of recruitment was definitely towards increasing the proportion of workers. During 1975, of the 108,000 new members admitted, 67 percent were workers, 12.5 percent peasants, and 20.5 percent intellectuals. The nationality composition had undergone a slight change during the year. At the end of 1975, 87.67 percent of all RCP members were Romanians, 7.68 percent Hungarians, and 1.94 percent Germans.[31]

By the end of 1976, the Romanian party had grown to 2,655,000 members. Of this number, 72.9 percent were workers and peasants; women now constituted 25.8 percent of all members. During 1976, 106,000 new members joined the ranks of the RCP. Once again, the emphasis was on recruiting workers and peasants (83.5 percent of the new recruits) rather than intellectuals (16.7 percent of the new members). The proportion of women among the new entrants was 33.7 percent. In terms of nationality, the proportion of Romanians was back up to 89 percent after a slight reduction in 1975; about 7.4 percent of all members were Hungarians, and 1.6 percent Germans.[32]

While the party structure has been expanded to include new geographical areas and new social and age strata, there has been a considerable reorganization of other administrative structures which constitute an important part of the vast organizational network at the disposal of the party in Romanian society. As indicated above, many of the overstaffed cadre ministries and economic organizations have been reorganized during the last three years, with a view towards reducing administrative overhead. Thousands of cadres with technical training or production experience have been transferred to work outside of Bucharest although primarily in their respective fields of expertise. The new functions of such personnel are primarily in the production process rather than in administration so that their skills can be better utilized for the sake of fulfilling the ambitious economic plans of the last decade. At the same time, many top party cadres have been reassigned to administrative or state bodies under the slogan of "rotation of cadres," which prescribes that individuals primarily in party administration at the political center should also have some expertise in work in the regional organizations of the RCP or in functionally different occupations, such as supervisory work in state or administrative units. An example of this kind of transfer was Virgil Trofin, who lost his position as RCP Central Committee secretary in 1971, went to the trade unions as head of the trade union council (USGR), and in 1973 was transferred to a somewhat minor ministry in charge of commerce and provision of consumer goods for the population.[33]

The constant rearranging of party and administrative cadres may have been ostensibly directed at persistent inefficiency and overadministration, but it also had an important political effect which certainly was not unintended. By constantly moving personnel around, the general secretary has enhanced his ability to control the main cadres, and thus to prevent any possible coalitions from forming against him, at least by individuals whose positions were based on longstanding leadership of major structures or groups. This has been an important stabilizing factor for Ceausescu, and the process of rearrangement continues, despite the fact that there are strong indications of severe strains in economic administration as a result of such frequent personnel transfers. It is, of course, ironic that the removal of thousands of individuals from administrative positions, originally undertaken to provide more production, has had the opposite effect in many fields of activity, but the *political* payoffs are apparently considered to be of greater importance. Besides, tinkering with the administrative system is a favorite remedy utilized by many of the political leaders in Eastern Europe in lieu of more direct solutions of fundamental problems, such as commitment and productivity.

3. *The continuation and expansion of economic development to "lay the material base" for multilateral development and, ultimately, socialism and communism.* The ambitious policies of the RCP in the political and social fields are only conceivable if the requisite material base can be achieved. The concept of the "multilaterally developed society" emphasizes the need for an economic system in which *all* branches are developed to a high level, indeed to such a level that they are self-sustaining and capable of continuous rapid growth while at the same time providing increasing benefits and a rising standard of living for the population. This concept assumes that agriculture and consumer goods industries will be given much more attention than has been the case in the past, while at the same time heavy industry must be developed further, since Romania is still one of the least developed states among the socialist countries. The RCP, therefore, will continue to be the chief overseer of the economy, and it is symptomatic of the present leadership in the party that a policy of incrementalism (whereby certain neglected sectors of the economy, such as agriculture and light industries, would be allowed to "catch up" with heavy industry) has been rejected in favor of a broad attack on the problems of underdevelopment. This Herculean task is only feasible through a continuation of strict centralization, mobilization of the citizenry, and even an expansion of the political penetration of the party into strata of the population hitherto inadequately covered, coupled by an intensification of organizational and ideological work among those elements of the masses

(as well as activists) already mobilized. The RCP's insistence on organizational expansion and ideological offensives, then, is intimately tied in with an extremely ambitious program designed to raise Romania to an economic level comparable with the most advanced countries in the West. As is often the case, the RCP and its general secretary are in a hurry to accomplish this goal. The time frame for achieving "multilateral development" has been set with the end of this century as the absolute deadline.[34]

The enormously ambitious program of economic development outlined above can be illustrated by the achievement figures for the 1971–75 Five-Year Plan, in the process of completion at this time (December 1975). At the Eleventh RCP Congress, Nicolae Ceausescu reported that the total value of industrial production in 1975 would be 580 billion lei, as compared to 18 billion lei in 1938, the last prewar year with reliable statistics. During the 1971–75 Plan, more than 2,400 new industrial plants were put into operation, which meant that at the end of this period, more than 50 percent of the total industrial capacity would be less than five years old, while only 19 percent of existing plants were more than ten years old. The general secretary's report also emphasized a series of other major achievements in the period 1971–75: electrical power was expanded by 5,000 billion watts; the average yearly increase in the production of the machine-building industry was 18.6 percent; in electrotechnics the increase was 20 percent; in electronics, 27 percent; fine and optical mechanics, 33 percent; installations of machinery, 33 percent; technological installations, 25 percent; and shipbuilding 19 percent. Furthermore, in the chemical industry, the yearly increase averaged 19 percent; in the construction materials field, the increase was 10 percent; in light industry, 14 percent; and in the food industry, 9 percent. Local and cooperative industries experienced a production increase of approximately 10 percent.

The production increases in agriculture were considerably less impressive. The general secretary stated that in the 1971–75 period, the annual production of grains and cereals was 15 million tons, as compared to 8 million tons in 1934–38, 10 million tons in 1961–65, and 12.7 million tons in 1966–70.[35]

The size of the Romanian economy can best be comprehended by an examination of the 1973 figures of total production in selected fields (table 7.1).

Table 7.1. Production of Selected Items, 1973

Iron	5,713,000 tons
Steel	8,161,000 tons
Aluminum	141,241 tons
Coal	26,664,000 tons
Electrical energy	46,779,000,000 kw/h
Chemical fertilizers	1,242,000 tons
Tractors	38,800
Locomotives (Electric and diesel)	311
Automobiles and trucks	106,555
Shoes	85,311,000 pairs
TV sets	397,453
Refrigerators	221,960

SOURCE: *Anuarul Statistic al Republicii Socialiste Romania 1974*, pp. 106–10.

The 1976–80 Five-Year Plan envisions continued rapid development along the lines of earlier long-range plans. Table 7.2 shows the projected figures for production increases in a series of key fields.[36]

The 1976 plan called for increases in strategic fields (table 7.3).

The general Secretary also maintained that by 1990, the per capita GNP is to be raised to $2,500–$3,000. This figure, if achieved, would represent a tremendous achievement for Romania, although it would fall short of catching up with the more advanced countries of Western Europe and North America.[37] Nevertheless, the economic program represents an integral part of the ambitious nation-building program supervised by the RCP, and many of the other manifestations of that program, be they in the field of organization or supervision or in other areas of endeavor, are decisively influenced by the ambitious economic targets outlined above.

Table 7.2. Projected Increases in Production in Selected Fields, 1976–80

Industry and Fuels

Field	Projected Increase over Period 1976–80	Projected Increase (%/Year)
Coal	56,000,000 tons/year by 1980	
Electrical energy	75–80 billion kwh/year by 1980	
Machine-building		11.5–12.5
Technological installations, ship-building, electrotechnics and electronics industry, finer mechanics	2–3 times	
Steel	17,000,000–18,000,000 tons/year by 1980	
Chemical industry	1.6–1.8 times	
Wood products and building materials		8.0
Light industries	1.4–1.5 times	
Food industries	1.5 times	
Cost of production		6.5–7.0 reduction
Labor productivity	38–42%	
Total industrial production		9–10

Agriculture

Field	Projected Increase over Period 1976–80
Grains and cereals	Up to 18,000,000–20,000,000 tons/year
Cattle	Up to 8,000,000
Sheep	Up to 18,000,000–20,000,000
Pigs	Up to 12,000,000
Poultry	Up to 45,000,000–50,000,000
Reclamation of land	Up to 2,000,000 hectares
Newly irrigated land	Up to 1,000,000 hectares
Total agriculture production	25–34% as compared to 1971–75 period

Table 7.2. Projected Increases in Production in Selected Fields, 1976–80

Work Force and Standard of Living

Field	Projected Increase/Decrease over Period 1976–80
Industry and other non-agricultural fields	1,300,000 Increase (up to 62% of total labor force)
Higher education	180,000–200,000 (80,000 with technical specialty)
Students	Up to 160,000 by 1980
Nominal income) industry	24–26% over period
Real income) industry	18–20% over period (projected inflation: 5% over period)
Real income–agriculture	20–25% over period
Pensions	15–16% over period
Apartments	815,000 over period
Working week	Reduced to 42–44 hours by 1980
Provision of commodities for the population	40–45%
Services	10–11%/year
Investment	30–32% of GNP over period
Consumption	68% of GNP over period

Table 7.3. Total Production of Selected Items and Projected Increases, 1976

	Total Production	Percentage Increase over 1975
Total industrial production	641.0 billion lei	10.2
Total agricultural production	108.3–119.3 billion lei	15–26.6
Total transport	84.2 ton/km	5.8
Investments	159.5 billion lei	19.4
Foreign trade	60.7 billion lei	17.8
Domestic commerce and trade	154.8 billion lei	10.0
Services for the population	31.5 billion lei	13.8
No. of employed	6,655,000	5.6
Productivity	254,500 lei per person employed	8.5
National income	400.0 billion lei	10.5
Real monthly income per person	1,030–1,035 lei	8–8.5

While the 1976 economic plan was ambitious, fulfillment was spotty, as reported by *Scinteia* on February 6, 1977. Total industrial production increased more than planned, but there was underfulfillment in such important categories as steel, trucks, chemical fertilizers, and in the extraction of several minerals. Furthermore, the perennial bottlenecks of consumer goods and agriculture remained problematic. Specifically, the production of footwear and several other consumer items was short of target, and output in virtually all categories of agricultural commodities was below the plan figures (e.g. cereals, sunflower seed, sugar beets, potatoes, vegetables, fruit, grapes, and livestock).

Part of the problem stemmed from failures in the investment sector, where the plan was seriously underfulfilled. Lagging investments in turn had a depressing effect on construction in all sectors, especially in the completion of new production facilities. Labor productivity continued to be low.[38]

The major earthquake which struck Romania in early March 1977 had a devastating effect upon the economy. Over 1,500 people were killed, 33,000 dwellings were destroyed, hundreds of economic units were damaged, and scores of important research facilities with their precious equipment were leveled. Estimates of the total damage suffered range from 10,000 to 12,000 million lei.[39] As a result of this major setback, there was a need for some reallocation of investments to ensure rapid reconstruction of housing and factories. Economic recovery and momentum were thus gradually restored, but despite regime assurances to the outside world that production would meet the plan in 1977, it seems unlikely that this was actually achieved. The analyst must await the figures for 1977 plan fulfillment sometime in the first quarter of 1978.

When the official communiqué on 1977 plan fulfillment was reported in *Scinteia*, February 5, 1978, serious shortcomings were revealed in almost all fields of economic activity. Total industrial production did rise more than planned (12.5 percent versus a planned increase of 10.5 percent), and labor productivity gains also outstripped the plan. Agricultural production, on the other hand, fell short of the targets, and there were deficiencies in investments, foreign trade, services, national income, and real remuneration (as opposed to nominal wage increases). Some of these problems are certainly attributable to the earthquake of early 1977, but more fundamental and long-range deficiencies were clearly to blame for part of the shortfall.

4. *A concerted campaign to enhance the image of the RCP as a national force which is carrying on the traditions of the great liberators of Romanian history, such as Stephen the Great and Michael the Brave.* The Ceausescu regime has consistently emphasized that the modernization process in the economy and the emphasis on ideological orthodoxy in the political realm are the concrete manifestations of the Romanian road to socialism and communism, and that this road is consistent with Romanian national traditions of development and nation-building. Ceausescu frequently invokes the eventful and heroic past of Romanian history to justify his rule, and there is considerable emphasis on archaeology and historical research which can draw the connecting lines between the past, the present, and the future as envisioned in various regime statements and the party program.

This heavy emphasis on traditional Romanian nationalism has had a profound effect on the many ethnic minorities living on Romanian territory. There is considerable resentment against a policy which is perceived as intense Romanian nationalism and chauvinism in Marxist-Leninist garb, and this resentment has in turn necessitated increased regime efforts to mobilize the minorities, hopefully ensuring their continued support for the socioeconomic and political programs established by the RCP. Thus, the party has been engaged in a massive recruitment campaign in areas heavily populated by minorities, and a concerted effort is made to ensure some minority representation at the intermediate levels of the party as well. In such areas, there is apparently a scrupulous "balancing of the ticket" in terms of national representation. At the top level of the RCP, however, Romanians occupy all the crucial positions, and the policies of centralization and control by Bucharest ensure the conformity of regional, non-Romanian elites; in fact, non-Romanian leaders tend to go out of their way to "prove" their loyalty by strict adherence to all major policy decisions (and minor ones) made in Bucharest.[40]

The quest for the national heritage and the attempt to cast the RCP in the image of a political movement carrying on the struggle of heroes of the past have given rise to a series of practical policies with profound effects, both domestically and in foreign policy. The effects have perhaps been most noticeable in foreign policy and in relations with the ethnic minorities in the country, but there are ample manifestations in other fields as well. A striking example is the tone of political discourse in contemporary Romania. Ceausescu never makes a major speech on any subject without discussing the "organic links" between past national heroes and political movements, on the one hand, and the RCP and his own position in the party, on the other. Party programs, resolutions and decrees of the Central Committee, the State Council, or other official bodies frequently deal with the same subject, and the massive campaign of political socialization and indoctrination constantly emphasizes that the present policies of the RCP constitute the Romanian national road to socialism and communism.[41]

The educational system is also very much steeped in nationalism, as is much of academia. The school curriculum at the primary and secondary levels is clearly nationalistic in the treatment of archaeology, anthropology, and history, and the RCP version of modern history is also sharply geared towards the "national road" and an explanation of events during the last thirty years in terms of this political parameter. A considerable amount of scholarly work is being undertaken in archaeology to show the ethnic and cultural connections between the Romans and the contemporary population of Romania. Folklore and peasant art and costumes, as well as fairy tales, have become major areas of research. All in all, the national element in all areas of contemporary political and cultural activity is being emphasized to an extent unprecedented in the postwar era.

In the fields of economic production and science and technology, a similar spirit of nationalism prevails. The economic plans are designed to develop Romania as an industrial power in its own right, and it is precisely on this point that Bucharest has its main quarrel with the policies of specialization and integration currently emphasized by the Soviet Union and the COMECON. Fulfillment (and overfulfillment) of the economic plans constitutes a major ingredient in the Romanian quest for autonomy in foreign affairs, and the RCP utilizes rather frank nationalistic exhortations to increase production. Similarly, Ceausescu has repeatedly lamented the tendency for Romanian scientists to import technology and know-how without attempting to develop processes, formulas, and patents on their own. In this context, his criticism of the low productivity of Romanian research institutions is particularly poignant; Romania's quest for autonomy and stature in the international community simply cannot be properly enhanced as long as the low level of technological innovation hampers development in other fields. On this basis, Romania has emphasized import of know-how primarily through joint ventures of various kinds, ventures in which the Romanian state becomes an active partner. Another major approach has been that of long-range agreements in which Romania will pay for technology by export of finished products (rather than agricultural commodities or other raw materials).[42]

The nationalistic emphasis of the current regime has also had major ramifications for relations among the ethnic groups in Romania. While Ceausescu emphasizes that the multilaterally developed society will have a superior culture which is socialist rather than national in the traditional sense, it is abundantly clear that most of the basic elements of this society in the cultural sphere are in fact Romanian and thus the old problems of multiple ethnic groups coexisting under the leadership of a dominant nationality have come to the fore once again. There are strong hints of this kind of problem in most of Ceausescu's statements on the subject, where he consistently attacks remnants of "bourgeois nationalism" in Romania, and he has also frequently discussed the need for all citizens of the country to learn Romanian, at least as a "business language." Manifestations of ethnic consciousness must therefore be limited to form, whereas the content must be "socialist." Given the Romanians' domination of the top party bodies in the RCP, the definition of "socialist culture" is inevitably colored by the viewsd views individuals who are strong Romanian nationalists.

In addition to the indirect evidence of ethnic separation contained in many of the statements emanating from the top RCP leadership, there are more direct indicators of the same phenomenon. An examination of the 1956 and 1966 census data shows that there has been little movement of Hungarians and Germans, for example, into areas heavily populated by Romanians, while the influx of the latter into minority areas has been heavy, partly as a result of official encouragement, and partly because of the march of industrialization into new areas. The minority groups seem to prefer to stay in their "own" areas. For some time in the 1960s, the statistical yearbooks of Romania contained information on intermarriage between several of the major nationalities, but this kind of statistic is no longer available—perhaps an indication that there is little interaction in this respect. A confirmation of this indication is the residential pattern found in almost any village or city in the areas of Romania traditionally inhabited by Hungarians and Germans; here, there are clearly delineated sections for each group, although the new housing projects in the outskirts of industrial cities seem to be somewhat more mixed in terms of population. Similar observations (which must be rather unsystematic under the present circumstances), can be made concerning lifestyles, recreational habits, and friendship patterns.[43]

It is this kind of persistent problem which the RCP is attempting to solve through an increased ideological campaign and massive efforts to instill national values in all citizens, no matter what their ethnic background. At the same time, the predominantly Romanian values which have dominated the cultural and political programs of the RCP in the Ceausescu era have undoubtedly contributed significantly to the relative popularity of the general secretary and his party among the masses of the ethnically Romanian population, which constitutes some 87 percent of the total population of the country.

The quest for national consciousness and the emphasis on the

Romanian heritage currently in vogue in the RCP have had a curious, mixed effect on the relations between Romania and the West. On the one hand, Bucharest has actively pursued a policy of expanded relations with the industrialized countries of Western Europe and the United States. This kind of policy has enhanced and accelerated the modernization process in Romania through the importation of technology and credits. On the other hand, these expanded relations have provided the political leadership in Bucharest with considerable problems of political control, a syndrome quite familiar to the Soviet Union and the other socialist states in Eastern Europe. Expanded relations means an increased flow of people and ideas, and the centralized regime finds itself in the unenviable dilemma of risking the influx of Western, "capitalistic" ideas, books, and individuals which are bound to have a detrimental effect on domestic political control. Nicolae Ceausescu is not interested in a Western road of development (just as he rejects a Soviet-sponsored road), and during the last two to three years, there have been tendencies to restrict the flow of ideas and people, especially in academic exchanges and the import of books, films, and plays, while at the same time the *official* economic ties have been maintained or expanded. Controlled technology, credits, even scientists and other experts who are living apart from the general population—these are aspects of the relationships with the West which are encouraged, but a freer flow of ideas and people on an informal basis is discouraged. In the latter case, the RCP leadership is apt to stress the need for self-reliance and a better understanding of one's own culture and heritage rather than senseless kowtowing to the West.[44]

The Romanian overtones of the "socialist culture" promoted by the RCP became even more strongly accentuated during the 1976 ideological conference and its aftermath and in the campaign which developed around the slogan, "Hymn to Romania." The musical festival associated with the "Hymn" was strongly imbued with Romanian patriotism and reference to the glorious past of Romania, coupled with exhortations about the need for ever greater efforts of a political, economic, and social nature for the socialist fatherland. During much of 1977 there was also a concerted and harsh regime campaign against emigration from Romania, particularly designed to reduce outmigration of ethnic Germans to the Federal Republic.[45] All of these events made it abundantly clear that the nationalistic policy of Nicolae Ceausescu was being followed with determination and persistence.

5. *A foreign policy emphasizing increasing autonomy and influence for Romania in foreign affairs.* The Romanian quest for autonomy in foreign affairs is manifested in practical terms in a whole set of policies. First of all, the RCP has steadfastly refused to accede to the Soviet-sponsored quest for a world conference of Communist parties, at least in the form prepared by Moscow. On numerous occasions, Ceausescu has spelled out the preconditions for Romanian participation in such a conference: there must be no attempt to condemn any of the world's Communist parties at such a parley, and the concept of "national roads to socialism and communism" must be accepted as a guiding principle of the proceedings; there must be no effort to establish any central leadership of the world movement, and therefore, no party can be classified as deviationist either on the right or on the left; the principles of noninterference in internal affairs and the right of each party to conduct policies according to the conditions in its own society must be made fundamental bases of any negotiations.[46]

In addition to his emphasis on the individual national road to socialism and communism for each national party, Ceausescu has attempted to project an image of the RCP as a mediator in the ideological struggle between Moscow and Peking. The general secretary has repeatedly pointed out that internal strife among the "progressive" political elements in the world can only reduce the effectiveness of such forces in the struggle against "imperialism." Bucharest has criticized both of the Communist giants for their tendency to put national interests above the interests of the world progressive movement. There is more than a hint in this that the Romanian approach may be more conducive to the unity of *all* peace-loving forces.[47]

With such a set of preconditions, the RCP has effectively

precluded any unanimity in the effort to weed the Chinese party out of the movement, and in his rejection of the concept of one center of world communism, Ceausescu has effectively blocked one of the major Soviet objectives in international communism. Furthermore, the RCP has become the center of a group of parties, such as the French and Italian parties, which loudly and eloquently reject both the principle of Soviet supremacy and also many of the practical manifestations of Moscow's foreign policy. Together with the Yugoslav League of Communists, the RCP has thus become a major obstacle to Soviet policies in this field.

In fact, the RCP has begun to expand its relations with most of Europe's Communist and "progressive" parties (this includes also the left-wing socialist groups now existing in abundance in Western Europe). It is clear that Bucharest is moving towards a position in which it could become the pivot of a wide circle of relationships which would cut across ideological borders and spheres of influence. If this were to be the case, Soviet influence among the Communist parties and other left-wing movements in Western Europe would likely diminish. Ceausescu's visit to Portugal in 1975, for example, produced political messages from both the Romanian leader and Portugal's president which seemed to assume a "special relationship" in the making.[48]

A similar Romanian deviation from Soviet policies is clearly visible in the field of general foreign policy. Here, Bucharest has carried out an imaginative policy during the last decade, one which has significantly increased Romanian autonomy in many areas. Of particular importance has been Ceausescu's ability to improve relations with the West, especially West Germany and the United States, but with most other countries in Western Europe as well.

Romania has become one of the most active participants in international organizations such as the UN, and Nicolae Ceausescu has made several highly publicized trips to the United States, West Germany, and other countries in Western Europe, while numerous delegations from practically all of the capitalist world have visited Bucharest. Trade relations have been expanded significantly, and Romania is now involved in a wide net of cooperative ventures, many of which are clearly designed to diminish Bucharest's dependence upon the Soviet Union and the COMECON. Considerable amounts of Western credits have flowed into Romania, and there is little indication that this trend will be reversed in the near future, although the expansion of economic relations with Western countries has slowed somewhat during the last two years.[49]

The display of Romanian autonomy in security policies has been perhaps even more dramatic. At the SALT and MBFR negotiations during the last few years, Romanian representatives have displayed a remarkable initiative, continuously emphasizing the need for all deliberations to pay due regard to national sovereignty and the principle of noninterference in domestic affairs. In fact, Bucharest has repeatedly emphasized the need to diminish the power of blocs and regional organizations, so that Europeans and others can settle their differences without "bloc influence." At the same time, Ceausescu has inveighed against "big-power chauvinism," emphasizing the need for all small and medium-sized powers to increase their cooperation and thus expand their influence while reducing their dependence upon large states. One of the most significant elements of this Romanian quest for increased cooperation has been Bucharest's willingness to disregard ideological and political boundaries. According to Ceausescu, improved relations among all states in this category must proceed without regard to social and political system. This approach is in direct contradiction to the Soviet position, which has increasingly emphasized regional and bloc agreements in the large international negotiations which have taken place in Europe during the last few years.[50]

Just as Ceausescu had expanded his relations with the West, he has kept the supernational tendencies within COMECON and the Pact at arm's length. This has been quite noticeable in Romania's reluctance to accede to specialization of production within the COMECON, as discussed above, but Bucharest has also balked at military and security coordination. Romanian participation in joint maneuvers of the Warsaw Pact is minimal, usually restricted to map exercises and observers, and there has indeed been an attempt by the Romanians to expand their own armaments production, thus reducing their dependence upon Soviet spare parts and hardware.

While expanding ties with the West and at the same time maintaining at least tolerable relations with the fraternal socialist states, Romania has, in fact, attempted to act as a mediator between the two sides, insofar as Bucharest has strenuously argued for the gradual dismantling of all military and economic blocs, with a corresponding expansion of so-called "free relations" between all states. (It should be pointed out that Ceausescu declined to let this principle escalate to a really free flow of people and ideas; that would be perceived as a major danger to the internal stability of the regime.) In addition, the RCP general secretary has acted as a liaison and a mediator in the Middle East conflict through the maintenance of cordial relations with both Israel and the Arab states. The rôle of Nicolae Ceausescu in helping to establish closer relations between Washington and Peking has been downplayed in the United States, but the general secretary himself makes occasional references to his beneficial influence in this relationship.[51]

Perhaps the most imaginative aspect of Romanian foreign policy under Ceausescu has been Bucharest's expanded ties with the developing countries of Africa, Asia, and Latin America. During the last three to four years, the RCP general secretary has visited many of the countries in these areas, and it is unlikely that this kind of travel diplomacy will cease in the near future. In fact, travel schedules for the 1970s envision even more Romanian visits to these countries and more delegations arriving in Bucharest from the Third World.

The objectives of Romanian foreign policy in these areas have been a curious mix of economic pragmatism and idealism. On the pragmatic side, Ceausescu has concluded several important economic agreements with countries in the Third World, agreements which have provided the expanding Romanian industries with raw materials and at the same time have established important markets for Bucharest's finished industrial products.

Economic relations with developing countries have been steadily increasing in the 1970s, and the increase in foreign trade for the second half of this decade allows for a continuation of these trends.[52]

A counterpart of economic expansion in the developing countries has been Bucharest's quest for increased political influence in the same area. Ceausescu has repeatedly spoken of the "special relationship" between Romania and the countries of Africa, Asia, and Latin America, and he has steadfastly emphasized that the Romanian road of development is one that has lifted an underdeveloped Balkan country up to a level of development which is now characterized as mixed industrial-agrarian, but will be predominantly industrial and service-oriented by the turn of the century. Although the RCP general secretary is careful not to offer the Romanian "model" directly to jealously nationalistic leaders in the Third World, there is nevertheless a hint of such a possibility in many of his statements, and this inclination is given practical manifestations by the increasing amount of Romanian foreign aid and the expanding number of Romanian technicians and other personnel in many aid programs now being established in several countries.

In the final analysis, Romanian foreign policy in the developing countries represents a challenge, however muted, to both the Chinese and the Soviets in these areas. Both Peking and Moscow have attempted to expand their influence in these areas by stressing the developmental model of Marxism-Leninism (variously interpreted in the two Communist capitals) as a viable alternative for the new nationalistic regimes struggling to cope with independence. The Romanian message is quite simple: the basic elements of Marxism-Leninism do indeed represent a viable alternative for rapid socioeconomic development, but in the case of great powers, the model is always tinged with chauvinism and the interests of expansionism, whereas Romania stands before the developing countries as a medium-sized power without ulterior motives in its aid and in its propagation of the Marxist-Leninist model of development. Ceausescu is therefore beginning to produce policies which are designed to make Romania a "central" power whose moderate views allow it to establish good relations with *all* major power constellations in the world, such as the socialist camp, the capitalist camp, and the developing countries. Such a position, if it can be achieved, would be a pivotal one indeed, and it would significantly advance Bucharest's prestige in the world. While the achievement of such a position is still in the future, Nicolae Ceausescu appears right now as a major ideological competitor with the Soviet Union in some of the countries of the Third World, and this development must certainly be seen in a less than favorable light in Moscow.

The semiautonomous position of the RCP in the international Communist movement has been considerably moderated during the last few years. During 1976, a series of important meetings took place between the Soviet and Romanian parties, and contact was lively at the government level as well. In the fall of that year General Secretary Leonid Brezhnev undertook a "friendship visit" to Bucharest which emphasized the trend towards closer relations between the two countries.

The turn towards partial Romanian reintegration into the bloc in foreign policy questions occurred during the summer of 1976. As late as the end of April of that year, Vadim Zagladin, an official of the CPSU Central Committee section on international relations, visited Bucharest, and the reports emanating from that meeting reiterated traditional Romanian views of foreign policy, including the emphasis on national sovereignty.[53]

During the following few months, however, quiet diplomacy and considerable Soviet pressure produced a modification of Ceausescu's position in this field. During the first half of August 1976, the Romanian party leader made a trip to Soviet Moldavia (a considerable part of which is made up of the former Romanian province of Bessarabia), and Ceausescu also met Brezhnev in the Crimea that month. An official visit to Moldavia must be seen as at least implicit recognition of Soviet sovereignty of the territory after years of "hidden" polemics (in the form of historical and ethnographic disputes) about this very question. The meeting between the two leaders resulted in statements pledging improved relations at all levels, including interparty relations.[54]

The Crimea meeting set the stage for Brezhnev's visit to Bucharest in late November 1976. The carefully worded statements emanating from this meeting showed increased willingness on both sides to continue and indeed to expand the dialogue, and there is little doubt that relations between the two parties have improved considerably.[55] On the other hand, there were significant nuances in the views expressed by the two leaders, and Ceausescu's statements clearly showed that Romania intends to follow its basic foreign policy while making concessions in matters which are not considered vital. One such field of expanded relations is economic cooperation. Sharp differences on international communism and nationalism have been toned down. Thus, the balance has once again been restored between the two countries; some Romanian concessions have averted the danger of forceful Soviet intervention, concessions which are interpreted in the most favorable light by Brezhnev.

"Ceausescuism"

The many variegated strains of policy discussed above bear the unmistakable mark of the RCP general secretary, Nicolae Ceausescu. It can indeed be safely stated that the unique mix of factors coalescing in the policies of this remarkable brand of policy can be termed "Ceausescuism." In no other country in Eastern Europe can one find this kind of blend of situational, ideological, external, and personal factors shaping the policies of the Communist party and thereby setting the parameters for development in society.

One of the main factors influencing contemporary Romanian society is Nicolae Ceausescu's "populism" and his distrust of bureaucracies and their occupants. Ceausescu likes to rule directly, if at all possible; he frequently leaves the RCP headquarters and makes "flying visits" to factories, collective farms, and regional party headquarters. At times, such visits are unrehearsed and can best be characterized as inspection visits, in which the general secretary personally examines the performance of the local bureaucrats. The feedback received from the rank and file of the party and the economic units visited serves as an important control factor in Ceausescu's constant battle with a top-heavy bureaucracy which he apparently fears to be in danger of ossification and declining performance; complaints received during such visits are of considerable importance in his continuous quest for expanding personal power. At the same time, there is some record of rectification undertaken as a result of rank-and-file complaints, and this has helped ensure the general secretary's position with the masses of the population.

More often than not, the flying visits are carefully staged shows of popular support for the RCP leader. Under this scenario, the local party leaders are informed well in advance of the planned visit, and massive preparations are undertaken, with posters, pamphlets, and carefully rehearsed demonstrations by the masses. Upon Ceausescu's arrival, the "spontaneous" outpouring of popular support for the leader will act as further reassurance that there is no possible opposition, no feasible counterelite which may attempt to limit the enormous power now concentrated in the hands of the general secretary. This reinforcing mechanism clearly serves as a reminder to all ambitious societal elites that they have a few chances in the face of such massive popular support for the leader and his close entourage. The show of solidarity, indeed of love, which such flying visits produce, is also an important agent of nation-building and legitimacy in the Romanian tradition of great leaders and populism. Together, these factors combine to increase the political position of Nicolae Ceausescu.

Another important aspect of Ceausescu's approach to politics in his strong attachment to traditional Romanian values and styles of leadership, on the one hand, and the continuation of other traditional values among the masses of the population, on the other. The enormous concentration of power in the hands of one individual is clearly in the Romanian heritage of personalized leadership, basing itself on the boyar tradition and that of the village head, with power based on charisma and coercion rather than institutionalized procedures. The Ceausescu emphasis on Romanian history and his quest for the fulfillment of the "glory of Romania" are other basic elements of the general secretary's traditionalism. Such a leadership style is likely to be critical of institutionalization, since complex structures and bureaucracies tend to develop their own styles and procedures, thereby producing a certain amount of insulation from the political head. The Ceausescu approach of frequent institutional change, reorganizations, and the establishment of everchanging new committees and commissions represents a concrete example of strongly held personal values being made operant in society, with considerable dislocation among bureaucrats and producers alike.

While the Ceausescu approach to political leadership strongly resembles the practices of previous regimes, the general secretary is outspokenly critical of the remnants of traditional values in the general population. Many of the outlooks of traditional Romanian peasant society are indeed considerable obstacles to modernization as perceived by the current RCP leadership. Raised in a tradition of exploitative political leadership, the Romanian peasant is reluctant to "get involved" in political matters, especially activities that have a bearing on all of society, rather than the village itself. The Romanian tradition of corruption and inefficiency has fostered a life-style based on informal arrangements rather than clear rules of behavior in political, economic, and social affairs. Localism and attachment to one's piece of land have persisted.

The modernization process, as conducted by the RCP during the last thirty years, has done little to break down such traditional values. Because of the heavy element of coercion involved in the forced industrialization of society and the consolidation of the Communist party in the political realm, the man in the street became extremely reluctant to get involved in public matters, and the traditional chasm between the regime and its citizenry was reinforced. The incessant politicization of all areas of social and economic activity in fact produced strong tendencies towards depoliticization. The collectivization of agriculture reinforced the traditional attachment to *private* land in Romania as elsewhere in Eastern Europe and the Soviet Union. All of these factors have remained important in the minds of the masses in Romania, and industrialization has not been able to eradicate them, but has instead produced a situation where traditional values have invaded the modern setting of the city and the factory, often with rather devastating effects on productivity and orderly industrial procedures. In addition to all these elements, the continued scarcities of the Romanian economy have enforced behavior patterns based on hoarding, "deals," and corruption, all of which run counter to the main values emphasized by the RCP leadership.

The massive ideological campaign carried out during the last four years in Romania represents both an established party program and the result of Ceausescu's personal impatience with the "remnants of bourgeois-landowner mentality" in the masses of the population. Ceausescu the activist is constantly frustrated by the nonperformance of his executors or the intervention of the "deal" in economic intercourse; Ceausescu the populist, with his firm belief in the innate goodness of the average man, frets at this exhibition of "antisocial" behavior among the very mainstay of his society, the average worker and collective peasant. Thus, the RCP is constantly being utilized for the supervision of a massive ideological campaign which has produced few tangible results, at least in the political sphere.

In foreign policy and in ideological matters, too, the unique blend of orthodoxy and the personal twist permeates the policies of the RCP. All the major statements by top RCP leaders, all the party platforms, and the RCP program itself, are models of ideological orthodoxy; the foreign policy emphasis on close relations among fraternal socialist states, the emphasis on a common front against imperialism, and reference to the Soviet Union as one of the main progressive forces in the world all contain ingredients familiar to students of any Communist party in Eastern Europe. Yet the RCP in many respects constitutes a special case in terms of policy output. The unusual combination of strict centralization and party control in domestic affairs, on the one hand, and the highly imaginative and maverick foreign policy of the party, on the other, carries the distinct stamp of the general secretary himself. Such a personal influence on policy production and execution is of course much more likely when the concentration of power in one hand reaches the proportions it has in contemporary Romania. Thus, personal leadership produces a special set of policies which in turn help reinforce that leadership. This kind of combination is the essence of political dynamics in contemporary Romania.

The RCP and Romanian Society: A Balance Sheet

The ambitious policies of Ceausescu and the RCP have met with a mixture of success and failure. In the multifaceted policy outputs examined above, it is necessary to distinguish between the political ambitions of the general secretary, the political position of the RCP domestically and in foreign policy, and the social and economic impact of the Communist party upon Romanian society. At all levels, considerable successes in some fields are somewhat offset by failures in other areas. Among the most significant successes enjoyed by Ceausescu personally has been his policy of gathering a maximum amount of political power in his own hands, a mission which has been accomplished to such an extent that there are few serious groups, groupings, or individuals who can conceivably threaten his personal power at the present time. This, of course, does not mean that Ceausescu is in a totally impregnable position; a number of events or sets of circumstances could occur which would undo his power, either in a rapid loss or over a more protracted period of time. Some of these circumstances would include a decisive Soviet move, perhaps involving military intervention, in retaliation against the independent foreign policy pursued by Bucharest—a possibility which is more remote today than it appeared to be in the summer of 1971. A more likely circumstance leading to Ceausescu's fall or the reduction of his power would be the accumulation of enough resentment in elements of the political leadership and the technical/managerial intelligentsia because of the general secretary's high-handed methods of personnel administration and bureaucratic reorganization. A third possibility would include a coalition between disenchanted political and administrative cadres and elements of the military in opposition to an "adventurist" foreign policy. All of these circumstances, although feasible, seem somewhat remote at this time, and Ceausescu continues in his position as perhaps the most powerful figure in a European socialist state since the death of Stalin.

While Ceausescu has been highly successful in acquiring power within the RCP, the Communist party has had spectacular success in establishing itself as the supreme leader of political, social, and economic matters in Romania. Much has been written about the relative decline of the Communist party in East European societies during the last decade; many scholars have instead focused on the increasing pluralization of these societies, a process which has cast up a number of societal elites that are seen as potential or actual competitors with the Communist parties even in the political realm (let alone in the social and economic spheres of activity). In Romania, this process has to sacrifice some economic growth for the sake of maintaining its position in society, as illustrated by the current reorganization campaign and the ideological offensive which have seriously upset economic production in several fields. There is no prospect of the top leaders of the RCP accepting greater political pluralization, with a concomitant reduction in its own power, in the immediate future.

Ceausescu and the RCP have also been extremely successful in major areas of their modernization program. Thousands of new factories have been erected, total production has increased many times over during the period of RCP rule—in short, Romania has made the decisive step from being basically an agrarian country with pockets of industrial activity to a system with a mixed agrarian-industrial base, but with a rapidly increasing industrial and service sector. Literally millions of people have moved from the countryside to the cities, and millions more have been exposed to modern ideas and life-styles through the spread of mass communications and better transportation links. The RCP has also managed to break down some of the localism which existed in previous times through an ambitious program of organization and mobilization. It can safely be said that the Romania of today bears little resemblance to the impoverished country of 1944, at least in terms of the outward manifestations of economic activity.

In the realm of nation-building, the achievements of Ceausescu and the RCP would have been unthinkable without the heavy emphasis on traditional Romanian nationalism, an emphasis which has achieved the important step of eliciting considerable mass support, at least among the ethnic Romanians of the country. In its quest for legitimacy, the RCP has scored one of its most significant successes in the period of socialism. At the same time, there are indications that some of the ethnic minorities have viewed this process with some misgivings, since many of the regime policies must be characterized as manifestations of Romanian nationalism. The continued scarcity of many consumer goods and agricultural products has also made the regime less credible among many citizens. The most important drawback for the regime, however, has been its failure to create a real sense of community between the general population and the political leadership. Romania is an authoritarian dictatorship, despite its populist traits, and there are severe limitations to the possibilities of genuine political participation by the man in the street. Under such circumstances, the political system is correctly perceived as a regime which attempts to mobilize the citizenry for the execution of preset policies with real possibilities for mass input. Such a political system experiences severe strains in terms of the flow of information necessary to make decisions, as well as the popular perception of the legitimacy of the regime itself. Another major problem arises from the social pluralization of a rapidly modernizing system, a phenomenon which creates entire new societal elites without the corresponding access to political power. The next decade, with its accelerated modernization and expanding societal pluralization, will represent an acid test for the Ceausescu regime. Ways must be found to accommodate the new elites while maintaining essential control over them. Given the imaginative approach of Nicolae Ceausescu to political leadership, it is likely that the RCP will have the adaptive ability required to meet this challenge.

NOTES

1. See, for example, Stephen Fischer-Galati, *Twentieth-Century Rumania* (New York: Columbia University Press, 1970).

2. For a Western discussion of this period, see Ghita Ionescu, *Communism in Rumania 1944–1962* (London: Oxford University Press, 1964), esp. pp. 107–47. Official Romanian views on this can be found in Andrei Otetea, ed., Istoria Poporului Roman (Bucharest: Biblioteca De Istorie, 1972).

3. Fischer-Galati, *Twentieth-Century Rumania*, pp. 109–28.

4. Ionescu, *Communism in Rumania*, esp. pp. 210–14.

5. See Stephen Fischer-Galati, "The Socialist Republic of Rumania," in Peter A. Toma, ed., *The Changing Face of Communism in Eastern Europe* (Tucson: University of Arizona Press, 1970), pp. 19–22.

6. *Ibid.*

7. *Ibid.*

8. This statement was published in *Scinteia*, March 9, 1963.

9. This position has been reiterated on many occasions; perhaps the most forceful statement came at a Central Committee Plenum in November 1971, when Ceausescu castigated the party for inadequate ideological work (see *ibid.*, November 4, 1971).

10. The general secretary discussed some of these measures in his report to the Eleventh RCP Congress, November 1974. See *Congresul al XI-Lea al Partidului Comunist Roman* (Bucharest: Editura Politica, 1975), esp. pp. 75–79.

11. An interesting discussion of this from the point of view of a well-known writer is a book by Aurel Dragos Munteanu, *Opera si Destinul Scriitorului* (Bucharest: Editura Cartea Romaneasca, 1972), esp. pp. 1–91.

12. Once again, this is a frequently stated goal, e.g., by Nicolae Ceausescu at the 1972 RCP National Conference; see *Conferinto Nationala a Partidului Comunist Roman, 19–21 Iulie 1972* (Bucharest: Editura Politica, 1972), pp. 51–67.

13. *Congresul al XI-Lea*, pp. 75–79.

14. The November 1971 Central Committee meeting was the scene of much criticism of this phenomenon (*Scinteia*, November 4 and

5, 1971). The dismissals have been published in *ibid.* at various times, e.g., May 16 and 17, 1973, June 22, 1973.

15. The Romanian press gave the conference (as well as its preparation), top billing, e.g. *Scinteia,* first half of June, 1976.

16. The Ceausescu vision of the festival was neatly summarized in his speech to a public rally in Satu Mare, October 22, 1976 (see *ibid.*, October 23, 1976).

17. See, for example, *ibid.*, April 19, 1977.

18. Particularly serious were the strikes of coal miners in the Jiu Valley, as reported by *ibid.*, August 4, 1977.

19. This is graphically illustrated by the organizational chart to emerge from the Eleventh RCP Congress, in *Congresul al XI-Lea*, pp. 834–42. (At this Congress it was also proposed that Ceausescu be made president of the republic for life, but he declined).

20. See *Congresul al X-Lea al Partidului Comunist Roman* (Bucharest: Editura Politica, 1969), pp. 751–58.

21. See Gilberg, *Modernization in Romania since World War II* (New York: Praeger, 1975), pp. 39–46.

22. The death of Miron Constantinescu was announced by *Agerpres* on July 18; *Scinteia* February 19, 1975 reported Chivu Stoica's death.

23. *Congresul al XI-Lea* pp. 834–42.

24. Gilberg, *Modernization in Romania*, pp. 60–64.

25. Most of the changes were announced and discussed in some detail in *Scinteia*, January 26 and 27, 1977. I am also indebted to Robert R. King for his excellent analysis, "Comprehensive Romanian Party and Government Reshuffle," *RAD Background Report/33 (Romania)*, February 9, 1977.

26. See *Rad Background Report/33*.

27. See *Scinteia*, January 26 and 27, 1977.

28. *Congresul al XI-Lea*, pp. 68–70.

29. For figures on the RCP composition at the time of the Tenth Congress, see *Congresul al X-Lea*, pp. 128–29; corresponding figures for the Eleventh Congress are in *Congresul al XI-Lea*, pp. 68–70; for the 1972 RCP National Conference, they can be located in *Conferinta Nationala a Partidului Comunist Roman*, pp. 58–60.

30. See Gilberg, *Modernization in Romania*, pp. 60–64.

31. *Scinteia*, April 24, 1976.

32. *Ibid.*, April 7, 1977.

33. *Ibid., pp.* 57–60.

34. This has been stated on numerous occasions; see, for example, Nicolae Ceausescu at the Eleventh Congress in *Congresul al XI-Lea*, pp. 45–68.

35. *Ibid.*, pp. 16–21.

36. *Ibid.*, pp. 44–68.

37. *Ibid.*, p. 85.

38. The problem of labor productivity is especially acute in agriculture. For a discussion of this problem, see Ceausescu's speech to the

Congress of Management Councils of Socialist Agricultural Units, April 18, 1977, as reported in *Scinteia,* April 19, 1977.

39. Based on reports in *ibid.*, March 6, 1977, *Agricultura Socialista,* March 8, 1977, and *Revista Economica,* March 11, 1977.

40. See, for example, the general secretary at the 1972 RCP National Conference, in *Conferinta Nationala a Partidului Comunist Roman,* pp. 72–80; see also his speeches in the collection *Romania: Achievements and Prospects. Reports, Speeches, Articles, July 1965–February 1969* (Bucharest: Meridiane, 1969).

41. This is clearly reflected in many of the official party documents, e.g., *Documente ale Partidului Comunist Roman: Natiunea Socialista* (Bucharest: Editura Politica, 1972).

42. See, for example, *Radio Free Europe Research,* Rumania/14, April 23, 1974, discussing the visit by U.S. Secretary of Commerce Frederick B. Dent to Bucharest to discuss expanded economic cooperation.

43. Such observations are backed up by statistics on residential patterns and population migration, culled from the 1956 and 1966 official censuses (see Gilberg, *Modernization in Romania,* pp. 207–31).

44. E.g., *Documente ale Partidului Comunist Roman: Morala Comunista* (Bucharest: Editura Politica, 1972).

45. This campaign was particularly virulent during the month of April 1977, e.g., Friedrich Bömches in *Scinteia,* April 13, 1977, on the conditions of Romanian Germans in West Germany.

46. See, for example, statement by Gheorghe Macovescu, Romanian Foreign Minister, in *Le Monde Diplomatique,* January 5, 1973.

47. E.g., *Scinteia,* September 8 and 9, 1973, reporting on Ceausescu's visit to Latin America.

48. *Ibid.*, October 30 and 31, 1975, reporting on the general secretary's visit in Portugal and quoting speeches by Ceausescu and President Da Costa Gomes.

49. Even so, considerable economic ties do exist, as demonstrated by numerous agreements made during the last few years (e.g., decision by the Council of Ministers to invite Western firms to participate in a joint venture to produce small cars, reported in *Radio Free Europe Research,* Rumania/12, April 8, 1974).

50. These major points have been constantly repeated by the RCP leadership, e.g., Ceausescu in *Scinteia,* July 20, 1972 (his speech to the RCP National Conference, and Gheorghe Macovescu in *Le Monde Diplomatique,* January 5, 1973.

51. These references are usually couched in terms of Romania's beneficial influence on expanding cooperation between East and West, e.g., *Congresul al XI-Lea,* pp. 21–23, 31–38.

52. *Ibid.*, pp. 23–25.

53. Zagladin's visit was reported in *Scinteia* and other Romanian papers on May 1, 1976.

54. For detailed reports on the visit and the meetings with Brezhnev, see *ibid.*, first week of August 1976. *Lumea,* August 5, 1976 had a detailed commentary on the meeting.

55. *Scinteia* published the text of the speeches made by Ceausescu and Brezhnev in its issue of November 23, 1976. For an excellent analysis of the Brezhnev visit, see Robert R. King, "Soviet Party Leader Brezhnev Pays First 'Friendship' Visit to Romania," *RAD Background Report*/247, December 2, 1976.

Paul Shoup

8. The League of Communists of Yugoslavia

Among the Communist parties of Eastern Europe, the Yugoslav League of Communists (LCY) occupies a special position. It was the first party to break with the Soviet Union, the first to espouse the cause of economic reform, and the first and as yet only party to curtail its own powers in a meaningful fashion.

Given this unique background, comparisons of the structure and function of the Yugoslav party with that of other parties in Eastern Europe (and with the Soviet party) take on a special importance. How, and to what degree, has the introduction of market socialism and self-management changed the role of the party, and with this, the party's structure? To what extent can the party relinquish control to other bodies without losing its position as the dominant political force in society? And, once the party has given up its dominant position, how can it retain its sense of revolutionary purpose and direction? While the remaining parties of Eastern Europe have had to consider such problems largely in the abstract, the LCY has been face to face with these issues for at least twenty years, since the first reforms of the party took place in the mid-1950s.

To understand the problems which the Yugoslav party has faced, and to make meaningful comparisons with the experience of the remaining parties in Eastern Europe, one must understand the history of the Yugoslav party since 1948, the year of the break with the Soviet Union. This task, rendered difficult by the absence of any comprehensive history of the LCY, will be attempted in the first part of the discussion that follows. The second part will concern itself with the organization and operation of the party, focusing on the manner in which the party's structure has been adopted to meet the challenges of altered economic, social, and political conditions in Yugoslavia. Finally, in our concluding remarks we shall turn to the main issues now facing the LCY. To the extent that space permits, we shall analyze the implications of these problems for the future of the party and for our understanding of the other Communist parties of Eastern Europe.

Party History and Development

The Yugoslav Communist party traces its origins to a congress of leftist socialists held in 1919, from which there emerged a Socialist Workers Party of Yugoslavia. A year later the party officially adopted the name Communist and approved a statute modeled after that of the Soviet party. The party operated legally for only a brief time; in 1920 its activities were drastically curbed, and in August 1921, the CPY was outlawed. For the remainder of the prewar period internal party struggles, complicated by the interference of the Comintern and the complexities of the national question, plagued the party and rendered it largely ineffective.[1]

With the outbreak of World War II, the position of the party altered dramatically. The invasion of Yugoslavia, followed by the German attack on Russia in the summer of 1941, provided the CPY with an opportunity to extend its base to the peasantry and to build up a well disciplined fighting force capable of seizing power when the occupation troops withdrew in 1945. The party's role in organizing the partisan units on the one hand, and the national liberation front groups on the other, stands as a textbook example of the successful combination of military and political methods in waging guerrilla warfare.

With the end of the war and the seizure of power, the party rapidly expanded in size. By 1946, the party numbered 258,303 persons, and by 1948 this number had climbed to 482,938. Notwithstanding this growth, the party remained an elite group whose leaders remained wedded to conspiratorial forms of behavior. For many years little was known about the backgrounds of leading party figures. Rather than participate directly in elections, the CPY chose to conceal itself behind the national front organization. While party leaders quickly commandeered the villas of the prewar upper classes, they pursued a rough and ready style of life reflecting their rural origins and their predilection for military diversions.[2] In domestic and foreign policy, the CPY gained a reputation as the most radical of the parties of Eastern Europe and a belligerent but loyal ally of the Soviet Union.

We now know that these postwar years were also marked by growing friction between Yugoslavia and the Soviet Union, culminating in the expulsion of the LCY from the Cominform in June of 1948. The immediate effects of the dispute on the party were several. First, it led the party to strengthen its own internal organization. The establishment of national parties in Montenegro and Bosnia-Hercegovina date from this time, as do efforts to tighten party discipline by bringing the party apparatus more closely under central control. The conflict also led to extensive purges of persons loyal to the Soviet Union. Expelled from the party and incarcerated for long periods of time, these "Cominformists" survived as a miniscule but deeply alienated element in the political life of Yugoslavia.

At the same time the Yugoslavs, facing growing pressure from the Soviet Union and her satellites, were forced to chart their own path in foreign and domestic policy. The results in the realm of foreign policy are well known and need not be recounted here. In the area of domestic policy the effect of the Soviet actions was to encourage the Yugoslavs to develop their own distinctive brand of socialism. In this fashion the Yugoslavs hoped to win sympathy abroad, find a solution to the country's pressing economic problems, and retain a revolutionary legitimacy in the face of Soviet criticisms of the Yugoslav leaders for isolating themselves from the rest of the socialist camp.

It is important to note that many of the most significant efforts at party reform date from this early period when Yugoslavia was trying to pioneer in the development of a new, non-

Soviet form of Communist rule. Between 1950 and 1952, party and administrative posts were separated, party activity in the villages was substantially reduced in connection with the decision to give up collectivization, the practice of employing political commissars in the army was eliminated, and the first steps were taken to reduce the size of the party bureaucracy.[3] These changes, initially of a pragmatic character, soon became associated with attempts to alter the basic character of the party itself. Party organizations were urged to be more democratic and to hold open party meetings. The future of the party began to be viewed in the context of the development of workers' self-management, and the concept of the withering away of the party began to gain acceptance. These currents came to expression at the Sixth Congress of 1952, perhaps the most reform-minded congress in the history of the LCY.

The first of a number of ideological deviations which were to appear in the party in the post-Cominform period also dates from this time. After the Sixth Party Congress, widespread confusion was apparent over the role the party was to play in Yugoslav society. Many party organizations lapsed into inactivity, and it proved necessary for the Central Committee to circulate a special letter condemning the passivity of the rank-and-file party members.[4] It was against this background of confusion that the articles of Milovan Djilas appeared in the summer of 1953.[5] In these well-known theoretical discussions, Djilas demanded a fundamental change in the role of the party, a transformation which would result in the organization losing its monopoly on political power and becoming largely a group for influencing public opinion.

Djilas was disciplined in January 1954.[6] His followers, few in number, were quickly dealt with.[7] While the personality and methods of Djilas were important factors in limiting his influence (Djilas was essentially a propagandist and intellectual not interested in organizing a faction to support his views), it seems in retrospect that the revisionist doctrines he espoused were launched prematurely. Yugoslavia was just entering into a period of rapid economic growth in which the energies of the party were absorbed by developmental tasks. The reforms approved by the Sixth Congress, although not repudiated, were by and large disregarded. Party bureaucrats, moved from their positions in the party apparatus, quickly found jobs as directors of the new factories springing up around the country. A mood of self-satisfaction and confidence in the Titoist system—while giving party reform low priority—was expressed at the Seventh Congress of the LCY held in 1958. It was at this meeting that a new party program was adopted in the face of Soviet opposition, incorporating the basic tenets of the Titoist political creed.[8]

At the same time, the end of the 1950s saw the emergence of many problems generated by overly rapid economic growth and shortcomings inherent in the political and administrative system of the period. Differences over foreign policy date from this time, as do disputes over the course of economic reform, and rivalries between the developed and underdeveloped republics. These pressures came to a head as the result of setbacks experienced by the Yugoslav economy in 1961 and 1962. The liberal faction within the party leadership wished to deal with the problem by carrying out further economic reforms. The conservatives opposed such changes and called for a greater degree of administrative and party control over the economy. At a dramatic encounter which took place within the Executive Committee in March 1962, the conservative group, led by Aleksandar Ranković, temporarily gained the upper hand.[9] In the course of the struggle, Ranković came to be recognized as Tito's successor, and for several years enjoyed the position of being acknowledged as Number Two in the Yugoslav Party.[10]

The ascendancy of Ranković in Yugoslavia in the early 1960s reflected the underlying conservatism of the party bureaucracy and secret police, both of which were under Ranković's control. The situation was not unlike that in other countries in Eastern Europe at the time, where conservative leaders, in many cases backed by the secret police, were opposing reform.

Two factors peculiar to Yugoslavia nevertheless worked to limit the power of the conservatives within the party: fear that the victory of Ranković would provoke a major crisis in national relations by opening the door to a new form of Serb hegemony; and widespread opposition to a return to Stalinism, or to the quasi-Stalinism which Ranković seemed to favor. Ranković, recognizing that the charge of bureaucracy was undermining his position, initiated a campaign to reinvigorate the party by attacking corruption, the accumulation of functions in the hands of a few party functionaries, and other abuses. This effort, which reached a high point in the spring and summer of 1962, seems to have backfired.[11] Few of the objectives of the campaign were attained, while revelations concerning corruption and the amassing of privileges by party members simply confirmed the liberal charge of excessive bureaucracy in the Yugoslav political system. On the economic front, the conservative forces could not provide an effective program (or a coherent ideology) to counter the policy of reform; in the last analysis, the reintroduction of party and state controls promised only to plunge the economy still further into confusion.

The period of Ranković's ascendancy was brief. By the time of the Eighth Party Congress in 1964, the liberals had staged a comeback. The economic measures advocated by the congress reflected, for the most part, the liberal philosophy of economic decentralization. Reforms, far-reaching in scope, were officially adopted by the government a year later.

The conservative forces were nevertheless firmly enough entrenched to block the implementation of the new economic measures. In the spring of 1966, the struggle between the two factions shifted to the republics, as the liberal leadership attempted to oust the conservative groups that dominated the republic parties in Serbia, Montenegro and Bosnia-Hercegovina. This tactic failed, and in the summer of 1966 a committee was hurriedly formed to investigate the activities of the secret police. Following the Committee's report, the Executive Committee voted on June 16 to relieve Ranković of his party and government posts. This decision was ratified by the Fourth (Brioni) Plenum of the Central Committee held in July, at which time Ranković's fall from power was publicly announced.[12]

The purge of Ranković and his supporters marked a crucial

stage in the evolution of the LCY, for it cleared the way for a more widespread modernization of the party than had been possible in the earlier period of reform in the mid-1950s. The impact of this altered situation was felt most profoundly in Serbia, where the liberal, modernizing elements in the party were able to gain the upper hand, removing the conservative, pro-Ranković forces from most top and middle-level positions. Nevertheless, the conservative elements proved extremely tenacious, and even managed, because of their identification with Serbian nationalism, to gain considerable popular support. In the elections of 1967, this conservative "underground" managed to elect sympathizers to the local government assemblies, and at least one deputy to the federal parliament.[13] They were even more successful in having supporters chosen as presidents of the local government assemblies, thus creating a rivalry between the more liberal party secretary and the conservative district assembly president which persisted through the period of liberalism in the late 1960s.[14]

The victory of the liberals was also marked by renewed discussion of the question of party reform. A full-fledged debate developed over the role of the party in Yugoslav life, much of it sharply critical of the monopoly of power enjoyed by the party. Proposals for a two-party system were put forward, and a number of prominent party leaders associated themselves with the idea of permitting opposition groups to develop within the one-party system.[15]

The debate over party reform continued until the fall of 1967, but by the spring of that year any possibility of real reform seems to have disappeared, perhaps because of the success of the conservative underground in the April elections. The "theses" for the reorganization of the LCY, when published in April, proved to be a restatement of existing practices and theories rather than a blueprint for reform.[16] The July 1967 Central Committee meeting stressed the need for the local party organizations to take the initiative in strengthening their control over party organizations in the enterprises.[17] Because the party leadership permitted the discussion over reform to continue, but did not propose any new policies of its own, it proved impossible to obtain a clear picture of the direction in which the party was to develop. This was especially evident when the Executive Committee issued a set of directives in early June 1968 meant to guide party work. The document urged that the party pay greater attention to ideological questions, but failed to adopt clear-cut policies on the issues of economic reform or the future role of the party.[18]

The student demonstrations of the spring of 1968 and the invasion of Czechoslovakia by the Soviet Union in August shook the party leadership into action. Elements in the party that sided with the students were purged from the party's ranks; but purges aimed at the conservatives were also initiated in the fall of 1968. Patriotic sentiment, aroused by the invasion of Czechoslovakia, contributed to an influx of persons into the party. This in turn enabled the LCY to launch a drive for rejuvenating the party by encouraging the admission of young persons and workers. The republic party congresses held in the fall of 1968 carried this policy forward by replacing older political figures in leadership positions with younger and less well-known Communists. The Ninth Congress of the LCY, meeting in March 1969, adopted a new party Statute which completely reorganized the top party bodies of the LCY, introduced new procedures governing debate within party organizations, and provided for guarantees of the rights of individual party members.[19] The role of the republic parties in choosing the leadership of the LCY was greatly enhanced—with dramatic consequences, as we shall see shortly.

Like the Sixth and Eighth Congresses, the Ninth was devoted to reform. The impact of the Ninth Congress was nevertheless quite different from that of the two liberalizing congresses which preceded it. The Sixth Congress had been concerned with the role of the party in Yugoslav society and politics. The Eighth Congress spelled out the principles of economic reform on which market socialism was to be based. The Ninth Congress was focused primarily on problems of internal party democracy, rejuvenating the party leadership, and granting the republics a greater role in the affairs of the LCY. The change in emphasis from problems of the party's role in society to issues of membership was not entirely fortuitous, for by 1969 the question of basic party reform was far more sensitive than it had been seventeen years earlier. Unlike the early 1950s, there now existed numerous groups in Yugoslavia, ranging from leftist intellectuals and students to neo-Stalinists and Western-oriented political scientists, who were raising basic questions concerning the nature of the one-party system in Yugoslavia. More and more, the party began to see its future task as one not of reforming the one-party system, but of increasing the chances for survival of that system through improving party morale, bringing fresh blood into the leadership, and giving the republic parties a greater voice in the affairs of the LCY.[20]

In fact, it was not long after the Ninth Congress that policy towards the role of the party took a conservative turn. Tito helped set the tone in two speeches delivered in August 1969, in which he called for increased party discipline and stressed the need to struggle against antisocialist elements.[21] At the Seventh Plenum of the Presidium held in December, it was emphasized that the party would play a greater rather than a lesser role in decision-making at all levels.[22]

The reasons for the new policy could be traced in part to foreign policy considerations (Tito's speeches preceded, by several weeks, a visit of Gromyko to Yugoslavia), Tito's own concern over the diminishing influence of the party in Yugoslav society, and most important of all, developments related to the national question. In July 1969, Slovenia had been rebuffed by the federal government in connection with a bid to obtain part of an international loan, made available earlier to Yugoslavia, for road construction. The Slovenian government protested strongly and threats of "secession" were voiced by some of the more hot-headed Slovenian Communists.[23] The affair set in motion a policy of cracking down on the republics (to be described shortly); it also apparently swung some of the liberal but pro-

Yugoslav Communists in the Executive Bureau, including Kardelj and Todorović, into an alliance with the group favoring more vigorous party leadership.[24]

The emergence of the national question as the major issue dividing the party can be traced back to the early 1960s, when the efforts of Ranković to implement his conservative line became entangled in debates over the future of the federal system. It was alleged by the liberals and nationalists in Slovenia and Croatia that Ranković wished to abolish the federal system, that is, to do away with the republics entirely. Direct proof of this charge is lacking. The stormy confrontation at the 1962 Plenum must nevertheless have convinced the liberals of the threat that the unitarian forces behind Ranković posed to republic rights, and not incidentally helped persuade Ranković and his allies that the liberals in Croatia and Slovenia were dangerous separatists.

Republic rivalries did not cease with the removal of Ranković. On the contrary, Slovenia and Croatia continued to oppose the policies of the federal government. A crucial role in this development was played by the partial failure of the economic reforms introduced in 1965. As economic difficulties mounted, each republic was compelled to pursue its own short-term self-interest; agreement over economic policy became more and more difficult. Federal commitments to large projects, especially the Djerdap hydroelectric complex and the Belgrade-Bar railway, continued to drain investments away from modernization of existing plants, striking a severe blow at the economic interests of Slovenia and Croatia. At the same time, the position of the underdeveloped republics worsened as a result of the reforms; industry in the south found itself unable to compete with the more efficient enterprises located in the developed republics. Only Serbia clearly benefited under the new economic system, largely by virtue of the growing concentration of banking activities and the presence of highly profitable commercial enterprises in Belgrade. Warnings by the Croatian and Slovenian party leadership as early as 1968[25] concerning growing federal commitments to special projects—the so-called "extra-budgetary accounts"—were rejected as unfounded, preparing the way for the Slovenian outburst a year later over the exclusion of Slovenia from the international loan for road construction and the Croatian demand to retain control over foreign currency earned within the territory of the republic.

Republic rivalries worked to fragment the party leadership and encouraged the republic parties to assume greater initiative. The struggle for power prior to 1966 was accompanied by the drawing up of special agreements on economic and cultural cooperation between the republic Central Committees of Serbia and Montenegro, and between Serbia and Macedonia.[26] Following the downfall of Ranković, the Croatian and Slovenian Communists pushed for a greater role for the republic parties as a way of curbing the conservative forces remaining in the central party apparatus. The results of these trends could be seen in the party statutes adopted at the Eighth and Ninth Congresses.[27] The former specified that republic congresses were to be held before the congress of the LCY, and granted republic parties greater freedom to develop policies to deal with republic problems. The statute adopted at the Ninth Congress took the novel step of making the selection of Presidium members a republic responsibility. The Executive Bureau chosen by the Presidium at the Ninth Congress, although not chosen directly by the republics, was partially under republic control; as a consequence, the Bureau largely failed in its responsibility to provide the party with leadership, leading to its eventual reorganization when the crisis had passed.[28]

The attack on the Slovenians in the summer of 1969 altered the situation once more. As we have seen, a number of liberals were now to be found in a position critical of the republics and the threat they posed to party unity. The issue was brought to a head late in the year when Mološ Zanko, under the pretext of an attack on the Croatian cultural society *Matica Hrvatska*, published a series of articles in *Borba* critical of Croatian nationalism.[29] Appearing shortly after the Seventh Plenum, the articles appeared to be part of a campaign aimed at strengthening the party center at the expense of the Croatians. The Croatian party leadership, under the direction of Miko Tripalo and Savka Dapčević-Kučar, responded vigorously. The Tenth Plenum of the Croatian Central Committee, which met in January of 1970, demanded the recall of Žanko from Belgrade and stated the Croatian argument for the devolution of the economic powers of the federation to the republics.[30] With this step, the Croatian party was launched on an independent course which, in the months to follow, became a crusade for national rights. At the federal level, efforts to regain control over the republic parties were put aside, and the emphasis shifted to constitutional reform.

The constitutional reforms, appearing at a time when the party was in disarray, appear to have been a calculated effort to shift the search for consensus from the organs of the central Party (the Presidium, the commissions, and the Executive Bureau) to the governmental apparatus. The creation of the presidency, announced by Tito in his speech in Zagreb on September 21, 1970, was the first step in this direction. The new body was meant to ease the succession problem, but at the same time provided a new method for resolving deadlocks among the republics outside the framework of the party. The system of "coordination" of republic views before the submission of legislation to the federal parliament—spelled out in Amendment 33—was also designed to cope with a situation in which the federal government could no longer rely on the party to overcome republic resistance to federal legislation.

Republic rivalries nevertheless grew more, not less, severe following the announcement of the constitutional reforms. The threat these rivalries posed to the unity of the party can hardly be overestimated. We may note, in passing, the hostility of the Serb Communists to the new constitutional order and the alarming growth of Serb-Croat hostility in this period (1971); the split within the provincial party organization in Kosovo between its Albanian and Serb factions; and the growing nationalism of the Macedonian party which, under the leadership of the liberal Crvenkovski, edged closer to the Croatians in a reenactment of the traditional Croatian-Macedonian alignment of prewar Yugoslavia. In Croatia, by the spring of 1971, Tripalo and Dabčević-

Kučar found themselves at the head of a movement which was growing increasingly and alarmingly nationalist and anti-Yugoslav in tone.

A temporary truce in republic rivalries was effected at the Seventeenth Plenum of the Presidium in April, when the republic party leaders reaffirmed their support for the contentious constitutional amendments. On July 5, Tito held a meeting with the Croatian Executive Committee which resulted in the purge of several of the less important, but very vocal, nationalists in the Croatian party and a visible softening in the pronouncements of the Croatian leaders on the national question. But by September, the Croatian position had hardened once more. The immediate controversy centered around the failure of the constitutional amendments to effect reform of the currency system and to curb the power of the banks and the commercial institutions located in Belgrade. The more fundamental issue, which brought the Croats into direct conflict with the Serbian Communists as well as with a majority of the older party leaders, was the future of Yugoslavia. There was a growing fear that if the Croatian demands were met, Yugoslavia would become a loose confederation of quarreling republics. The Croatian Communists, for their part, saw the problem almost exclusively in terms of the protection of Croatian national interests against the political, financial, and administrative centers of power located in Belgrade. In November, the Twenty-second Plenum of the Croatian Central Committee, taking advantage of Tito's visit to the United States, restated the Croatian position on the national question, first set out at the Tenth Plenum of 1969–70.[31] The meeting was particularly significant in accepting the view of Dapčević-Kučar that a "general national movement" was emerging in Croatia under the leadership of the party. Later one of the principal accusations directed against Dapčević-Kučar was her espousal of this movement.[32]

The exact calculations of the Croatian Party leaders in encouraging the escalation of the national question in the fall of 1971 will always be a matter of debate. The Croatian Communists had won a major victory in gaining acceptance of the constitutional amendments and might have been expected, with a show of patience, to have received satisfaction on the issues of foreign currency reform and control over the banks. Evidently the mood in Croatia in 1971 made rational calculations impossible. The Croatian party, long suffering from an inferiority complex within the LCY and for many years lacking broad popular support in Croatia, suddenly found itself at the head of a mass movement. The effect, in the words of the Croatian Communists, was a "euphoria," of which the decision to support the idea of a national movement was one sign. When the students took to the streets in November, the Executive Committee of the CLC temporized, allowing the demonstrations to continue unchecked, although they were a clear challenge to the party, not to speak of being directed against the federal government in Belgrade. Tito reacted to the crisis brought about by the student demonstration by meeting with the Croatian leadership in a marathon session lasting twenty hours. The meeting, which took place in Karadjordjevo, Serbia, has subsequently been referred to as the Twenty-first Plenum of the Presidium, although there is some doubt concerning the presence of the entire Presidium membership.[33] The Executive Committee of the Croatian party issued a statement supporting the decisions of the Twenty-first Plenum several days later, but the meeting (and a meeting of the Zagreb city organization which took place at the same time) failed to resolve the conflict within the Croatian party. A second meeting of the LCY Presidium (the Twenty-second Plenum) quickly followed, demanding action on the part of the Croatians; this in turn was followed by the Twenty-third Plenum of the Croatian Central Committee on December 12, at which the resignations of Kučar, Tripalo, Pirker and Koprtla were accepted, and Milka Planinc was chosen president of the Croatian party to replace Kučar (Josip Vrhovec was appointed secretary of the Executive Committee). This action was quickly followed by purges at all levels of the Croatian party, confirmed at the party's Fifth Conference, meeting in January 1972.

The spectacular rise and fall of the Croatian national movement marked a turning point in Yugoslav politics. The alliance between the liberal elements and the nationalists had brought the party to the brink of political disaster; both groups, greatly discredited, were forced into retreat, while those who favored a strong party and more state control of society were given an opportunity to see their policies put into practice. The role of the army became increasingly important, as did that of the secret police. Veterans' organizations, embittered by the actions taken against their members in the 1960s, sought revenge against the liberal party leaders and "technocrats" who had led the campaign for the removal of unqualified cadres from positions of responsibility in the enterprises and in government. Although not directly behind the demands of these groups, Tito gave them indirect encouragement by choosing the crisis of the fall of 1971 to carry out a purge of liberal elements in the party, and by supporting the policy of a larger role for the party. These changes were not totally unexpected; as we have seen, warnings by liberals in the party against the resurgence of the conservatives and the policy of the "Firm Hand" date back to 1969 and earlier.[34] Still, the vigor of the attack on the liberals, the often irrational lashing out at technocrats (accompanied by the widespread purge of enterprise managers), the fierce criticism of intellectuals, and the rise to positions of influence of the mysterious Mišković brothers—all these events took the mass of party members by surprise and injected a deep note of uneasiness and foreboding into the political atmosphere of Yugoslavia in the early 1970s.

The retreat of the party from liberalism and nationalism after 1971 nevertheless had its limits. The purge of liberal elements in the party did not open the door to the return of the conservative forces supporting Ranković, as many had feared. Rather, important party posts were filled with individuals who had remained outside the factional struggles of the preceding decade. Often these were young party functionaries or persons who had careers outside of politics. As in the past, the party operated through a series of compromises between those of more conservative and more moderate persuasion, although the political tone was, until 1974, definitely set by the former of the two elements.

The events of the last few years on which these observations are based are well known and need be only briefly alluded to here.[35] Following the purge of the Croatian party, top party bodies were reorganized at the Second Conference of the LCY held in February 1971. The Presidium was reduced somewhat in size but retained its largely liberal complexion. The Executive Bureau, however, was drastically altered by the removal of all its former members and their replacement by a group of persons without established political reputations. The core of this group was a number of younger party functionaries, headed by Stane Dolanc and Jure Bilić, who were eager to cooperate with Tito in halting the decine in the fortunes of the party. In the fall of 1972, Tito and the Executive Bureau turned their attention to the Serbian League of Communists. A fierce struggle was waged over a period of several weeks, leading to the resignation of Marko Nikizić, president of the Serbian LC, and other top party figures. Liberal leaders in the mass media in Serbia were either removed or resigned from their posts. Purges in other republics led to the resignation of Krste Crvenkovski and Slavko Milosavlevski in Macedonia, and Stane Kavčič and Leopold Krese in Slovenia. In Vojvodina, the conservatie faction, supported by veterans' organizations, waged a particulalry bitter campaign against the liberal leadership, which was removed from power in December 1972.

The purges of 1972 were followed by a period of relative stability in the top party leadership posts. At the Tenth Party Congress of May 1974 a new Presidium of 48 members was chosen in which both liberal and conservative tendencies were apparent, but extremes from both groups were excluded. In the Executive Committee there was little change; most members continued to fall into the category of "party technocrats," persons skilled in politics or economics but without prominent political roles in the party.

The period after 1972 was also marked by indirect pressures

from those on the right of the political spectrum. This became apparent after attacks on "centralistic" forces were launched by the moderate Croatian party leaders in 1974. Concurrently, a group of Soviet sympathizers organized a secret "congress" in Bar, Montenegro; the existence of this group became known when thirty-two of the participants were arrested by Yugoslav authorities. There followed, during the course of 1975, a full-fledged campaign against pre-Soviet Cominform elements, leading to the rearrest of many persons jailed in the 1940s and 1950s. The result of these incidents and of developments on the foreign scene was to strengthen somewhat the position of the moderates in the party leadership; there were even signs at this time that the liberals in Serbia were staging a minor political comeback.

The relative political calm following the events of 1971 and 1972 suggested that Tito had succeeded, for a time, in imposing his solution of the "Firm Hand" over the party. In so doing, his most important achievement was to curb the potentially ruinous political rivalries among the republic parties, while permitting those who believed in a stronger role for the party—but within the context of Yugoslav pluralism—an opportunity to put their theories into practice. These efforts to rebuild the party are best understood, in the light of changes in the organization and operation of the LCY resulting from the reform movements of the 1950s and 1960s. It is to these latter problems that we shall now turn, reserving consideration of how the party leadership has sought to rebuild the party in the context of a pluralist society for our concluding remarks.

Party Organization and Operation

The organization of the LCY has undergone frequent changes, in part as a result of reform of the party and in part as a consequence of the attempt of factions within the leadership to gain an advantage by reorganizing leading party bodies. Although since the war each of the six party congresses has introduced changes into the party's organization and adopted new statutes, many of the most important alterations were made between congresses and in complete disregard of statutory provisions.

The leading party organs of the CPY in 1948, as provided in the statute adopted by the Fifth Congress, resembled those in existence in the Soviet Union. At the apex of the system stood the Politburo and Orgburo; below these two bodies was the Central Committee, and, as the broadest forum for registering support of the policies of the leadership, the Party Congress, which was to meet every three years. The leading organs of the republic parties were identical to those of the CPY, although no provision was made for an Organizational Bureau.[36]

The 1948 statute also provided for a Party Conference at the federal level made up of representatives of local party organizations. The Central Committee was to call this conference into session at least once between congresses; delegates were to be chosen at meetings of the Central Committees of the republics. In practice, no union conference was ever convened, and reference to the body was omitted from subsequent statutes until 1968, when the idea was incorporated into the new republic and union party statutes.

At the Sixth Congress of 1952, the Politburo became the Executive Committee with thirteen members, while the Secretariat was placed directly under the control of the Executive Committee. Leading party organs remained unchanged at the Seventh Congress; however, the Executive Committee was given the power to form its own Secretariat, thus creating a system of dual Secretariats which lasted until the Eighth Congress of 1964. In addition, the statute adopted at the Seventh Congress spelled out the power of the Central Committee to choose a General Secretary of the LCY and other secretaries of the Central Committee. At the Eighth Congress, the existing system of leading party bodies remained unchanged. Reflecting the trend toward greater republic participation in decision-making, the Political Secretary of the Central Committee of each republic was now made a member of the Executive Committee of the LCY.[37]

The reorganization of the party bodies carried out at the Fifth Plenum of the Central Committee in October 1966 reduced the size of the Executive Committee from nineteen members to eleven.[38] Tito and Kardelj no longer held positions in the Executive Committee, but were made members of a newly created body, the Presidum (*predsedništvo*). The Presidium was to set the general political line while the Executive Committee was to act in a purely administrative capacity. The Secretariat was reorganized; in place of three party secrtaries, a new post was formed, that of Secretary of the Executive Committee. In place of the General Secretary, the office of president of the LCY was now created.

These changes were considered temporary at the time they were introduced. They represented a deviation from party tradition by shifting the locus of power from the Executive Committee to the newly created Presidium. The purpose behind these moves, it can be surmised, was to facilitate the removal of Ranković supporters from the party leadership, partly through the elimination of the political secretaries of the republics from the Executive Committee.

The statute adopted at the Ninth Congress in 1969 made entirely new provisions for leading party organs. The familiar institution of the congress (which was now to meet every five years) was retained; its most important function, besides adopting a party statute, was to elect the president of the LCY. Now, however, the institution of the conference was reintroduced; its task, according to the statute, was to define the policies of the party between congresses. A more significant change was the elimination of the Central Committee and its replacement by a smaller Presidium of fifty-one members. While performing most of the same functions as the Central Committee, including choosing the Executive Bureau, the Presidium was a unique institution because its members were chosen by republic party congresses from persons nominated by district conferences of the party. Thus, the body assuming the functions of the Central

Committee was no longer responsible to the LCY Party Congress, but to the republic parties.

Although not provided for in the party statute, an Executive Bureau of fifteen members, chosen by the Presidium, was formed after the Ninth Congress. The statute did spell out the powers of the president of the LCY in some detail; this represented the first time that the responsibilities of the party leader were made explicit in the statute itself.

The Second Conference of 1972 witnessed the reduction of the Executive Bureau from fifteen to eight. Leading party figures were no longer to be found in the Bureau but in the Presidium. The change was similar to that which took place in 1966 in which the Executive Committee was reduced to an administrative body with no real political power. Tito's long-term objective, meanwhile, was to strengthen the Executive Bureau. This was partially achieved at the Tenth Congress in 1974, when the Executive Committee (as it was now called) was mentioned in the new party statute, and the party commissions and committees attached to the Presidium were in large part placed under the new Committee. At the same time, the Tenth Congress witnessed the reestablishment of the Central Committee, while the practice of calling party conferences was dropped. The result of these changes was a four-tiered system at the top of the party's organizational structure: Congress, Central Committee, Presidium and Executive Committee.

Despite frequent organizational changes, a hierarchical pattern of relationships among party bodies of a kind common to all the Communist parties of Eastern Europe persists in the LCY. Decisions are customarily the result of consultation among a small group of party leaders. Larger and more representative party organs are transmission belts without independent decision-making powers. Changes in the conditions under which decision-making takes place have largely been the result of the transformation of party organs into bodies representing the republics, of a better system of gathering information, and of a retreat from the practice of turning over whole areas of responsibility, such as the economy or security, to a single, all-powerful individual. Thus, despite the great transformations the Yugoslav party has undergone, it remains basically faithful to the principle of democratic centralism, according to which all power remains concentrated at the center. (The power of the republics in decision-making, because it is exercised primarily at the very top of the party through leading republic party representatives, does not change the picture fundamentally.)[39]

The role of the Central Committee over the years illustrates this point. There have been few, if any, occasions on which the Central Committee of the LCY has played an independent role. It appears that in 1948 the Central Committee was in fact unaware of the correspondence that was being carried out with the Soviet Union in its name.[40] Decisions crucial for the development of the party—for example those announced at the Fourth Plenum of 1962 and the Twenty-first Plenum of 1971—were in fact taken by meetings of the Executive Committee several days or even months before the Central Committee (or after 1969, the Presidium) met.[41] The same relationship seems to have prevailed in the republic parties between the central committees and the republic party leaders; we have the testimony of Bakarić that "I barely needed the plenum of the [Croatian] Central Committee. I needed it only as a political support."[42]

It is true that voting in the Central Committee of the LCY has not always been unanimous, and that on occasion, meetings of the Central Committee or the Presidium have been marked by debate.[43] This seems to have occurred, for example, at the Seventeenth Plenum of the Presidium in 1971, when a variety of views were expressed on the national question. Debates have also, on occasion, taken place in meetings of the republic central committees: the Macedonian CC, for example, adjourned in the spring of 1966 without issuing a resolution after lengthy controversy over the issue of nationalism and economic reform. In addition, we know that the political complexion of the Central Committee has sometimes placed obstacles in the path of one or another of the factions contending for party leadership; in the conservative-liberal struggle of the mid-1960s, the CC seems to have leaned toward the Ranković camp, thus necessitating its reorganization after the liberals' victory. (This may have in part been due to the fact that at the time the majority of the CC members lived and worked in the capital, where they were under the influence of the Ranković faction.)[44]

The Presidium between 1969 and the end of 1972 represents a special case. As a result of the fact that its members were, after 1969, chosen by the republics, and thanks to divisions within the Executive Bureau, the Presidium took on added importance as a locus of power within the party. Before 1972 the Presidium does not seem to have exercised its power in defiance of the party leadership. Following the emasculation of the Executive Bureau in early 1972, a split emerged between the Executive Bureau and the Presidium. The former body became an instrument for carrying out Tito's plan to purge and strengthen the party, the latter a place of refuge for party notables under attack. The conflict reached a high point in September, 1972, when the Presidium refused to approve a letter issued by Tito, with the support of the Executive Bureau, criticizing the party and calling for purges of party members associated with the liberal wing. Only after the purge of the Serbian members of the Presidium was completed did the body give belated approval to the Tito letter.

In contrast to the Central Committee and the Presidium, the Executive Committee (between 1969 and 1974, the Executive Bureau) has been a focal point of decision-making, and debates within that body have often been sharp. The power of the Executive Committee has not, however, been unlimited. We have seen that in 1967 the party leadership chose to bypass the Executive Committee entirely. The Executive Bureau formed at the Ninth Congress encountered grave difficulties in functioning properly. Created at the last moment (discussions by Congress had given the impression that the Presidium would be the leading party body), the Executive Bureau was made up of party notables and leading representatives of the republics, and was intended to serve as a place where republic differences could be resolved in an authoritative fashion. In fact, just the opposite occurred, as controversy among republic representatives led to paralysis in the Executive Bureau. In part, the Executive Bureau's role as a decision-maker in the Yugoslav political system was assumed by the government; in part, decisions were simply delayed or initiative was seized by the republics. The twenty-first Plenum criticized this situation, and promised to strengthen the Executive Bureau. As we have seen, the actual result was not quite as anticipated, and involved transforming the Executive Bureau into an instrument of Tito's own personal policies by excluding all party notables from its ranks.

Since 1972 the power of the Executive Bureau and Executive Committee have grown steadily, encouraged by the purge of the Presidium of its liberal members, the reorganization of top party bodies in 1974, and the growth in the number and responsibility of the organs of the Executive Committee. The greatest weakness of the Executive Committee lies in the absence of party notables from the older generation in its ranks, paralleled by the presence of these notables in the party Presidium and the state presidency. On the other hand, the younger generation of party professionals, under the vigorous leadership of Stane Dolanc and Jure Bilić, is strongly represented in the body. With Tito's support, this younger group of party leaders has been able to use the Executive Bureau and Executive Committee to dominate the political scene from 1972 to the present.

Tito's overwhelming prestige and his unchallenged role as party leader have, of course, shaped the decision-making process in the Yugoslav party profoundly, placing a great deal of emphasis on maneuvers designed to win Tito's support—or to turn him against rivals and foes. Tito has, nevertheless, followed the practice of allowing his subordinates great freedom in decision-making, even to the extent of permitting policies to be adopted with which he himself did not agree. Perhaps because of this, but more likely out of a desire to conform to the practice of other Communist parties, the powers which Tito enjoyed as General Secretary of the party were for many years never explicitly set forth in the party statute. The statute adopted at the Ninth Congress broke with this tradition. Under Article 66, the powers of the president of the party were spelled out in some detail. The president was to direct the work of the Presidium, represent the LCY in dealings with other parties, and determine questions to be considered by the Party Congress and meetings of the Presidium. These and other powers were again granted the president of the LCY in the statute adopted at the Tenth Congress. While the formal grants of authority under the provisions of the party statute do not underlie Tito's position as unchallenged leader of the party, these powers are important as a prize to be grasped by the individual who succeeds Tito to the post of party president.

The post of president was introduced in the republic parties in early 1967. The position of party secretary was retained, resulting in a system of dual leadership at the republic level. While the president was the more important of the two posts, it appears that the secretary may have had greater responsibility for internal party affairs at the republic level, permitting the president to devote his energies to representing the party in dealings with the LCY.

The Party Secretariat—the heart of the party apparatus—has been frequently reorganized. A directive of June 10, 1948, provided for three sections (*uprava*) within the Secretariat: Cadre, Agitprop, and Organizational-Instructional Questions.[45] Following the Sixth Congress, the Secretariat was reorganized and its activities limited mainly to the area of internal party organization and responsibility for cadre selection. A basic reorganization of the Secretariat was again carried out in June 1958. The creation of an Organizational-Political Secretariat at this time, followed by the establishment of a special "secretariat" responsible to the Executive Committee, marked a growth in power of the party bureaucracy. For several years the Organizational-Political Secretariat, headed by Ranković, dominated the party bureaucracy. The 1964 statute adopted by the Eighth Congress broke up the power of the Organizational-Political Secretariat by dividing its responsibilities among numerous commissions; at the same time the Secretariat of the Executive Committee was abolished.[46] In the course of the 1966 reorganizations, the commission structure was consolidated, but by 1969, the number of commissions had risen to fifteen. The Twenty-eighth Plenum of the Presidium, meeting in March 1972, reduced the number of commissions to nine.

Since 1972, the Executive Bureau and Executive Committee have assumed greater direct responsibility for the work of the apparatus of the party. By 1976, six commissions were to be found attached to the Executive Committee, headed by those members of the Executive Committee who were not occupying posts as secretaries.[47] The secretaries, in turn, were given areas of responsibility often overlapping with those of the commissions and their heads. The apparatus of the Presidium by this time had been reduced to three departments and four standing committees.[48] It is difficult to determine precisely what the roles of the commissions, committees, and departments are, and how the chain of command among them operates. It may be surmised, nevertheless, that the secretaries of the Executive Committee for International Relations and for Ideological Work and Propaganda are in charge of the corresponding departments of the Presidium, and that the remaining secretaries supervise the work of the Presidium Standing Committees. There remain the commissions, whose task appears to be that of keeping track of developments in important areas such as civil defense and the implementation of the new constitution. As previously noted, the commissions are now under the direct supervision of members of the Executive Committee. The practical consequence appears to be a sharp limitation on the independence of the commissions, which had operated with a considerable degree of freedom under the loose supervision of the Presidium in the period between 1964 and 1972.

Among the responsibilities of the party most affected by organizational changes over the years is that of cadre placement. Responsibility for cadre decisions was decentralized during the 1950s, but a tendency toward recentralization was discernible after the June 1958 reorganization of the Secretariat. In the early 1960s, cadre commissions were reestablished in sectors where they had been abandoned earlier, especially in institutions of public administration. The existence of a multiplicity of cadre organizations changed the nature of the task of the Secretariat from one of direct ordering to one of coordination. A great deal of the supervision exercised by the party in the field of cadre placement came to focus on problems of rotation, "de-professionalization," and of assuring a proper national balance in federal institutions and elective organs.

The party made a significant reduction in its cadre placement responsibilities after the Eighth Congress; from this point on there is no reference in accounts of the party's organization to a body performing this function.[49] Further evidence of the party's retreat from cadre placement and selection activities came at the Ninth Plenum (1968).[50] This meeting referred to the vacuum which had been created in the preceding years by the democratization of cadre policy; while it was stated that the party should by all means avoid having a monopoly over cadre placement, the Plenum did reaffirm the right of the party to play a leading role in cadre questions. The Ninth Plenum position seemed to call for a sharing of responsibilities between the party and other bodies in respect to cadre placement; at a minimum, the party would exercise a veto over decisions of other bodies in this field, especially the SAWP (Socialist Alliance of the Working People). This conclusion, however, requires further corroboration; the exact mechanisms by which cadre decisions were made in the party in the 1960s are not easy to discern.[51]

After 1972, cadre questions once again became of prime concern to the LCY. Purges of enterprise managers were carried out under the party's direction, and efforts were made to staff the new self-managing bodies (the BOALs, the Interest Communities) with workers. To this end, an attempt was made to compel institutions to sign self-managing agreements stipulating that workers were to be placed in leading positions in the enterprise or organization in question. Whether the party succeeded in its objective of bringing workers into positions of leadership is doubtful, however, and a good deal of confusion and opposition accompanied efforts of the party to dictate to other bodies in matters of cadre policy.[52]

The size of the party bureaucracy has varied greatly over the years. As might be expected, it was greatest in the immediate postwar period, suffered a sharp decline in numbers after the Sixth Congress,[53] and then remained stationary, or even increased slightly, in the early 1960s. Data is scarce for recent years, but in early 1975 Jure Bilić referred to the existence of 1,500 professional party workers—[54] a figure greater than that of the mid-1950s, but not greatly exceeding the number that can be estimated, from scattered republic data, for the mid-1960s.[55]

Up to 1974, the trend in party-military relations was marked by a reduction in party controls.[56] Immediately after the war, party organizations in military units were directly responsible to the Political Administration, or Main Political Administration, as it was known after 1948. In February 1949, the MPA was abolished. In its place there was created a party body known as the *Opunomocstvo;* this organ was in turn replaced, at the First Conference of the League of Communists in the Yugoslav Peoples Army (YPA) in 1969, by a Committee of the League of Communists in the YPA, with a membership of thirty-five chosen by a Conference of the LCY in the YPL. Party controls over the officer corps were reduced in the spring of 1953, when the post of political commissar was abolished and military commanders given responsibility for the moral-political education of their men. From this time on, party units placed their emphasis on work with party members rather than engaging in political education and other activities among the troops. At the same time the army increased its participation in local government; in 1957 there was a total of 15,225 party members from the military elected to local organs of government (by 1968, this number had dropped to 2,729).[57]

The freeing of the army from direct party control did not lead to the divorce of the army from political life, for factionalism in the party encouraged a greater role for the military in politics. The full story of the military's involvement in party affairs has yet to be written; Fejtö's account of politics in Eastern Europe contains brief reference to the role of Slovene army units in support of the liberal party faction in the struggle with Ranković,[58] and there have been references to the existence of an alliance between Serbian units and Kardelj at the time of the Žanko incident.[59] The crisis of 1971 gave birth to a number of reports that the military had assumed a major role in Yugoslav politics.[60] It is difficult to confirm these journalistic accounts; on the other hand, there is little question that the failure of the party to deal with the national crisis forced the military into the political arena. Tito, in several highly publicized speeches held at the height of the national crisis in December 1971, made clear his willingness to use the military to crush the dissident national Communists in Croatia, if necessary.[61] The military, for their part, appealed to Tito to take firm action against nationalist forces in Croatia.[62]

Since 1971 the influence of the military has been manifest in the power of the Counter Intelligence Service (KOS), whose head, General Ivan Mišković, was Tito's close adviser until 1973, and in the presence of military figures in the Executive Committee and the Presidium of the party.[63] At the same time, an effort has been made in recent years to strengthen the basic party organizations in the army, while the military appears to be divided on its approach to major issues facing the government and the party, thus blunting somewhat the effect of the armed forces on the shaping of policy.

The dramatic increase in the power of the republic parties, especially after the Ninth Congress, has already been alluded to. The party statute adopted at that time spelled out, in explicit terms, the manner in which the Presidium of the LCY (formerly the Central Committee) would be chosen by the republics. No such specific guidelines were drawn up for the Executive Bureau, whose selection was left in the hands of the Presidium. The evidence is overwhelming, nevertheless, that voting in the Executive Bureau was decisively influenced by the clash of interests which characterized relations among the republics at this time. Undoubtedly, this reflected divisions along republic lines within the Presidium, as well as the fact that republic party presidents served ex officio in the Executive Bureau.[64]

The crisis of 1971, followed by the confrontation between Tito and the Serbian party in 1972, was a test of the republic parties' strength. The successful purge of the two leading republic parties restored the central party organs to a position of predominance. On the other hand, the statute adopted at the Tenth Party Congress made a major concession to the republics by allowing them to determine the selection of the Central Committee members, and in this way, to influence the make-up of the Presidium. Important decisions of the Executive Committee are usually made in consultation with the presidents of the republic parties. Finally, the federal system in Yugoslavia has placed a great deal of responsibility in the hands of the republic governments and, therefore, the republic parties. While the Executive Committee of the LCY momentarily gained the upper hand after 1974, the republic parties remain extremely powerful, and seem destined to grow even more influential in the future.

In addition to the six republic party organizations, there exist two provincial party organizations, in Kosovo and Vojvodina. Until 1971, both were under the firm control of the Serbian party. Following this date, the positions of the provincial parties were greatly strengthened, thanks to the representation of the provinces in inter-republic coordinating committees of the federal government, in the new state presidency, and in leading party organs. In the case of Kosovo an especially delicate political situation developed as the result of a revival of national feeling among the Albanians. This led to antagonism between the Albanians and the Serbs in the province and a struggle for control of the provincial party. The crackdown against national elements in Croatia was also felt in Kosovo, where a purge led to the victory of the moderate elements, restoring a degree of harmony to the provincial party organization.

Basic and local party organizations in the LCY have also undergone considerable transformation over the years, although many features common to other East European parties remain. After seizing power, the Yugoslav Communists set up a comprehensive network of local and regional organizations based on the model of the Soviet party.[65] This system received its first shock with the termination of collectivization in 1950; village party organizations set up to carry out collectivization were allowed to stagnate, or were abandoned altogether, thus decisively weakening the ties of the party with the countryside, a source of party strength since the beginning of the partisan struggle.[66] In 1952 and 1953, reforms instituted by the Sixth Party Congress fundamentally altered the structure of the party at the local level. Party cells were dissolved in many areas; the party bureaus were abolished; new basic organizations, formed around an area generally corresponding to the electoral district, were organized. In addition, provisions were made for the establishment of *aktivs* in certain types of institutions where cells had been abolished. Most far-reaching in its implications was the decision to give the basic party unit—the cell—a new role. Instead of transmitting orders from above, the cells were to play an educational role. In the words of the party congress, "the main task of the basic party organization [is to act] as a political organization in the fight for the socialist consciousness of the working people."[67]

The reforms of the Sixth Congress caused considerable confusion at the local level, and it was not long after that steps were taken to reassert the position of the party. At the Fourth Plenum of the Central Committee of March 1954, the decision was taken to reintroduce party cells into certain areas—newspaper editorial boards, theaters, and hospitals—where they had been abolished in 1952. The statute adopted at the Seventh Party Congress made provisions for a network of local party groups which included basic party organizations set up on the production and the territorial principle, temporary and permanent *aktivs*, and regional party organizations at the level of the commune (*opština*) and district (*srez*). In the district and commune organizations the basic organ of the party was the conference, meeting every two years, which chose the party committee. The committee was in turn empowered to choose its political secretary and a secretariat. Between the Seventh and Eighth Party Congresses, an attempt was made to reduce the party bureaucracy at the local level by abolishing the commune and district secretariats.[68] At the same time, this period witnessed a great increase in the number of basic party organizations due to the spread of self-management and the founding of new enterprises requiring party organizations.

The party statutes adopted by the Eighth and Ninth Party Congresses made no dramatic changes in this organizational structure; nevertheless, steps were taken to strengthen the commune party organization. This was most noticeable in the statute adopted by the Ninth Congress which stressed the role of the commune party organization as the guiding force for all local institutions.[69] The Ninth Party Congress statute also strengthened the conference, focusing on this body as the representative of the broad rank and file of party members at the local level.

The impact of the post-1971 events on local party organizations and their role was evident in the statute adopted at the Tenth Party Congress. The new statute stressed the importance of the basic party organization, which was no longer to be limited to ideological work. In the new self-management unit within the enterprise—the Basic Organization of Associated Labor—party members were to concern themselves with all major questions touching on the development of the BOAL (Article 35). In other units in which basic organizations were to be formed—self-managing workers' communities, territorial communities, and military units—the party was also to play a more active role.[70] Stress was placed in the statute on the responsibility of the party organization for seeing that the activities of the institutions or organs in which they were situated were harmonized with the broader interests of the community and with the need to develop self-management relations. At the local government level, party organization remained basically unchanged. The mandate of the *opština* conference was extended to four years and provision was made for the workers' *aktiv*—a device for allowing workers in each *opština* to discuss matters of importance under consideration by local party and state organs.[71] As in the past, provision was made for the formation of *aktivs* in institutions where basic party organizations were not considered appropriate—in sociopolitical organizations, in organs of interest communities, in territorial defense units, and the like.

These alterations in the organization and structure of local party organizations over the years were bound up with far-reaching changes in the local power structure in Yugoslavia. It was at the local level, above all, that the party had to face the problem of maintaining discipline in the face of a sharp curtailment of party responsibilities. It was at this level, too, that a sharp struggle broke out between the party and "underground elements" in the latter half of the 1960s, with the result that local politics was often tempestuous and bitter (especially in Serbia).[72] In these complex circumstances, the party sought to develop flexibility and responsiveness to local needs by stressing the role of the Party Conference, the Conference Presidium, and the president of the Conference. In some districts for which data is available there was a discernible trend for the Presidium of the Conference to represent "notables" of the area from the realm of politics and economics. The president of the Conference appears to have been the spokesman for this group: a nonprofessional politician, he could not at the same time be a member of the Party Committee. The party secretary, on the other hand, was always a professional party employee. Rather than representing the old guard, he was usually a young man (often an engineer by training), aided by a district committee drawn largely from the local technocratic managerial class.[73] At the level of the enterprise, there appeared an informal organization, the political *aktiv* (not to be confused with the workers' *aktiv* described earlier), made up of leading persons in the enterprise, which to some extent replaced the functions of the basic party organization.[74]

Investigations of the power structure at the local level carried out by sociologists in the 1960s were unanimous in their conclusions concerning the drastic decline of party influence.[75] Further investigation may show that the role of the party at the *opština* level was nevertheless not insignificant in this period.[76] In any case, it is clear that the late 1960s were marked by the growth of new centers of power at the local level, and that this provided the new technical-managerial groups with an opportunity for greatly strengthening their position and influence—especially through local government organizations and the Party Committee.[77]

Figures on party membership are provided in Table 8.1. While a great deal of information has been published on the social composition, age, and job qualifications of party members, there are gaps in the data, especially for recent years. Our discussion will therefore focus on the period up to 1971.

It can be seen that after the war the party was an elite organization, comprising only 2 percent of the population of the country. A rapid growth in membership in the period 1948–50 broadened the party's base. There followed a period of declining membership between 1952 and 1956, followed by a continuous expansion during the period of the Second Five-Year Plan, broken only by a brief downturn in 1962. Two years of stagnation (1966 and 1967) were followed by a sharp growth in party membership in 1968, when a record for the time of 1,146,084 members was reached. During the early 1970s, a purge of party members took place, followed by a rapid increase.[78] In 1976 the party, with 1,302,843 members, was the largest in its history, constituting approximately 6 percent of the population.

In analyzing the reasons for the growth of party membership, one can point to economic factors (the party has grown faster during periods of rapid economic expansion), the political climate, and deliberate party policy. Over the years the impact of the Yugoslav-Soviet dispute can be clearly discerned, especially in 1968, when the invasion of Czechoslovakia encouraged young people to join the party in great numbers. Until 1973, the party remained small in relation to total population. In part, this reflected a desire to retain an elite status in society for party members. On the other hand, this policy tended to favor the white-collar elements in the party at the expense of the working-class membership. The recent policy of expanded recruitment may signal a change in outlook toward the question of membership; if so, the number in the party may be permitted to increase beyond the present 6 percent level in order to make room for more workers and other manual elements.

Prior to 1973, the party was aging. In 1958, 23.6 percent of

Table 8.1. Social Composition of the Party
(By current occupation)

	1948	1956	1960	1966	1970	1976
Total Party Membership	482,938	648,616	1,006,285	1,046,018	1,049,184	1,302,843
% of population	3.0	3.7	5.5	5.3	5.2	6.2
Workers	145,226	206,697	363,420	355,022	324,459	366,272
% of party	30.1	31.9	36.1	33.9	30.3	28.1
Peasants	231,032	111,915	131,206	77,134	68,425	65,910
% of party	47.8	17.2	13.0	7.4	6.5	5.1
White-Collar & Intelligentsia	65,665	211,325	321,800	408,378	473,128	542,248
% of party	13.6	32.6	32.0	39.0	45.1	41.8
a) Intelligentsia	–	–	–	–	187,800	–
% of party	–	–	–	–	17.8	–
b) White-Collar Workers	–	–	–	–	211,958	–
% of party	–	–	–	–	20.2	–
c) Leaders	–	–	–	–	74,070	–
% of party	–	–	–	–	7.1	–
Others	41,015	118,679	189,859	205,484	189,472	–
% of party	8.5	18.3	18.9	19.6	18.0	–
a) Students	–	–	–	34,657	51,331	96,139
% of party	–	–	–	3.3	4.9	7.5
b) Housewives	–	–	–	31,604	–	–
% of party	–	–	–	3.0	–	–
c) Pensioners	–	–	–	74,610	91,067	–
% of party	–	–	–	7.1	8.7	–
d) Military	–	–	–	52,842	–	–
% of party	–	–	–	5.1	–	–

the party was under twenty-five years of age; in 1966 the proportion had dropped to 11.5 percent. Following the rapid expansion of party membership in the mid-1970s, the age of party members dropped significantly. By 1975, 28.5 percent was under 28 years of age (as compared to 24.6 percent in 1968). At the same time an effort was made to enroll younger technical and professional personnel in the party. Although precise figures are lacking, this campaign seems to have met with considerable success, if only because the supply of trained cadres in Yugoslavia considerably exceeded demand, permitting the party to insist on party membership as a precondition for employment.

The data on the social composition of the party show that a dramatic change took place in the make-up of the party between 1952 and 1954, when the peasants dropped from 48.8 percent of the party to 22.6 percent, and the white-collar and "Others" increased from 25.0 percent to 49.0 percent. From 1954 onward trends are more gradual. In the two and a half decades covered by the data there has been a slight increase in the percentage of workers, a sharp decline in the percentage of peasants, and a major increase in the percentage of white-collar and "Others."

The functionaries, or white-collar workers, together with the intelligentsia, are clearly the dominant group in the party. This fact has been confirmed over the years by complaints concerning the easier terms of entry for such persons and their relative immunity from expulsion. As a whole, the white-collar group is better represented in the party than are other social strata. In 1966, the last year for which we have reliable data, 21.5 percent of the manual workers employed in the socialist sector were party members, while 39 percent of the white-collar employees were members. Among the nonmanual workers, penetration was particularly high in positions not requiring a high level of education. In such low-level white-collar jobs, 64.6 percent were party members![79]

Data on job qualifications reveal that the party members are, as a group, better educated than the population as a whole.[80] The extremely low educational levels of the postwar period, when Tito had to report that in 1948 only half of the party membership had a basic education, are a thing of the past; today most party members have a secondary or basic education combined with some form of vocational training. Those with a university education are well-represented in the party, but still not a dominant element.[81] The penetration data cited earlier also reveal that in the 1960s and early 1970s a disproportionate number of party members had low-level white-collar jobs, a fact supported at the time by evidence from the republic parties and by remarks by Tito concerning the role of "semi-intellectuals" in the party.[82] Meanwhile, this problem has been alleviated, if not completely resolved, by the influx of young professional and technical personnel into the party alluded to above.

Data on the national composition of the party show that although all major national groups are well represented, Serbs, Macedonians and especially Montenegrins make up a larger share of the party than their numbers in the population would lead one to anticipate.[83] In 1967, those of Serb nationality constituted slightly over one-half of the party membership, while making up 43 percent of the population of the country as a whole. Minorities have been significantly underrepresented. There are, in addition, deviations from the norm of balanced national representation in the republics. This is especially true in Bosnia-Hercegovina, for which no statistics on the nationality of party members have been published, but where it is known that the Serbs have been the dominant group in the party.

The data just presented highlight the fact that the Yugoslav party, notwithstanding its revolutionary origins, has successfully coopted modernizing elites into its ranks. Its younger leaders appear to be dynamic and well educated. Emprical data from the 1960s suggest that the party represents the modernizing, upwardly socially mobile elements of Yugoslavia.[84] The anti-technocratic campaign of the early 1970s, although it led to a sharp deterioration in relations between the party and the modernizing elites in Yugoslavia, does not seem to have resulted in a mass defection of this latter group from the party.

On the other hand, it is clear that the party has not simply been transformed into the tool of an elite bent on modernizing Yugoslavia. We have seen how, in recent years, tensions have built up between the party leadership and the new technical and managerial elites in Yugoslav society. Also, many members join the party in order to advance their careers; the result is that opportunism is common, and this in turn encourages bureaucratic and even corrupt practices which tarnish the image of the party as a force for progress and change.

Nowhere is this more evident than in respect to the accumulation of privileges. The existence of costly summer villas, the use of luxury cars, the practice of sending children to expensive boarding schools abroad—all of this has been described by Djilas and others,[85] and from time to time has been the object of campaigns by the party leadership.[86] Nevertheless, these practices persist. It may be that the peasant background of many party leaders has helped make the accumulation of privileges such a problem, but it must also be recognized that Tito has contributed indirectly to the spread of abuses of this kind by his luxurious style of life and his expensive tastes—habits which others, not surprisingly, try to emulate.

With the accumulation of privilege has come corruption. A communication of the Central Committee in 1963 warned of the existence of widespread fraud in sociopolitical organizations, in particular in the veterans' organizations, the unions, and the Red Cross.[87] From 1961 to June 1963, according to this communication, 3,462 criminal acts were uncovered, with the loss of over 400 million dinars. Criminal prosecutions notwithstanding, the problem of corruption has proved insoluble, in part because it extends to the top leadership itself. The most serious among several cases involving important party leaders concerns Boris Krajger, the party's expert on the economy in the 1960s, whose death in an auto accident led to the uncovering of huge sums apparently which he had swindled from the government.[88]

The party leadership has been acutely aware that bureaucratic manifestations in the party conflict with the professed goals of the self-management system. The campaign of the period

1962–64 against abuses in the party included efforts to pension off older party functionaries, to "deprofessionalize" party bureaucrats, and other measures. The downfall of Ranković made it possible to extend the scope of this campaign to the very highest echelons of the party, leading to the removal of practically an entire generation of older party leaders. Ironically, however, the problem of corruption, influence peddling, and the like grew after 1966, and became one of the central issues in the national controversy. This was because many of the pensioned and "deprofessionalized" party leaders (as well as former secret police officials) used their influence to gain lucrative positions in the new commercial and banking structure growing up in Belgrade. Having passed through a period of debureaucratization, the LCY threatened to become a spoils party whose members operated in the economy in such a way as to amass enormous profits for their enterprises and, of course, for themselves. The problem of controlling the informal power structure built around party rule therefore remained acute. It is a subject to which we shall now return in our resume of the party's role in Yugoslavia.

CONCLUDING REMARKS

The many changes which have taken place within the LCY since the early 1950s are eloquent testimony to the adaptability of East European Communist systems, given the proper political conditions. To summarize these changes once more is unnecessary. Rather, we shall limit ourselves to several observations concerning the role of the LCY as a revolutionary party, and its similarities to and differences from the remaining parties of Eastern Europe. The problem, first of all, is whether the LCY has retained its Leninist features or, on the contrary, has become a new type of party, one different in a fundamental sense from the remaining parties of Eastern Europe.

Although the Yugoslav party has changed in many respects, it still bears the signs of its origins. In ideological matters the

LCY, while no longer blindly adhering to Leninist principles, upholds a Marxist viewpoint which remains in essence antidemocratic and antiliberal.[89] The party leadership remains deeply influenced by elitist principles, notwithstanding its efforts to encourage self-management and decentralization. Although there have been many changes in the organization of the LCY, the party's insistence on adhering to the principles of democratic centralism, the retention of party cells in places of work, and the assumption that the party rather than the government is ultimately responsible for enforcing the regime's decisions, all testify to the continued influence on the LCY of past practices derived from the Leninist model.

In adhering to this model, it has been vitally important for the LCY that it retain control over the individual party member, and that it be able to transmit orders down to individuals in responsible positions with the expectation that these commands will be obeyed. As long as the party has this capacity, it can act directly on institutions and groups in society, and its coordinating, mobilizing, and controlling functions remain intact.

Control over the individual party member did decrease significantly after 1966. Democratic centralism came under criticism, the cadre responsibilities of the party were greatly reduced, and the spread of factionalism within the party meant that an individual in disfavor with the leadership could often find political support from some other quarter. A major goal of the party after 1971 was, as we have seen, to tighten discipline, to expel those who defied party orders, and to regain control over persons in key positions. By and large these efforts succeeded: party discipline was tightened, those opposed to the new policies dismissed, and party control over other institutions increased.

Still, there remains room for doubt that the LCY regained full control over persons in posts of responsibility after 1971. There were reports that many persons purged from the party in 1972 and 1973 retained their positions—a development which, if widespread, could have had the unintended effect of increasing the number of persons in positions of responsibility outside the party's control. The successful defiance of the party for many years by a group of Belgrade professors—the Belgrade Eight—also suggests that the ability of the party to remove persons from positions of responsibility was not without its limits.[90]

Thus, while the party today defends what are essentially Leninist principles in respect to its control over party members and the right of the party to transmit orders to its members in their place of work, one can legitimately raise the question of whether these principles have not been undermined too greatly in practice to be retained over the long run. Clearly the Yugoslav party is faced with a dilemma, in this respect, which lies far in the future for the other parties of Eastern Europe.

The Yugoslav party is also subject to group pressures to a degree unknown in the rest of Eastern Europe. Politics in Yugoslavia at times seem to be dominated by the activities of groups—be they representatives of regional interests, branches of industry, or some other element. The emergence of this phenomenon is in fact hardly surprising, for the self-management system and the corporate structure of local, republic, and federal assemblies, as well as the multinational character of the country, have helped to create a society of interest-oriented associations which can usually justify even the most selfish demands by appealing to the right of self-management or the principle of equality among nationalities.

As a result of this development, the party finds itself deeply enmeshed in the task of mediating among competing groups in Yugoslavia. At least two groups—the republic parties and the military—are now represented within the party's leadership. Party commissions provide a mechanism for articulating and expressing interests at the highest levels. Personal ties—for example, between the party organization of a locality and an important political personage in Belgrade—are very effective in generating informal pressures and gaining decisions favorable for special groups, enterprises, or localities. Complaints on the part of the party leaders indicate that they are acutely aware of the dangers facing the party from the activity of various groups pressing for special favors.

As we have seen, the rise in group activity in the 1960s was paralleled by a sharp reduction in the party's cadre responsibilities, and a sharing of decision-making with other bodies, chiefly the federal, republic, and local governments. In the end, the party felt so threatened by these developments that it sought to reimpose controls. The device chosen was the expanded system of self-management introduced between 1971 and 1974.

This move to strengthen itself is a reminder of the continued revolutionary vitality of the Yugoslav party. The attempt to build a system of self-managing bodies parallel to the existing interest group structure (the core of which are the managerial and technical groups and the local and republic governments), and then to place these bodies under party control, is a bold strategy, and is very much in keeping with the innovative character of Yugoslav communism in the past. More broadly, this may be considered a unique response to the challenges facing a Leninist party in an interest-oriented society. Indeed, the LCY is in this connection showing itself to be more revolutionary than the other parties of Eastern Europe, to whom the notion of voluntary self-management agreements, even under party sponsorship, is quite foreign.

It is all the more unfortunate, therefore, that the evidence on which to make a judgement of this experiment in party rule through self-management organizations is so scanty. The party has succeeded in setting up primary organizations in most BOALs. The influence of the party in the interest communities is less clear but is presumably substantial. The influence of the party can also be seen in the frequency with which "self-management agreements" are concluded in Yugoslavia today.

In support of this new approach, it can be argued that there is an indisputable need for the party to act as an integrating force in Yugoslavia, and that the present method of working through the self-management structure frees the party, to some degree at least from the control of established interest groups in the enterprises and in local and republic governments. On the other hand, there are clearly problems involved with the new stratgegy. In trying to by-pass the established managerial and local governmental elites, the party has set the stage for a clash of interests among the self-managing institutions themselves. Having accepted responsibility for creating and guiding these new organizations, the party finds itself drawn into the conflicts of interest it was supposed to control, resulting in the identification of party members with the interests of the self-managing groups.

Indeed, one is forced to come to the paradoxical conclusion that the great differences between the LCY and other East European parties notwithstanding, the Yugoslav party has yet to resolve the basic dilemma of whether it is to continue as a party in the Leninist mold or not. The present strategy is an attempt to answer this question in the affirmative. It rests on a policy of strengthening central party organs, extending control over the new pluralistic society through self-management organizations and self-management agreements sponsored by the party, and tightening party discipline through emphasis on democratic centralism and party control over career opportunities in Yugoslav society. It is, however, an inherently difficult strategy to pursue in a pluralistic society. Furthermore, it has the effect of weakening, if not destroying altogether, the "old-boy network" which operated so effectively in the past to maintain party influence behind the scenes, for many members of that network now find themselves on the opposite side of the fence, that is, among the managers and others who have been subject to continuing criticism during the past five years.

An alternative view of the party's role does exist and has considerable support. It is not the revisionist approach of Milovan Djilas, but the more moderate position espoused by those given the task of proposing party reform in 1967. This view was later endorsed by the more liberal republic leaders in Serbia and Croatia. Under this approach, the party would cease trying to impose its will on other organizations, even indirectly. Internal party democracy would be encouraged and democratic centralism deemphasized. Outside the purely political realm, the party would divest itself of cadre responsibilities. Attractive as this view might seem because of its liberal features, it also has its shortcomings. Such a party would enhance the position of the republic parties and the managerial groups, the two beneficiaries of the weakness of the LCY in the late 1960s. It would also allow more scope for corruption and the operation of the old-boy network, thus encouraging the evolution of the party into essentially a political machine or spoils party. Also, such a party would probably lack the ability to play an integrating role in the Yugoslav system; by default such responsibility might then have to be assumed by the army, the federal bureaucracy, or perhaps the secret police.

The problem of the role of the party in contemporary Yugoslav society thus remains unresolved. In the last analysis, it appears that the party will be compelled to play a major role as an integrative force in the Yugoslav political and social system, simply because no other institution is capable of performing this function effectively. It may be, nevertheless, that the task of checking pluralistic forces may fall to the republic parties, acting both as spokesmen for the new elites in Yugoslav society and for the party as a mediating and integrative institution. Such a development would reduce the friction now evident between the party and other groups, but would impose a heavy burden on the republic party leaders, who would have to find ways of reconciling their differences while retaining the support of their own rank-and-file party members. Such a system would probably not succeed if there were not other forces for stability and order present at the highest level of the system. If the present constitutional structure is any clue, the task of providing such stability could fall to the state presidency, the federal bureaucracy, and the military.

Making all these elements harmonize will surely tax the political skills of the LCY to the utmost. It may well be that the future of the party lies in a situation of contrived ambiguity, in which the present tensions—between the new self-management institutions and the party, on the one hand, and the local enterprise, and regional elites, on the other—remain a permanent fixture of the Yugoslav system. For this solution to work, however, it is necessary that factional warfare within the party be kept to a minimum, for a renewal of the struggle between the liberal and conservative wings of the party would be sure to lead to a debate over the role of the party in the Yugoslav political system—one far more serious than took place in 1953–54 or 1966–67. To predict such a factional struggle is premature. Meanwhile, as the date for Tito's departure from the political scene draws closer, it seems increasingly likely that the party will have to reexamine its role, and that this will inevitably involve clashes of opinion within the leadership. On the outcome of that debate could rest, in turn, the future of the party either as a revolutionary institution retaining its Leninist features, or as a one-party system of a nonrevolutionary type, closer in most essentials to the one-party systems of the non-Communist world.

NOTES

1. On the prewar history of the party, see Ivan Avakumović, *History of the Communist Party of Yugoslavia* (Aberdeen: Aberdeen University Press, 1964); Istorijsko odelenje Centralnog komiteta KPJ, *Istorijski Arhiv Komunisticke Partije Jugoslavije*, 6 vols. (Belgrade: 1949–1951; Edib Hasanagić, ed., *Komunisticka Partije Jugoslavije, 1919–1941* (Zagreb: Skolska Krj. 1959); Rodoljub Čolaković et al., *Pregled Istorije Saveza Komunista Jugoslavije* (Belgrade: 1963).

2. The best Western source on the life-style of the party leadership after the war is Josef Korbel, *Tito's Communism* (Denver: University of Denver Press, 1951). See also Phyllis Auty, *Tito: A Biography* (Harmondsworth: Pelican, 1974), p. 268, as well as the works of Djilas cited below.

3. See the author's article, "Problems of Party Reform in Yugoslavia," *The American and Slavic East European Review* (October 1959), 18(3):334–50.

4. *Komunist*, no. 7, pp. 430–31.

5. Translated in *Anatomy of a Moral* (New York: Praeger, 1959).

6. At the Third Plenum of the CC. Djilas was arrested a year later for statements to the *New York Times*, then was put on trial a second time in December 1956 for articles appearing in *The New Leader* on the Hungarian revolution. In October 1957, he was once more put on trial for writing *The New Class*. In January 1961, he was released but was again arrested in 1962 and sentenced to five years' imprisonment for his book *Conversations with Stalin*.

7. In Croatia, *Naprijed*, the Croatian party journal, was banned, and its editor, Dušan Diminić, was jailed. In Serbia, Djilas was given some support by Vladimir Dedijer. For Djilas's own brief account of his writings and the response to them, see *The Unperfect Society* (New York: Harcourt, Brace, 1969).

8. Savez komunista Jugoslavije, *VII Kongres Saveza Komunista Jugoslavije* (Belgrade: 1958), pp. 926–1105.

9. For the circumstances under which this meeting took place, see the discussion of leading party organs to follow.

10. A sign of the shift in the balance of power within the party at this time was the stiff sentence given Djilas in May of 1962 for publishing abroad his work *Conversations with Stalin.*

11. With Tito's speech at Split, in the spring of 1962. See *Komunist,* May 10, 1962. This speech can be compared with Tito's speech in the spring of 1969 and the letter of the Executive Bureau of September 1972 (infra.).

12. *Komunist,* July 7, 1966. An account of these events can also be found in Fejto, *A History of the People's Democracies* (New York: Praeger, 1969) and Nenad Petrović, "The Fall of Aleksandar Ranković," *Review* (published by the Study Centre for Yugoslav Affairs, London), no. 6, 1967, pp. 533–51.

13. Radivoje Jovanović beat out four other candidates in Lazarevac to win the seat in the Federal Assembly. He was subsequently recalled, but only after he had put up a fierce battle against the party in which he successfully joined forces with the president and vice-president of the communal assembly. See Radio Free Europe bulletins for April, May, and June 1967 for this and other cases.

14. More will be said on this dispute in the section dealing with party organization. This debate produced a great amount of material, much of it of great interest for those concerned with the problems of the evolution of Communist one-party systems.

15. Among the leaders of the party, Krste Crvenkovski was notable for suggesting, in October 1966, that the party allow different views to coexist within its own ranks. *Politika,* October 23, 1966. In *Socijalizam* (1967), (10):1322, Crvenkovski went a step further, questioning the need for democratic centralism in the party. Todorović also spoke out for reform at this time, and suggested that a multiparty system was not inconceivable in Yugoslavia; he himself supported the idea of a free expression of the views of different interests in Yugoslavia in the Socialist Workers Alliance (SAWP). For his views, see his work, *Preobrazaj Saveza Komunista Jugoslavije* (Belgrade: Rad, 1968). Dobrivoje Radosavljević, at the time secretary of the Serbian party, suggested in an article in *Komunist,* January 26, 1967, that Communists should be ready to accept decisions by a majority, even if by non-Communists. Vukmanović-Tempo fought to give organizations in the enterprises freedom to follow their own policies without direction from the center (*Nin,* September 10, 17, and 24, 1967). Numerous articles criticized the party's monopoly of power in outspoken terms. Note the suggestions

for a two-party system made by the political scientist Steven Vračar, "Partijski monopolizam i politička moć društvenih grupa," *Gledištà* (August–September 1967), 8(8):1053–66. Other important contributions to the debate include Svetozar Stojanović's article in *Praxis*, no. 5–6 (September 1967), pp. 680–92; Predrag Vranicki, in *Kniževne Novine*, October 14, 1967, and Rade Dumanić, "Prakticna pitanja reorganizacije Saveza komunista," *Naše Teme* (May 1967), 11(5):850–58. See also Dimitar Dimitrov et al., *Za Preobrazba Na Sojuzot Na Komunistite Na Jugoslavija I Na Opsteštvoto: Zbornik* (Skoplje: 1967).

16. *Politika*, April 27, 1967.

17. *Borba*, July 2–3, 1967.

18. "Saopštenje Izvršnog komiteta Sk Jugoslavije," *Komunist*, June 6, 1968, p. 3.

19. For the statute, see *Deveti Kongres Saveza Komunista Jugoslavije* (Belgrade: 1969), pp. 279–308. The changes in party organization adopted by the statute are discussed in more detail below.

20. The party was not afraid to raise the ideological issue, at least on its own terms, and frequently spoke of launching an "ideological offensive" to strengthen the party. This theme was most fully explored at the Eighth Plenum of the Party Presidium held in April 1970. See *Politika*, April 23 and 24, 1970, and numerous articles appearing in *Socijalizam* on the question of ideology in the period 1969–70.

21. At Split and Zadar, August 28 and 29. See *Politika*, August 29 and 30, 1969.

22. *Komunist*, December 11 and 18, 1969.

23. *Politika*, July 31, 1969.

24. On August 26, Kardelj delivered a sharp attack against Slovenian nationalism at a broadened session of the secretariat of the Slovenian party. It was published several months later in *Komunist*, October 2 and 9, 1969. Kardelj, Todorović, and others continued, in the year that followed, to warn against nationalist feelings and to call for decisive action to solve the developing political crisis. While their remarks still show a desire to liberalize the political system, the predominant tone is one of fear, lest the party and government become paralyzed. See especially the speeches of the Thirteenth Plenum of the fall of 1970 in *Borba*, October 15–17, 1970.

25. See Miko Tripalo, *Aktuelna Pitanja Razvoja Sistema Samoupravljanja* (Zagreb: 1970), pp. 23–24. A good source for the Croatian complaints is Savez komunista Hrvatske, *Savjetovanje U Centralnom Komitetu Saveza Komunista Hrvatske 22 I 29 Svibnja 1968* (Zagreb: 1968).

26. See *Komunist*, February 6, 1964, for the agreement of 1963 between Serbia and Montenegro. The 1966 agreement between the Serbian and Macedonian parties was described in *Komunist*, March 24, 1966.

27. The party reorganizations carried out at the Eighth and Ninth Congresses are discussed more fully in the section on party organization.

28. See the discussion to follow.

29. See *Borba*, November 17–21, 1969. Žanko was deputy chairman of the Federal Assembly and Croatia's representative to the Party Conference, as well as Croatian delegate in the Council of Nationalities.

30. *Borba*, November 17–21, 1969. See also Savez komunista Hrvatska, Centralni komitet, *Deseta Sjednica Centralnog Komiteta Saveza Komunista Hrvatska* (*Prema Autoriziran Tekstovima Magnetofonskog Zapisnika*) (Zagreb: 1970).

31. See *Vjesnik*, November 6, 1971.

32. Published versions of the speeches made at the Plenum do not refer to the "general national movement." Bakarić, in his December 7 speech, nevertheless traces the origins of this phase to the Twenty-second Plenum. *Foreign Broadcast Information Service* (hereafter referred to as FBIS), December 9, 1971.

33. FBIS December 2 and 3, 1971. Tito, in referring to the meeting, says he met with the Croatian Executive Committee and leaders of "socio-political organizations." See FBIS, December 3, 1971. The Yugoslav radio reported December 2 that the meeting was attended by republic secretaries, the presidents of the two provincial parties, the secretary of the committee of the League of Communists of the army (possibly a reference to the Opunomočstvo), and representatives of the SAWP, trade unions, veterans, and the president of the youth organization.

34. Note especially Mijalko Todorović's speech of February 1967, in which he warned of those who favored the policy of the "Firm Hand" "to save the situation." See Todorović, *Preobražaj*, p. 81.

35. For accounts of this period, see Dennison I. Rusinow, "Yugoslavia's Return to Leninism," *The American Universities Field Staff, Southeast Europe Series*, (June 1974), 21(1); K. F. Cviic, "Turning the Clock Back in Yugoslavia," *World Today* (May 1974), 30(5):206–13; Slobodan Stankovic, "Jugoslawien—ein Jahr nach dem X. Parteitag," *Osteuropa* (1975), 25(7):491–501.

36. *V. Kongres*, p. 163.

37. *Osmi Kongres*, p. 226.

38. Savez komunista Jugoslavije, Centralni komitet, *Politički Izveštaj O Radu Centralnog Komiteta Sky Od Osmog Do Devetog Kongresa* (Belgrade: 1969), p. 22.

39. The principle of democratic centralism was examined most closely at the Ninth Party Congress in connection with the extension of the rights of the minority to take positions contrary to that of the majority of the party. Article 9 of the statute provided for democratic discussion before decisions are made, the full participation of the party membership in elections of officers, and the informing of members of the activities of the party, but made all decisions taken by the majority obligatory on the minority. Article 17 dealt with the rights of the individual party member to bring a matter up once a decision had been reached, but forbade a person from continuing to hold a minority position once a decision had been reached, or to practice factionalism or *grupaško*. *Deveti Kongres*, pp. 239–45. The statute adopted by the Tenth

Congress, reflecting the turmoil of the preceding years, placed great emphasis on the importance of democratic centralism, stressing the obligatory nature of decisions of higher bodies for lower ones (Article 9). At the same time, the right of party members (and basic party organizations) to raise issues and have them discussed in party forums was retained (Articles 13 and 15 of the statute).

40. Adam Ulam, *Titoism and the Cominform* Cambridge, Mass: Harvard University Press, 1952, p. 113.

41. The showdown between the liberals and conservatives in the early 1960s is often referred to as having occurred at the Fourth Plenum. This plenum met in July 1962; the famous confrontation actually took place at a "broadened" meeting of the Executive Committee March 14–16. See Zvonko Staubringer, SKJ *Izmedju VII I VIII Kongresa* (Belgrade: 1964), p. 18. Having prevailed at the EC meeting in March, Ranković then imposed his views on the Fourth Plenum in July.

42. *Vjesnik*, September 17, 1966.

43. Tito first made this complaint at the Second Plenum of the CC in 1959; this charge was repeated in the letter of the EC to party members published in June 1962. See *Drugi Plenum Centralnog Komiteta Saveza Komunista Jugoslavije* (Belgrade: 1960), and *Komunist*, June 14, 1962, p. 3.

44. Valuable information on the work of the Central Committee and the background of its members in the early 1960s is to be found in *VIII Kongres* SKJ*: Izveštaj Centralnog Komiteta I Centralne Revizione Komisije*, chap. 3. Forty-nine of the total of 135 members were party professionals, and 63 were deputies to the federal assembly. The report characterizes the CC of the time as being made up of "distinguished" party members, usually leaders of various "sectors," with an average age of 52. It also stresses the difficulty the CC faced in reaching a united position because of the fact that its members all were leaders in their own right in some branch of government or the party.

45. *V. Kongres*, p. 166. The statute adopted at the Fifth Congress provided (Article 24) for four sections: Organization-Instructors Administration; Administration of Agitation and Propaganda; Administration for Cadre; and Economic-Financial Section..

46. There remained, however, a group of four persons who were referred to as belonging to the secretariat until the reorganizations of 1966: Tito, Kardelj, Ranković, and Vlahović.

47. Coordinating Commission for the Study and Direction of Activity in the Implementation of the New Constitution; Commission for All People's Defense, Commission for Current Socioeconomic Questions and Economic Policy, Commission for the Development of the LCY and Personnel Policy, Commission for International Relations, and Commission for Propaganda and Information Activity. Information on the organization of the EB and Presidium apparatus given below is taken from Central Intelligence Agency, *Reference Aid: Directory of Officials of the Socialist Federal Republic of Yugoslavia* Washington, D.C., (February 1976).

48. Department for Ideological Work, Department for International Relations, Department for Political Propaganda and Information; Standing Committee for Administrative and Financial Affairs, Standing Committee for Science and Culture, Standing Committee for Socioeconomic Relations, Development of the Economic System and Long-Term Economic Policy, Standing Committee for the Sociopolitical System and International Relations.

49. A Commission for Cadre Policies was established by the Eighth Congress, but this body seemed to be primarily concerned with general policy, not actual cadre selection.

50. SKJ, Centralni komitet, *Politički Izveštaj O Radu Centralnog Komiteta SKJ Od Osmog Do Devetog Kongresa,* p. 28, and *Borba,* July 17, 1968.

51. By a decision of the EC of October 1962, a cadre commission was formed in the SAWP; this body seemed to take over some of the functions of the Organizational-Political Secretariat in the party. However, not all the republic parties eliminated their cadre sections in the 1960s; in Montenegro a commission for cadre questions was still in existence in 1968. The role of the SAWP in cadre questions was subsequently reduced, and the matter was left to the personnel services of individual institutions, until organs for coordinating cadre policy were set up in the SAWP; these coordinating bodies had representatives of the LCY, the unions, youth organizations, and even, in some republics, of the economic chambers (*komori*). For a discussion that sheds some light on these problems, see *Kadrovska Politika U Organima Federacije* (Belgrade: 1970).

52. It is not clear at present which bodies have day-to-day responsibility for cadre selection. There is no department or standing committee attached to the Executive Bureau or the Presidium with responsibility in this area. There is a Commission for the Development of the LCY and Personnel Policy which may have some oversight functions.

53. F. W. Neal, *Titoism in Action,* (Berkeley: University of California Press, 1958) pp. 50–51, cites Ranković to the effect that by November 1952, 860 persons had already been dismissed from the central apparatus, and that after the Sixth Congress, the republic secretariats were "decimated"—Montenegro having only two [sic] full-time employees. At the Fourth Plenum of 1953, Ranković reported that there were 369 persons left working full-time in the apparatus. See Shoup, "Problems of Party Reform in Yugoslavia," pp. 339–40. Slovenia reported that the number of persons in the republic apparatus dropped from 660 in the summer of 1950 to 16 in the summer of 1954; in Macedonia the number fell from 643 in 1949 to 42 in 1953.

54. *Komunist,* March 3, 1975, p. 7.

55. In Serbia in 1961 there were reported to be 393 professional party workers; this number had risen to 405 by 1964. In 1962, the reported size of the Croatian party apparatus was 267; in 1967 it had dropped to 200.

56. An excellent account of party relations with the military is to

be found in Sveto Kovačević, "Koncipiranje uloge komunista u posleratnom razvitku Jugoslovenske Narodne Armije," in *Politička škola Jna, Zbornik Radova*, no. 1 (Belgrade 1968), pp. 7–35.

57. *Prva Konferencija SKJ U JNA* (Belgrade: 1969), p. 19.

58. Fejto, *History*, p. 138. Auty, *Tito*, p. 283, calls the reports of troop movements in 1966 "unconfirmed."

59. See accounts of the Zanko case in Radio Free Europe Bulletins of the time, especially January 21, 1970.

60. See, for example, the discussion in Radio Free Europe Bulletin of June 28, 1972, on the report in *Giornale d'Italia* of June 11 concerning a supposed coup attempt by certain pro-Ranković forces in the military.

61. See Tito's two speeches of December 21 (given in Sarajevo) and December 22 (in Rudo), in which he made reference to his willingness to use the military. *Politika*, August 29 and August 30. Bakarić also makes reference to Tito's conversations with military commanders in Karadjordjevo which, although not reported in the press, were widely known. FBIS, December 9, 1971.

62. It appears that on December 9, 1971, 63 prominent veterans and generals wrote Tito a letter, appealing for firm action against the Croatians. For reference to the letter, see Radio Free Europe Bulletin no. 1994, February 1974.

63. Military representation in the Party Presidium has already been alluded to. In the Executive Bureau, the military is represented by one active general, Ivan Kukoc. Fifteen officers were to be found in the Central Committee chosen at the Tenth Congress. See Slobodan Stankovic, "Jugoslawien—ein Jahr nach dem X. Parteitag," pp. 496–97.

64. The question arises as to whether the republic parties—especially the Croatian party—pressed for federalization of the party. This charge was made after the Twenty-first Plenum of the Presidium in 1971. The writings of Tripalo prior to the fall of 1971, however, show a very cautious approach to this problem and no outright call for federalization of the LCY. See his work, *Aktuelna Pitanja Razvoja Sistem Samoupravljanja;* his article, "Još jedan put o reorganizaciji Saveza komunista," *Naše Teme* (January 1968), 12(1):1–21; and "Problemima daljeg razvoja i aktivnosti Saveza komunista," *Komunist*, December 11, 1969. For reference to those who suggested that the party should become a "federation of republic organizations," see Stane Dolanc in *Politika*, October 28, 1971, p. 8.

65. From the basic level upward, this organization included cells in the enterprise, local and district party committees, *okrug* committees, provincial and *oblast* committees (one each in Vojvodina and Kosovo Metohija), city and raion committees and, of course, republic and central party organizations. *Okrug* organizations were eliminated in 1948. A system of control was instituted over the committee through the bureaus, of which there were some 2,000 at the time of the Fifth Congress in 1948. The basic source for the party structure at the local level in this period is *V Kongres*, pp. 168–69.

66. The problems of the party in the countryside are described in

Stipe Šuvar, Jordan Jelić, and Ivan Magdalenić, *Društvene Promjene I Djelovanje Komunista U Selu* (Zagreb: 1969). See also *Savez 'komunista Na Selu I Društveno Ekonomska Reforma* (Belgrade: 1967); Vlado Cvijetičanin, "Komunisti u selu," *Sociologija Sela* (April–June 1967), 5(16):3–14.

67. *VI Kongres Komunističke Partije Jugoslavije* (*Savez Komunista Jugoslavije*) (Belgrade: 1953), p. 427.

68. *VIII Kongres SKJ*, p. 32.

69. This approach was first incorporated into Article 20 of the 1964 statute, which emphasized the role of the *opstina* organization, especially its right to determine where cells and other basic organizations were to be created. The approach embodied here was further developed in Articles 34 through 36 of the 1969 statute, which made the *opština* organization responsible for coordinating the views of all party groups and sociopolitical bodies in the commune, strengthened the role of the local *aktivs*, whose decisions were made binding on all communists in the *aktiv*, and gave the *opstina* organization the right the draw up its own statute. *Deveti Kongres*, p. 249.

70. The terminology of self-management in Yugoslavia today is complex and confusing. Basic Associations of Associated Labor, or BOAL, are formed inside the enterprise. Self-managing workers' communities are apparently identical to the enterprise in scope. Interest communities represent associations of enterprises, or of other self-managing institutions, either at the local or republic level.

71. Workers' *aktivs* were introduced in the early 1970s, prior to the adoption of the new statute in 1974. As is the case with many recent innovations in the party structure, they seem to have met with considerable difficulties, and their exact role and mode of operation are not entirely clear.

72. *Nin* is an exceptionally good source for the intricate political problems that arose in the course of the struggle with the "underground" (that is the conservative forces defeated in 1966). For one of the more celebrated cases (in Kragujevac) see "Nesporazum oko predsednika," January 23, 1972, pp. 12–13. The account is interesting because it reveals the importance of the enterprise *Crvena Zastava* in local politics; the company directed "its" deputies to vote against new social services for the town in the local assembly, for example. According to this account, both sides were girding for a test of strength in the 1973 elections. For a similar power struggle in Kraljevo, see *Politika*, July 23, 1968. The problem was not confined to Serbia. For a typical struggle pitting the president of the local assembly against the party in Macedonia, see the case of Radovista, reported in *Politika*, August 6, 1970; in Karlovac, Croatia (where the struggle had a strong national element), *Politika*, August 4, 1970; in Montenegro, *Komunist*, February 5, 1970.

73. Material on local party organizations in the 1960s can be found in local yearbooks and similar publications. A valuable source on political organizations of all types at the local level is Zdenko Stambuk, ed., *Društveno-Političke Zajednice* (Belgrade: 1968), vol. 4, *Opštine* (books 1 and 2).

74. The role of the political *aktiv* is described in Ichak Adizes, *Industrial Democracy: Yugoslav Style* (New York: Free Press, 1971), p. 100.

75. The most important of these studies by a Yugoslav is Janez Jerovsek, *Structure of Influence in Local Communities*, published by the American-Yugoslav Project in Regional and Urban Planning (Ljubljana, 1969). See also: Albert Meister, *Socialisme et Autogestion* (Paris: Editions du Seuil, 1964); Jiri Kolaja, *Workers Councils: The Yugoslav Experience* (London: Tavistok, 1965), p. 34; Jovo Brekić, "Kadrovska politika u teoriji i praksi," *Kadrovi I Rad* (January–February 1971), 1(1):15.

76. As an example of an active local party organization—probably more influential than the average—we may take the information provided on Sisak in its 1969 almanac, *Almanah Sisak 69* (Sisak: 1969). The *opština* committee, with 18 members, had, under its direction, 8 committees, each with about a dozen members. They included the Commissions for Ideological-Political and Organization Cadre Construction of the SK; for Social Economic Relations and Actual Ideological Political Questions in the Economy; For Development of Social Relations and Actual Ideological Political Questions in the Economy; For Development of Social Relations and Actual Social Political Questions in the Social Services; For the Development of the System of Social Self-Management in the Commune; For Ideological Political Movement, Publications, Opinion, and Information; For Agriculture and Socialist Transformation of the Village; For Activity of the SK in Respect to Questions of the Younger Generation; and a Statutory Commission. The Party Conference of 155 members held 21 meetings during 1969; matters covered in debates in the conference included (1) party matters, including elections to higher party bodies; (2) social problems of the *opština*, including discussion of the law on financing education in Croatia; (3) party attitudes toward decisions of the Educational Chamber of the *Opština* Assembly on raising funds for education in the *opština;* (4) organizing the party in connection with "national loans" for improving roads; (5) the position of the party in respect to the appointment of the local school director; (6) carrying out the local action program in respect to the *opština* economy, and so forth. The Sisak party included 32 party cells in factories, institutes, hotels, and other places of work; 4 cells in noneconomic institutions—basic schools, middle schools, and faculties; 22 territorial party organizations; and 4 *aktivs* in the Public Auditing Service, the Communal Social Insurance Office, the Ministry of the Interior, and the local government assembly.

77. The question of new power centers in the *opština* appears to have been closely tied to the debate over whether to reorganize local party organizations in the spring of 1967. The issue was whether to strengthen the cell as the basic party or to reorganize the party around the commune. The debate was partially tied into the problem of dealing with the defeated conservative faction and the struggle against the "underground," as well as touching on the role of the party organizations in large, integrated enterprises. See the draft theses, *Komunist*, April 27, 1967. In October 1967, the Croatian Central Committee passed a reso-

lution favoring the enterprise as the unit where the organization should be located. See *Borba,* October 12, 1967.

78. Incomplete data makes it difficult to give precise estimates of the numbers involved.

79. See Paul Shoup, "The Social Structure of the Communist Parties of Eastern Europe and the Soviet Union: An Analysis of the Data," paper delivered at the 1976 annual meeting of the American Political Science Association, September 2–5, p. 36.

80. "Membership of the League of Communists of Yugoslavia," *Yugoslav Survey* (November 1967), 8(4):44.

81. In 1966, 15 percent of those party members working in the socialist sector were to be found in jobs requiring a higher education. The actual percent of those party members who had a higher education would, however, have been less than 15 percent. No statistics have been published on the percentage of total party members with a higher education.

82. See Milija Komatina in *Komunist,* June 3, 1971.

83. Data published in 1967 gave the following breakdown: Serbs: 51.77 percent of the party (42.08 percent of population); Croatians: 18.13 percent of the party (23.15 percent of the population); Slovenians: 6.74 percent of the party (8.57 percent of the population); Macedonians: 6.46 percent of the party (5.64 percent of the population); Montenegrins: 6.13 percent of the party (2.77 percent of the population); Moslems: 3.58 percent of the party (5.24 percent of the population); Yugoslavs: 1.43 percent of the party (1.71 percent of the population); Albanians: 3.04 percent of the party (4.93 percent of the population); Hungarians: 1.21 percent of the party (2.72 percent of the population); *Pripreme 9 Kongresa Saveza Komunista Jugoslavije,* p. 53. For earlier data on the national composition of the party and of the leading party bodies, see Shoup, *Communism and the Yugoslv National Question,* (New York: Columbia University Press, 1968) Appendix B.

84. See Meister, *Socialisme et Autogestion,* Bogdan Denitch, *The Legitimation of a Revolution* (New Haven: Yale University Press, 1976) and M. George Zaninovich, "Party and Non-Party Attitudes on Social Change," in R. Barry Farrell, ed., *Political Leadership in Eastern Europe and the Soviet Union* (Chicago: University of Chicago Press, 1970), pp. 294–334.

85. Milovan Djilas, *The New Class* (New York: Praeger, 1957); Nenad Popovic, *Yugoslavia: The New Class in Crisis* (Syracuse: Syracuse University Press, 1968).

86. See references earlier, and in the pages to follow, to the campaign against privileges launched in 1962. For an excellent account of the life-style of the local elites, see "Opštinske oligarhije," *Politika,* October 10, 1971.

87. *VIII Kongres SKJ,* pp. 284–85.

88. The incident was never discussed publicly, but it became widely known, and the party was compelled to hold special meetings of party organizations in Belgrade to caution against discussing the case.

89. For a defense of the position that the LCY was no longer a "Leninist" party, see Prvoslav Ralić, "Dogme u revoluciji," *Socijalizam* (1969), 14(3):377–86. Note, however, that the party statute adopted at the Ninth Congress in its "general principles" identified the party with "Scientific Socialism, that is, Marxism-Leninism." A return to Lenin and his concept of the party can be seen in more recent theoretical writings. See, for example, Fuad Muhić, "Demokratski centralizam i tendencije njegovog negiranja," *Socijalizam* (1975), 18(2):183–92.

90. After a campaign of several years, in which the party committee in the Philosophical Faculty refused to obey party orders and expel the professors from their posts, a law was passed by the Serbian legislature in 1975 to effect their removal.

Index

JN 96 .A979 C65
(91-742)
The Communist parties of
Eastern Europe